CW00780984

George Newnes and the New Journalism in Britain, 1880-1910

Culture and Profit

Kate Jackson

Ashgate

Aldershot • Burlington USA • Singapore • Sydney

© Kate Jackson, 2001

All rights reserved. No part of this publication may be reproduced, stored in a retrieval system, or transmitted in any form or by any means, electronic, mechanical, photocopying, recording or otherwise without the prior permission of the publisher.

Kate Jackson has asserted her moral right under the Copyright, Designs and Patents Act, 1988, to be identified as the author of this work.

Published by
Ashgate Publishing Limited
Gower House
Croft Road
Aldershot
Hants GU11 3HR
England

Ashgate Publishing Company
131 Main Street
Burlington
Vermont, 05401–5600
USA

Ashgate website: http://www.ashgate.com

British Library Cataloguing in Publication Data

Jackson, Kate
    George Newnes and the New Journalism in Britain, 1880–1910: Culture and Profit – (The Nineteenth Century Series)
    1. Newnes, George. 2. Journalism—Great Britain—History—19th century. 3. Journalism—Social aspects—Great Britain. I. Title.
    072'.09034

US Library of Congress Control Number

The Library of Congress Control Number was preassigned as: 00–108812

ISBN 0 7546 0317 2

This book is printed on acid free paper.

Printed and bound in Great Britain by MPG Books Ltd, Bodmin, Cornwall

Contents

Figures

The Nineteenth Century
General Editors' Preface

The aim of this series is to reflect, develop and extend the great burgeoning of interest in the nineteenth century that has been an inevitable feature of recent decades, as that former epoch has come more sharply into focus as a locus for our understanding not only of the past but of the contours of our modernity. Though it is dedicated principally to the publication of original monographs and symposia in literature, history, cultural analysis, and associated fields, there will be a salient role for reprints of significant texts from, or about, the period. Our overarching policy is to address the spectrum of nineteenth-century studies without exception, achieving the widest scope in chronology, approach and range of concern. This, we believe, distinguishes our project from comparable ones, and means, for example. that in the relevant areas of scholarship we both recognise and cut innovatively across such parameters as those suggested by the designations 'Romantic' and 'Victorian'. We welcome new ideas, while valuing tradition. It is hoped that the world which predates yet so forcibly predicts and engages our own will emerge in parts, as a whole, and in the lively currents of debate and change that are so manifest an aspect of its intellectual, artistic and social landscape.

Vincent Newey
Joanne Shattock

University of Leicester

Acknowledgements

I wish to thank Ken Macnab, from whose always constructive and practical advice and unfailing support I have benefited considerably in the writing of this book. I am extremely grateful to my family for their support and encouragement, and especially to my father, Rob Jackson, who has been both an inspiration and a knowledgeable and patient sounding board. I also wish to acknowledge the assistance of Richard White and Stephen Garton, both of whom made valuable contributions towards my final revisions. For thoughtful and meticulous help with formatting and indexing I am indebted to Susan Hunt, and for expert assistance in the production of my illustrations to Michael Shaw and Eleni Tsomis. Thanks also to John Travis for giving and arranging permission to reproduce the Lynton photographs. Finally, I would like to express my appreciation of the financial assistance given to me by the University of Sydney and the History Department for an extended research trip to Britain.

Introduction

George Newnes was one of the most influential British publishers of the late Victorian and Edwardian periods. He established a vast number and variety of journals in the years from 1881 until his death in 1910, personally editing some of these, shaping the character and format of others, and leaving an impression upon all of them. By 1905, only Alfred Harmsworth was producing more newspapers and magazines than Newnes. The periodicals that George Newnes created included *Tit-Bits* (1881), *The Strand Magazine* (1891), *The Million* (1892), *The Westminster Gazette* (1893), *The Wide World Magazine* (1898), *The Ladies' Field* (1898) and *The Captain* (1899). This list covered a diverse range of journalistic prototypes: the penny weekly, the sixpenny illustrated magazine, the colour-printed paper, the penny evening newspaper, the true story magazine, the women's magazine and the boys' paper. It therefore represents an immensely rich archive of journalistic and cultural material. Many of these publications achieved and sustained substantial circulations. Through them, Newnes pioneered new styles, formats and journalistic techniques, and accessed new audiences. And he flavoured everything he published with his own views of people and the world they inhabited and were shaping. The personality and innovative flair of George Newnes thus pervaded British journalism for thirty years.

When asked to account for his own success in periodical publishing, Newnes replied:

> Most people have no idea of doing anything beyond what they may have seen done before, and what they are told to do. They are frightened by originality, lest it might be disastrous. I suppose I have been inclined to do things differently from, rather than in the same way as, other people, and I have always struck while the iron was hot. That, I think, to put it briefly, is the secret of any success which has attended my efforts.[1]

---

[1] Hulda Friederichs, *The Life of Sir George Newnes, Bart*, London: Hodder and Stoughton, 1911, p.144.

The ingredients of Newnes's success as an entrepreneurial publisher and the rules of his engagement with his readers were, as he saw them, originality and timing.

Alfred Harmsworth said of Newnes, in the obituary he wrote for *The Times* in 1910:

> Most of [his] earlier publications were new ideas hitherto untried in English journalism, and their distinguishing mark was a striking and unusual success. Mr Newnes had found a market which had been created by the spread of popular education, and he proceeded to extend still further the operations of his publishing house.[2]

Harmsworth was one of the first to place Newnes as a key figure of the so-called New Journalism that ushered in the modern age. Since then, a succession of twentieth-century journalists, historians and critics has invoked the name of George Newnes as one of the creators of modern journalistic practice.[3] Not everything Newnes produced was 'new', and the way in which Newnes's publications represented a marriage of new and old practices will be a major theme of this book. Nor were his journals entirely unique. Yet according to Joel Wiener, he was one of a number of leading New Journalists whose innovations were critical to the formation of the modern popular press:

> These men experimented with new techniques and drew on American examples at a time when a considerable expansion of the press was taking place. They were innovators in a new type of journalism and deserve to be remembered as such.[4]

Despite this recognition, there has been no systematic study of the diverse range of Newnes's periodical publishing career. There remains only one biography of Newnes, written by his friend and colleague Hulda Friederichs in the year after his death.[5] Friederichs made use of Newnes's own autobiographical jottings, written in preparation for an autobiographical work which was never completed. This has been supplemented by various references

---

[2]   *The Times*, 10 May, 1910.

[3]   See for instance, Harold Herd, *The Making of Modern Journalism*, London: Allen and Unwin, 1927; T.H.S. Escott, *Masters of English Journalism*, London: T. Fisher Unwin, 1911; Hulda Friederichs, op. cit.; E.T. Raymond, *Portraits of the Nineties*, London: T. Fisher Unwin, 1921; Brian Braithwaite, *Women's Magazines: The First 300 Years*, London: Peter Owen, 1995.

[4]   Joel Wiener, 'How New was the New Journalism?', in Joel H. Wiener (ed.), *Papers for the Millions: The New Journalism in Britain, 1850s-1914*, New York: Greenwood Press, 1988, pp.58-59.

[5]   Hulda Friederichs, op. cit. Friederichs was German by birth, and possessed a knowledge of many languages. She became acquainted with W.T. Stead upon her arrival in England, and obtained a post on the *Pall Mall Gazette*, then edited by Stead. She subsequently wrote for Newnes's *Westminster Gazette*, and edited its sister publication *The Westminster Budget* for many years.

to Newnes and his publishing activities in biographies of other editors, publishers, proprietors and journalists and in general histories of journalism, and by the chapter on Newnes in John Travis's recent local history of Lynton and Lynmouth, twin towns in North Devon in which he is still remembered as the towns' biggest benefactor.[6]

The publications of the House of Newnes have attracted some attention in the historiography of the late nineteenth and early twentieth-century periodical press. *Tit-Bits* has been noted for its novelty, circulation and influence on successive journalistic enterprise. Its character and circulation have placed Newnes at the centre of a long-running debate on the expansion of the popular press in the late nineteenth and early twentieth centuries. *The Million*, on the other hand, has received virtually no mention. *The Strand Magazine* has assumed some importance in the historiography of periodical literature because of its literary reputation, built upon the status of its contributors, and the popularity that it sustained for more than half a century. It has been examined by Reginald Pound, in *Mirror of the Century: The Strand Magazine, 1891-1950*. Pound was a later editor of *The Strand*. His book, part history and part autobiography, contains a wealth of invaluable material now unavailable: archival evidence relating to the House of Newnes as well as *The Strand* itself (such as share prices, annual profits and the sums paid to authors for their various contributions), and anecdotal evidence gleaned from many contemporary journalists and from members of Newnes's family.[7] *The Strand* has also been selectively indexed by Geraldine Beare.[8] *The Wide World Magazine* has been cited as a 'story magazine' and noted for its publication of the controversial story of Louis de Rougemont in the 1890s.[9] *The Westminster Gazette* has been examined, though far from exhaustively, in the light of its political connections and influence, and as the organ of its well-known editor, J.A. Spender. *The Captain* has been acknowledged as one of the most successful juvenile periodicals of the early twentieth century, but has remained unresearched. However, none of these publications have been incorporated into a comprehensive and interdisciplinary study of the periodical publishing activities of George Newnes.

---

6   See Reginald Pound and Geoffery Harmsworth, *Northcliffe*, London: Cassell, 1959; T.H.S. Escott, op. cit.; Harold Herd, *The March of Journalism: The Story of the British Press from 1622 to the Present Day*, London: Allen and Unwin, 1952; Alan J. Lee, *The Origins of the Popular Press*, London: Croom Helm, 1976; Stephen Koss, *The Rise and Fall of the Political Press in Britain*, Chapel Hill: University of North Carolina Press, 1984, vol. 2; John Travis, *An Illustrated History of Lynton and Lynmouth, 1770-1914*, Derby: Breedon Books, 1995.

7   Reginald Pound, *Mirror of the Century: The Strand Magazine, 1891-1950*, London: Heinemann, 1966.

8   Geraldine Beare (comp.), *Index to the Strand Magazine, 1891-1950*, Westport, Connecticut and London: Greenwood Press, 1982.

9   Q.D. Leavis, *Fiction and the Reading Public*, London: Chatto and Windus, 1932, p.11.

This book aims to elucidate the significance of George Newnes to British journalism and culture in the late Victorian and Edwardian periods. The figure of Newnes is its binding thread. It evaluates a collection of seven periodicals which differ in frequency of publication, audience, appearance and appeal. *Tit-Bits*, for example, was a penny weekly largely aimed at a lower middle-class readership; *The Strand* a sixpenny illustrated monthly with an essentially upper middle-class circulation; *The Westminster Gazette* a penny Liberal evening paper with a small but dedicated readership; and *The Ladies' Field* and *The Captain* both specifically-targeted and well-produced illustrated magazines.[10] These publications were linked, however, by the involvement of Newnes in their creation and production, his influence manifested in a multitude of ways. Many of them have received little historiographical attention or, if they have been examined, can be further illuminated through a methodology which locates them within a range of Newnes periodicals with linking features, and analyses them through a combination of various critical, historiographical and methodological perspectives available to the contemporary historian.

Historiography

The historiography of periodical literature has included a range of studies of individual periodicals or of a limited period in the life of a magazine; celebratory studies of various journals, commissioned to mark publication anniversaries; and biographies of founders or notable editors.[11] Monographs have generally been limited to magazines deemed particularly influential in their age and belonging to a particular, generally middle and upper class, cultural ethos (although the influence of 'cultural populism' has led to a number of more recent studies examining 'popular' publications). Most scholars, as Brian Maidment has pointed out, have 'come at periodicals obliquely' through an interest in an individual who contributed to periodicals, in an event or issue that was described in periodicals, or in pictures, books and performances reviewed in periodicals. Many articles, books and essays have employed evidence drawn from periodicals for illustrative or substantiative purposes.[12] Histories of publishing houses have tended to rely heavily on manuscript sources, and have often been biographical in

---

[10] *C.B. Fry's Magazine* was another of Newnes's most successful specifically-targeted magazines. It was a monthly illustrated sporting journal, established by Newnes in 1904, and edited by the famous sportsman C.B. Fry. This magazine is not discussed extensively here for reasons of space, but is the subject of a number of articles by the author of this book.

[11] J. Don Vann and Rosemary T. Van Arsdel (eds), *Victorian Periodicals: A Guide to Research*, New York: Modern Language Association, 1978, p.105.

[12] Brian Maidment, 'Victorian Periodicals in Academic Discourse' in Laurel Brake, Aled Jones and Lionel Madden (eds), *Investigating Victorian Journalism*, New York: St Martin's Press, 1990, p.144.

orientation, and descriptive in style rather than thematic, conceptual or theoretical.[13]

Since the 1960s, a number of research societies and journals have been established, all of them attempting to open up the vast uncharted territory of research into newspapers, periodicals and the history of publishing.[14] The pioneering work encouraged by the Research Society for Victorian Periodicals in the 1960s tended to take the form of archival research, and included indexes and bibliographic research guides such as The *Wellesley Index*, *The Waterloo Directory*, *Victorian Periodicals: A Guide to Research* and *Victorian Periodical Press: Samplings and Soundings*. It also included surveys of the nineteenth-century press, and many articles and books describing the careers of individual editors, authors, and periodicals.[15] The history of print culture has burgeoned in the last ten years, and national 'histories of the book' (as they are known to scholars in the field) have proliferated.[16] Such studies, examining issues of production, distribution, formal character and reception, represent the intersection of economic, literary and social history. Whilst various recent research initiatives have sought to address the problem of locating, indexing and recording the archives of British and American publishers and related groups such as Publishers' and Writers' Associations, none have sourced material relating to George Newnes, Ltd.[17] This is a reflection of the fact that such material is scarce,

---

[13] See, for instance, Charles Morgan, *The House of Macmillan*, London: Macmillan, 1943; Patricia Thomas Srebrnik, *Alexander Strahan: Victorian Publisher*, Ann Arbor, Michigan: University of Michigan Press, 1986; F.A. Mumby, *The House of Routledge, 1834-1934*, London: Routledge, 1934; Leonard Huxley, *The House of Smith Elder*, London, 1923.

[14] The Research Society for Victorian Periodicals was established in 1968, and began producing the *Victorian Periodicals Newsletter*, which later became the *Victorian Periodicals Review*. The *Journal of Publishing History* was established in 1977, and the *Journal of Newspaper and Periodical History* in 1984. The Society for the History of Authorship, Readership and Publishing began bringing out its quarterly newsletter (*SHARP News*) in 1992, and launched its annual journal, *Book History*, in 1997.

[15] Walter E. Houghton (ed.), *The Wellesley Index to Victorian Periodicals, 1824-1900*, Toronto: University of Toronto Press, 1966; *The Waterloo Directory of Victorian Periodicals, 1824-1900*, Waterloo, Ontario, 1976; J. Don Vann and Rosemary T. Van Arsdel (eds), op. cit.; Joanne Shattock and Michael Wolff (eds), *The Victorian Periodical Press: Samplings and Soundings*, Leicester: Leicester University Press, 1982. See also Alan J. Lee, op. cit.; Lucy Brown, *Victorian News and Newspapers*, New York: Oxford University Press, 1985.

[16] A collaborative project on the History of the Book in Australia (HOBA), for instance, was begun in 1996.

[17] Chadwick-Healey are engaged in producing vast collections of microfilm reels including Richard Bentley and Son, 1829-1898; George Allen, 1893-1915; Macmillan, 1854-1924; and George Routledge, 1853-1902. Simon Fraser University began the 'Publisher's Papers Project' in 1994, developing a database that locates Canadian publishing company records in both public institutions and the offices of Canadian publishers, personal papers of individuals involved in publishing, and the papers of related groups. The author made a number of visits to IPC Magazines, into which George Newnes, Ltd was incorporated in 1958, in an effort to obtain such material. It appeared that the bulk of the records of the company had been placed in storage in a disused underground tunnel during the Second World War, and that it was now impossible to locate or view them.

a fact which has influenced the nature of this book inasmuch as its focus is on textual rather than archival sources.

The period under scrutiny was one of the most dynamic periods in British journalism and culture. Many argued that it saw the invention of a new journalism which was to diversify the field of periodical publishing and shape all subsequent journalistic development. The historiography of New Journalism has included a number of essay collections which have proved useful for this study, such as *Newspaper History from the Seventeenth Century to the Present Day* (edited by Boyce, Curran and Wingate), *Papers for the Millions* (Joel Wiener) and *Investigating Victorian Journalism* (Brake, Jones and Madden). Many scholars have made useful contributions to the debate over the novelty of the New Journalism. Francis Williams has asserted that New Journalism was responsible for, amongst other things, the dichotomy in the British press between 'quality' and 'popular' newspapers. Examining typographic trends in newspapers from 1622, both Stanley Morrison and Allen Hutt have shown that the innovations of New Journalism helped to create a lively press. Cynthia White, Margaret Beetham and Brian Braithwaite have all discussed the emergence of mass periodicals for women.[18] Personality, both editorial and within the proliferating 'human interest' stories, was a prominent feature of the New Journalism, and innovative editors such as W.T. Stead and T.P. O'Connor marketed themselves strenuously to the public. There have been many studies of both of these men. Joseph Baylen, for instance, has argued that the New Journalism was defined primarily by Stead, who employed popular methods of journalism to achieve moral goals.[19] Despite the existence of various volumes of memoirs, biography and autobiography, there has been relatively little treatment of other leading New Journalists. And of the leading press magnates only Northcliffe (Alfred Harmsworth) has attracted significant attention.[20]

---

[18] Francis Williams, *Dangerous Estate: The Anatomy of Newspapers*, London: Longman, Green, 1957; Stanley Morrison, *The English Newspaper: Some Account of the Physical Development of Journals Printed in London Between 1622 and the Present Day*, Cambridge: Cambridge University Press, 1932; Allen Hutt, *The Changing Newspaper: Typographic Trends in Britain and America, 1622-1972*, London: Gordon Fraser, 1973; Cynthia White, *Women's Magazines, 1693-1968*, London: Michael Joseph, 1970; Margaret Beetham, *A Magazine of Her Own? Domesticity and Desire in the Woman's Magazine, 1800-1914*, London and New York: Routledge, 1996; Brian Braithwaite, op. cit.

[19] Joseph O. Baylen, 'The "New Journalism" in Late-Victorian Britain', *Australian Journal of Politics and History*, 18 (1972), pp.367-385. See also Joseph O. Baylen, 'W.T. Stead and the New Journalism', *Emory University Quarterly*, XXI (1965), pp.196-206; 'The Press and Public Opinion: W.T. Stead and the "New Journalism"', *Journalism Studies Review*, 4 (July 1979), pp.45-49; Frederic Whyte, *The Life of W.T. Stead*, 2 vols, London: Jonathan Cape, 1925.

[20] See, for example, Reginald Pound and Geoffrey Harmsworth, op. cit.; Paul Ferris, *The House of Northcliffe: The Harmsworths of Fleet St*, London: Weidenfeld and Nicolson, 1971; R.D. Blumenfeld, *The Press in My Time*, London: Rich and Cowan, 1933 and *R.O.B.'s Diary, 1887-1914*, London: William Heinemann, 1930; Sidney Dark, *The Life of Sir Arthur Pearson, Bt, G.B.E.*, London: Hodder and Stoughton, 1922; Henry Lucy, *Sixty Years in the Wilderness*, London: Smith, Elder, 1909 and *The Diary of a Journalist*, 3 vols, London: John Murray, 1923.

In one respect, this study is a contribution to the debates surrounding New Journalism and the history of the popular periodical press. It will explore the nature of authorship as it relates to Newnes's periodicals, covering such issues as editorial voice and the authority structure of the late nineteenth-century periodical press. It will examine the evolution of new formats, focussing on the significance of advertising, and the emergence of popular and innovative features such as the interview, the character sketch, the competition, the portrait series and the correspondence column. And it will interrogate the character of journalistic developments and techniques of the period: the distinctions and continuities between the old journalism and the new, serious journalism and commercial journalism, and the popular and quality presses; the use of commercial and promotional schemes; the development of new technologies of colour and photographic reproduction; the development of different types of journals such as the penny weekly and the true story magazine; and the development of journalistic specialisation and market segmentation (the journalistic version of 'divide and conquer'). Illustrations from both textual and other sources have been included at the end of the chapters to which they refer. The photographic prints relating to this Introduction underline the connection between Newnes's public image and the persona he developed as a periodical editor and proprietor. In other sections, magazine covers, pictorial headers and illustrations have been selected to evoke the material appearance of the various publications and impress upon the reader the importance of the periodical's visual impact. The captions which accompany the illustrations locate, describe, and, in some cases, briefly comment upon the various visual features and techniques employed by Newnes. The analysis of the periodical publications of George Newnes will consist in the interweaving of arguments relating to production, distribution, reception and the nature of the periodical as a cultural text.

This is, in many ways, an interdisciplinary study, which crosses the boundaries between history, literary criticism, cultural and media studies and intellectual biography. The scholarship of these fields has both provided some of the methodologies which it utilises and suggested some of the themes which it explores. It attempts to answer, for instance, the challenge posed by recent work in cultural studies and literary criticism concerning the relationship between the industrial production of cultural forms and the consumption or reception of those forms, and offers a model of the periodical text (especially with respect to *Tit-Bits* and *The Million*) which is a dialectical combination of creation and reflection; of production and reception; of openness and closure. The periodical, it is argued, is a culturally-embedded social object which is a product of negotiation and interaction between editor-proprietor and audience, and is as much context as text. The analysis of *The Wide World Magazine* is a clear example of the interweaving of text and context.

In the recent scholarship of periodical literature, empirical studies have been supplemented by and conjoined with a developing 'metacriticism' of periodical research, focussing on the methodology of periodical research.[21] Scholars within media studies have debated whether the media sustains and reflects a consensual reality already in existence, or whether it produces or manufactures that consensus. Revisionist reception theorists have recently argued that production-centred studies have overstated the power of culture industries to exert ideological control over the meaning of their products. They have suggested that the audience of any cultural performance are social subjects who actively and variably engage with cultural texts on the basis of their lived experience. Reader-response critics contend that a text's 'effects' or results - psychological or otherwise - are essential to an analysis of its meaning since the effective existence of any text is limited to its realisation in the mind of the reader.[22] Their comments suggest a methodology within which the cultural text should be examined with reference to its place within a wider social, cultural and ideological formation.

It was this kind of approach that the founding texts of cultural studies - Richard Hoggart's *The Uses of Literacy*, E.P. Thompson's *The Making of the English Working Class*, and Raymond Williams' *Culture and Society* and *The Long Revolution* - attempted to bring to the history of popular culture, in the late 1950s and early 1960s. Hoggart, for instance, focussed on *lived cultures* and on the *relation* between texts and contexts. He demonstrated the kind of impulse towards the sociological reconstruction of British society that underpinned the Mass Observation project of the 1930s, when hundreds of Britons kept diaries of their daily lives for inclusion in a general sociological survey.[23] Raymond Williams emphasised the communicative, creative nature of art and culture, arguing that 'communication is the crux of art, for any adequate description of experience must be more than simple transmission, it must also include reception and response'. When popular literature communicates, he concluded, 'a human experience is actively offered and actively received. Below this activity threshold there can be no art.'[24] These scholars shared an interest in analysing the textual forms and documented practices of British culture. Where Matthew Arnold had associated popular culture with 'anarchy', and the *Scrutiny* school of critics with standardisation, 'levelling down' and cultural decline in general, these scholars found in popular culture a measure of positivity, stressing human agency and the

---

[21] Laurel Brake and Anne Humpherys, 'Critical Theory and Periodical Research', *Victorian Periodicals Review*, XXII, 3 (Fall 1989), p.94.

[22] They have employed such concepts as Walker Gibson's 'mock reader', and Gerald Prince's three classifications of 'narratee'. See Jane P. Tompkins (ed.), *Reader Response Criticism: From Formalism to Post Structuralism*, Baltimore and London: Johns Hopkins University Press, 1980. Reader-response critics also differ amongst themselves in the way in which they conceive the act of reading in relation to the creation of meaning.

[23] See Richard Hoggart, *The Uses of Literacy* (Intro. Andrew Goodwin), New Brunswick: Transaction Publishers, 1992, p.xvi.

[24] Raymond Williams, *The Long Revolution*, London: Penguin, 1961, pp.46, 42.

active production and reception of popular culture.[25] Some critics have attacked the consumptionist perspective of cultural populism, and pleaded for a return to Arnoldian certainties about culture: 'culture is the best that has been thought and said in the world'. Yet it is difficult to disagree with John Storey's response to this:

> cultural populism's refusal to judge a text or practice 'good' or 'bad' is not in my opinion a crisis, but a welcome recognition that there are other, sometimes far more interesting, questions to be asked.[26]

Such historiographical debates have significantly influenced the methodology of this book: the questions to be asked. It aims to forge links between extensive empirical research on the outstanding examples of the periodical genre fashioned by George Newnes (after all, theoretical developments do not obviate the need for detailed and thorough empirical research), and more abstract theoretical notions about the nature of periodical literature. And it seeks to place Newnes's periodicals within a dynamic system of discursive and cultural interaction that included new technological developments, educational systems, social and political movements, oral cultural forms, tourist literature and imperialist propaganda, urban segregation and patterns of class formation, new patterns of leisure, changing notions of time and space, the evolution of a consumer culture, and the construction and dissemination of cultural stereotypes. This study will examine the manner in which Newnes's publications function historically as 'social discourse', and will assess the significance of his publications to the historiography of print culture, New Journalism and periodical research.

As a literary and popular form, periodical literature presents the historian with a particular set of methodological concerns revolving around the issue of the relationship between the text itself and the culture that produced it. One model for the interpretation of periodical literature has been the reflection model employed by Michael Wolff in his pioneering essay entitled 'Charting the Golden Stream'. Wolff suggested that 'The years that we call Victorian are best mirrored in the serial publications - literature, argument, the tastes and preoccupations of just about every level and sort of society, all display themselves in the newspapers and journals.' Walter Houghton adopted the reflection model in his introduction to the *Wellesley Index* in which he stated that periodicals were 'a remarkable record of contemporary thought' which 'reflect[ed] the current situation'. And John North described the periodical

---

[25] In *Culture and Anarchy* (1869), the term 'anarchy' operates essentially as a synonym for popular culture, denoting Arnold's fear of the disruptive nature of a working-class lived culture and of political and social disorder. It is significant that he was writing amidst the suffrage agitation of 1866-1867.

[26] John Storey, *An Introductory Guide to Cultural Theory and Popular Culture*, New York: Harvester Wheatsheaf, 1993, p.183.

press as a 'sensitive ... record of a civilisation'.[27] This model obviously has a certain value. Yet it is problematic insofar as it implies that the media are secondary and derivative, existing above and beyond the 'real world' and passively mirroring society rather than forming an active and integral part of it. Victorian and Edwardian periodicals were, by their very nature (their appearance at regular intervals and dependence - financial and otherwise - upon reader response, and their varied composition) an extremely interactive and intertextual medium. This was something that Newnes understood and exploited very successfully.

Recent redefinitions of the methodological challenges of periodical research by structuralist, post-structuralist and a diverse collection of Marxist theorists within historiography, literary studies, and cultural and media studies have entailed a rethinking of the reflection model. Periodicals are no longer deemed mere *reflective evidence* through which to *recover* the culture that they *mirror*. They have come to be viewed as a central component of that culture; an 'active and integral part' of it to be understood only as part of that society and its discourses about the periodical press.[28] Thus Shattock and Wolff have redefined the press and periodical study in the following terms:

> The press, in all its manifestations, became during the Victorian period the context within which people lived and worked and thought, and from which they derived their sense of the outside world.[29]

The periodical press is neither a mirror *reflecting* Victorian culture, nor a means of *expressing* Victorian culture, but an 'inescapable ideological and subliminal environment, a (or perhaps *the*) constitutive medium of a Victorian culture which is now seen as interactive.'[30] It is part of a matrix of meaning that encompasses the total semiotic field.

This theoretical position is the logical outcome of the process by which, through the impetus provided by social history and cultural studies, the literary source gained recognition as a viable source of evidence for historical analysis: an expression, not merely of the consciousness of the author, but of the relationship between authorial consciousness and social formation. We have now arrived at a point at which the literary source has been transformed from

---

[27] Michael Wolff, 'Charting the Golden Stream', in Joanne Shattock and Michael Wolff (eds), op. cit., pp.26-27; Walter E. Houghton (ed.), op. cit., p.xv; John North, 'The Rationale - Why Read Victorian Periodicals?', in J. Don Vann and R. Van Arsdel (eds), op. cit., p.4.

[28] Lyn Pykett, 'Reading the Periodical Press: Text and Context', *Victorian Periodicals Review*, XXII, 3 (Fall 1989), p.102. See, for instance, Mikhail Bahktin, *The Dialogic Imagination* (ed. Michael Holquist, trans. Caryl Emerson and Michael Holquist), Austin: University of Texas Press, 1981. See also Michel Foucault, *The Archaelogy of Knowledge* (trans. A.M. Sheridan Smith), New York: Pantheon, 1972.

[29] Joanne Shattock and Michael Wolff (eds), op. cit., pp.xiv-xv.

[30] Ibid.

acceptable *text* (representing or reflecting an historically significant reality) into quintessential *context* (constituting the very essence of that reality). Interdisciplinarity - in the form of semiology, structuralism, post-Foucauldian and formalist historiography - has altered our thinking so that literature and context are viewed, in the words of Lyn Pykett, as 'indivisible elements of a signifying system, or ideological or discursive formation'.[31]

A range of cultural critics from Matthew Arnold to Q.D. Leavis and beyond have constructed an opposition between art and mass culture in which the market relationship has provided the principle for a hierarchical division of the cultural field into high and low forms. Within this critical tradition, high culture, 'Literature' or (genuine) 'Art' has been theorised as a specialised discipline, pursued and defined by 'English Literature' and the academy. It has been dissociated from the realm of the common reader. 'Journalism', on the other hand, and especially 'New Journalism' (so designated by its critics) has been defined as a mass-produced cultural commodity, and writing for a mass audience (of 'consumers' rather than readers) has been viewed as an intrinsically debased cultural form, determined by market rationality, and potentially subversive in its implications for literary standards.

Within the historiography of the press itself, there has been a certain pessimism about the commercial press that was born of the repeal of the 'taxes on knowledge'(abolition of the advertisement duty in 1853, stamp duty in 1855, paper duty in 1861 and the security system in 1869). In an analysis of the commercial changes affecting the press in the half century after the repeal of the newspaper tax, Alan Lee has argued that the liberal ideal of an independent press broke down in the 1880s and 1890s when capitalism encroached strongly. The establishment of a free press also brought the establishment of a cheap one. The effect, according to Lee, was to create an 'intellectually more passive and morally less confident readership'. The newly commercialised press served the ends of an increasingly powerful capitalist class. Commercial motives had always underpinned the foundation and management of newspapers, but the abolition of what opponents called the 'taxes on knowledge' heralded a new phase of development in which, according to Lee, 'economic forces would gradually dominate political ones'.[32] This argument has resonated through the historiography of periodical literature from the late nineteenth century to the present day.

Yet Stephen Koss has emphasised patterns of continuity in press development, in a work that is particularly relevant to Newnes's *Westminster Gazette*, pointing out that many organs of the so-called New Journalism were as representative of an old tradition of political journalism as of a new journalistic

---

[31] Lyn Pykett, op. cit., p.103.

[32] Alan Lee, 'The Structure, Ownership and Control of the Press, 1855-1914', in George Boyce, James Curran and Pauline Wingate (eds), *Newspaper History from the Seventeenth Century to the Present Day*, London: Constable, 1978, p.117.

model.[33] Koss's argument will be taken up in Chapter 3, as will the work of Piers Brendon in *The Life and Death of the Press Barons*. Brendon has chronicled the rise and decline of the 'press barons' in the U.S. and Britain, suggesting that the press baron was 'a lone pioneer of outstanding journalistic ability, a man of mercury who invested his entire personality in his newspaper', and that collectively,such men transformed the landscape of journalism in the nineteenth century. They were defeated, however, by a sharp change in the economic climate and were overrun by twentieth-century 'media conglomerates'.[34] Although Newnes was not a 'press baron' in the strictest sense (he owned only one major *news*paper), Brendon's argument is remarkably pertinent to the process of mapping Newnes's progress from editor of *Tit-Bits* to owner of an extensive periodical publishing empire. This book seeks to interrogate the relationship between the New Journalism and the old, and between 'serious' or 'quality' journalism and popular or commercial journalism. It offers *The Strand* and *The Westminster Gazette*, in particular, as products of the cross-pollination between the old and the new, ideology and profit, and artistic quality and journalistic innovation.

Contemporary scholars in media and cultural studies have noted the way in which producers in what they call 'the culture industries' (televisual media networks, the film industry and the magazine industry) have increasingly attempted to appeal to niche audiences through more tightly-focussed cultural products, targeting ethnic, youth, female and various other audiences. This strategy has been labelled 'narrowcasting'. It is a policy, however, that can be traced to the magazine industry of the 1890s, an industry that was heavily influenced by the expansion of the advertising business.[35] Newnes targeted a range of specialised markets at the turn of the century (thus attracting substantial advertising revenue) with a range of periodicals including *The Ladies' Field* and *The Captain*. This represented a departure from the inclusive strategies that had made *Tit-Bits* such a success. These two periodicals represent points of access into a range of views, anxieties and preoccupations relating to the niche audiences at which they were targeted: upper middle-class and society women and youth (primarily boys, but with some appeal to girls).

Methodology

One of the most frequently acknowledged problems of Victorian periodical research relates to the sheer mass and variety of material available to the scholar,

---

[33] Stephen Koss, op. cit.

[34] Piers Brendon, *The Life and Death of the Press Barons*, London: Secker and Warburg, 1982.

[35] See, for instance, Michael Curtin, 'On Edge: Culture Industries in the Neo-Network Era' and David Shumway, 'Objectivity, Bias, Censorship', in Richard Ohmann (ed.), *Making and Selling Culture*, Hanover and London: Wesleyan University Press, 1996.

much of it uncatalogued in bibliographical indexes. Indeed, the abundance of potential source material beckons new scholars to the field. Nineteenth-century Britain was a 'journalising society', and periodicals were an important form of entertainment for people for whom there were few alternatives to the written word as a method of mass communication. Reviewing the literary history of the nineteenth century in 1896, George Saintsbury suggested that: 'perhaps there is no single feature ... not even the enormous multiplication of the novel, which is so distinctive and characteristic as the development in it of periodical literature'.[36] The journals established between 1824 and 1900 numbered between 125,000 and 150,000.[37] In fact, periodicals were more widely read than books. This book offers a thorough and original examination of seven periodicals established in the years from 1881 to 1899, making them available, at least in some speculative way, to the researcher of periodical literature. It offers, in a sense, a method of organising what is a vast quantity of source material.

More specifically, the methodology of this book will consist of three approaches: an examination of the production of the periodical publication involving issues of proprietorial and editorial control, authorial and artistic input, and technical and journalistic development; an exploration of the periodical as a social object embedded in contemporary discursive and cultural practices, encompassing issues of readership, circulation, reception and cultural formation; and an interrogation of the distinctive properties of the periodical text and the 'personalities' (to use Joel Wiener's term)[38] of Newnes's periodicals, involving a combination of close-reading and critical theory, and utilising the heterogeneity of the late nineteenth and early twentieth-century periodical as a means of locating it within its journalistic, cultural and commercial context.

There are various problems associated with the investigation of the input of journalists and others as it relates to the study of Victorian and Edwardian periodicals. One of these is the anonymity often exercised by journalists, editors and sub-editors in the nineteenth century. This has meant that the assumption that Newnes himself edited *The Million* has been based upon the fact of its similarity to *Tit-Bits* in editorial style and format rather than on archival evidence. Another problem is the complexity of the authority structure of the press as it became increasingly capitalised, and thus of the connection between proprietor, editor, sub-editor and publisher's reader.[39] This issue has become part of the

---

[36] George Saintsbury as cited in Joanne Shattock and Michael Woolf (eds), op. cit., p.3.

[37] Joanne Shattock and Michael Woolf give an estimate of 50,000 (ibid. p.3), but more current research puts the number of Victorian periodicals at triple that figure.

[38] Joel Wiener, 'Sources for the Study of Newspapers' in Laurel Brake, Aled Jones and Lionel Madden (eds), op. cit., p.155. The *Pall Mall Gazette*, for instance, had been under W.T. Stead 'a demon for work, insatiable in curiosity and interest, and ceaseless in its interrogation of public opinion', according to E.T. Cook. Under John Morley, on the other hand, it had been 'grave', 'deliberate', 'weighty' and 'subdued' (p.161).

[39] See Linda Marie Fritschner, 'Publisher's Readers, Publishers, and their Authors', *Publishing History*, 7 (1980), pp.45-100.

conceptual framework and thematic development of this book. Newnes was more evidently the source and fount of *Tit-Bits*, which he established, financed and edited himself, than of *The Strand*, a later publication over which he exercised general editorial control but for the production of which he employed a powerful editor in Greenhough Smith, and many sub-editors, journalists, artists and compositors. He is thus central to the chapter on *Tit-Bits* and *The Million* whereas the chapter on *The Strand* encompasses a good deal of material on the hierarchy of constituents involved in the magazine's production. *The Westminster Gazette*, over which Newnes allowed his editors (E.T. Cook and then J.A. Spender) considerable editorial control and freedom from proprietorial intervention, has been depicted here as a textual site through which issues of proprietorial control were explored and mediated. And the two later Newnes publications, though still inspired by Newnes, have been shown to be the logical outcome of the process by which the responsibilities of the editor were gradually separated from those of the proprietor, as the rule of proprietors gave way to corporate management.

Comments about the reception of periodicals are limited by the absence of reliable and detailed information about circulation. From the abolition of the stamp tax on newspapers (a system which had provided some information, though not entirely reliable, about circulation) until the 1890s, sales figures for newspapers were not audited or certified. It is therefore difficult to obtain authoritative circulation figures. A few papers published certified figures, although these were sometimes contentious.[40] Papers often made exaggerated claims about their circulation in order to attract a profitable advertising trade. Yet another complication relates to the ratio of readers to each copy in a period when papers were sometimes read aloud, and were often read by multiple readers, especially if they were 'family papers'. It is thus difficult to establish both the size and the composition of a publication's readership.

Moreover, for all the merit in recent theoretical developments, penetrating the social meaning of periodical discourse is by no means an easy task. And for all the talk of the cultural text and its effects on its audience, the periodical text is a complex form and understanding the reading process, as it relates to the periodical, a considerable challenge. The historian of the nineteenth-century press often has no archival source for *actual* as opposed to *implied* or *constructed* reader response (diaries, oral evidence, or unpublished reader correspondence, let alone real sales figures). Furthermore, the Victorian period was characterised by a well-tried convention of fabricating letters from readers to generate sales. There is no evidence to suggest that this technique was routinely employed by Newnes.[41] Yet neither is there any record of the correspondence

---

[40] Kennedy Jones claimed that it was common practice in the 1890s for newspapers to overprint an edition to increase 'sales' figures and therefore advertising, despite the financial loss entailed in destroying excess stock. See Joel Wiener 'Sources for the Study of Newspapers' in Laurel Brake, Aled Jones and Lionel Madden (eds), op. cit., p.159.

[41] The only reference to the use of such a practice in a Newnes publication comes from C.B. Fry, who referred to 'the intelligent questions' of *Captain* readers, '*real as well as*

that was rejected, and the act of reader response was itself selectively represented in the text. What is employed here is thus a rather transmission-centred approach to readership. It relies on internal textual evidence (the images of readership fostered and sustained by the text, visually, and through the various correspondence columns, competitions, circulation figures, narratives, editorials) to suggest an implied or imagined readership. (For, as Wolfgang Iser points out, the reader is not independent of textual constraints, but participates in interpretative activity within the manifold possibilities implied by the text. The text's intentions are always circumscribed by it and traceable to it.)[42] And it offers both anecdotal and secondary evidence for readership as far as is possible.

'Literacy', as well as literature, is dynamic and contextual. It is also a concept very much enmeshed in the history and historiography of the years 1880-1910, when successive Education Acts and the expansion of the popular press focussed attention on the spread of the reading habit. The debate over *Tit-Bits*, to which Chapter 1 is a contribution, clearly demonstrates this. Literacy, as David Vincent and Gerd Baumann have argued, must be placed in its historical context, and it must be seen as a social practice within the context of other social practices, power structures, institutions and organisations in order for its diverse uses and meanings to be understood.[43] *The Strand*, *The Million* and *The Wide World Magazine*, for instance, appealed to an audience with a considerable degree of *visual* literacy, fostered throughout the century by cultural texts which included ballads and broadsheets, advertising and illustrated papers such as *Punch* (1841) and *Illustrated London News* (1842). Crime fiction and crime news had been associated with a semi-literate working and lower middle-class audience in the mid-nineteenth century. But by the late nineteenth century, as A.E. Murch has pointed out, it was becoming acceptable and popular amongst a more 'respectable' readership.[44] Hence middle-class periodicals such as *The Strand* incorporated a huge crime fiction component. The concept of literacy was subject to challenge and change, and went beyond the mere ability to read.

Yet despite being somewhat problematic and complicated, reader-response criticism does seem to offer a model of interpretation that is particularly appropriate to the periodical form, given that readers create a periodical in a way that is manifest (through buying it week after week). And the notion, derived from this critical tradition, that 'reading and writing join hands, change places,

---

imaginary' (my italics). See C.B. Fry, *Life Worth Living: Some Phases of an Englishman*, London: Eyre and Spottiswoode, 1939, p.154.

[42] Wolfgang Iser, 'The Reading Process: A Phenomenological Approach' in Jane P. Tompkin (ed.), op. cit., p.50.

[43] David Vincent and Gerd Baumann, 'Abstracts from 1993 SHARP Conference', *Publishing History*, 34 (1993), pp.86-87.

[44] A.E. Murch, *The Development of the Detective Novel*, London: Peter Owen, 1968, p.9. There was a tradition of literacy associated with the self-educated reader, whose repertoire included the Bible and *Pilgrim's Progress*. W.T. Stead's survey of Labour MPs revealed that they had educated themselves through a common set of seminal texts. Newnes's competitions in *Tit-Bits* to name the 'Ten Best Books' and the like were an appeal to this tradition and an attempt to define it.

and finally become distinguishable only as two names for the same activity' offers a valuable perspective from which to survey the effect of a large and dynamic readership upon Newnes's publications.[45] It is of peculiar relevance to *Tit-Bits*, in which readers actually become writers in the 'Answers to Correspondents', 'Legal Tit-Bits' and 'Tit-Bits Inquiry' columns, and in which the act of editorial selection and the process of writing become very transparent and very personalised. In *The Wide World Magazine* too, readers were writers (in the sense of being contributors), and the magazine's readers strongly identified with the various narrators as they travelled imaginatively to all corners of the 'wide world'. In *The Ladies' Field*, readers' interests, as revealed in the many columns in which they participated through correspondence, constituted the magazine's field of reference: 'the ladies' field'. In *The Captain* and *C.B. Fry's Magazine* the relationship between author-editor and readers, closely allied to the relationship between the sporting or popular hero and his adoring crowd, was vital to the text's psychological effects and to its popularity. It was derived from the social fabric of a society shaped by consumerism, anxiety about youth problems, and mass spectator sport. In general, the most important methodological hint which critical theory offers in the case of this particular study concerns the importance of interrogating the way in which periodicals function as social discourse rather than as direct 'social statement'. The study of periodical literature entails a process of mediation between the discourse of certain magazines and the discursive practices of their readers.

The periodical text itself is a complex form, difficult to define. The 'text' is both the single issue, and the run of numbers of each magazine. The complex nature of the periodical text thus necessitates a mixed analytical approach. Individual issues and stories require some detailed critical analysis with attention to such devices as simile and literary allusion, to narrative technique and narratorial voice, and to the linguistic structure of reference employed. *The Wide World Magazine*, for example, was structured by the language of imperialism. Terms such as 'penetration', 'opening up' and 'civilising', and oppositions such as 'civilised' and 'savage', 'heathen' and 'Christian' were commonplace. This sort of approach provides access to the cultural and ideological interplay occurring between author and readers with a common ground of language, expectation and literary tradition (the traditions of literary structure and form).

A whole run of numbers, linked by form (format, length of stories, size of pages), regular features ('Legal Tit-Bits', 'Answers to Correspondents', 'Continental Tit-Bits', 'Inquiry Column', 'Tit-Bits of General Information' in *Tit-Bits*; the map-contents in *The Wide World Magazine*) and material characteristics (green paper for *The Westminster Gazette*, quality of paper and photographic reproduction for *The Wide World* and *The Ladies' Field*, coloured illustrations for *The Million*) would seem to present a whole new set of analytical problems. This text represents a market relationship between producer and

---

[45] Jane P. Tompkin (ed.), op. cit., p.x.

consumer; a phenomenon related to demand, anticipation and familiarity, loyalty and time.

The fundamental characteristic of the periodical text in this second definition is the way in which it engages with its readers across time and thus involves them in the development and character of the text. Margaret Beetham has examined the formal qualities of the periodical text and explored the way in which the periodical functions as both open and closed text.[46] Beetham has demonstrated that the periodical is, in one sense, 'not only characteristically self-referring but is by definition open-ended and resistant to closure'. The serial form of the periodical implies a resistance to closure, and can thus be read as a sign of its strength as a potentially creative form for its readers, implicated in a continuing history which it both responds to and helps to define. Furthermore readers rarely read an entire periodical, nor do they read in the order of printing, or even at one sitting. They select and construct their own order. Thus the periodical is a form which openly offers readers the chance to construct their own texts (though their capacity to do so is, of course, necessarily limited by the 'text' out of which they make their own 'text').[47] The interactive character of periodical literature, of which Newnes's work provides some interesting examples, thus defies conventional models of interpretation relating to literary production. Periodical literature offers openness, fluidity and the possibility of alternative meanings. Hence the reaction of readers could influence the conclusion of a serial, as in the case of the Sherlock Holmes stories in *The Strand Magazine*, in which Holmes was resurrected after his death at Reichenbach Falls in order to satisfy public demand for more Holmes stories. *Tit-Bits* has been characterised in this study by the way in which it emphasises the open, serial qualities of the form: the predominance of competitions, question/answer formats and regular features. These qualities reinforced the dynamic nature of the publication.

At the same time, the periodical form implies structure and closure inasmuch as the economics of periodical literature - the fact that success is dependent upon the maintenance of a constant, loyal readership - entails the reproduction of successful features and the linking of separate issues. Temporality endows it with a regularity of structure and a continuity of format (regular columns, page size, shape, pattern of contents), the consistency of which attracts a regular weekly or monthly readership. And the periodical form goes hand in hand with other structures in industrial society by which work and leisure have become regulated by time.[48] Despite its publication in serial form, *The Strand Magazine* represents, in some sense, a closed text, each issue

---

[46] Margaret Beetham, 'Open and Closed: The Periodical as Publishing Genre', *Victorian Periodicals Review*, XXII, 3 (Fall 1989), p.97; and Margaret Beetham, 'Towards a Theory of the Periodical as a Publishing Genre', in Laurel Brake, Aled Jones and Lionel Madden (eds), op. cit, pp.30-35.

[47] Ibid., pp.97, 98.

[48] See E.P. Thompson, 'Time, Work-Discipline and Industrial Capitalism', *Past and Present*, 38 (1967), pp.56-97.

remarkably complete. The self-sufficiency of the monthly number was created by the standardisation of the bound text, and by the wide use of the serial short story form pioneered by A.C. Doyle and others (a form which, as Doyle pointed out, bound the reader to the magazine without excluding the reader who had missed an issue).[49]

Difficulties of definition arise partly out of the fact that the periodical is a mixed genre. Like the novel in Bakhtin's exposition on *The Dialogic Imagination*, it is 'a phenomenon multiform in style and variform in speech and voice'.[50] It contains a heterogeneous combination of text, pictures, maps, diagrams, rubric and captions, and is compounded of a diversity of voice and authorial contribution. The concept of authorship is problematic in the context of periodical literature because each number involves the consciousness of a number of writers, in addition to that of the editor and that of the proprietor. Thus there arises a difficulty in situating the periodical text within the locus of a particular author. In this study, editorials and correspondence columns will be closely analysed on the assumption that they represent a relatively direct and familiar form of interaction. The text's complexity will also be addressed through the examination of some particular editors, writers and illustrators in detail.

Yet the heterogeneity of the periodical text actually offers a key to engaging with the form as it developed in this period. The progress of mass culture was intimately associated with a general cultural reorientation that was, as Stephen Kern points out, essentially pluralistic and democratic.[51] Periodical literature became a vehicle for maintaining and exploiting the pluralism of the market, and Newnes established a range of publications, including *The Ladies' Field*, *The Captain* and *C.B. Fry's Magazine*, that catered to various different reading communities. It is significant in this context that Newnes published a variety of types of periodicals, their issues separated by different intervals of time. *Tit-Bits* was a weekly (published on 'Thursday for Saturday') as was *The Ladies' Field*. *The Westminster Gazette* an evening daily, and *The Strand*, and *C.B. Fry's Magazine* monthlies.[52] The material characteristics of each text were intimately related to the rhythms and class habits of late nineteenth-century life, work and leisure. *The Westminster Gazette* was printed on green paper to prevent eyestrain for readers travelling home on dimly lit suburban trains in the evening. *Tit-Bits* was published so that its distribution coincided with the

---

[49] Doyle claims, in *Memories and Adventures*, that it was his idea to publish stories, in monthly instalments in a monthly magazine, which used the same familiar character and thus bound the reader to a particular magazine, and yet were complete in themselves. *The Strand Magazine* was the first to put Doyle's idea into practice. See Arthur Conan Doyle, *Memories and Adventures*, London: Greenhill, 1988, pp.95-96.

[50] M.M. Bakhtin, op. cit., p.261.

[51] Stephen Kern, *The Culture of Time and Space, 1880-1918*, Cambridge, Massachusetts: Harvard University Press, 1983, p.152.

[52] See J. Willing, *Willing's Press Guide and Advertisers' Directory and Handbook*, London, 1903.

Saturday half-holiday obtained by workers in the 1860s, and it was substance for a week's varied reading for the commuting market. Newnes's monthlies were more complex publications, diverse and substantial enough to occupy the leisure time of a month and sustain repeated reference. The multiform and heterogeneous character of the periodical text thus represents the key to understanding its formal and commercial development, and its social meaning in the late Victorian and Edwardian periods.

Biography

This book highlights Newnes's evolution as a periodical editor, publisher and proprietor in an age in which proprietors became especially significant as popular journalism was transformed by capitalisation and the forces of commercialism. The profession of publishing only developed into a vocation in its own right in the early nineteenth century, pioneered by such enterprising and speculative venturers as John Murray and Archibald Constable. Even in those early years the issue of whether publishing (and authorship) belonged to the province of business or the realm of art was a constant pressure on publishers.

The House of Cassell expanded into periodical and serial publishing in the 1860s and 1870s, founding a variety of periodicals. In 1865 Cassell were publishing three magazines, never producing more than twelve part issues per month. By 1888, they were publishing seven magazines, never producing fewer than forty part issues per month.[53] In the 1880s, Cassell's lead in periodical publishing diminished as its proprietors failed to adapt to public taste and underestimated rival publishing enterprises. The slack was taken up by George Newnes and other innovative publishers such as Harmsworth and Pearson, who captured and retained the market through a constant stream of innovation in periodical publishing.[54] They began, often with very little capital, not in bookselling or general publishing, but in periodical publishing. And they capitalised one successful periodical to establish others. Various measures paved the way for the development of the press along capitalistic lines. The Companies Act (1866) made it easier to form joint stock companies and over the next fifty years, over 4,000 newspaper companies were formed in England and Wales.[55]

---

[53] See Simon Nowell-Smith, *The House of Cassell, 1848-1958*, London: Cassell, 1958, pp.113-116.

[54] Both Harmsworth and Pearson were given their first openings in the journalistic field by Newnes, then editor and proprietor of *Tit-Bits*. Arthur Pearson began his career by winning a salaried position on Newnes's paper in one of the *Tit-Bits* prize competitions. He went on to establish *Pearson's Weekly* (1890) and many other journals. The young Harmsworth, attracted by the fact that Newnes offered to pay a guinea per short column to *Tit-Bits* contributors by return of post, collaborated with Max Pemberton to write an article about jerry-builders which Newnes agreed to publish in *Tit-Bits* (Max Pemberton, *Lord Northcliffe. A Memoir*, London: Hodder and Stoughton, 1922, pp.28-29)

Before the 1880s, a printer, printing family or joint stock company had ownership of a single paper. By the end of the nineteenth century, according to Raymond Williams, 'whole groups of papers and periodicals were being collected or begun' around 'a new kind of speculative owner'.[56]

George Newnes was such a 'speculative owner'. An idiosyncratic publisher, a Liberal MP, and a business-minded but public-spirited man, Newnes is the binding thread of this book. For the realm of Newnes's experience represents a crucial perspective on the social meaning of the periodical text as he fashioned it. If the periodical press was an interactive medium which constituted the context within which people 'lived and worked and thought', then George Newnes was an important factor in that context, and an important component of the process of interaction. And if the 'personality' of a periodical encompasses the predominant influence of the proprietor in shaping its characteristics, then Newnes was integral to the entire series of House of Newnes publications. Each section introduction will thus include an exploration of the ways in which Newnes's own experiences, preoccupations and public personality were played out in the establishment, naming and progress of his publications.

Born in 1851 at Matlock in Derbyshire, George Newnes was the son of a Congregational minister. He was educated primarily at a Congregational school in Derbyshire and then for a short time at the Shireland School in Birmingham and at the City of London School. And he spent his early working life in the wholesale business. In 1881, using money he had raised by opening a vegetarian restaurant in Manchester, he started a weekly paper called *Tit-Bits*. The establishment of *Tit-Bits* marked the beginning of a remarkable career in editing and publishing. Politically, Newnes was firmly tied to the Liberal Party. He entered Parliament as the member for the Newmarket division of Cambridgeshire in 1885 and remained until 1895, when he lost his seat, but gained a baronetcy in recognition of his services to the party. In 1900 he re-entered Parliament as the member for Swansea and represented that constituency until 1910. He was also a JP at Lynton, in North Devon, where he built a country house in 1893.

Newnes's formative years are illuminating in relation to his later success as an editor-proprietor. Being reared in a Congregationalist religious environment meant that Newnes was also exposed to Liberal political principles very early in life. Congregationalism and Liberalism were closely associated, and Newnes's father was an ardent Liberal. Silcoates School, which Newnes attended from the age of 6, was a school for the sons of Congregational ministers and missionaries. In the register of the parents, distant places such as Chinsura, Madras and Mauritius were represented. Many of these places were later to feature in *The Wide World Magazine*. At Silcoates, the spirit of broad liberalism prevailed, and the school's popular principal, Dr J. Bewglass, was a

---

[55] Other measures included the abolition of the advertisement duty in 1853, stamp duty in 1855, and paper duty in 1861. See George Boyce, James Curran and Pauline Wingate (eds), op. cit., London: Constable, 1978, pp.68, 151.

[56] Raymond Williams, *The Long Revolution*, pp.200-229.

staunch Liberal. When there was an election at Wakefield, masters and boys all joined in the excitement and enthusiastically supported the Liberal candidate. It is not, therefore, surprising to find Newnes entering parliament as a Liberal MP in 1885, becoming a member of the National Liberal Club (founded in 1882, and opening its first premises in June 1887), and establishing *The Westminster Gazette*, a Liberal evening newspaper, in 1893. Assessing the legacy of his time at Silcoates, W.T. Stead, who was Newnes's contemporary at the school, said that he learnt three important things: 'Christianity, cricket and democracy'.[57] Many Newnes publications may be seen as products of that legacy: the *Sunday Strand* as a medium of Christianity; *C.B. Fry's Magazine* and *The Captain* as purveyors of the cricketing ethos; and *Tit-Bits, The Million* and *The Westminster Gazette* as attempts to publicise and exploit democratic principles.

When George Newnes was a boy in the late 1850s and 1860s, he was an avid reader of Fenimore Cooper stories and had visions of embracing a life of heroic adventure. He later provided generations of boys with such stories in *The Wide World Magazine* and *The Captain*. As a schoolboy, he soon became 'profoundly impressed with the importance of religion' (not surprising, since his father was a Congregational minister). He held weekly prayer meetings at his school and aspired to become a preacher, an aspiration of which his parents strongly approved. Whilst he did not follow such a career path, he did later provide the religious with a popular medium of communication in the *Sunday Strand* (1900). The adolescent Newnes subsequently became, as he put it, 'stage-struck', and went to the theatre four nights a week with a friend in pursuit of the kind of familiarity with the stage that he saw as a necessary grounding for a theatrical career.

> We knew better than many of the critics the plot of every play that came out about that time, and the characteristics of every actor and actress upon the London stage.[58]

It is significant, in this context, that *The Strand*'s popular 'Portraits of Celebrities' series featured many celebrities of the London stage.

In 1899, Newnes wrote, for a series entitled 'What I Wanted to Be' in *The Captain*:

> My next ambition was destined to take practical shape. I became a greedy devourer of all kinds of periodical publications. Besides my own purchases I used to pay my Newsagent a shilling to let me spend a couple of hours in his shop, turning over the pages of the various publications, and, as he took most of those issued, it was very interesting. There I examined them, criticised them, and tried to improve upon them.

---

[57] W.T. Stead as cited in Reginald Pound, op. cit., p.14.

[58] *The Captain*, 1 (August 1899), p.493.

> In fact, at that time my thoughts were largely upon journals and magazines, and I suppose they have been largely upon them ever since.[59]

Newnes went on to establish dozens of successful periodicals, improving upon old formats and developing new ones.

As an employer, George Newnes acquired a reputation for benevolence and collaboration that matched the editorial image he cultivated in *Tit-Bits*, *The Million* and *The Strand*. He was regarded with respect and affection as a just and benevolent leader. A volume presented to him by his employees in 1900 to celebrate the thousandth issue of *Tit-Bits*, and addressed to 'Sir George Newnes, Bart, MP', resembled a petition of thanks to the lord of the manor:

> ... we, who have been associated with you so intimately at the offices of George Newnes Ltd, would ask you to accept this as a personal token of the pleasant relations, indeed, one might almost say respectful affection, which has always existed between employer and employed. This is a unanimous feeling. There are those who have been with you for years, there are others who have been with you for a little while. But this gift is one which represents the esteem and regard of all. We sincerely appreciate your kindness and thoughtfulness in all matters affecting the welfare of your employees here. As the head of this great firm you have a well-deserved reputation for energy and business enterprise. In all dealings with us you have won our sincere regard for your justice and generosity.
> Permit us to wish you and yours every happiness in life.

Newnes acted out his seigneurial image. 'Quite unconsciously', observed Friederichs, 'the founder and first proprietor of *The Westminster Gazette* had a lordly way about him.' When E.T. Cook suggested that the former editorial staff of the *PMG* would be willing to transfer their services to the new publication, Newnes said only, 'Well, bring them all over.'[60] Busts of Newnes were distributed about the country, at the places to which he made substantial benefactions (Putney, Lynton and Matlock), in a manner which reinforced his local connections as well as his national reputation (*see Figure 1*).

Newnes's editorial image also paralleled his local reputation in Lynton, North Devon, where he built a country residence. And his journalistic method paralleled his devotion to championing the interests and winning the approval of the local population. 'Never in Lynton and Lynmouth's long history', John Travis has recently remarked in a Churchillian manner, 'has so much been owed to one man':

---

[59] Ibid.

[60] Hulda Friederichs, op. cit., p.224.

> From the moment George Newnes first set foot in the town, he
> played a leading part in its development. He spent freely,
> exerted enormous influence and brought about major
> changes.[61]

On Hollerday Hill, just above the town of Lynton, Newnes built a beautiful
country mansion called Hollerday House. It was built by local workmen and
completed in 1893. With views of sea, rock, moor and woodland, established
gardens, woods, tennis courts, bowling greens and croquet lawns, it was the kind
of residence that might have appeared in *Country Life*, founded jointly by
Newnes and the firm of Hudson and Kearns in 1897. To Hollerday House,
Newnes and his family and friends adjourned each summer to escape the noise
and crowds of London. It was a tangible form of the kind of escapism that he
provided in *Country Life* and *The Wide World Magazine*. In a gesture that was
typical of this instinctive host and paternalist, Newnes opened Hollerday Hill to
the general public, stipulating only that visitors should not pick the ferns and
other rare plants he had planted. He paid for Warren Field, in the Valley of the
Rocks, to be levelled for a cricket ground in 1891 (the year that the *The Strand*
was established), and arranged to have a cricket pavilion erected. In May 1894,
he performed the opening ceremony at the new golf course on Martinhoe
Common, which he had helped to pay for. He also funded a new bowling green,
on a site immediately below Hollerday House, in 1904 (the year that *C.B. Fry's
Magazine* was established).

Newnes found that Lynton lacked the kind of public building requisite for
a fashionable watering place and that the inhabitants were unable to raise the
funds necessary to build one. So he bought a plot of land on Lee Road and
offered to build an impressive town hall as a gift to the community. The
foundation stones were laid by Lady Newnes and another prominent local
woman, Mrs Jeune, on 11 May, 1898, the same year in which two new Newnes
publications were established: *The Wide World Magazine* and *The Ladies'
Field*. The town hall took two years and cost £20,000 to build.[62] It was opened
in the same year that the *Sunday Strand* was established. On 15 August, 1900,
Sir George Newnes performed the opening ceremony (*see Figure 2*). He
formally handed over the building to the town, expressing the hope that it would
be 'a source of instruction and recreative pleasure, not only to the present
inhabitants, but to future generations'.[63] Such rhetoric echoed his publishing
manifesto: that his journals provided 'wholesome instruction and
entertainment'. The building's cornerstone bore the words 'Erected by Sir
George Newnes baronet, JP and presented by him to Lynton and Lynmouth For
Ever'. And in 1902, a bust of Newnes was placed at the site 'by the inhabitants
of Lynton', as the inscription read, 'in recognition of the many benefits he has

---

[61] John Travis, op. cit., p.96.

[62] The local building firm of Jones Bros. obtained the contract.

[63] It now houses the public library, council rooms and cinema.

conferred on them including the gift of this hall'. It was unveiled by Arthur Conan Doyle.[64] The name of George Newnes was thus as familiar to the people of Lynton as it was to the periodical-reading public. T.H.S. Escott observed that the donation of Lynton Town Hall and Putney Library (opened in 1899) were 'two specimens of conduct which made George Newnes the most widely popular as well as prosperous newspaper runner of the new era'.[65] They were, of course, good publicity as well as good deeds.

Approached by local Congregationalists in 1903 for a donation towards the cost of a new church, Newnes offered to pay for a larger site and for the construction of a spacious church, as a memorial to his father and an expression of his commitment to Congregationalism and the local community. The new church was opened in 1904. The Reverend R.J. Campbell, a famous London preacher, conducted the opening services. Newnes was later to make him a present of a new car. This scenario of organising the appearance of a celebrity and dispensing a lavish gift resembled one of Newnes's journalistic schemes. It serves to underline the connection between Newnes's public personas, editorial and seigneurial, and adds a new dimension to Stead's representation of the editor as 'the uncrowned king of an educated democracy'.

The clarity of this connection between the social and journalistic spheres is only enhanced by an understanding of the pivotal social role that Newnes and his family played at Lynton. 'George Newnes was a national figure who brought prestige and excitement to a small provincial resort', observes John Travis.[66] Many famous people, including Conan Doyle, gravitated to Lynton to be entertained by Newnes, just as authors and illustrators gravitated to his publications. Every summer, the arrival of the Newnes family was greeted with great rejoicing. Flags were flown, and a canon fired. On major occasions organised by Newnes too, such as the opening of the Lynton-Barnstaple railway, houses were decked with flowers and bunting, floral arches were suspended across the streets, bands played, and the people formed into long processions. At the coming of age of Frank Newnes, in September 1897 (the year that *Country Life* was founded), the Royal North Devon Hussars Band led a long procession through the town and up to Hollerday House, where Frank was presented with a silver salver from the inhabitants. The procession then returned to a field in town where upwards of 2,000 people were treated to a feast of turkey, goose, duck, beef and ham. In the evening, Hollerday Hill was illuminated with 14,000 electric lights. And the celebrations were rounded off with a fantastic display of fireworks and the firing of a huge bonfire. It was a day that remained long in local memories and an extravagant feat of publicity worthy of the great publisher. Newnes was much moved by the affection shown by the local people.

---

[64] According to the *Lyn Journal*, Sir George said on thanking them that it was so life-like that, when leaving the studio, he absentmindedly put his hat on the bust and walked out bare-headed. See Frederick Juniper, *The Lyn Journal* (handwritten), 1956, Lynton Library.

[65] T.H.S. Escott, op. cit., p.258.

[66] John Travis, op. cit., p.104.

It was hardly surprising that he offered to build the town hall later that month.[67] As a Liberal MP, Newnes had organised many similar occasions in an effort to rally support for the Liberal party. In June 1895, for instance, he had organised a demonstration in his seat in Cambridgeshire on Whitsuntide Feast Day, providing tea for 1,200 people, and organising for John Burns to give the public address.[68]

Newnes was very much aware of the transformations wrought by the communications revolution, and was a great devotee of new technologies (not only of printing technology, but of the automobile, the telephone, and of electric light). This aspect of Newnes, characteristic of his generation, was represented in *The Wide World Magazine*. When he made his first visit to Lynton to stay with Thomas Hewitt in September 1887, he had been shocked at the sight of the horses toiling up the steep hill from Lynmouth to Lynton. He immediately entered upon a scheme for a cliff railway in partnership with Hewitt and Bob Jones, the local engineer, putting up most of the capital himself. 'This was the way George worked', according to Travis:

> He saw an opportunity and took it. Schemes which met a public need and at the same time made him a profit appealed to him. He was quick to realise that the novelty of a cliff railway would bring in many visitors and might restore local prosperity, while at the same time providing him with a good return on his investment.[69]

There was thus a significant parallel between Newnes's publishing ventures, in which he combined business and benevolence with great success, and his other investment schemes. An Act of Parliament to build the Cliff Railway was obtained, at considerable expense, in 1888, and the work was completed by 1890. George Newnes presided at the opening ceremony in April 1890. Newnes was also chairman of the company which devised a scheme to build a narrow-gauge railway between Lynton and Barnstaple, and was the leading financier of the railway. The cutting of the first sod was seen as an occasion for much celebration and Newnes was honoured by the local population as the father of the scheme, again playing a major part in the festivities (*see Figure 3*). The railway was opened in 1898, the same year that *The Wide World Magazine* was established.

In public life, Newnes was thus a figure of benevolent paternalism, dispensing great gifts to an admiring public just as, in the guise of the New Journalist and through the medium of the popular periodical, he promoted various philanthropic causes and bestowed many lavish prizes.[70] His acts of

---

[67] Ibid.

[68] Newnes to John Burns, 30 May, 1895, Burns Papers BL, Add. MS. 46295. ff.104b.

[69] John Travis, op. cit., p.114.

[70] The technique of employing the widely-circulating organs of New Journalism as agencies of publicity and support for philanthropy and social reform was particularly characteristic of the period. Note, for instance, the journalistic reform campaigns waged by

charity, public and private, are too many to enumerate. Among the causes he supported were the Salvation Army and the Boys' Empire League. One West Country paper published an article, entitled 'The Story of Sergeorge the Giver' and written in the style of the monastic chroniclers, which depicted Newnes as a medieval Christian knight. It described his many gifts to Lynton, and the esteem in which he was held there. The community's reception of the cliff railway, for instance, was rendered in biblical language: 'And the people who were glad spake unto him and thanked him, and they stood before him and blessed his name.'[71] George Newnes, otherwise known as 'Sergeorge the Giver' in the West Country and 'Gentleman George' in his electorate of Swansea, played the part of the editor-squire instinctively and in multifarious settings.

Newnes was a self-made man: the very embodiment of the liberal, self-help ideology which he so strongly advocated. There was a distinctly educational, self-improving flavour about the popular knowledge volumes which he began producing at the turn of the century. And with his 'Household Series', his 'Pocket Classics', and his 'Red Cloth 6d. Library', Newnes offered the lower middle and upper working-class reader, and the female or juvenile reader, the status of the self-educated specialist.[72] His journalism was also informed by an awareness of the urge towards self-improvement which pervaded mid-Victorian morality and contemporary business instincts. Upbringing and temperament rendered Newnes open to the self-help gospel proclaimed by Samuel Smiles in his popular book of 1859, *Self Help*. He was a methodical man with a deep sense of personal integrity and a breadth of knowledge in the areas of law and business.[73] His *Sunday Strand*, begun in 1900, was overtly religious in tone, but his other publications tended to be imbued with general moral ideas rather than being directly concerned with piety. Newnes's Congregational associations, however, were a bar to his developing the *Weekly Dispatch* along the sensational lines of its chief competitors, *Lloyd's Weekly Sunday News* and *News of the World*, and after failing to make a success of this paper, he sold it to the Harmsworths.

The fortunes of the House of Newnes closely mirror the biographical bell curve inscribed by George Newnes, lending an intrinsic logic and symmetry to the chronological scope of this study. Beginning as a commercial traveller with a

---

W.T. Stead through the *Pall Mall Gazette*, and the philanthropic schemes administered by Cyril Arthur Pearson through *Pearson's Weekly*.

[71] Hulda Friederichs, op. cit., pp.195-197.

[72] Newnes published sixpenny volumes of the works of contemporary novelists such as Rider Haggard, Hall Caine, A.E.W. Mason, W.W. Jacobs, Stanley Weyman and Edgar Wallace. The Household Series included practical manuals on a range of subjects such as dog-care, home medicine, household management, gardening, cookery, needlework, and even a pronunciation dictionary. The ideology of professionalism and the rhetoric of expertise were thus extended to encompass novel reading, household work, popular music, patterns of speech and so on.

[73] Newnes's concern with legal issues relating to publishing is also apparent in a number of letters written to G.H. Hoyle of the *Devon and Exeter Daily Gazette* in November 1887, and held by the Secretary of the Lynmouth and Lynton Lift Company.

clerk's salary and limited career prospects, Newnes entered the publishing profession with a modest publication that appealed essentially to the lower middle-class reading public. The next ten years constituted a building stage, as *Tit-Bits* gathered momentum, and its editor-proprietor began to rise in social and financial status. Newnes built a magnificent house at Putney Heath and, in the 1885 General Election, won the Tory stronghold of Newmarket for the Liberals.

The next decade constituted a sort of 'Golden Age' for Newnes. In 1891, Newnes's publishing business was flourishing, and was floated as a company. The annual dividend of 10 per cent which he guaranteed for the next five years was consistently earned. This was a period of journalistic experiment and success, confidence, wealth and generosity for George Newnes. He established a succession of new, innovative and profitable publications, and the fruits of his success were amply distributed at Lynton, Matlock (his birthplace) and Putney (his London address) into divers other business projects, and amongst family, friends, employees and philanthropic organisations. 'George Newnes was building up a publishing empire', observes John Travis. 'Soon he branched into other forms of business. Everything he touched seemed to turn to gold .... George Newnes had become a celebrity.'[74] '*The Million*' was undoubtedly a name that bespoke Newnes's confidence in his financial prospects.

Yet in the last few years of his life, Newnes's ability to make money seemed to desert him. A number of unsuccessful business ventures and investments led to his losing much of the fortune he had accrued. A venture in oil-shale mining in New South Wales cost him £240,000. His temporary partnership with Lord Northcliffe's younger brother, Leicester Harmsworth, promoting the Darracq motor car to the British market, met with some success. But he forfeited most of his gains with a heavy investment in Peruvian rubber. A number of shaky speculative schemes in London for which he provided capital - a hammock-sprung motor-car seat, the 'Ever-clean' collar for men, and a device to equip motor-car wheels with springs in place of pneumatic tyres - were also failures. Even some of his schemes for new ventures in the book publishing field were doomed to failure. 'Thin Paper Classics' and 'The Art Library', both beautifully produced series, were nevertheless totally uneconomical at their selling price, and caused the company heavy losses.[75] The effect of these ventures was to decrease the value of the Newnes shares, and the dividend rate reached its lowest at 2.5 per cent. George Newnes personally contributed an

---

[74] John Travis, op. cit., p.98. In these years, Newnes bought Weldons Ltd, and secured the purchase option for the company of the French manufacturer of motor-cars, Mr A. Darracq, immediately raising the necessary subscriptions for the purchase of the company which flourished afterwards, providing considerable returns.

[75] A book department was established in 1895, and various projects in book publishing, such as Newnes's Penny Library of Famous Books (1895), Newnes's Pocket Classics (1903), Newnes's Devotional Series (1906), Newnes's Household Series (1910), and Newnes's Playtime Series (1910), followed.

undisclosed sum to bring the profits for 1906 up to £57,000. By 1907 they had dropped to £32,000.[76]

A report of the tenth AGM, published in *The Times* on 10 August 1907, offered an explanation of the company's inability to add to the dividend paid on ordinary shares in the first half of the year:

> In their desire still further to increase the business of the company, the board had embarked on enterprises on which they had lost considerable sums of money. It was there that the loss had been. Their magazines and periodicals were thoroughly prosperous. They would in future concentrate their energies on their serial publications .... Desirous not to lag behind they had spent considerable sums on advertising .... All their machinery was up to date and efficient. The only department of machinery which was not saving them money was the bookbinding, and they had consequently given it up, thus effecting a welcome economy.[77]

In August 1909 it was announced that the profits of the flagship company, George Newnes, Ltd, had fallen dramatically due to increased competition in the magazine business.

Newnes himself was a victim of diabetes, drink and a failing mind. In the last years of his life, he received a letter from the Prime Minister, intimating that his name was being put forward for a barony. He showed the letter to Sir Grimwood Mears, an old barrister friend who had been in the Indian civil service for many years. He decided to be known as Lord Wildcroft. At the Speaker's Dinner at the House of Commons, however, he drank to excess and had to be led away. His name was absent from the next Honours List. Sir Grimwood later recalled Frank Newnes's reaction: 'He has ruined my life.'[78] Lady Newnes enlisted the aid of the Reverend R.J. Campbell to help restore her husband's sense of responsibility to his family, his friends and his business. But the attempt was a failure, and Newnes acquired a habit of disappearing for extended periods without notice, leaving important decisions in suspense.

When, in the General Election of January 1910, Frank Newnes lost the seat that he had held for four years as MP for Bassetlaw in Nottinghamshire, Newnes was bitterly disappointed. He died on 9 June, at Hollerday House, and was buried at Lynton.[79] When his will was published it was apparent that most of the family fortune had gone. Made in 1895 on a sheet of foolscap paper, it was proved at £174,753, an amount which went towards debts to the company. Lady Newnes was to receive £3,000 a year. The bequest could not be made. Frank Newnes, still a board member for George Newnes, Ltd, was forced to

---

[76] Reginald Pound, op. cit., pp. 111-112.

[77] *The Times*, 10 August, 1907, p. 14.

[78] Reginald Pound, op. cit., p. 112.

[79] Hollerday House was destroyed by fire on 4 August, 1913. See John Travis, op. cit., pp. 105-107.

seek a personal loan guarantee for £1,000 from Leicester Harmsworth.[80] Frank was to spend most of his life paying back the debts left by his father.

Despite the injurious effects of these latter events on the company's affairs, many preferred to remember Newnes for his contribution to publishing, his acts of public benevolence, and his generosity to the vast numbers of people whose lives were touched, in various ways, by his activities. 'The news of Sir George's death', according to one North Devon paper, 'caused a profound feeling of regret in Lynmouth and Lynton, where flags were flown at half-mast as a sign of public grief':

> By all classes he was beloved for his broadmindedness, generosity, and particularly for his kindly interest in the working people, which was a most notable trait in his character. Large as his private benefactions were, his gifts to Lynton were on an almost princely scale.[81]

George Newnes was remembered as publisher, proprietor and editor, paternalist, gentleman and squire. But he was also remembered as an innovator, as the *Daily Graphic* emphasised in its obituary of him:

> Something more than a notable figure in journalism has passed away with the death of Sir George Newnes. An innovator has gone, though he has left his influence behind .... it was the application of Sir George Newnes of innovation to the monthly magazine, to the picture photograph, and to other subjects connected with journalism, that turned his enterprises into gold.[82]

Newnes has frequently been associated with the legendary Greek king Midas. He employed a creative approach to publishing and journalism which resulted in the accumulation of a vast fortune, and in this way represented an ideal of entrepreneurialism that had gained remarkable currency in the nineteenth century (*see Figure 4*).

Terms, Scope and Structure of this Study

In order to clarify the thrust of this book, it is necessary to introduce and define some of the central terms used, such as 'British society', 'class', 'the reading public' and 'popular culture'. 'New Journalism' will be defined in the introduction to Part I, to which it is most relevant. In this period, the concept of 'British society' was particularly difficult to define, because it embraced four

---

[80] *Wandsworth and Putney Borough News*, 12 August, 1910, p.144; Reginald Pound, op. cit., p.113.

[81] Cited in Hulda Friederichs, op. cit., p.296.

[82] Ibid., pp.144-145.

national cultures, was affected by transnational forces common to all European societies and, as Jose Harris has pointed out, 'stretched from the village street to the African veldt, from the parish to the globe'.[83] In this study, the way in which 'British society' was extended to include nations with which it traded or which it governed, or which in some sense shared in the identity of Britons, and in which the term came to encompass the prospect of an expanding but interconnected world, is discussed in the chapter on *The Wide World Magazine*.

The term 'reading public' has a long and varied history, but is insufficiently flexible to be used in this study.[84] On the other hand, the notion of 'reading communities', derived from reader-response theory, has significantly influenced the way in which readership has been conceptualised here. This term describes categories of readers linked together by a common experience or expectation of reading, and by common social, political, ideological or cultural objectives or bonds rather than by physical proximity. It offers an alternative both to the excessively generalised (and historically class-laden) notion of a 'reading public', and to theories which revolve around the concept of the individual 'reader' who relates to the text independently and unambiguously. It is particularly appropriate to the periodical text, which aims to make contact with a large and essentially (but not exclusively) coherent body of readers by tapping into the realms of their common experience. Newnes's rendering of the readerships of *Tit-Bits* and *The Million* as 'loyal Tit-Bitites' and 'trusty Millionaires' is the most transparent example of his own attempt to develop and exploit the concept of a community of readers. The other terms employed here to describe periodical readers include 'circulation' and 'the market for periodical literature'. They are equally applicable to the concept of readership, in an age in which circulations increased and were crucial to advertising revenue, and an increasingly commercialised publishing industry sought to exploit the full extent of the market for newspapers and magazines.

The notion of 'class' is employed frequently here in discussions of reception and readership, and in the elaboration of the cultural context from which each periodical derived its meaning. 'Class', to draw upon E.P. Thompson's definition, is an historical phenomenon which happens within human relationships and human experience. Class consciousness - 'the way in which these experiences are handled in cultural terms: embodied in traditions, value-systems, ideas and institutional formations' - is central to the notion of

---

[83] Jose Harris, *Private Lives, Public Spirit: Britain 1870-1914*, Harmondsworth: Penguin, 1993, p.4.

[84] For Q.D. Leavis the reading public was a social and intellectual entity which had forfeited its claims to literary authority as a result of the incursions of a commercial ethos and a consumer culture. It had 'split', 'spoilt', 'collapsed' and 'disintegrated', wrote Leavis in *Fiction and the Reading Public*. See Q.D. Leavis, op. cit., pp. 31, 96, 117, 172, 181. In a rather more optimistic study, Richard Altick described the growth of the reading public as a symbol of democratic development. See Richard D. Altick, *The English Common Reader. A Social History of the Mass Reading Public*, Chicago: University of Chicago Press, 1963.

class, and to its application to periodical research.[85] This study emphasises the way in which 'class' was rendered within the context of an interactive and discursive relationship between proprietor, editor, author, illustrator or advertiser - the producers of the periodical text - and the publication's readers. It relies on both subjective measures (attitudes and values, language, education, leisure activities) and objective measures (income, occupation) in its use of the term. As has been suggested here in challenging the historical myth surrounding *Tit-Bits*, for example, the language, competitions, illustrations and advertisements employed in a magazine tell the historian as much about its audience as does its price.

Harold Perkin has demonstrated that late Victorian Britain remained an extremely segregated society, although the rise of professional society, and the continuing tensions between entrepreneurial and professional ideals, tended to complicate class distinctions.[86] Perkin's argument has particularly informed my discussion of *The Strand Magazine*. In fact, various social, political and economic movements transcended class boundaries to some extent. One challenge to the assumptions of class society came from what Beatrice Webb described in her autobiography as a 'class-consciousness of sin' amongst 'men of property and intellect'.[87] This notion of a negative class image has also proved suggestive in relation to *The Strand*. Nevertheless, aside from the stratifying impact of distribution and large-scale production, the organisation of work, schools, housing, welfare and recreation all conspired to compartmentalise British society along class lines. The notion of 'class' will thus be used throughout this book.

'Culture', according to Raymond Williams, is 'one of the two or three most complicated words in the English language'.[88] Williams suggests two broad definitions which may be of use here, both of which he explored in his own work, and which have also informed the work of scholars in the field of cultural studies. 'Culture' suggests 'a particular way of life, whether of a people, a period or a group', according to Williams. This definition encompasses cultural practices or what cultural theorists often refer to as lived cultures, such as youth sub-cultures, home-ownership, industrial and urban cultural practices. 'Culture' can also be used to refer to 'the works and practices of intellectual and especially artistic activity'. This definition can be used to refer to signifying practices or cultural *texts*, such as soap opera, comics, or, in this case, magazines and newspapers. There has tended to be a division in cultural theory between the study of *texts* and the study of *lived* cultures or cultural practices. This study lays emphasis on the cultural texts which constitute its main source of evidence

---

[85] E.P. Thompson, *The Making of the English Working Class*, London: Penguin, 1968, pp. 9-10.

[86] Harold Perkin, *The Rise of Professional Society: England Since 1880*, London and New York: Routledge, 1989.

[87] Beatrice Webb, *My Apprenticeship*, Penguin, 1938, vol.1, p.204.

[88] Raymond Williams, *Keywords*, London: Fontana, 1983, p.7.

(Newnes's various periodicals), but makes significant reference to the way in which those texts connected with lived cultures (commuting practices, professional society, work and leisure patterns, youth sub-cultures).

'Popular culture' then, is a term which brings into play a complex combination of the meanings attached to the terms 'popular' and 'culture'. Williams suggests four current meanings for the term 'popular': 'well-liked by many people'; 'inferior kinds of work'; 'work deliberately setting out to win favour with the people'; and 'culture actually made by the people themselves'.[89] In the sense that it represents a culture which is widely favoured, popular culture can be quantitatively assessed to determine its 'popularity'. In the case of magazines of the Victorian and Edwardian periods, however, for which accurate circulation figures are rarely available, the quantitative dimension is problematic. While the term 'popularity' will be used in this sense, with reference to circulation estimates, its use will necessarily be rather loose.

A second way of defining 'popular culture' is by contrasting it to high culture, as a kind of residual category of cultural texts and practices which fail to meet certain criteria - 'moral worth', for example, or 'formal complexity' - which would qualify them as high culture. This definition entails a notion of the 'exclusivity' of the audience which, according to Pierre Bordieu, has been used largely to support class distinctions. Indeed, it often relies on the claim that popular culture is mass produced for mass consumption. And it carries the implication that such culture is, in some way, irredeemably commercial, imposed and impoverished, formulaic and manipulative; its audience a mass of non-discriminating readers. The term 'mass literacy' is generally associated with this conceptualisation of popular culture, and it has been integrated into the debate over New Journalism. In this sense, the terms 'popular' and 'popular culture' carry connotations of inferiority. They are used to describe a kind of second-rate or consolatory culture catering to those unable to comprehend real culture - that which Matthew Arnold calls 'the best that has been thought and said in the world'. Newnes self-consciously played upon this tradition when he introduced *Tit-Bits* as a paper whose producers would 'find out from this immense field of literature the best things that have been said or written, and weekly ... place them before the public for one penny'.[90] This book attempts to dismantle this definition of 'popular culture', and to employ the very terms in which it is couched to analyse the complexities and contradictions inherent in the way in which the rise of a mass consumer culture was handled in cultural terms.

Finally, in his political discussions, the Italian Marxist Antonio Gramsci, suggested that popular culture is neither the imposed culture of the mass culture theorists, nor a spontaneously emergent and oppositional 'culture from below' (a culture made by the people themselves), but a terrain of exchange between

---

[89]   Ibid.

[90]   *Tit-Bits*, 1, 1 (October 1881), p.1.

dominant and subordinate classes and cultures.[91] This takes us back to the debate in cultural and media studies over the balance between production and reception in the creation of meaning through cultural texts. And it takes us back to one of the central methodological themes of this book: the periodical text as a mechanism of exchange and negotiation between producer and consumer; editor-proprietor and reader.

The period covered by this book, chosen because it represents the three decades of Newnes's publishing career, from the invention of *Tit-Bits* to his death in 1910, was a tremendously rich, dynamic, crowded and tumultuous period in British history. Jose Harris has argued that:

> In so far as there have ever been great chasms rather than mere subterranean murmurings in the deep structures of British social history, it seems to me that they occurred in the 1870s and 1880s ... rather than in the apparently more dramatic and cataclysmic happenings of either of the two world wars.[92]

This may sound like an attempt to defend the historian's specialisation in the period. Yet these years saw many significant developments: the extension of the franchise through the 1867 and 1884 Reform Acts, and other legislation relating to political representation with which Newnes was involved as a devotee of radical liberalism; the global revolution in food production; the centralisation, urban transformation and imperial rise of Britain, and especially London; and the onset of mass education, mass culture and mass leisure. Gender roles, and the legal and personal relations between men and women, were increasingly contested and uncertain. These changes created new and distinctive class, status, cultural and consumer groups (or in journalistic terms, 'reading communities') to which George Newnes catered through a variety of periodical publications.

In the 1890s in particular, as the end of the nineteenth century approached, there was a widely diffused sense that Britons were participating in the emergence of 'modernity'. The attention focussed on the development of the 'New' Journalism and the representation of Newnes as the creator of modern journalistic practice were symbolic of this. And *The Wide World Magazine* was infused with a spirit of enthusiasm for various modernising developments in science, technology, transportation and communication, and for the evolution of a distinctively modern culture of time and space. Yet there was much in the cultural, journalistic and social life of the period that combined the continuity of established tradition with 'modern' innovation. In a journalistic context, *The Westminster Gazette* represented the combination of old and new.

One key aspect of modernisation was the so-called consumer revolution. The 1880s, John Benson has argued, saw the beginnings of Britain's evolution into a consumer society with a consumer culture, in which choice and credit were

---

[91] See Roger Simon, *Gramsci's Political Thought: An Introduction*, London: Lawrence and Wishart, 1982.

[92] Jose Harris, op. cit., p.252.

readily available, social value was defined in terms of purchasing power and material possessions, and there was an overriding focus on that which was new, modern and fashionable.[93] This 'revolution' encompassed, for instance, the growth of advertising and the department store trade in women's fashion (central to *The Ladies' Field*), the creation of a distinctive youth culture (central to *The Captain*) and the commercialisation of sport (central to *C.B. Fry's Magazine*).[94]

Given the complexity of the subject, the structure of this study will integrate the major interpretative themes with the textual sources and their historical and biographical contexts. Groups of thematically-linked chapters have been divided into sections, the conceptual and contextual core of each established in a short introduction. The seven chosen periodicals (Newnes's best-known publications) will be examined in the order in which they were established, one in each chapter (except for Chapter 1, which examines two publications closely linked by style, features and audience). It is hoped that this structure will clarify the various themes and arguments of this book, and emphasise the way in which the evolving role of George Newnes in the field of periodical publishing gave structure to his publications and captured the diversity of his world.

Part I, entitled 'The New Journalism: A Liberal Profession or a Branch of Business?', discusses the ways in which Newnes established and consolidated his place in the so-called New Journalism through his early publications: *Tit-Bits* (1881), *The Million* (1892) and *The Strand Magazine* (1891). All three were owned, published and edited by George Newnes himself, and were heavily dependent upon Newnes's editorial personality and his promotional skills. They offer an insight into the interactive nature of the periodical text as Newnes created it and his audience received it, into some of the techniques of the New Journalism, and into the ways in which debates over journalistic developments were handled in textual and discursive terms.

Part II, 'Liberalism and Imperialism: Developing Formats and Expanding Horizons', explores the relationship between developments in New Journalism and the character and evolution of liberalism and imperialism in late Victorian and Edwardian Britain. It examines two publications which were owned and managed but not edited by George Newnes, and which bore the mark of his experience, views and affiliations. In many ways an old-style political journal, with political connections and a political purpose, a relatively small (if influential) circulation and no commercial benefits for its proprietor, *The Westminster Gazette* (1893) represented Newnes's commitment to Liberalism. Yet this paper employed popular commercial techniques and innovative features, and this,

---

[93] John Benson, *The Rise of Consumer Society, 1880-1980*, London and New York: Longman, 1994. The revolution's starting point has been a matter of considerable contention.

[94] S.H. Benson compiled and published *Benson's Facts for Advertisers* in 1905 in an attempt to make facts about the various advertising mediums available to would-be publicists. Newspaper and magazine publicity was deemed particularly potent, and Benson attempted to provide relevant information about the various publishing houses to advertisers. Circulation figures, however, were notable for their absence. See S.H. Benson, *Benson's Facts for Advertisers*, London, 1905, p.i.

combined with the reticence of its producers to admit to the direct influence of party ties, demonstrated that it equally had connections with newer, more popular journals which aimed at a commercially-sustained independence. *The Wide World Magazine* (1898) was at one level an expression of the proprietor's patriotic enthusiasm for Liberal imperialism, and in a wider sense, it reflected and shaped new ways of experiencing time and space, echoing the enthusiasm of his generation for the transport and communications revolution which had brought the 'wide world' within the experience of so many Britons.

Part III, 'Specialisation and Diversification: Targeting Niche Audiences and Exploiting a Segmented Market', explores the ways in which Newnes, as an established publisher, expanded his business to cater to a growing variety of interest, social, professional and consumer groups in order fully to exploit the market for periodical literature. It was in this period that magazines were first targeted positively towards specific classifications. The key to success was to compartmentalise and specialise. Newnes was involved in this process at a conceptual and business level, although he had little to do with the ongoing work of producing this batch of magazines. Of the many weekly and monthly publications established by Newnes, two successful magazines will be examined closely: *The Ladies' Field* (1898), a weekly illustrated journal for middle-class and society women; and *The Captain* (1899), a monthly illustrated magazine for public school boys and for the vast number of juvenile readers who shared in an admiration for the public school 'gentleman', the 'sportsman' and the 'Empire Boy'. These publications engaged with a variety of cultural practices, preoccupations, anxieties, and journalistic techniques. They represent the expansion of George Newnes's publishing operations, and reflect the convergence of culture and profit within an ever-increasing range of periodical prototypes.

This book emphasises a number of underlying processes, in addition to these three major themes of New Journalism, Liberalism/imperialism, and marketing. Such processes include the continuing tensions between entrepreneurial and professional ideals in the period; the relationship between class and culture (and between high and popular culture) in the context of late nineteenth-century commercialism and Newnes's radical aspirations towards 'community' and 'fellowship'; the development of new patterns in political, urban and industrial life; and the cultural effects of modernisation. The various phases of George Newnes's periodical publishing career are linked to broader developments in the world of journalism and publishing. Ultimately, this book seeks to demonstrate the ways in which Newnes's experiments in New Journalism were successfully poised, as were those of other New Journalists, between culture and profit.

Figure 1. Bust of Sir George Newnes in the entrance to Putney Library, commemorating his donation of the library to the people of Putney, in 1899. A similar bust now stands in the boardroom at IPC Magazines, the company into which George Newnes, Ltd was incorporated in 1958. The motto 'Festina Prudenter' appears with the Newnes family crest, presumably chosen by Newnes in 1895, when he was awarded the baronetcy.

Figure 2. Opening of Lynton Town Hall, August 1900. George Newnes leans from the balcony.

Figure 3. A triumphal arch erected to celebrate the cutting of the first sod for the Lynton and Barnstaple Railway. It was placed above the entrance road to Hollerday House, and carried the deferential message, 'Honour to Whom Honour is Due'. Reproduced by kind permission of Paul Gower.

Figure 4. George Newnes, from the cartoon by 'Spy' in Vanity Fair. *Newnes bore all the marks of the successful entrepreneur, in his grey frock coat with silk-faced lapels, grey silk cravat and double-breasted waistcoat.*

PART I

The New Journalism:
A Liberal Profession or a Branch of
Business?

Introduction to Part I

George Newnes embarked upon *Tit-Bits* and *The Million* in a late Victorian atmosphere that Paul Ferris has so evocatively recreated in his study of the House of Northcliffe, spurred on by 'the glowing prospects of the coming age':

> Those morning commuters in their black coats and top hats, pouring into the smoky vale of London by steam train and horse bus, were a new generation of educated citizens. Their children would read, learn, grow, multiply, and cover the face of the earth with literate Britons. More and more of them would live in cities, in rows of pink and yellow houses with net curtains on the windows. *A sense of people, of gathering millions with names, voices, votes, desires, and money, was in the air .... The mass market for everything was trembling on the edge of being born.* Beecham's Pills were making a fortune for Mr Beecham. Railway companies competed to take working men and their families to the seaside. Mr Lever was selling four hundred tons of soap a week .... Leisure would percolate the masses as thoroughly as Fry's Cocoa and Will's Woodbines. They would have time, the commodity that only the rich had had before.[1]

The 'gathering millions' were members of the expanding lower middle class: a commuting, educated, urban, increasingly enfranchised and consumerist public, with access to leisure time. To George Newnes, with the advantage of commercial training and a knowledge of the tastes of the lower middle classes, they represented a vast pool of potential periodical readers. And he sought to appeal to their desires with two penny weekly papers: *Tit-Bits* and *The Million*. Thus Reginald Pound observed that *Tit-Bits* 'quickened life for a vast mass of lower-middle class readers of all ages'.[2]

The late Victorian and Edwardian middle class, as defined by Chiozza Money, was composed of taxpaying families with an income of between £160 (the income tax threshold in 1905) and £700 a year. At the lower end, the middle class included shopkeepers, schoolteachers, clerks and white-collar workers, often struggling to maintain middle-class status on insufficient incomes. Professional society, spanning the upper ranks of the middle class, was on the rise in the late nineteenth century, its growth stimulated by the rapid expansion of the service occupations, and its interests defended by a range of newly formed collective associations. At the upper end, the middle class included senior civil servants, clergymen, lawyers, doctors, local manufacturers and wholesalers, university vice-chancellors, public-school headmasters and national newspaper

---

[1]   Paul Ferris, Paul Ferris, *The House of Northcliffe: The Harmsworths of Fleet St*, London: Weidenfeld and Nicolson, 1971, p.3. My italics.

[2]   Reginald Pound, *Mirror of the Century: The Strand Magazine, 1891-1950*, London: Heinemann, 1966, p.11.

and periodical editors. At this level, the middle class could merge with the fringes of 'Society'. 'Society', or 'the upper ten thousand' as *The Queen* and Karl Marx labelled this set, was comprised of rich and powerful landowners and businessmen, together with some very successful lawyers, engineers, architects, authors, artists, judges, fashionable physicians, editors and university men. By the time *The Strand* was established in 1891, Newnes had risen from the ranks of the lower middle class to become a wealthy publisher and a Liberal MP, and, during the next decade, acquired all the trappings of a 'Society' man: a yacht, a car, a country house, an influential political paper (*The Westminster Gazette*) and a positive plethora of other successful publications, various domestic and foreign business concerns, a substantial fortune, a wide circle of well-connected friends and a baronetcy. He was thus ideally placed to create the kind of publication that would appeal to this class. *The Strand*, a sixpenny illustrated monthly magazine, was just such a publication.

Conditions of reception and distribution were integral to the success of Newnes's magazines. In the second half of the nineteenth century, as Gareth Stedman Jones has shown, the work-centred artisan culture that had prevailed amongst the upper-working class in the first half of the century gradually yielded to a culture oriented towards the family and home, as working hours were reduced, and workers who had lived in the immediate vicinity of their work began to live further away.[3] The increase in the number of family papers like *Tit-Bits* and *The Million*, designed to appeal to a varied reading community, was intimately related to such a cultural climate. W.H. Smith had established his first railway bookstall on Euston Station in November 1848, and in the same year, Routledge had launched its 'Railway Library' to meet the needs of a growing travelling public. By the following year, Smith had established 144 shops on stations or station approaches. The rapid and comprehensive development of a country-wide network of railway bookstalls was crucial to the expansion of periodical publishing. And *Tit-Bits*, distributed through such outlets, consisting of brief, easily digestible portions, and popularising the notion that every copy constituted a railway insurance policy for readers, was intimately linked to the commuting phenomenon.[4] It appeared on Thursday, and was designed to provide reading matter for the weekend and ensuing week. *The Strand*, too, a best-seller at all the main-line bookstalls and throughout the empire, was a favourite amongst the travelling public.

---

[3]   Gareth Stedman Jones, 'Working-Class Culture and Working-Class Politics in London, 1870-1900: Notes on the Re-Making of a Working Class', *Journal of Social History*, 7, 7 (Summer 1974), p.486. For Stedman Jones, the significance of this cultural shift lay in the fact that it undermined working-class radicalism.

[4]   W.H. Smith took 135,000 copies of *Tit-Bits* per week in 1897. Newnes even published the story of an American who auctioned a copy of *Tit-Bits* in a tramcar in the U.S. for 25 cents. See *Tit-Bits*, 15, 382 (February 1889), p.285.

Many critics have commented that *Tit-Bits* 'revolutionised' popular journalism, and that Newnes was the founder of modern journalistic practice.[5] Whilst Newnes's paper did not cause the kind of complete historical break associated with the term 'revolution', it initiated and reflected many changes in the world of journalism, and was integral to the New Journalism emergent in the late nineteenth and early twentieth centuries. In the 1880s, English journalism was transformed by technological innovation (the introduction of the telegraph, telephone, typewriter, high-speed rotary press and half-tone photographic block), commercialisation (substantial profits, through large sales and advertising becoming a major objective of newspaper proprietors) and a shift in the market for journalism. 'In readership terms', Joel Wiener has suggested, 'classlessness edged past class as the circulation of papers soared into the millions.'[6]

In May 1887, Matthew Arnold unleashed a cultural debate on the state of journalism, in which he and W.T. Stead were to be two of the greatest protagonists. Arnold represented the traditionalist arbiter of culture, fearful of the effects of the 'new democracy'. 'New Journalism' was, in fact, a term Arnold coined, in a derisory (and much-quoted) article in *The Nineteenth Century* (May 1887). 'We have had opportunities of observing a new journalism which a clever and energetic man has lately invented', wrote Arnold. He was referring to Stead, then editor of the *Pall Mall Gazette*:

> It has much to recommend it; it is full of ability, novelty, variety, sensation, sympathy, generous instincts; its one great fault is that it is *feather-brained* .... Well, the democracy, with abundance of life, sympathy, good instincts, is disposed to be, like this journalism, feather-brained.[7]

Arnold criticised the features which he saw as characteristic of the 'New Journalism': a 'popular' tone, an excessively dramatic reporting style, a lack of editorial responsibility and the transparent pursuit of profit.

Stead, on the other hand, was determined to transform journalism into something which gave expression to the democratic culture of the time. He expatiated continually on the illimitable range of the editor's powers and responsibilities. In an article on 'Government by Journalism', published in 1886, he argued that the newspaper editor was 'the uncrowned king of an educated democracy', receiving a daily mandate from his people, who re-elected him every time they bought his paper. Through his paper, the editor could inform and represent the public, conduct social missions, expose abuses, judge grievances and right wrongs. The press was the 'engine of reform', the 'Chamber of

---

5   See, for instance, *Public Opinion*, 19 August, 1904, p.236; Harold Herd, *The Making of Modern Journalism*, London: Allen and Unwin, 1927, p.13; and R.A. Scott James, *The Influence of the Press* (1913) as cited in Reginald Pound, op. cit., p.17.

6   Joel H. Wiener (ed.), *Papers for the Millions: The New Journalism in Britain, 1850s-1914*, New York: Greenwood Press, 1988, p.xii.

7   Matthew Arnold, 'Up to Easter', *Nineteenth Century*, XXI (May 1887), pp.629-643.

Initiative', the 'voice of democracy', the 'apostle of fraternity' and the
'phonograph of the world'.[8] Stead, a school friend of George Newnes, might
almost have been invoking the language of *Tit-Bits*.

The editor was accorded increasing social and professional status in the
Victorian period.[9] Thus, the editorial voice was a major factor in the method by
which *Tit-Bits* (in particular), *The Million* and *The Strand* connected with readers.
Yet the journalist, associated with a form of writing seen as ephemeral, unfinished
and uncrafted by contrast with authentic 'literature', and identified with a
Bohemian way of life, faced something of a crisis of respectability. In the
discourse of the developing journalistic profession, the distinction between the
socially respectable 'amateur' and the 'professional' journalist was rigidly
preserved. By the 1880s, however, professionalism was acquiring positive
connotations as Britain developed into a professional society. Periodical writers
had struggled throughout the century with the nomenclature of their craft. They
had generally opted to nourish their associations with literature and 'higher
journalism', but they now began to extract value from their status as
'professionals'. This process was integral to the success of *The Strand*.

The so-called New Journalism has been comprehensively defined within
the historiography of periodical research. It was heavily influenced by American
journalism. And it was increasingly dependent on visual innovation, featuring
novelties of typography and make-up: banner headlines, news and parliamentary
reports spread across unbroken columns; attractive display advertising; and a
range of illustrations, some of them produced by new techniques. Late
nineteenth-century journals featured a brighter, clearer style of writing, devoted
less space to leaders and cultivated a more standardised style of reporting news,
influenced by news agencies such as Reuters. In content, there was a shift from
parliamentary and political news to sport, crime, gossip and sexual matters.
Published excerpts such as those printed in *Tit-Bits* proliferated. And there was
an increase in the number of columns catering to readers' specific tastes
(women's pages, children's pages, comic strips), and in the publication of
correspondence pages and serialised popular fiction. The press became
increasingly commercialised, and vast increases in circulation and advertising,
aided by prize competitions and insurance schemes, guaranteed substantial
profits for proprietors. In the context of these transformations in the business
and style of journalism, George Newnes established his place alongside other
leading New Journalists such as Stead, O'Connor, Pearson and Harmsworth as
an innovator whose contributions were critical to the formation of the modern
press.

The main point of difference between the New Journalism and the old,
according to T.P. O'Connor, was 'the more personal tone of the modern

---

    8   W.T. Stead, 'Government by Journalism', *Contemporary Review*, XLIX (May
1886), pp.653-674.
    9   See Joel Wiener (ed.), *Innovators and Preachers: The Role of the Editor in Victorian
England*, New York: Greenwood Press, 1985.

methods'.[10] Newnes certainly employed such a tone in his early publications. Anonymity gradually lost ground in the 1870s and the New Journalism employed correspondence columns, signed articles and personal detail extensively. In this way, it substituted pluralism - the explicit identification of many authors and spokespeople - for a notion of single authority implicit in Victorian journalism. Interviews and investigative stories, modelled on American examples, were pioneered by journalists such as Stead and O'Connor. (Stead's series exposing juvenile prostitution, entitled 'The Maiden Tribute of Modern Babylon', attracted extensive publicity, especially when the campaign leader was imprisoned in fighting for the cause. It has generally been viewed as a crucial episode in the development of the New Journalism.) The interview, in fact, became one of the chief journalistic forms of the period.[11]

The rhetoric of personality and individual responsibility transformed the field of journalistic production. The success of *Tit-Bits* thus relied upon Newnes's ability as editor to create and maintain a bond of sympathetic intimacy with his readers. This paper contained many correspondence columns. *The Million* offered hundreds of biographical sketches. And *The Strand* was famous for its interview series. And all three of these publications relied heavily on editorials. It is curious to note the contradiction between the rhetoric of 'personalised journalism' and the developing structure of the modern press: heavily capitalised and syndicated, hierarchically organised and technically complex.

Yet the New Journalism was not entirely new. Many of the changes that seemed to usher in a modern press were anticipated by the old journalism. And the old journalism was itself affected by developments in the radical and popular press of the 1830s, by the success of the Sunday papers from the 1840s onwards, by the influence of sub-literary forms (chapbooks, almanacs, broadsheets) and of cheap fiction upon popular culture, and by a general expansion in the press resulting from the repeal of the taxes on knowledge and from increasing editorial opportunities. The so-called 'bohemian journalism' of journalists such as George Augustus Sala, Frederick Greenwood and Edmund Yates in the decades after 1850 laid the foundations for the New Journalism.[12]

---

[10]   T.P. O'Connor, 'The New Journalism', *The New Review*, 1 (1889), p.423.

[11]   'If you do anything on earth the world is interested in, the world demands nowadays to know when and where and how and why you do it', wrote Grant Allen in the preface to a a a collection of interviews by Raymond Blathwayt:

> To answer all these biographical inquiries, the Great Republic invented the Interviewer; and Britain, ever ready to annex whatever it can lay its hands upon, immediately annexed and adopted him from her. (Raymond Blathwayt *Interviews: By Raymond Blathwayt*, (Preface by Grant Allen), London: A.W. Hall, 1893, pp.11-12)

Blathwayt did many of the interviews in *The Strand* and *The Million*.

[12]   Greenwood, the first editor of the *Pall Mall Gazette*, introduced a number of innovations, including 'Occasional Notes' and sensational articles. Yates pioneered 'keyhole journalism': gossip columns and celebrity interviews. See B.I. Diamond, 'A Precursor of the New Journalism: Frederick Greenwood of the *PMG*', Joel Wiener, 'How New was the New

Himself a practitioner for thirty years of what was, by implication, the 'old journalism', Matthew Arnold had sought to elevate his own journalism into 'criticism' and lend it the authority of 'literature', by distinguishing it from a new style of journalism. He created a model of journalistic development within which New Journalism was associated with a clear historical fault line.

Arnold inaugurated a new critical tradition in discourse about the press, complicated by the fear that 'the common reader' represented a threat to both quality and order, that was to persist into the twentieth century. George Gissing's novel *New Grub Street* (1891) evoked images of mechanisation and decline. And Edward Dicey, a prominent contemporary journalist, concluded in 1905 that 'the newspaper-reading public of today wants to be amused, not instructed .... They like to have their mental food given them in minces and snippets, not chops and joints.' Dicey could well have been referring to *Tit-Bits*. Writing in 1917, T.H.S. Escott contended that 'journalism has sunk, or at least is in danger of sinking, from a liberal profession to a branch of business'. In the *Oxford History of England, 1870-1914*, R.C.K. Ensor referred to this period as a watershed in which 'a dignified phase in English journalism' was destroyed and *Tit-Bits*, catering to a new class of uncritical reader, inaugurated a new tradition.[13] More recently, Alan J. Lee concluded pessimistically: 'In the simplest terms, the press had become [by 1914] ... a business almost entirely, and a political, civil and social institution hardly at all.' Lee conceded, however, that the New Journalism was creative in its introduction of typographic and stylistic changes.[14] Writers as politically diverse as José Ortega y Gasset, T.S. Eliot, F.R. Leavis and George Orwell all shared a pessimism about mass society and the onset of 'mass culture'. They saw the industrialisation of culture as a key element in the decline of civilised values and practices. George Newnes, embarking upon a career in periodical publishing, was well aware of the critical climate. In his three earliest publications - *Tit-Bits, The Million* and *The Strand* - he engaged with both the innovative techniques and forms of the New Journalism, and the contemporary debate over those techniques and forms.

Biographical detail is crucial to an understanding of Newnes's editorial persona, and of the success of publications such as *Tit-Bits* and *The Million*, which were extremely interactive and dramatic, and which depended upon the editor securing, in a very active and transparent fashion, 'the suffrage of the crowd'. Newnes had always loved good stories. At Silcoates he was, according to Friederichs, 'the *raconteur* of his time, who swayed the hearts of a crowd of little boys at will; who made them laugh and cry and tremble as he chose, and who was himself as thrilled by the creatures of his imagination as was the

Journalism?' and Laurel Brake, 'The Old Journalism and the New: Forms of Cultural Production in London in the 1880s' in Jole Wiener (ed.), *Papers for the Millions*.

[13] Edward Dicey, 'Journalism, New and Old', *Fortnightly Review*, LXXXIII (1905), p.917; T.H.S. Escott, 'Old and New in the Daily Press', *Quarterly Review*, 227, (1917), p.368; R.C.K. Ensor, as cited in Raymond Williams, *The Long Revolution*, p.196.

[14] Alan J. Lee, *The Origins of the Popular Press*, London: Croom Helm, 1976, p.232.

audience hanging upon his lips'.[15] When he left the City of London School, he took away with him the prize for the best-told story, eclipsing the efforts of his fellow pupil H.H. Asquith, with whom he was to continue on friendly terms as an MP. Later, 'thrown, largely upon his own resources and guidance, into the vortex of City life', Newnes frequented debating-societies and lecture halls, and the performances of open-air preachers and speakers such as those that occupied Speaker's Corner in Hyde Park on a Sunday. He regularly took issue with 'some voluble would-be instructor of his fellow-men', according to Friederichs' account, 'and the lad's keen wit and humour would often secure the suffrage of the crowd, to the discomfiture of his opponent'.[16] As a successful publisher, MP and public man, he went on to speak at many dinners, political meetings and Lantern lectures, and at home he demonstrated a taste for charades and other indoor entertainments. The link between the popular oral culture in which Newnes participated as a young man in London and later as an MP and public man, and the kind of journalism that he created in *Tit-Bits* is quite tangible. Practice at narrative, role-play, ready repartee and impromptu argument served him well in his career as an editor-proprietor.

Newnes's experiences as an apprentice to a London firm of haberdashers in their fancy goods department offer an insight into the successful publisher's aptitude for business. Acquiring a reputation for being extremely quick at arithmetic, and therefore being indispensible in the annual stock-taking, the young Newnes rose rapidly within the firm to the position of 'Entering Man', and was given charge of the whole department (consisting of between twenty and twenty-five men). He negotiated himself an annual salary of £100. He remained in the city for one year in this position, and was then sent to the country to open up business for the firm. He made a success of his position as a commercial traveller, and when his apprenticeship was completed, was offered a similar position with another London firm, representing it in Manchester and Liverpool, and 'pushing' the business in the surrounding districts.[17] This experience in sales promotion, combined with his innate business instinct, was undoubtedly of considerable significance to Newnes in his publishing career. And it earned him an insight into the preferences and prejudices of the lower middle classes, whom he was to target with his first publication.

The inspiration for *Tit-Bits* sprang very much out of Newnes's own personal experience, as well as his understanding of the needs of the lower-middle classes. In London in the late 1860s, during the period of his apprenticeship, Newnes haunted the newsagents shops and bookstalls in search of periodical literature that satisfied his desire for amusement and instruction.

---

[15] Hulda Friederichs, *The Life of Sir George Newnes, Bart*, London: Hodder and Stoughton, 1911, pp.49-50.

[16] Ibid., p.35.

[17] Ibid., pp.36-43. There is a parallel here between the career of Newnes, and that of John Cassell, 'the Manchester carpenter' who moved from selling tea and coffee by mail order and through local agents into publishing.

Magazines such as *Reynold's Miscellany, Cassell's Magazine* and *Lloyd's Weekly News* would no doubt have met his eye. Young readers of his type, according to Friederichs, 'desire to follow the events and happenings of the day':

> but unless these are put before them in a compressed and
> simple form, they have neither the time nor the taste to acquaint
> themselves with what is going on in the world. They also care
> for things that cheer and make them laugh, and lead them
> momentarily away from their own more or less drab lives, into
> an atmosphere of fun and merriment.[18]

Newnes himself adopted this line of argument in characterising the *raison d'être* of *Tit-Bits*.[19] He identified a gap in the market for periodical literature between mid-Victorian family papers such as *Reynold's Weekly*, which supplied sentimental, highly-coloured fiction appealing largely to female and juvenile readers, and the sporting papers, which boasted a 'low', racy style and emphasised turf news, racing tips and *double entendre*. There was little that was compressed and light enough, and yet neither excessively pedestrian nor evidently 'pernicious', to appeal to lower middle-class readers. The thoughtfully-written and carefully-edited magazines that were available were pitched too high to meet their requirements, and were generally inaccessible because of cost.

One contemporary commentator said of *Tit-Bits* that it was 'the greatest literary fluke of the century'.[20] It was, in fact, no fluke, but a carefully calculated play for the periodical market. It was significant that Newnes began his publishing career in Manchester, one of the busy, densely-populated northern towns where the passion for reading was even greater than in the south. Late nineteenth-century Manchester was distinguished by a strong appreciation of the arts which earned it a reputation as one of the provincial capitals of Europe. Newnes was not a journalist by instinct or training. But he was an intuitive businessman and an experienced salesman. He devised innovative and original schemes for advertising, promoting and formatting *Tit-Bits*, and his paper was quickly and widely imitated. Even Newnes's practice of printing the cover of *Tit-Bits* in colour was imitated by Harmsworth, whose paper *Answers* was published with an orange cover (the cover of *Tit-Bits* had been green), earning it the title 'The Golden One'. Such competition, however, forced Newnes into the constant invention of new schemes to maintain and increase circulation. It was a task to which, as a businessman, he was particularly well-suited. It was four years later that Newnes transferred his activities to London, where he rented a ramshackle building in Farringdon St and secured a trestle table as a desk. In June 1886, he

---

[18]   Ibid.

[19]   See Newnes's well known sermonette to W.T. Stead on the difference between journalism which 'directs the affairs of nations' and his own 'quite humble and unpretentious' journalism (Chapter 1).

[20]   Reginald Pound and Geoffery Harmsworth, *Northcliffe*, London: Cassell, 1959, p.73.

moved the offices of *Tit-Bits* to Burleigh St, where *The Globe*, the *Guardian*, *Church News* and the *Court Journal* were also based.

Newnes's publishing career expanded after this first stroke of initiative. In 1889, according to Sidney Dark, 'George Newnes, having firmly established *Tit-Bits* as a paying property, was looking out for other worlds to conquer.'[21] In 1890 he founded the *Review of Reviews* with his schoolfriend W.T. Stead, but the partnership was dissolved after three months, Stead buying Newnes's share of the magazine for £10,000.[22] Its dissolution was precipitated by a 'character sketch' of the *The Times* which Stead was preparing for the March issue, and which Newnes feared might provoke a libel action from the controllers of the paper.[23] The natures and ideas of the two men were so completely at variance that they could never have collaborated for long. Newnes was diplomatic, determined, businesslike and idealistic in a deliberate, methodical kind of way. Stead was ebullient, passionate, wilful and charismatic, and had a penchant for controversy. A series of letters in which they discussed the publication reveal a rather emotional exchange, with Newnes staunchly defending his business interests in this 'most valuable property'. The letters highlighted the other major difference between the two. Newnes's own journalism, as he pointed out, brought in 'the sheckels'. Stead, preoccupied with his devotion to 'high ideals', was financially careless, and his excesses tended to throw his publishing enterprises into a state of financial disequilibrium that subsequent business managers only barely managed to contain.[24] Newnes's skill lay in his sound business sense and his steady idealism. He employed the large additional staff engaged for the *Review of Reviews* to put into practice a long-cherished project to start a sixpenny monthly which combined popular illustration with popular literary matter.

When the first number of this new magazine was in preparation, and its name was discussed, Newnes toyed with the titles 'Burleigh Street Magazine' (his publishing offices were in Burleigh St) and 'New Magazine' (the magazine was to be a novel one, reflecting contemporary American innovations). When his friend and neighbour L.R.S. Tomalin (who later became a director of George Newnes, Ltd) suggested the name 'Strand Magazine', after that great London thoroughfare, intimately associated with London journalism, Newnes took up the name at once. He introduced Tomalin to Greenhough Smith (who was to be the Literary Editor of the magazine) as the godfather of the new publication. Where the cover illustration was concerned, he was equally particular, rejecting many of Gordon Haite's early sketches. At last he found a large oil painting, representing

---

[21] Sidney Dark, *The Life of Sir Arthur Pearson, Bt, G.B.E.*, London: Hodder and Stoughton, 1922, p.45.

[22] J.R. Tye, *Periodicals of the Nineties*, Oxford: Oxford Bibliographical Society, 1974, p.353.

[23] The two men also disagreed over Stead's arrangement to publish a condensation, and then a translated and unexpurgated version of Tolstoy's provocative story *The Kreutzer Sonata*, despite the objections of the Tsarist government.

[24] Newnes-Stead Correspondence, Churchill College Library, Cambridge. See also, Frederic Whyte, *The Life of W.T. Stead*, London: Jonathan Cape, 1925, vol.2, pp.319, 220.

a street in Liverpool, which conveyed the impression of life and energy that he sought to convey. He carried it in a brougham to the office, where he showed it to Haite. 'In time to come', he remarked, 'I should like the cover of the *Strand* to become as familiar to the mind of the public as is the cover of *Punch*.' [25] It did indeed become very familiar.

In the early years of the *The Strand*, Newnes was closely involved in its production. As with *Tit-Bits*, he operated upon the principle that individual features should be changed as soon as the public tired of them. While visiting Sir Richard Webster, he casually opened an album containing a number of photographs of his host at various ages. From this chance occurrence sprang the idea, the popular appeal of which Newnes saw intuitively, of the famous and successful series 'Portraits of Celebrities' and 'Illustrated Interviews'. It was also Newnes, according to Friederichs, who 'discovered' Arthur Conan Doyle. He was thorough and persevering in his role as editor, always taking it upon himself to read the piles of manuscripts that flowed into the editorial offices of *The Strand*. With the arrival of Sherlock Holmes upon the scene, *The Strand* entered upon a period of almost unrivalled success during which it had to be sent to press a month before the day of its appearance on the bookstalls. Circulation rose to well over half a million. *The Strand* became a forum for a large and popular circle of literary and artistic men and women, an organ central to upper middle-class life which retained its reputation and popularity for more than fifty years.

Newnes's publishing firm was floated as a limited company with £400,000 capital in 1891, with Newnes as the sole director. In 1897, George Newnes, Ltd was capitalised at £1,000,000, from which 900,000 shares were issued in order to obtain further capital for expanding the business. George Newnes, Ltd was one of the first publishing houses to receive a Stock Exchange quotation, the company's £1 shares being marked up to £2 12s. 6d. in conformity with the profit trend, then exceeding £60,000 per year.[26] Two new directors were added: Tomalin (also managing director of the Jaegar Clothing Company) and Edward Hudson (of the Southwark printing firm of Hudson and Kearns). Newnes lunched with both of these men daily at the Hotel Cecil. Frank Newnes later replaced Tomalin, after finishing his education in law at Cambridge. George Newnes, Ltd continued to produce new publications.

The Million (1892) was a penny weekly paper boasting the novelty, for 1892, of coloured illustrations. It bore many similarities to *Tit-Bits*, and represented a further attempt to exploit the expanding lower middle-class market for cheap, entertaining and innovative periodical publications. As a term for the popular audience, 'the million' was in use from as early as 1855, when Moses Levy's penny daily *Telegraph* claimed that: 'This journal not only circulates

---

[25]   Hulda Friederichs, op. cit., p.121.

[26]   Reginald Pound, op. cit., pp.49-50. In 1959, the company, including its subsidiaries (of which C. Arthur Pearson, Ltd was one) was acquired by Odhams Press, Ltd for upwards of 12 million pounds. By then, it was publishing fifty-three periodicals.

with the million, but it is taken in the very highest circles.' As a circulation figure, it should not be taken too literally. The *Telegraph*'s circulation was around 50,000.[27] Yet by the time *The Million* was established, the term had acquired a variety of associations relating to the growth and commercialisation of the press and the democratic development of British society, lending Newnes's paper a peculiarly contemporary significance.

Newnes was editor, publisher and proprietor of all three of his early publications: *Tit-Bits*, *The Million* and *The Strand*.[28] Through *Tit-Bits* and *The Million*, both of which were weekly publications, relatively cheap to produce and priced at a penny, Newnes established his place in modern British journalism. Through *The Strand*, he consolidated that place. The first two publications were heavily dependent upon Newnes's editorial personality and his promotional skills. *The Strand* relied on the professional reputation, editorial techniques and financial gains that Newnes had developed and secured through *Tit-Bits*. Whilst Newnes's influence was central to *The Strand*, its popular status was equally a product of the contributions of the increasingly professionalised body of authors, artists and editors whom Newnes recruited and patronised as editor-proprietor. *Tit-Bits*, credited with founding a new era in popular journalism, brought into focus contemporary debates about the effects of mass literacy and popular journalism on literary standards. In *The Strand*, Newnes offered a compromise between artistic 'quality' and journalistic innovation. New Journalism, as Newnes's early publications demonstrated, whilst associated with the commercialisation of the press, occupied the journalistic ground somewhere between 'a branch of business' and 'a liberal profession'.

---

[27] Matthew Engel, *Tickle the Public: One Hundred Years of the Popular Press*, London: Victor Gollancz, 1996, p.33.

[28] Although there is no concrete evidence as to who edited *The Million*, the editorial language and style of the publication and its format and features indicate that it was almost certainly Newnes himself.

1

Securing the Suffrage of the Crowd:
Tit-Bitites and Millionaires

Tit-Bits (1881) and *The Million* (1892)

George Newnes, who often spoke in homilies, assessed his contribution to periodical literature in 1890, when he separated from W.T. Stead over their joint venture, *The Review of Reviews*:

> There is one kind of journalism which directs the affairs of nations; it makes and unmakes cabinets; it upsets governments, builds up Navies and does many other great things. It is magnificent. This is your journalism. There is another kind of journalism which has no such great ambitions. It is content to plod on, year after year, giving wholesome and harmless entertainment to crowds of hardworking people, craving for a little fun and amusement. It is quite humble and unpretentious. This is my journalism.[1]

Newnes was to become one of Britain's first media magnates, publishing a huge number and variety of publications. But it was through his first publication, *Tit-Bits* (1881), that he established his place in British journalism. *The Million* (1892) represented Newnes's attempt to augment the reputation for popular journalistic innovation that he had secured through *Tit-Bits*. The two publications were of a distinctly similar mould, and will thus be treated jointly in this chapter.

In this instance, drawing a distinction between the conventional nineteenth-century model of the press as an estate of the realm - a fourth branch of government which acted as a safeguard against misrule and despotism by provoking social inquiry - and his own seemingly less ambitious journalistic endeavours, Newnes conceptualised *Tit-Bits* as a kind of familiar companion. It was integral to the very rhythms of its readers' lives and to their sustenance, reflecting, Newnes implied in a characteristically self-effacing comment, even their humble position in society. 'I *am* the average man', Newnes always maintained, 'I am not merely putting myself in his place. That is the real reason why I know what he wants.'[2] Just as Raymond Williams has

---

[1] Hulda Friederichs, *The Life of Sir George Newnes, Bart*, London: Hodder and Stoughton, 1911, pp.116-117.

[2] Ibid., p.188.

viewed popular literature as inseparable from 'the cognate forms of other writing, publishing and reading ... other kinds of political and cultural formation and organisation', so Newnes envisioned his publication as a social object, firmly rooted in contemporary culture: an extremely contextualised text.

One of the most significant emphases of the developing metacriticism of periodical research has been an awareness of the uniquely interactive, open and self-referential form of the periodical text; the way in which it functions as social discourse rather than as direct social statement.[3] This chapter is an attempt to demonstrate the ways in which the weekly papers *Tit-Bits* and *The Million* functioned within this paradigm of social discourse, with special reference to their creator and editor, George Newnes. It examines the ways in which they offered connection, interaction and creative potential to a community of readers, and enabled Newnes to establish a responsive editorial presence as the reader's friend, adviser and representative. It offers an analysis which defines *Tit-Bits* as a source of cultural identification, a supplier of social services, a popular social educator, a legal and moral bond between readers and editor, and as a pluralistic discursive sphere regulated by a communal sense of mutual responsibility. And it characterises *The Million* as a kind of multi-coloured extension of Newnes's first periodical publishing venture. Through these two periodicals, representing the combination of commercial transaction and cultural exchange, George Newnes demonstrated that he was possessed of both business instincts and editorial flair.

Historiographically, *Tit-Bits* has been enmeshed in the historical myth of the so-called 'Northcliffe Revolution'. Some contemporary social critics believed that journalism of the *Tit-Bits* mould perverted the aims of the 1870 Education Act and supplementary legislation which followed it. They argued that New Journalism offered information at the expense of knowledge and encouraged the kind of cultural Philistinism feared by Matthew Arnold. It was 'cheap', 'low' and 'trivial', they complained, and it undermined literary standards by playing to the lowest common denominator. The rival 'quality press' was especially fond of spreading this myth. According to the common formula, there was a direct causal connection between the Education Act of 1870 (by means of which, the story goes, the common people learnt to read) and the spontaneous birth of the 'cheap' popular press. The coming of *Tit-Bits* and *Answers* in the 1880s, and Northcliffe's *Daily Mail* in 1896, heralded this latter event. In fact, Northcliffe himself gave expression to the myth in a conversation with Max Pemberton in 1883, although he viewed it in terms of journalistic and commercial opportunism rather than 'deculturisation':

---

    3   See, for instance, Lyn Pykett, 'Reading the Periodical Press: Text and Context', Margaret Beetham, 'Open and Closed: The Periodical as Publishing Genre' and Laurel Brake and Anne Humpherys, 'Critical Theory and Periodical Research' in *Victorian Periodicals Review* (Special Critical Theory Issue), XXII, 3 (Fall 1989); Brian E. Maidment, 'Victorian Periodicals and Academic Discourse', in Laurel Brake, Aled Jones and Lionel Madden (eds), *Investigating Victorian Journalism*, New York: St Martin's Press, 1990.

> The Board Schools are turning out hundreds and thousands of girls
> and boys annually who are anxious to read. They do not care for
> the ordinary newspaper. They have no interest in society, but they
> will read anything which is sufficiently interesting. The man who
> has produced this *Tit-Bits* has got hold of a bigger thing than he
> imagines. He is only at the beginning of a development which is
> going to change the whole face of journalism. I shall try to get in
> with him.[4]

And in Richard Altick's 'Chronology of the Mass Reading Public', 1880 is
registered in the following terms: 'Elementary education made compulsory.
Newnes's *Tit-Bits* starts a new era in popular journalism.'

The equation is reductive, and its presuppositions manifestly untrue. The
Education Acts of 1870 and 1880 did not suddenly and comprehensively result
in the creation of a mass literate audience. Other social and political
mechanisms had contributed to the growth in literacy throughout the century.
And both the popular press *and* a substantial level of working-class literacy go
back well before 1870.[5] But the extension of education did increase the
numbers of the literate, and perhaps more importantly, as John Goodbody has
pointed out, 'focussed entrepreneurial attention on the reservoir of public
literacy that was available'.[6] The popular literature and journalism of the late
nineteenth century, dubbed 'New Journalism' by Matthew Arnold, exploited
the increasing size and diversity of the reading public. *Tit-Bits*, along with its
imitators *Answers* and *Pearson's Weekly*, achieved circulations that would
have been inconceivable earlier in the century. Yet the readership of *Tit-Bits*
was not composed of the 'newly literate masses'. It was predominantly drawn
from the ranks of the upper working-class 'aristocracy of labour' (a class with
a tradition of self-education) and the lower middle-class (urban workers such
as clerks and shopkeepers, who formed part of a new commuting population).
Tit-Bits catered to a range of readers. Furthermore, far from lowering the
standards of popular journalism, it undoubtedly raised them.[7]

---

[4]   R.M. Wilson, *Lord Northcliffe: A Study*, London: Ernest Benn, 1927, p.63.

[5]   The mechanisms through which working people learnt to read included Sunday
schools, dame schools, charity schools, fireside Bible reading circles, workingmen's clubs and
a thriving radical popular press. Cheap literature sold by hawkers and peddlers on the streets
included chapbooks of popular ballads and stories, and the extremely popular 'Last Dying
Speeches' of convicted murderers. Even in 1840, 70 per cent of men and 50 per cent of women
could sign their names on marriage registers, and these figures were rising rapidly well before
1870. (See Matthew Engel, *Tickle the Public: One Hundred Years of the Popular Press*,
London: Victor Gollancz, 1996, p.24.)

[6]   John Goodbody, 'The *Star*: It's Role in the Rise of the New Journalism', in Joel
Wiener (ed.), *Papers for the Millions: The New Journalism in Britain, 1850s-1914*, New York:
Greenwood Press, 1988, p.145. Note the title of this examination of the New Journalism.

[7]   See Harold Perkin, *The Structured Crowd: Essays in English Social History*, Sussex:
Harvester Press, 1981, pp.47-55.

Acknowledged by many historians and contemporaries to be the most popular penny paper of the late nineteenth century, *Tit-Bits* appeared on the publishing scene on 22 October, 1881. It was essentially a paper of the miscellany variety that became popular in the late nineteenth century: a sixteen page patchwork of advice, humorous anecdote, romantic fiction, statistical information, historical explanation, advertisement, legal detail, quips and queries, and reader correspondence. Competitions were a central feature. Regular columns and serials were interspersed with short jokes and sallies of the kind frequently furnished to newspaper and magazines by literary types. Its readership consisted of the expanding lower middle and upper working classes. It was a family paper, and it catered for the male, female and juvenile reader, and the white-collar commuter.

The average weekly circulation of *Tit-Bits* during the years of Newnes's involvement (1881-1910) was 400,00 to 600,000 copies, but this figure fluctuated as circulation-boosting schemes came and went. By 1890, according to Geraldine Beare, its sales had exceeded 500,000 and by 1893 it was considered to be the world's most popular penny paper.[8] A competition in Easter week, 1897 increased circulation to 671,000.[9] These figures were on a par with the other most successful papers of the *Tit-Bits* variety, *Answers* and *Pearson's Weekly*, with weekly circulation figures of 400,000-600,000.[10] *Tit-Bits* also maintained a substantial overseas circulation.

In fact, as far as the reception of *Tit-Bits* was concerned, it was transformed from printed text into embedded cultural reference. The cultural absorption of *Tit-Bits* encompassed many mentions of it in novels, historical texts, biographies and periodicals, and it has been integral to the misrepresentation of George Newnes as a mere businessman, and the dismissal of his journalism as 'cheap'. In Joyce's *Ulysses*, one character reads *Tit-Bits* whilst engaged in his private ablutions - a rather unflattering image of Newnes's paper. The words 'Tit-Bits' became synonymous with the miscellany or encyclopaedic tradition, the paragraphic technique and the 'popular' paper. This publication was thus an accepted cultural symbol of the New Journalism, its name widely known.[11]

The Million, established in March 1892, was a penny weekly magazine. It was published and edited by Newnes; another text in the increasingly complex narrative of his journalistic career. This paper was introduced at a

---

[8]   Geraldine Beare, 'Indexing the Strand Magazine', *Journal of Newspaper and Periodical History*, 11 (Spring 1986), p.20.

[9]   Richard Altick, op. cit, p.396.

[10] Ibid. These figures are for 1897.

[11] Mr Trout', wrote Etta Close in 1924, 'is not a great reader, still he has brought a library of sorts with him. It consists of two copies of a newspaper, a sort of evangelical *Tit-Bits*, giving information in Dutch as to how many different languages the bible has been translated into, how many missionaries had been cooked and eaten, and so on.' See Etta Close, *A Woman Alone in Kenya, Uganda, and the Belgian Congo*, London: Constable and Co., 1924.

time when rapid colour printing, as required for reproduction in magazines, was in its very early stages of development. And its major appeal lay in the novel visual impact of the full-page colour pictures that adorned its cover and some of its inside pages. 'We'll do it better than they', Newnes said. 'We'll have better work both for the illustrations and the letterpress, and we'll be able to print better; it will be an entirely new, and a very cheerful and entertaining paper.'[12] It was intended as a kind of British equivalent to the French paper *Petit Journal*, a paper with a vast circulation which featured coloured pictures and light literature. In fact it was very much the precursor to the modern comic, with comic sketches being another feature. *The Million* consisted, by the editor's own account, of 'bright, coloured pictures and healthy, entertaining reading' and catered to a 'wide and expanding circle of readers'.[13] Its title was significant, placing the magazine within an evolving discourse of journalistic development, democratic liberalism, commercialisation and mass culture.

According to all the indications given in the texts, in the language, competitions, illustrations and formal characteristics, the reading community engaged by *Tit-Bits* and *The Million* consisted of a lower middle and aspiring middle-class, largely commuting, often salary-earning, consumerist, self-helping public: Newnes's 'crowds of hardworking people'. Many were 'constant subscribers'; that is, middle-class readers with a regular income and the means to subscribe. Competition prizes and contribution payments offered in *Tit-Bits* were expressed in guineas, a fact which implied a class of reader in possession of a salary (middle class or professional) as opposed to a wage (always expressed in pounds, shillings and pence). The success of the *Tit-Bits* Villa Competition reflected the aspirations of readers towards home-ownership, an essentially middle-class ideal. And the popularity of the *Tit-Bits* Insurance Scheme was an indication that the audience of the paper was a commuting population, a pool of potential readers that substantially increased in the late nineteenth century.[14]

The prizes and incentives offered to *Million* readers - silver-plated jewellery and Christening mugs made of 'elegantly-chased "Queen's plate"' - appealed to an audience characterised by consumerist instincts and middle-class aspirations.[15] The lower middle class, in particular, was rapidly

---

[12] Hulda Friederichs, op. cit., p.133.

[13] *The Million*, 2, 49 (February 1893), p.405. Unfortunately, due to the lack of facilities for colour reproduction at the British Newspaper Library at Colindale, I have been unable to obtain colour copies of illustrations. The novelty and impact of the paper was, in fact, heavily dependent upon vivid colour printing.

[14] In fact, the number of passengers carried by the railways increased dramatically from around 500 million in 1878 to around 1,000 million in 1898, and had reached 1,250 million in 1908. See E.J. Hobsbawm, *Industry and Empire*, London: Penguin, 1968, Figure 17.

[15] The quality and commercial value of the Christening mugs which Newnes awarded to loyal readers were described in great detail: 'The nickel silver foundation is coated with pure silver of such a thickness that the inscription engraved upon the mug does not penetrate through the outer covering.' See *The Million*, 2, 44 (January 1892), p.347.

expanding in the latter decades of the nineteenth century, and was one to which Newnes himself belonged (as a commercial traveller), before rising to the top of the professional middle class in becoming a self-made entrepreneur. This class was often the backbone of university extension courses and vocational evening classes, the taste for which was met by Newnes in the '*Tit-Bits* Inquiry Column'. And they were prevalent in new constituency organisations of both the major political parties, a fact which seems to have strongly influenced the language and editorial style of both papers.[16]

Newnes's readers were depicted visually, as well as represented discursively (through the competitions and correspondence columns) in the text of this publication. A pictorial canvas entitled 'A Few Incidents in Connection with *Tit-Bits*' provided an insight into the readership of this publication (*see Figure 5*). It depicted well-dressed, bonneted women, obviously of the middle class; men in the bowler hats, top-hats, collars, ties, waistcoats and black suits that were the characteristic attire of the same class; and well-dressed children wearing hats and the latest in sailor-suit fashion. Clerical types, distinguishable by their hats and collars, also appeared. The 'prudent family' at the railway station 'prepared for anything', with each member sporting a copy of *Tit-Bits* in accordance with the *Tit-Bits* Insurance Scheme, was emblematic of the paper's readership. Whilst these images might, in some sense, represent an idealised readership or a standard to which to aspire, they also indicate the character of the 'crowd' to whom Newnes sought to appeal.

The management of demarcated time (within demarcated space) - the ethos of work-discipline which E.P. Thompson has so clearly explained - was the very *raison d'être* of *Tit-Bits*.[17] 'It is impossible for any man in the busy times of the present', opened the editor when it appeared on the publishing scene on 22 October, 1881, 'to even glance at any large number of the immense variety of books and papers which have gone on accumulating, until now their number is fabulous.'

> It will be the business of the conductors of *Tit-Bits* to find out from this immense field of literature the best things that have been said or written, and weekly to place them before the public for one penny.[18]

---

[16] See Harold Perkin, *The Origins of Modern English Society, 1780-1880*, London: Routledge and Kegan Paul, 1969, pp.92-99.

[17] E.P. Thompson, 'Time, Work-Discipline and Industrial Capitalism', *Past and Present*, 38 (1967), pp.56-97.

[18] *Tit-Bits*, 1, 1 (October 1881), p.1. Note that my own rendition of textual material does not always reproduce the typographical and formatting features of the source exactly, but only those deemed particularly meaningful or characteristic. Bold lettering was often used in rendering the name of a publication ('THE WESTMINSTER GAZETTE', for instance). Bold lettering was also employed as a highlighting technique (as in *Tit-Bits* competitions or in citing the names of public or political figures in *The Westminster Gazette*), but is only selectively used here in quotations. Occasional footnotes make reference to this issue.

The notion of industrial time, implicit in Newnes's sermonette upon the two types of journalism, permeated the text from the outset. The editor's comments invoked the language of industrialisation, conjuring up images of oversupply and surplus stockpiling. The editor's 'business' was to rationalise: to manufacture a marketable commodity for the busy consumer with limited time and limited means. *Tit-Bits* reduced the complexities of modern life, distilling and synthesising information relevant to its readers after the fashion of the more middle and upper-class Review, but in such a way as to appeal to an upper working and lower middle-class audience. A series of literary excerpts, drawn from the works of various well-known authors, mostly middle-class canonical writers such as Dickens, Disraeli, Macaulay and Arnold, exemplified this process of manufactured synthesis.

The late Victorian period was one in which, according to Raymond Williams, the struggle for democracy, the extension of the communications network, and a dramatic increase in capitalisation were the major forces of cultural change.[19] In this cultural context, the notion of 'the Million' - the democratic masses - was central. 'The Million' represented the expanding political electorate, whose allegiance was to be courted in the quest for parliamentary power. Two Gladstonian Reform bills of 1884 and 1885 had extended the vote to (male) agricultural workers and redistributed seats in favour of the larger at the expense of the smaller towns. They represented the mass market, possessing newly acquired purchasing power and leisure time, and ripe for commercial exploitation.[20] And they constituted an expanding reading public. Various measures relating to the press, including the Companies Act (1866), paved the way for its development along capitalistic lines. Circulations soared. A circulation of a million, unimaginable earlier in the century, suddenly seemed possible, and editors and publishers employed various new technological, journalistic and commercial methods in an attempt to attain such heights. In London in particular, the tradition of buying street literature and the spread of transportation (which created a commuting population and conditions of accessibility) aided circulation. Newnes offered to donate £10,000 to the Hospitals Fund in 1889, if readers of *Tit-Bits* took the circulation of the paper to one million. But *Lloyd's Weekly News* was the first

---

[19] Raymond Williams, *The Long Revolution*, London: Penguin, 1961, p.12.

[20] Gareth Stedman Jones has labelled working-class culture of the late nineteenth century a 'culture of consolation', and described it as a culture based upon 'pleasure, amusement, hospitality and sport'. See Gareth Stedman Jones, 'Working-Class Culture and Working-Class Politics in London, 1870-1900: Notes on the Re-Making of a Working Class', *Journal of Social History*, 7, 7 (Summer 1974), p.486. See also Paul Thompson, *The Edwardians: The Remaking of British Society*, London: Weidenfeld and Nicolson, 1975 and P. Mathias, *The First Industrial Nation: An Economic History of Britain, 1700-1914*, London: Methuen, 1969.

paper to break through the mythical barrier of one million readers, in 1896.[21] George Newnes, with the advantage of commercial training, a sound business instinct and a capacity for 'securing the suffrage of the crowd' as a performer, was well-equipped to appeal to such an audience.[22]

Newnes quickly established a successful format for *Tit-Bits*. In the 'Inquiry Column', appearing on page 6, short questions were published each week with answers appearing two weeks afterwards. 'Any question, on any subject, may be asked', announced the editor in No.19, 'and each question will be published in the "Inquiry Column"'. Readers might 'depend upon receiving accurate replies'.[23] The column's format reflected the familiarity of this kind of exchange, typical of the examination, to an audience that was integrated into a system of compulsory schooling and sought further educational qualifications. As if to make the connection clearer, the best student - the reader who answered the largest number of questions correctly over a period of three months - received a reward of 10 guineas from the editor-teacher. The range of 'Tit-Bits of General Information', on page 15, was broad, and reflects the preoccupation of this society with the statistical assessment of progress and prosperity. 'Tit-Bits of Legal Information' appeared on page 14. From 1885 a column entitled 'Answers to Correspondents' featured on page 13. And on the front page, in a very visible position in the top left-hand corner, were notices to readers about upcoming and current competitions conducted by *Tit-Bits*.

Newnes also introduced commercial advertising on the front and back covers, and later the middle pages of the paper, as a means of raising capital for his publishing activities. The language and visual iconography emerging from the textual transaction between advertisers and consumers provide an insight into the tastes and preoccupations of the audience with whom the editor himself was engaged. The appeal of these advertisements lay in the bold visual techniques of formatting and headlining employed, and in the way in which they drew upon popular beliefs and ideologies. Advertisements for products such as 'Salt Regal' (prescribed as a cure for 'Infectious Diseases, Influenza, Malaria, Cholera' and even 'The Epidemic') drew upon a working-class tradition of self-medication. 'Frame Food Bread' derived its market credibility from its alleged scientific legitimacy, and was advertised within the rhetoric of anthropometrics, eugenics and efficiency, its nutritional value guaranteed by various medical experts. Advertisements for Pears Translucent Soap played upon popular racist ideology, suggesting that 'cleanliness [and therefore, 'whiteness', by a crude process of extrapolation] and godliness go together'. Newnes's audience were not only readers. They were consumers, and the

---

[21] Raymond Williams, op. cit., p.217. The circulation of Harmsworth's *Daily Mail* rose to over a million at dramatic moments in the Boer War. See Matthew Engel, op. cit., p.64.

[22] See Chapter 2.

[23] *Tit-Bits*, 1, 19 (March 1882), p.1.

advertisement pages of *Tit-Bits* were an attempt to gain their allegiance to the advertisers' product, through their allegiance to the paper.

As *Tit-Bits* evolved, it incorporated more original material, carrying an invitation to readers to send in literary contributions in a kind of journalistic recruiting campaign. In each issue appeared the announcement:

TO LITTERATEURS
The price we pay for original contributions specially written for *Tit Bits* is
ONE GUINEA PER COLUMN[24]

Thus began a tradition of publishing original material which was to lead Newnes to establish the highly successful *Strand Magazine* in 1890. Serial fiction, a form which engaged reader response on a weekly basis in a way which often allowed the reading public to mediate the production of the story, was introduced into *Tit-Bits* as an experiment in literary publishing. The first serial to be published, in 1889, was a piece by James Payn entitled 'The Word and the Will'.[25] By 1890, the format of the paper had evolved even further. On 27 September, 1890, remuneration of £1,000 was offered for a story of forty to fifty chapters averaging 2,500 words each, to be published later in book form by the proprietor of *Tit-Bits*. The editor was thus recruitment officer and employer, and *Tit-Bits* represented a form of exchange between employer and wage-earner - the 'cash nexus' - that was characteristic of urban industrial life.

Tit-Bits began as a collection of excerpts converted into 'text' purely by a process of creative editorial synthesis, and it was infused with a deep sense of editorial presence. Editorial interjection, often characterised by a familiar tone and containing references to readers as 'our friends', was the very essence of *Tit-Bits*: 'In consequence of the large numbers of queries we receive', intimated Newnes, referring to the 'Legal Tit-Bits' section, 'it is impossible to answer all we should like in this page.' Considerations of friendship, it was suggested, competed with the imperatives of economy.

> Those of our friends who find their questions omitted will please to understand that it is not from want of courtesy, but from want of space.[26]

A paper's 'personality', as Joel Wiener has pointed out, was partly a function of the editorial persona, and George Newnes, 'The Editor', was the very nucleus of *Tit-Bits*.[27] Through *Tit-Bits*, Newnes evolved as an editor and a

[24] Formatting as per original.

[25] *Tit-Bits*, 17, 418 (October 1889), p.17.

[26] *Tit-Bits*, 13, 313 (October 1887), p.14.

[27] Joel Wiener, 'Sources for the Study of Newspapers' in Laurel Brake, Aled Jones and Lionel Madden (eds), *Investigating Victorian Journalism*, New York: St Martin's Press, 1990.

publisher, and the reader of the paper was closely involved in this metamorphosis by virtue of Newnes's characteristically interactive, self-conscious, self-referential, editorially transparent, personalised, dramatic, earnest, innovative approach.

The 'Answers to Correspondents' column, conveying a sense of editorial presence and reader involvement, was the linchpin of the interactive posture that Newnes adopted in *Tit-Bits*.[28] Known at the office as 'corres.', this column was one of the most popular. 'For this page', according to Hulda Friederichs, 'the editor had a very special affection, together with very definite ideas as to the manner in which it should be conducted':

> He held that, first and foremost, all answers should be given in a manner which would make each correspondent feel that he was treated with special consideration; that here behind this newspaper page, there was somebody to whom the inquirer's affairs were of real human interest; who sympathised, and tried to give his advice a practical turn. Secondly, Mr Newnes held that the answers should be couched in such terms, whenever this was possible, as to make them interesting to the general reader as well as to the individual correspondent.[29]

Thus, the text of *Tit-Bits* represented both a medium for personalised editor-reader interaction and a commercial product with broad narrative and journalistic appeal to a diverse audience. These were characteristics which it shared with other products of the New Journalism.

This column was one which Newnes, with his 'vivid imagination, his innate good sense, his ready wit, and above all his unfailing social tact' was ideally suited to managing, according to Friederichs.

> For years, he took these letters, in bundles twelve inches high, and higher, went carefully through each, and answered them so fully, so wisely and so well, that in course of time people belonging to every social class sought help and advice through 'corres'.[30]

Newnes's editorial persona was multiform. He was 'innovator and preacher' (to borrow the title of a work on the Victorian editor), 'patriarch and pioneer', democratic representative, business partner, adviser and friend;

---

[28] The 'Notices to Correspondents' column had been a very popular department in the family periodicals of the 1840s and 1850s such as *Lloyd's*, *London Journal* and *Reynold's Miscellany*. According to Anne Humpherys, *Reynold's* acted as 'a stern adviser, a knowledgeable informant, an avuncular domestic manager'. See Anne Humpherys, 'G.W.M. Reynolds: Popular Literature and Popular Politics', in Joel H. Wiener (ed.), *Innovators and Preachers: The Role of the Editor in Victorian England*, New York: Greenwood Press, 1985, p.18.

[29] Hulda Friederichs, op. cit., pp.106-107.

[30] Ibid., p. 107.

sometimes upbraiding, sometimes cajoling, sometimes jesting, often avuncular.[31]

Through the editorials, competitions and serial features of *The Million* too, George Newnes interacted with 'Millionaires' (for so he called his readers) in a collaborative fashion. In an editorial column entitled 'To Our Readers', he made reference to the personalised style and innovative techniques of New Journalism, representing the publication of *The Million* as a kind of progressive and public-spirited initiative:

> In giving our second Double Summer Number to the world, we would briefly like to point out to Millionaires and their friends ... our coloured illustrations .... One of the objects of the starting of *The Million* was that of giving to the people a journal which should be an 'Academy of Popular Art', accompanied by literary matter of the highest class. We are ever striving to accomplish this object, and although here and there grumblers might exist, we think we may rest satisfied in having been able to please hundreds and thousands of readers.[32]

Thus the editor courted the support of 'hundreds and thousands' - if not millions - of readers, after the fashion of a political candidate seeking election. His platform: the reform of the press along popular and democratic lines, together with his claim to be introducing his readers to 'the best' ('literary matter of the highest class'). *The Million*'s illustrations were crucial to the editor's claims, journalistic innovation and social reform being conflated to foster the paper's image as an inclusive medium. 'No other paper in the world, except occasionally the sixpenny and shilling journals', wrote the editor, his claims moderated by his previous achievements in *The Strand*, 'has achieved the artistic work performed by *The Million*, and we are confident that few journals give for one penny so much high-class, sterling literary fare.'[33]

Newnes immersed his readers in the problems of production from the first. The editorial column constituted a narrative update on the actual technical process of creating the text, in which the editor elaborated upon the 'mechanical difficulties' experienced in connection with 'the new and intricate machinery which has been laid down', the 'difficult nature' of the work, and the patience he required of readers whilst his 'workpeople' developed their skills:

> We have already referred to the difficulties experienced at first, with regard to the machinery, and we ask the public to be patient with us for a little while, when we hope to produce an entire

---

31 See Joel H. Wiener (ed.), *Innovators and Preachers*; Helen Ogden Martin, *The Editor and His People: Editorials by William Allen White*, New York: Macmillan, 1924, p.xi.

32 *The Million*, 5, 120 (July 1894), p.130.

33 Ibid.

> edition of almost uniform quality .... It will readily occur to
> everyone that the production of 500,000 papers, such as *The
> Million*, was likely to produce some irregularity. Many of the
> copies were so well printed that they left nothing to be desired; in
> others, however, the colour ran a little, and spoilt the effects.[34]

Readers were led into familiarity with the technical developments
involved in journalistic production, and thence into a sense of personal
connection with the otherwise impersonal, capitalistic structure of the
developing press. New Journalism, as Brake, Wiener *et al* have shown, was not
an entirely novel phenomenon, but one that emerged out of an historical
process of journalistic and technological evolution.[35] Newnes extracted
publicity value from this process. Thus 'The Million' were involved in the
developments of New Journalism both as consumers, and as a critical audience
to whom the editor-publisher felt bound to account for himself. They, after all,
possessed the power to decide the fate of the experiment.

As the editorial voice of *Tit-Bits* developed, the editorial persona was
dramatised in various ways. In the pictorial canvas, he had appeared as the
'Fighting Editor' who dealt with disappointed competitors. In a series of
amusing episodes in 'Answers to Correspondents', the 'Fighting Editor' was
reintroduced, having not been heard of 'for some time past'.[36] It was suggested
by a fictional gatekeeper of productivity (that key imperative of industrial life)
that in order to 'earn his salary' during a quiet period of peace from
'malcontents', and to entertain his audience, he should utilise a disused balloon
allegedly stored in the *Tit-Bits* cellar to make 'daily descents from the top of
Tit-Bits Office in the excellent balloon' and return 'to earth in [an] elegant
parachute'. He refused, was remonstrated with, became angry, and was then
soothed and finally overcome with emotion.[37] In this case, the editor was
depicted as a rather argumentative, difficult character whose volatility was only
barely curbed by his diplomatic staff. Earlier, in the *Tit-Bits* Villa Competition,
the editor had appeared in 'all his editorial dignity' to inspect the prize villa.
He was introduced as an 'august personage' of the press and public life, but
was nevertheless discovered to be appealingly vulnerable as he trailed one of
the curtains to be used in photographing 'Tit-Bits Villa' on the ground, and
was reduced to contriving to disguise the damage.[38]

Such textual episodes confirm Raymond Williams' suggestion that the
products of 'New Journalism' had links with a popular oral cultural tradition.

---

[34] *The Million*, 1, 3 (April 1892), p.18.

[35] Joel Wiener (ed.), *Papers for the Millions*.

[36] The 'Fighting Editor' was also to feature in the correspondence columns of *Captain*.

[37] *Tit-Bits*, 15, 379 (January 1889), p.237. A kind of sequel episode, featuring a
redemptive debriefing between the editor and his staff was offered in a succeeding issue. See
Tit-Bits, 15, 381 (February 1888), p.269.

[38] *Tit-Bits*, 5, 117 (January 1884), p.203.

The print culture of books, pamphlets, magazines and newspapers that developed during the nineteenth century under the new urban conditions and spawned New Journalism, as he has pointed out, was very much interactive with a predominantly oral culture which encompassed such institutions as the theatre, the political meeting and the lecture, and such melodramatic forms as crime, scandal and romance.[39] It could be argued, however, that *Tit-Bits* had closer connections with music hall entertainment than with the more structured environment of the nineteenth-century theatre. As Newnes fine-tuned his individual act, he resembled one of the great variety entertainers popular amongst the working class in the later nineteenth century.

The Million engaged with these oral cultural traditions, employing dramatic techniques which often closely mirrored those of the music hall. News and social comment were rendered as short scenes, comic sketches and verse, and caricatures. Columns such as 'The Man in the Street' contained elaborate stage directions, Cockney accents, and dramatic monologues. A character of the music hall stage, *The Million*'s 'Man in the Street' verbally enacted dramatic scenes of urban life: the life of the streets, the clubs, the pavements crowded with people, and newsboys crying 'Pyper, sir - yezzir'. In the editorial column, 'Notes and Notions', anecdote, dramatic monologue, observation and role-play were combined to produce a serial performance that invoked the atmosphere of the pub and the stage. The column became a play in multiple 'acts' separated by 'an interval of one week'. (The editor even used these terms of reference himself.) It featured NYM as the editor-narrator and the slightly wayward but likeable 'Julius' as his larrikin private-secretary side-kick. The partnership was one that was characteristic of slapstick, pantomime and other music hall techniques, as well as of much popular fiction.[40] The characterisation of Julius as a slightly temperamental and disorganised but essentially good-natured adolescent represented an early attempt by Newnes to diffuse anxieties about the youth problem through humour. 'Julius' was, in fact, typical of a public school tradition of naming. *The Captain* was to offer a different and more comprehensive response.

That the accounts were fabricated was occasionally acknowledged, as in one commentary upon the spate of newspaper articles on suicide that had recently appeared. 'The following most interesting correspondence', wrote the editor, 'is perfectly genuine, having been entirely written by myself.' In fact, the correspondence columns and competitions that proliferated in these publications often revolved around the editor's invention of the reader, both through the selection of responses for publication, and (sometimes) through the fabrication of reader correspondence. This comment was thus an acknowledgment of the creative role of the editor as entertainer. This was a space in which disbelief was suspended, and both editor-author and audience

---

[39] Raymond Williams, op.cit., pp.43-46.

[40] *The Million*, 1, 21 (August 1892), p.206.

were imaginative constructions whose fictional existence revolved around role-play and performance. A sense of the immediacy of the dramatic performance was evoked by the editor-entertainer:

> We have at present a competition for pretty boys and girls, and
> when that is decided we may probably invite the Apollos of our
> great army of Millionaires to take part in a contest of good looks.
> Those who would like such a competition, hands up?[41]

The connection between the New Journalism and a popular oral tradition was manifest at another level too, with editors and journalists delivering lectures and performances based upon journalistic material to the popular audience at mutual improvement societies, clubs and schools. Newnes wrote Lantern Lectures on 'How Popular Periodicals are Produced' and 'Popular Authors and their Work', and the lectures, along with sets of slides, were made available for delivery at 'a public meeting of any duly authenticated literary, debating, or mutual improvement society, club, union, institute or school'.[42] And Harry How, one of the most prolific interviewers of the New Journalism, took his series of 'Illustrated Interviews', written for *The Strand*, 'all over the country' on tour. His exploits were described in *The Million* in such a way as to present him as a combination of commercial traveller, educative public lecturer and variety entertainer.[43]

The New Journalism, attacked by Arnold as 'feather-brained', was derided by its critics as 'low', 'cheap', sensational, irresponsible, and ephemeral - a transparent attempt to capture the market by playing to the lowest common denominator. In fact papers such as *Tit-Bits* and *The Million* made a feature of the trivial and fragmentary, as the name 'Tit-Bits' suggested. The titles of *The Million*'s columns emphasised the ephemeral, the fleeting, the insubstantial, the unformulated, the informal, personalised and colloquial: 'Notes and Notions'; 'Mems for the Million'; 'Thoughts and Thumbnails'; 'Queer, Quaint and Curious'; 'Fashions, Fads and Fancies: A Page for Everybody'; 'Rare, Racy and Readable: Items of Interest and Information'; 'A Weekly Chat on the Latest Fashions'; 'Gossip'. This was indeed a new kind of marketing that advertised the appeal - inherent in its very lack of pretence - of matter 'of fitting triviality and of no great account', and made much of the role of the editor in entertaining his readers through 'gossip', 'chat' and other informal and inclusive types of communication.[44] The organs of New Journalism cultivated an intimate rather than an authoritative tone.

Harry Schalck has argued that what both New and Old Journalism had in common in the transitional period at the end of the nineteenth century was a

---

[41] *The Million*, 2, 34 (November 1892), p.90.

[42] See *The Million*, 5, 127 (August 1894), p.268.

[43] See *The Million*, 3, 84 (October 1893), p.656.

[44] *The Million*, 1, 11 (June 1892), p.86.

serious interest in politics.[45] The vehicles of New Journalism, however, sometimes handled politics in very novel ways. In *The Million*, the serious political article or leader was transformed into a kind of parliamentary gossip column, in a series called 'Behind the Scenes of the House of Commons', written by T.P. O'Connor and illustrated by F.C. Gould. The articles were harmless enough but quintessentially trivial, and consisted of the kind of common gossip about the physical characteristics of parliamentarians that might have been heard in the public gallery: 'Beards in Parliament', 'Voices in Parliament', 'Sleepers in Parliament', 'Dandies in Parliament' and 'Noses in Parliament'. Newnes himself appeared in the series in March 1893 among the 'chess players of distinction' in the Chess Club at the House, of which he was Secretary. This column represented a kind of democratic popularisation of the parliamentary sphere. Newnes later developed the idea in *Picture Politics*, a penny illustrated monthly, featuring many political caricatures and cartoons by F.C. Gould, political anecdotes and commentary, a diary of the month's political events, and various regular features including 'Faces and Episodes in Parliament' and a 'Personal Page'.[46]

The organs of New Journalism were largely guided by the desire to take advantage of a lucrative commercial opportunity. *Tit-Bits* was no exception. 'Entrepreneurs such as Newnes and Lord Northcliffe stand out now', Stephen Elwell has observed, 'because they discovered in the 1880s and 1890s how to define and exploit the common interest of the middle class in *inclusive* rather than *exclusive* terms.'[47] After a period of class-based journalism, these years saw the emergence of a distinctly new editorial strategy. Magazines like *Tit-Bits* were able to speak to a broadly-defined reading community rather than to a discrete class of readers. James Curran has also pointed to the integrational themes stressed in the industrialised press.[48] 'The Million', for instance, were a diverse audience, and different columns, competitions and features were designed to appeal to different readers: 'A Weekly Chat on the Latest Fashions' to female readers and 'The Childrens' Hour' (a feature which, incidentally, was incorporated into *The Ladies' Field* after *The Million*'s demise) to juvenile readers. Later Newnes publications such as *The Ladies'*

---

[45] Harry Schalck, 'Fleet St in the 1880s: The New Journalism', in Joel Wiener (ed.), *Papers for the Millions*, p.73.

[46] This publication treated politics with a kind of humorous irreverence, and attempted to promote the Liberal cause amongst a broad readership through the comic tradition - 'the humours of Parliament and the amusing side of political controversies' were its substance - a personalised style and illustrative techniques which Newnes had developed in *Tit-Bits*, *The Million* and *The Strand*. Newnes also produced a series of lantern slides and lectures by F.C. Gould entitled 'Pictures in Liberalism', 'specially prepared for delivery, either in a hall or in the street, throughout the constituencies' (*Picture Politics*, 84 (October-November 1900)).

[47] Joel H. Wiener (ed.), *Innovators and Preachers*, p.40. My italics.

[48] James Curran, 'The Press as an Agency of Social Control' in George Boyce, James Curran, and Pauline Wingate, *Newspaper History from the Seventeenth Century to the Present Day*, London: Constable, 1978, p.70.

Field and *The Strand* were more specialised and were designed to appeal to particular sections of the market.

Newnes was an astute businessman, and *Tit-Bits* became a kind of 'promotional tool' (to use Elwell's term) in which new competitions and features appeared each week. He was the first publisher to apply shop window-dressing techniques to his circulation campaigns. The philosophy of the advertiser, as one article on 'Monster Advertising' in *Tit-Bits* pointed out, was 'notoriety and popularity'.[49] This might have been Newnes's motto. As he felt himself bound to confess in relation to one competition: 'there is no philanthropy about the matter. It is simply prompted by the advertising instinct, and there is no more generosity about it than if we had spent hundreds of pounds on bill-posting.'[50] Establishing *Tit-Bits* with a capital of £500, Newnes was offered £16,000 for outright purchase of the publication by a Manchester publishing firm six weeks after the appearance of the first issue.[51] Six months later, a London publishing firm offered £30,000. When he placed *Tit-Bits* in a green cover, on the advice of the advertising agent T.B. Browne, his personal income increased to £200 per week. It increased again when he established his own advertising department. His income from *Tit-Bits* in 1890, ten years after its establishment, was just under £30,000.[52]

Newnes employed various schemes to increase circulation and thus advertising revenue. The railway insurance scheme protected every commuter with a current copy of the magazine on his or her person whilst travelling on trains. The *Tit-Bits* Villa Competition offered a seven-roomed freehold house as the prize for a short story competition. It attracted a mention in the papers of every country in Europe.[53] And in another competition, a series of cryptic clues divulged the whereabouts of a buried tube of 500 gold sovereigns. In the ensuing years, £2,500 was hidden in different locations. 'Nothing has ever occasioned such passionate endeavour as this search for gold', wrote Friederichs in a kind of romanticisation of the acquisitive instinct, 'perhaps because it appeals to one of the most deep-seated elemental cravings of the human heart.'[54] This was what Newnes referred to as 'advertisement investment'.[55] The idea was not completely original, having been employed by a few earlier editors and publishers. Nevertheless Newnes exploited this technique in a new and comprehensive fashion. The story-writing competition won by Grant Allen attracted over 20,000 manuscripts from aspiring authors.

---

[49] *Tit-Bits*, 6, 141 (August 1884), p.172.

[50] *Tit-Bits*, 5, 115 (December 1883), p.168.

[51] The offer was made by the same Manchester businessman who had declined to take a half-share in the paper in return for providing the sum required for establishment.

[52] Reginald Pound, *Mirror of the Century: The Strand Magazine, 1891-1950*, London: Heinemann, 1966, p.25.

[53] 'The Science of Advertising' in *Tit-Bits*, 6, 137 (July 1884), p.101.

[54] Hulda Friederichs, op. cit., p.97.

[55] *Tit-Bits*, 6, 137 (July 1884), p.101.

For another competition, the G.P.O. delivered 300 mailbags full of entries.[56] *Tit-Bits* Christmas Numbers, in which the editor offered guinea prizes for contributions on seasonal themes, were household events.

In fact Newnes created a popular movement out of *Tit-Bits*, with his advertising stunts, his competitions and his stimulation of a sense of communality among those whom he referred to as 'loyal Tit-Bitites' - that commuters' club comprised of people who religiously carried a copy of *Tit-Bits* in their pockets in accordance with the conditions of the *Tit-Bits* Insurance Scheme. It resembled the 'Merrie England' movement which Robert Blatchford's series of that name in the *Clarion* inspired.[57]

It was these loyal readers - 'willing *Tit-Bits* canvassers' - whom Newnes had attempted to rally in support of his scheme to raise circulation by offering to benefit the Hospitals Fund. He promoted the scheme as 'a new kind of CO-OPERATIVE PHILANTHROPY' designed to benefit 'a good cause', cleverly drawing together working-class traditions of cooperation and solidarity and middle-class traditions of charity and philanthropy:

> There are thousands of people who, having no more of the world's goods than they require for themselves, are yet willing and anxious by personal effort in their leisure time to do what they can for promoting what they know to be good objects .... We wish to enlist the help of a large number of willing workers who will try and make this arrangement a practical success .... This may be described as a new kind of CO-OPERATIVE PHILANTHROPY. (The Lord Major of London is trying to get the working people to subscribe a penny a week to the Hospitals. We hope he will succeed in his efforts. Here is also a chance by which anyone, at the expenditure of a penny a week, for which he gets good value, can have the agreeable consciousness that he is helping a good cause ....)
> A few willing *Tit-Bits* canvassers, in each town and village in the Kingdom, will make success certain.[58]

The language in which the scheme was couched was a mixture of commercialism and conscience. 'Promoting', for instance, was endowed with philanthropic associations. And 'canvassing', usually associated with political campaigning, was transformed into a benevolent activity. Newnes attempted to co-opt his readers into a bond of mutual responsibility and communal identification, evoking an ideal version of a medieval or pre-commercial England (through the references to a fair share of 'the world's goods' and 'each

---

[56] Reginald Pound, op. cit., p.24; Hulda Friederichs, op. cit., pp.90-91.

[57] The *Clarion* was established ten years after *Tit-Bits*, in 1891, and was a very popular paper. See Nunquam, *Merrie England*, London, 1893. Reprinted by Journeyman Press, 1976.

[58] *Tit-Bits*, 16, 397 (May 1889), p.97

town and village in the Kingdom'), in an advertising stunt that was presented as a social initiative.

At the outset, Newnes had generated enthusiasm for his paper by sending out a squad of a hundred newspaper boys (the editor at their head), wearing hatbands which identified them as 'The *Tit-Bits* Brigade' and carrying bundles of the paper in their arms, to march up and down Market St.[59] To stimulate sales in Newcastle-on-Tyne, an army of sandwich-board men was engaged, the first of whom displayed the name *Tit-Bits*, the next 'I like it', the next 'My wife likes it', the next 'My daughter likes it', the next 'My mother likes it', and so on through a large family, ending with the assertion 'So do I'. This, the publisher stressed, was a *family* paper. There was even a *Tit-Bits* entry of horse and van in the newly instituted May Day procession at Newcastle.[60]

The editor became responsible for the guidance of his readers in multifarious settings, and the paper's name and cover became emblems of cultural identity for overseas readers, as well as in a domestic context. During the Paris Exhibition of 1889 Newnes provided a *Tit-Bits* Pavilion and Inquiry Office:

> having purchased a plot of land close to the central entrance to the Exhibition ... we have erected A LARGE BUILDING, the front of which will be a facsimile in design, colour, and every other way of the front page of *Tit-Bits*. This building will be placed at the disposal of readers of *Tit-Bits*.[61]

The office was described as 'a rendezvous for all readers of *Tit-Bits*, and a place for obtaining full information'. In an extension of its textual function as the site in which editor and reading public (producer and consumer) interacted on the printed page, *Tit-Bits* became associated with the physical and tangible act of 'rendezvous'.

The response from Newnes's readers to his initiatives was almost overwhelming. One reader, living in a remote corner of Cape Colony, South Africa, led an 'enthusiastic band of Tit-Bitites' (unsolicited) on a mountaineering expedition. On a rock overlooking the village and visible from all directions including from the Orange River, they painted, in letters 12 ft high, the words 'Read Tit-Bits', reclaiming the wild in a version of the imperial

---

[59] Hulda Friederichs, op. cit., p.70. In Glasgow, at the same time as Newnes brought out *Tit-Bits*, Thomas Lipton, the chain-store grocer, was having mammoth Canadian cheeses drawn by traction engine, and once by an elephant, from the docks to his warehouse. See Reginald Pound, op. cit., p.20. Such stunts made people talk. Newnes wanted them to talk about *Tit-Bits*.

[60] Hulda Friederichs, op. cit., pp.74-76. The May Day Procession was an innovation of 1890, designed, according to Friederichs, to rescue cart-horses and donkeys from eternal over-work and ill-treatment.

[61] *Tit-Bits*, 16, 394 (May 1889), p.49.

adventure in which the paper was a visible emblem of British civilisation.[62] Another devoted reader painted the word '*Tit-Bits*' in 'bold letters high up on the rocks of Great Orme's Head at Llandudno'. Newnes gracefully acknowledged such marks of esteem:

> We are very much obliged to those friendly readers who, when they go upon their travels, leave behind them some record of their favourite paper.[63]

The *Tit-Bits* offices themselves constituted a sizeable advertisement. 'Over the offices of *Tit-Bits*, 83, 84, and 85 Farringdon Street, London', wrote the Editor, 'has been recently fixed the largest letter sign in the world.' Newnes was certainly a master of self-publicity. The article, entitled 'The Largest Letter Sign in the World', offered the sign as a kind of addition to the Seven Wonders of the World:

> It is composed of seven letters, and is the word *Tit-Bits*. Each letter cost about £7. The sign took six men ten days to fix, and it may be said to be one of the sights of London. It can easily be seen from Ludgate Circus and from Holborn Viaduct, and those of our readers who are in that neighbourhood at any time, should not miss seeing the largest letter sign in the world.[64]

As display advertising increased in the later nineteenth century, public criticism of the excesses of advertisers took various forms.[65] One wonders what the reaction of locals to such signs as that described above would have been.

It is surely a sign of the widespread popularity of *Tit-Bits* and of the spread of what could almost be called the '*Tit-Bits* movement', that one manufacturer decided to produce little cigar ashtrays, costing sixpence, on which were printed a facsimile of the front page of *Tit-Bits*. These items were

---

62 *Tit-Bits*, 9, 234 (April 1886), p.408.

63 *Tit-Bits*, 14, 342 (May 1888), p.61.

64 *Tit-Bits*, 6, 137 (July 1884), p.101.

65 In two notable instances in the period, public outrage against the activities of advertisers was sparked by the erection of highly visible signs or hoardings within the jurisdiction of urban authorities. In 1897, the Bovril Company's plans to adorn the exterior of a building in Princes Street, Edinburgh with illuminated signs was abandoned because of public outcry. And four years later, a similar public reaction greeted the erection of an advertising sign for Quaker Oats in a prominent position on Dover cliffs. The Dover Corporation responded by promoting a local Act of Parliament to enable it to deal with such abuses. In 1893, the National Society for Controlling the Abuses of Public Advertising was formed, with an influential membership. It received, however, publicity out of proportion to its support. See T.R. Nevett, *Advertising in Britain*, London: Heinemann, 1982, p.117.

sold at the China Department at Whiteley's, Westbourne Grove.[66] Newnes had created out of *Tit-Bits* a kind of national symbol within popular culture.

Newnes suggested that *Tit-Bits* actually empowered the reader socially by providing him or her with a 'fund' of useful conversational material. His claim:

> Any person who takes *Tit-Bits* for three months will at the end of that time be an entertaining companion, as he will then have at his command a stock of smart sayings and a fund of anecdote which make his society agreeable.[67]

He thus projected his own ambitions onto the reader of *Tit-Bits*: his desire to combine the facility of entertainment with the ability to convert the paragraphic portions which he delivered in *Tit-Bits* into the material success associated with acquiring 'stock' and 'funds'. He himself was an interesting, entertaining and genial after-dinner speaker, according to Friederichs, and in *Tit-Bits* he was to create a kind of discursive version of the clubs he frequented: the National Liberal and Devonshire Clubs. Newnes was a natural host, and in some sense *Tit-Bits* represented his desire to entertain his 'friends': in this case the loyal readers of *Tit-Bits*.

Yet Newnes took the relationship between himself and his readers very seriously. He conceived of it as a relationship bound by legal and moral obligations, constantly invoking the idea of the contract which he strove to maintain with *Tit-Bits* readers. In the *Tit-Bits* Villa Competition, for example, he went into endless detail regarding the conditions of the competition, answered the questions of prospective competitors in the weeks leading up to the judging, and reported on the entire process of awarding and bestowing the prize, as 'an absolute guarantee to the public that it has been given without favour'. 'We shall take pride in seeing that the house is one which all will admit is a *fair and reasonable fulfilment of our contract*', he announced.

> Let everyone remember that we have pledged our reputation in this matter ... and all may be sure that we shall make this prize one which shall resound to the credit of *Tit-Bits*, and not one of which we shall be ashamed.[68]

The problem with journalistic competitions was that not only did they leave the publisher open to the allegation that he was undermining literary standards by employing cheap commercial ploys, but they left him susceptible to charges concerning the promotion of illegal gambling. 'We do not intend to have any more chance competitions', wrote the editor, tackling the issue head-

---

[66] *Tit-Bits*, 15, 378, (January 1889), p.221.

[67] *Tit-Bits*, 1, 1 (October 1881), p.1.

[68] *Tit-Bits*, 5, 112 (December 1883), p.120.

on, as was his wont, when it arose in 1889. 'We never cared for them, and only instituted them because, unlike literary contests, they seemed to give an equal chance.' He continued in a psuedo-reformist vein:

> But it has been pointed out ... that there is a danger of a demoralising effect from them, inasmuch as they encourage a tendency to gambling ... they may be injurious to some, and in any case they are unworthy of *Tit-Bits* and of its subscribers.[69]

Aware of the decision, derived from various common law cases of the period relating to promotional schemes and from Trade Marks Acts of 1875 and 1883, that a general offer in an advertisement could constitute part of an enforceable contract, Newnes made repeated reference to his legal obligations as a publisher-promoter within the text of *Tit-Bits*.[70] He elaborated upon the terms of the contract as time went on. 'The greatest care is taken to give correct answers to inquiries', he explained in one issue, 'but at the same time our correspondents must understand that we disclaim any responsibility in giving our opinions.' In the same issue it was stated that correspondents were required to 'give their names and addresses, not necessarily for publication, but as a guarantee of good faith.'[71] Later, when Newnes was negotiating the possibility of introducing advertising, he again employed the language of the law, explaining that he 'scarcely liked ... to intrude more pages of advertisements upon [his] readers without giving them full compensation'. To this end, the introduction of commercial advertising on the front and back covers of *Tit-Bits* was not permitted to reduce the number of printed pages in the paper. Every change in format or content in *Tit-Bits* was discussed at length. The process by which the publication, and indeed its editor, evolved, was therefore characterised by its transparency.[72] Newnes was engaged in establishing a relationship of trust and loyalty - a kind of moral bond as well as a legal one - with his readers. Manchester readers took this bond very seriously. When

---

[69] *Tit-Bits*, 16, 397 (May 1889), p.97.

[70] As the use of competitions increased towards the end of the century, a number of cases were brought before the courts as constituting lotteries. According to numerous Acts passed in the eighteenth and nineteenth centuries, the organising and advertising of any lottery was unlawful. The key question, for judges, was whether the distribution of prizes in various promotional schemes was dependent upon chance, and thus constituted a lottery. Competitions aimed at boosting newspaper circulations featured in the courts. Pearson, for instance, was taken to court in 1893 over the 'Missing Word' competitions which he organised through *Pearson's Weekly*, and as a result, such competitions were pronounced illegal. See R.D. Blumenfeld, *R.D.B.'s Diary, 1887-1914*, London: William Heinemann, 1930, pp.60-61. Trade Marks Acts of 1875, 1883, 1888 and 1905 restricted the kinds of claims that could be made, particularly regarding rival products, and enforced protection of the trader's name. The decision that a general offer in an advertisement could constitute part of an enforceable contract was the result. See T.R. Nevett, op. cit., pp.133-137.

[71] *Tit-Bits*, 13, 313 (October 1887), p.14.

[72] *Tit-Bits*, 17, 418 (October 1889).

Harmsworth introduced *Answers*, an imitation of *Tit-Bits*, they displayed their loyalty to Newnes by boycotting the newcomer.[73]

Newnes's investment in the moral bond between editor and readers, in many ways a relic of the old journalism and an extension of his own strong sense of public responsibility, led him to insist repeatedly on the 'clean' quality of *Tit-Bits*. With an excessive degree of moral earnestness, he scrutinised every line of the paper right down to the joke 'fillers' at the foot of the columns. In one instance, he blue-pencilled a query about kissing in public, writing against it on the page proof: 'We should avoid any subject that may have an injurious effect on our readers.'[74] His campaign to maintain his paper's impeccable moral standards and reputation was obviously successful. The manager of W.H. Smith's bookstall at Victoria Station, Manchester, said that he decided to 'push' *Tit-Bits* because he thought that it might, as Newnes had intended, provide much-needed opposition to the 'blood-and-thunders' which had led Smith to consider compiling its subsequently effective blacklist.[75]

Stephen Kern has suggested that the journalistic medium itself is both democratising and communal by virtue of the way in which it diminishes the distance between individuals - both social and geographical. It is equally accessible to all classes and decreases the isolation of individuals both in the city and throughout the whole country.[76] This was certainly true of *Tit-Bits* which had, as has been noted, a wide circulation. Social segregation and fragmentation had been the legacy of industrialisation and urbanisation. With urban segregation and urban spread, the wealthy employing class tended to move outside the boundaries of the larger towns and cities, and thus removed themselves from the responsibilities and networks of the communities they left behind. Only some, like Newnes, continued to engage in what Harold Perkin refers to as 'competitive philanthropy', giving hospitals, libraries, public parks, town halls and churches to the towns.[77] The appeal of *Tit-Bits*, it could be argued, lay largely in its recreation of this kind of community of mutual responsibility. It offered its readers engagement, interaction and connection.

---

[73] See Hulda Friederichs, op. cit., pp.80-81.

[74] George Newnes as cited in Reginald Pound, op. cit., p.25.

[75] Ibid., p.21. Initially, Newnes was impeded by concerns about the purity of *Tit-Bits* which sprang from the fact that to some potential readers, a 'tit-bit' was an off-colour anecdote, and to others it denoted prurience. A female newsvendor in Newcastle with a substantial sales round, whose customers relied on her personal recommendation of the papers they took in, contributed to initial sales resistance, thinking the title of the paper indecent. Newnes's brother-in-law, James Hillyard, made a special visit to persuade her of its purity. And Newnes consistently maintained that this was a paper 'as clean as a new pin, and as witty and humorous and brilliant as those the unclean minds could invent'. See Hulda Friederichs, op. cit., p.54.

[76] Stephen Kern, *The Culture of Time and Space, 1880-1918*, Cambridge, Massachusetts: Harvard University Press, 1983.

[77] Harold Perkin, *The Age of the Railway*, Newton Abbot: David and Charles, 1971, p.262.

Newnes's father had belonged to a generation of Free Church pastors who brought to their work a strong sense of personal responsibility for and intimacy with the individual members of their congregations. Through the secular medium of the popular periodical, Newnes replicated the bond of human connection which the Church had previously provided.[78] He also drew upon new social models. In the 1880s and 1890s, the settlement movement, a kind of secular replacement for religion, sought to assume responsibility for promoting this kind of 'fellowship'. Many educated men and women acquired a practical personal commitment to the ideals of human fellowship and social unity, and a number of middle-class students took up residence in newly-formed 'settlement houses' such as Toynbee Hall, which opened in 1885 and was followed by many more such houses. They provided a range of social services: health care, kindergartens, child-care classes, legal aid, lectures, libraries, concerts and recreational facilities. The gospel of fellowship even permeated public policy, and the move towards collectivism in public opinion and the law was a reflection of this. A.V. Dicey argued, in fact, that these years saw a transition from individualism to collectivism.[79]

Yet organic customary relations had been integral to earlier social models, which revolved around a notion of paternalism that was as much based on mutual responsibilities as on hereditary rights. *Tit-Bits* was thus a manifestation of both George Newnes's attachment to old local and parish community traditions, and his sense of new forms of collectivism. This paper, it is contended, was itself a kind of journalistic, discursive equivalent of a settlement house, providing social services, advice, participation and a sense of community and citizenship for its audience.

Newnes employed a variety of professionals to supply advice to and exert an educational influence upon his readers. A lawyer answered readers' legal queries, a doctor answered 'Medical Questions', and the editor himself supplied answers to readers' correspondence and inquiries. The editor-publisher introduced a column entitled 'Tit-Bits of Legal Information' in 1881, in response to requests from contributors for legal information to which he saw it as his duty to respond:

> We have received so many applications from our subscribers for tit-bits of legal information on matters important to our correspondents, that we have secured the services of a legal gentleman to give the required answers.[80]

---

[78] This point recalls Carlyle's comment that the Victorian editor constituted the Church of England.

[79] See A.V. Dicey, *Lectures on the Relationship Between Law and Public Opinion During the Nineteenth Century in England*, London: Macmillan, 1905, pp.281-300.

[80] *Tit-Bits*, 1, 4 (November 1881), p.14.

The column was a legal, journalistic version of the talkback radio programme. Over the early years of the paper's publication, a range of questions relating to urban, industrial life and to the legal preoccupations of this society emerged within it.

Questions relating to the right of a domestic servant to unpaid wages when dismissed, to debt recovery and the relationship between producer and consumer, to the right of a father to bind his son as an apprentice without the son's consent, to the obligations of a patent-holder, to the laws governing marriage and divorce, to the conditions attached to life insurance policies, to the issues relating to income tax and financial liability, crowded the columns. Questions concerning the ability of a married woman to make a will were common. The Married Women's Property Act of 1883 had only just granted her that right, and had also enabled women to initiate civil law suits, hence the significant contingent of female correspondents to this column. Divorce reform laws, however, had not yet emerged to alter the legal position of women. 'Your husband having deserted you without cause for upwards of two years', read the editor's response to one female correspondent, 'you are entitled to a judicial separation.'

> To enable you to marry another person, you would have to be divorced from your present husband, and you could only obtain such decree on proving that your husband had been guilty of both adultery and desertion.[81]

This advice column spawned other textual forms of social service and discursive interaction. The editor offered a secular substitute for pastoral guidance, with a series containing practical advice on 'How to Marry', including an account of the 'Legal Effect of Marriage' which was designed both to make the law intelligible to the paper's readers and to justify and promote recent Liberal reforms.[82] He also offered advice on emigration (in a series entitled 'Intelligent Emigration') and medical advice.

A two-part series on 'Medical Questions' supplied 'an explanation of the causes and cures of the various ailments of which our querists have complained' as well as 'knowledge on the general principles of health'. Once again, the column combined personal interaction with general appeal. The medical conditions treated included indigestion, headaches, 'noises in the ear', bunions and varicose veins, and the doctor's advice tended to take the form of a discourse on urban degeneration, social responsibility and temperance, with phrases such as 'irregular living', 'deficient care' and 'bad cooking' figuring heavily. Indigestion, it was suggested, was a result of urban conditions:

---

81 *Tit-Bits*, 1, 6 (November 1881), p.14.
82 See *Tit-Bits*, 4, 85 (June 1883), p.108.

> The hurried meals partaken of by a large number of clerks and
> warehousemen cannot but produce indigestion - all the laws of
> healthy digestion are violated. A run to a close restaurant, or a
> scramble to catch the bus or train, the food bolted, and then a
> smoke, and another scramble to get back to the office, is the daily
> routine of a large number of our townspeople.[83]

The column was almost reformist in tone. A later feature - a competition
to produce the best list of 'Ten Long-Felt Wants' - similarly precipitated an
exposition on social reform and social responsibility.[84] The discourse of these
columns was not partisan or directly political. But it created an atmosphere
conducive to the voicing of critical views, and to the participation and
representation of readers. And it reinforced the sense that editors and audience
were bound together in a community of mutual responsibility.

Newnes's innovative publishing strategies were the key to the success of
Tit-Bits. One scheme which guaranteed the paper's circulation was the novel
Tit-Bits Insurance Scheme, introduced in May 1885. Newnes announced 'The
New System of Life Assurance' in bold capitals, a characteristic journalistic
ploy for drawing attention to the innovation:

> ONE HUNDRED POUNDS WILL BE PAID BY THE
> PROPRIETOR OF *TIT-BITS* TO THE NEXT-OF-KIN OF ANY
> PERSON WHO IS KILLED IN A RAILWAY ACCIDENT,
> PROVIDED A COPY OF THE CURRENT ISSUE OF *TIT-BITS*
> IS FOUND UPON THE DECEASED AT THE TIME OF THE
> CATASTROPHE.[85]

Characteristically, the scheme had been suggested to Newnes by the
inquiry of a reader. The reader's husband, a devoted reader of *Tit-Bits* who was
almost due to be rewarded for his constancy with a sum of money (in
accordance with an incentive scheme for subscribers introduced by Newnes to
raise circulation), had been killed in a railway accident. She applied to Newnes
for some compensation and was sent £100.

Claims were always billed on the front cover of the paper, their visibility
guaranteeing their impact. The first insurance claim was paid in August 1885.
A 40-year-old coachbuilder with four children was killed when he was run
over by a train after falling between the train and the platform at Hatfield
Station. The Coroner's verdict was 'Accidental Death', and four witnesses
testified to the fact that 'a copy of *Tit-Bits* had been found upon the unfortunate
man at the time of the accident'. Thus the proprietor of *Tit-Bits* paid £100

---

83 *Tit-Bits*, 5, 125 (March 1884), p.333.

84 *Tit-Bits*, 6, 130 (April 1884), pp.221, 250.

85 *Tit-Bits*, 8, 189 (May 1885), p.97. Other publishers soon followed Newnes's lead.
Public Opinion, for example, ran a similar scheme in the 1890s and 1900s. It was a scheme
that was copied in a fiercely competitive fashion by the daily newspapers of the 1930s.

insurance money to the victim's widow, and the beneficiary's receipt of payment was published in *Tit-Bits* as proof of the transaction.[86] A series of claims followed at the rate of about one every two months, and by September 1891 a total of 36 claims had been paid. An advertisement for *Tit-Bits* in *Under the Union Jack*, another Newnes publication, in 1900, stated that £12,500 had been paid in insurance claims - proof of both supply and demand.[87] All claims generally followed the same format, and were decided by 'the proprietor of *Tit-Bits*'. Appended to the eighteenth insurance claim was a moral:

> We trust that the publicity which the *Tit-Bits* Insurance Scheme has been the means of giving to this lamentable occurrence may to some extent put a stop to the habit of leaping out of a train while in motion, which is so prevalent in young men. To jeopardise life in this reckless fashion is an act of which no sensible person should be capable.[88]

With comments such as this, the editor-proprietor of *Tit-Bits* established himself as investigator and judge in cases of accidents on the railways, taking the evidence, hearing the testimonies of the witnesses, and handing down a judgement. He set himself up as a guardian of social conscience and as a figure of paternalistic benevolence, fulfilling his responsibilities to his community of readers by dispensing insurance claims and advice. There is something symbolic (if a little morbid) in the fact that all of these victims were found with a copy of *Tit-Bits* on their person. Newnes's publication appealed to a commuting market, and to a public preoccupied with the notion of life insurance and concerned with the frequency of railway accidents.[89] But apart from anything else, the idea of railway insurance sold *Tit-Bits*, and the stories that emerged were gripping stories. Even agony columns, as Anne Humpherys has shown, depended upon the narrative gaps being filled by an audience with certain expectations about narrative form and convention. The power of such columns lay in the potential they represented for narratising.[90] Thus the *Tit-Bits* Insurance System was structured in such a way as to produce a series of

---

[86] *Tit-Bits*, 8, 198 (August, 1885), p.241.

[87] *Under the Union Jack*, 1, 1 (1900).

[88] *Tit-Bits*, 15, 387 (March 1889), p.353.

[89] This concern was considerable. According to a report compiled by the Board of Trade, the number of people killed on the railways in 1880 was 1,136, and the number injured 3,958. A public and parliamentary campaign to limit the hours worked by railwaymen (the main area of concern) and thus increase safety on the railways raged through the 1870s and 1880s. A Select Committee of the House of Commons was appointed to inquire whether working hours should be restricted by legislation. In 1893 the Railway Regulation Act was passed. It provided for the Board of Trade to inquire into cases of overwork, have access to duty schedules from offending companies and levy fines on such companies for failure to adhere to the Board's instructions. See Harold Perkin, *The Age of the Railway*, pp.292-296.

[90] Anne Humpherys, 'Popular Narrative and Political Discourse in *Reynold's Weekly Newspaper*', in Laurel Brake, Aled Jones and Lionel Madden (eds), op. cit., p.37.

parables in which the grieving relatives of the victim were invariably saved (in a financial sense) by the money provided by the editor of *Tit-Bits*.

In November 1883, a revolutionary competition was announced. A seven-roomed freehold dwelling-house was offered as a prize to the person sending in the story judged to be the best by the *Tit-Bits* adjudicators. The main stipulation made by Newnes was that the winner should call the house 'Tit-Bits Villa'.[91] The editor stressed that the competition was inclusive, being open to 'every member of every family in the Kingdom, from the highest to the lowest'. (The possibility of such inclusiveness was guaranteed by the extraordinary condition that entries could be selected from a published work rather than being original. Thus the competition required no great literary skill.) His approach to the conduct of the competition was typically interactive. Introducing a feature called 'More Questions Answered', he answered the queries of competitors, and throughout the competition was quick to retaliate to objections. He explained, berated, commented, appealed to his readers' better natures, and publicised editorial dilemmas, drawing on the idea of the competition as a 'transaction' entered into in 'good faith' and precluding 'any breach of faith with the public'.

The purpose of the competition, of course, was to raise circulation, but those who joined the 'followers of *Tit-Bits*' could expect an intimate and responsive relationship with their leader, the editor. At the conclusion of the competition, for instance, Newnes played policeman, prosecution and judiciary in passing sentence on the 'unprincipled miscreant' who had falsely informed a competitor that he had won the prize:

> ... we are of the opinion that an unnatural ruffian who would be guilty of such a dastardly act as this deserves punishment of the severest kind, and we offer £5 REWARD to anyone who will disclose to us the name of this viper. If we unearth him we shall spare no pains or expense to prove that this act was forgery, and comes under penal laws.[92]

The role of the editor-leader of this discursive community extended, it seems, even to the policing of community interests. And he addressed his audience in the language of popular melodrama ('unnatural ruffian', 'dastardly act', 'this viper').

Ultimately, Newnes published a 'Report upon the Competition'. Over 22,000 letters were received at the *Tit-Bits* offices, some containing up to twenty entries. 'Tit-Bits Villa', in Dulwich, was open for inspection, and

---

[91] The term 'villa' is significant. Originating in ancient Rome, in English it was initially a country mansion, seat, or estate - a sizeable house on its own grounds which symbolised social status. By the nineteenth century, the term began to be applied to middle-class housing, usually detached or semi-detached, (the 'suburban villa'), and the term 'villa Toryism' was coined around the turn of the century.

[92] *Tit-Bits*, 5, 117 (January 1884), p.205.

became a place of pilgrimage for day-trippers and tourists. Thousands of people took the trip by rail to visit. The villa was awarded in a public ceremony that must have resembled a political rally, and 100,000 photos of it were developed and sold as souvenirs of the competition. Even then, supply did not meet demand (*see Figure 6*).[93]

Various trappings were introduced for the photograph - curtains, for instance - in order to make the house, in reality unoccupied at this point, look 'inhabited' and homely. Furthermore, Newnes conducted an imaginary narrative tour of the house in *Tit-Bits*, in which he created an image of it that appealed to a long-held middle-class ideal of home-ownership and family life, and tallied exactly with readers' social ambitions. The conservatory was imagined as a kind of Garden of Eden, replete with daphne, carnation, heliotrope, stephanotis, mignonette and narcissus. The drawing room was imaginatively transformed into a room with a cheerful fire such as might have inspired the lines 'Home, Sweet Home'. The 'culinary department', by a process of mental projection, became the apartment where 'the roast beef of Old England will be cooked' and from whence, in a manner reminiscent of Dickens' Pickwickian Christmas, 'Christmas pudding will come all blazing, to the delight and wonderment of the little ones, and reviving bygone memories in the hearts of the old folk'.[94] Suburbanisation was the characteristic innovation of city life in the second half of the nineteenth century. Towns such as Croydon developed rapidly into dormitories for City clerks, and suburbs such as Dulwich were built on what was then the edge of the City. These areas consisted of rows of neat terraced or semi-detached houses with small gardens, and they testified to the successful propertied aspirations of a new army of City workers, trained at new polytechnics, employed in the growing service and commercial sectors, and commuting from their suburban homes.

Another competition, for which the prize was a £100 position at the offices of *Tit-Bits*, both appealed to the occupational aspirations of the magazine's upper working and lower middle-class audience, and functioned for Newnes as a method of recruiting journalists for his paper. It was announced in May 1884:

> It is stated throughout the country that there are at present over <u>one hundred thousand clerks out of employment</u>; the large majority of whom, though constantly endeavouring to obtain work, are unable to make a living. We therefore propose to put a SITUATION up to PUBLIC COMPETITION; and we offer as the FIRST PRIZE in the TENTH INQUIRY COLUMN COMPETITION A SITUATION in the offices of "TIT-BITS" at a salary of £100 per Annum. The said situation will be a permanent one, with prospect of increase, should that winner prove a trustworthy and competent

---

[93] The *Oxford Illustrated History of Britain* incorrectly identifies the Harmsworths as the publishers of *Tit-Bits* in the caption for this photograph.

[94] *Tit-Bits*, 5, 117 (January 1884), p.205.

> person. It will be guaranteed for one year. The winning of the Prize
> will secure the clerkship subject only to references as to honesty.[95]

The editor made sympathetic reference to contemporary economic and social conditions, and harnessed them for promotional purposes. *Tit-Bits*, as he later pointed out, was alive to the rhythms of industrial life and the needs of its readers. Eighteen-year-old Arthur Pearson won the competition. He made use of the library of his father's country rectory, and cycled a round trip of sixty miles, three times a week, to Bedford Free Library, which boasted an excellent reference department. Pearson answered 86 out of the 130 questions correctly. Eighteen of the remaining answers were very good, eight good, three fair, and only three absolutely incorrect. He went on to become the manager of the *Tit-Bits* offices, and remained on the staff for nearly five years before leaving to establish his own rival paper, *Pearson's Weekly*.[96]

In *The Million* too, Newnes hosted a vast number of competitions. He attempted to penetrate the lower middle and upper working-class home with a series of schemes in which 'a number of handsome presents, which, by their novelty and acceptability, will tend to spread the name and fame of this paper' were offered as prizes. Free birthday gifts were awarded to readers sending in a *Million* coupon, and parent-readers sending in large numbers of coupons were awarded Christening mugs 'made of elegantly-chased "Queen's Plate", bearing upon them, in ornamentally-engraved letters, the best wishes of *The Million* and the names of the little recipients.' The editor presented this promotional scheme as a kind of missionary project: 'Our circle of readers is now a wide and expanding one, but we are anxious to reach homes in which *The Million* is still unknown'. He claimed that the paper would be 'a sort of universal god-father to the children of its readers', drawing upon the language of kinship, paternalism and collectivism.[97] The editor also claimed the role of Executor of the common Estate, offering to assist readers who believed they were entitled to 'unclaimed property in Chancery or elsewhere' in the '"NEXT-OF-KIN" COLUMN', introduced in May, 1894.[98] As with the *Tit-Bits* Insurance Scheme, the stories of beneficiaries were published by way of advertising the good work of the column.[99]

'For many years', Friederichs wrote of Newnes's editorial role in *Tit-Bits*, 'not a line was published which he had not read and approved'. She went on to describe his method:

---

[95] *Tit-Bits*, 6, 135 (May 1884), p.97. Formatting as per original.

[96] See Sidney Dark, *The Life of Sir Arthur Pearson, Bt, G.B.E.*, London: Hodder and Stoughton, 1922, pp.29-47.

[97] *The Million*, 2, 49 (February 1892), p.405.

[98] *The Million*, 5, 112 (May 1894), p.12.

[99] See Kate Jackson, 'Securing the Suffrage of the Crowd: George Newnes and *The Million*', *Nineteenth Century Prose*, 24, 1 (Spring 1997), p.33.

> No detail was too slight to receive his personal attention, and at
> short intervals he made thorough inquiries as to his readers'
> opinion on this or that page or column, substituting new features
> for those which had obviously ceased to interest, and always
> inventing and adopting fresh ideas.[100]

A constant stream of invention and innovation followed. Newnes was
typically candid about this. 'We do not intend to allow it to hang fire', he
explained, in the introduction to one scheme. 'Let it run its reasonable course,
and then make room for some other novelty.'[101]

The competitions and correspondence columns of *Tit-Bits* and *The
Million* embodied the creative freedom of the open text as opposed to the
prescriptive reality of the closed text. They facilitated and symbolised the
participation of readers in the text. In July 1892, for instance, the publication of
'A NOVEL NOVEL' was announced in *The Million*:

> We want any of the readers of *The Million* to send us the
> succeeding chapters of this story. The first chapter presents a wide
> field for complication and intrigue, and we leave it to our readers
> to dispose of the characters as they please, with this stipulation,
> that the story must move on naturally from one stage to another
> without being concluded. The most reasonable and readable
> contributions to the second and following chapters will be inserted
> with the names and addresses of the authors.[102]

This was truly a multi-authored text, with readers being urged to interact
with the editor, audience and text in the production of a kind of progressive and
collaborative narrative. Their participation was acknowledged through the
publication of their names and addresses.

In the context of explaining the conditions of the *Tit-Bits* Villa
Competition, Newnes articulated the democratic ideal by making the
competition 'open to every one of our readers, irrespective of age, sex,
nationality or colour'. Thus creative freedom was transformed by the editor
into political and social equality, the market relationship becoming the basis of
a system of democratic representation. When a feature entitled 'Our Stamp
Album' was begun in *The Million* in July 1894, the editor introduced it in
terms which drew upon a connection between democratisation and journalistic
innovation: '*The Million* is impressed by the fact that up to the present time
this enormous constituency of people interested in a special subject has
received no attention of a regular kind from the periodical press.'[103] *The
Million*'s version of democracy was one which allowed and catered for special

---

[100] Hulda Friederichs, op. cit., p.109.

[101] *Tit-Bits*, 5, 112 (December 1883), p.120.

[102] *The Million*, 1, 19 (July 1892), p.186.

[103] *The Million*, 5, 120 (July 1894), p.130.

interest groups. The link between the political power of the democratic masses and the purchasing power of the new mass reading public was explicitly expressed by NYM (the editor), soliciting reader participation in one of *The Million*'s prize competitions by presenting himself as a candidate standing for election:

DON'T FORGET! BE IN TIME!
POLL EARLY
(And as often as you please)
VOTE FOR NYM,
AND PICTURES FOR THE MILLION
UNIVERSAL SUFFRAGE! ONE MAN ONE VOTE![104]

Tit-Bits and *The Million* constituted mediums of participation for their readers, and hence represented Newnes's attempt to create a pluralistic discursive sphere.

Newnes himself appeared as a 'benignant administrator' (a term used frequently in *The Wide World Magazine* to describe British administrators in the Empire) in these two papers, conducting the affairs of his publishing house in an interactive fashion as if he were administering a pluralist state. The written word became a vehicle and a symptom of democracy. Newnes rarely spoke in Parliament and became disillusioned after entering it with high ideals and a young man's social and political visions. His *journals* were his public voice. He forged such strong links with his readers - the noble band of constant subscribers' denominated 'loyal Tit-Bitites' and 'Millionaires' - that they came to be something akin to constituents. As a result, perhaps, of the relationship that he developed with the reading public through *Tit-Bits* and *The Million*, Newnes's received not less than thirty-three requests from constituencies wishing him to represent them during the years of his retirement from politics (1895-1900). He had, in effect, already done so.

The spectre of increasing working and lower middle-class political potency, in conjunction with increasing literacy and purchasing power, clearly impressed the editor. In 1890 he conducted a public opinion poll, in an attempt to gauge 'the feeling of the country' as regards the likely outcome of an election, amidst speculation about public confidence in the government. Claiming that *Tit-Bits* was 'the paper in this country which has the widest and most general circulation' and hence that an opinion poll conducted by him would constitute 'the very nearest approach that can be obtained to a General Election', Newnes instituted just that. He issued voting papers, counted the votes (the public were admitted for the counting and the Secretaries of the Conservative and Liberal Clubs invited to attend to ensure fair play), and publicised the results. The outcome was one by which Newnes, as a Liberal MP, would have been encouraged. A total of 35, 972 voting papers were

---

[104] *The Million*, 1, 23 (August 1892), p.230. Formatting as per original.

received. Of these, 17,086 voted 'Yes' to the question of whether they had confidence in the present Conservative Government, and 18,886 voted 'No'. In August 1892, Gladstone's Liberals were to be returned to office. Newnes's sensitivity to the currents of political and cultural change and the journalistic possibilities created by the development of the working-class political electorate, the mass market and the popular literate audience was to prompt him to establish *The Million* in 1892. And his enthusiasm for the ideas offered by democratic liberalism, many of them flavouring the language of *Tit-Bits*, led him to promote such ideas in *The Westminster Gazette*, established in 1893.

Yet neither *Tit-Bits* nor *The Million* featured anything that was partisan or even explicitly political, even whilst the general international and political climate did occasionally permeate their content. *Tit-Bits*, its editor claimed, fed not on current political crises, but on everyday life:

> *Tit-Bits* thrives best when the world moves on smoothly, and when people have to seek amongst its pages for that interest which is denied to them in the perusal of commonplace current events.[105]

Newnes's journalism was far removed from the kind of political potency that characterised the journalism of Harmsworth, and that of Newnes's friend W.T. Stead. It thrived in an atmosphere of sociability, and in catching and creating the rhythms of daily life.

The Million was a publication that brought into focus many contemporary preoccupations, drawing together the discourses of New Journalism, democratisation and consumerism. Like *Tit-Bits*, it offered the possibility of extensive reader interaction and an inclusive style and layout. Yet it was probably the very fact of its peculiarly contemporary appeal that ensured that it did not survive beyond the turn of the century, ceasing publication in March 1895, when the novelty of the concept of 'the Million' (and of the colour printing techniques which it had pioneered for the English popular audience) had worn off. The paper was expensive to produce; an experiment that was ceasing to be financially viable. *Tit-Bits*, on the other hand, continued to attract a wide readership, and Newnes continued to devote much of his attention to it. It is likely that he found that *The Million* did not differ sufficiently from *Tit-Bits* to earn him a substantially greater share of the market. *The Strand*, by contrast, established in 1891, had opened up a whole new market.

The key to the success of *Tit-Bits* was partly brevity and good humour. It was a mixture of light entertainment (following the 'gospel of fun' which Jonathan Rose has seen as a characteristic element of the 'Edwardian Temperament') and instruction.[106] 'Oh, you may call it cheap journalism;'

---

[105] *Tit-Bits*, 15, 385 (March 1889), p.333.

[106] Jonathan Rose, *The Edwardian Temperament*, Ohio: Ohio University Press, 1986, pp.163-169.

wrote its editor, 'you may say it combined lottery with literature.' 'But', he contended:

> it guided an enormous class of superficial readers, who craved for light reading, and would have read so-called sporting papers if they had not read *Tit-Bits*, into a wholesome vein which may have led them to higher forms of literature.[107]

The idea of 'giving the public what it wants' ('craved for light reading') is here combined with a more traditional ideal of educating the taste of the 'superficial' reader and guiding it towards 'higher forms'. Newnes denied the charge, laid by contemporary social critics and the rival 'quality press', and pervasive in the historiography of the 'Northcliffe Revolution', that his paper led to 'deculturalisation'. The commercial success of this publication was underpinned by a deep sense of editorial conscience and cultural awareness. Newnes, as Reginald Pound has acknowledged, 'might fairly have claimed that he was imbued by a desire for the betterment of his people'.[108] In *Tit-Bits* Newnes's marketing genius and his editorial flair coalesced. Above all, *Tit-Bits* was *inclusive*. The editor solicited the participation of readers in the creation of the text. This magazine represented a performance; a construction; a dynamic mechanism of communication; a carefully-balanced act of negotiation between editor-publisher and audience that was more than a timely but transient commercial triumph. Through it, Newnes secured a loyal readership, and pioneered habits of journalistic discourse that foreshadowed many of his own subsequent publications and many later developments in New Journalism.

---

[107] Hulda Friederichs, op. cit., p.97.

[108] Reginald Pound, op. cit., p.23.

Figure 6. The publicity photograph of the house in Dulwich which was won by Private Mellish in the Tit-Bits Villa Competition in 1884. The 'villa' was typical of lower middle-class suburban housing of the late nineteenth century. Original at Public Record office.

Figure 5. 'A Few Incidents in Connection With Tit-Bits'. This double-page spread, depicting scenes of editorial selection, as well as production, distribution and reception, appeared in 1887 (vol. 13).

2

A National Institution

The Strand Magazine (1891)

George Newnes, marking the publication of *The Strand Magazine*'s one hundredth number in 1899, wrote:

> The providing of the world's thought and reading whether it is of a light or serious type, is one of the most important professions; and it is a source of satisfaction with regard to *The Strand* that, whilst the tone has always been high, the interest has been continually retained.[1]

The Strand was an immensely popular monthly illustrated magazine that survived for over half a century, and was Newnes's most successful publication. Whilst its chief characteristic was readability (hence Newnes's self-conscious reference to contemporary journalistic labels - 'light or serious'), this magazine comprised material by some of the most talented, if conventionally respectable, authors and illustrators of the period. It numbered amongst its regular contributors fiction writers such as Arthur Conan Doyle, whose Sherlock Holmes stories were published in *The Strand*, Arthur Morrison, Max Pemberton, Sir Henry Lucy, Stanley Weyman, A.D. Hope, E.W. Hornung, P.G. Wodehouse, W.W. Jacobs, A.E.W. Mason, Grant Allen and Edith Nesbit, and illustrators such as Sidney Paget, H.R. Millar, J.F. Sullivan, J.A. Shepherd and W.S. Stacey.

If *Tit-Bits* had involved Newnes in a process of establishing and exploring his place in the world of journalism, then *The Strand* represented his consolidation and celebration of that place. 'From the beginning', wrote Reginald Pound, a later editor of the magazine:

> *The Strand* projected the sense of responsibility that was closely related to the moral temper of its founding year, when 'Mr Editor' was a vastly respected entity, infallibly wise and just, and always in the people's fancy, benignly bearded.[2]

[1] *Strand Magazine*, 17, 100 (April 1899), p.363.

[2] Reginald Pound, *Mirror of the Century: The Strand Magazine, 1891-1950*, London: Heinemann, 1966, pp.7-8. Pound's account contains valuable personal insights gathered from a range of people connected with the establishment, editing, publishing, selling, reading, writing and illustration of *The Strand*.

Newnes himself, the General Editor of *The Strand*, was a vital component of the method by which the magazine connected with its readers. His success as a publisher and editor, raising him from the ranks of the petty bourgeoisie to the upper ranks of the middle class, endowed him with professional and literary (and therefore social) status. In *The Strand*, Newnes played host to the members of the so-called 'intellectual class', the professional classes, and the upper and middle classes in general, confirmed their values, and fostered and celebrated their achievements.

Newnes's magazine was thus a powerful cultural determinant. 'Certainly', Pound has commented, 'the middle classes of England never cast a clearer image of themselves in print than they did in *The Strand Magazine*.' He went on to describe the way in which Newnes's magazine provided comfort and security to its community of readers:

> Confirming their preference for mental as well as physical comfort, for more than half a century it faithfully mirrored their tastes, prejudices, and intellectual limitations. From them it drew a large and loyal readership that was the envy of the publishing world.[3]

Despite Newnes's Liberal political affiliations, this magazine contained little that was reformist or controversial. Its authors were 'pedestrian writers in a non-derogatory sense', according to Pound. It was the very familiarity of their field of reference and the ease of their styles, he suggested, that constituted the influence of the magazine:

> Their feet were planted squarely on a common ground, where the surface was solid and familiar, where there was no need to look beyond the actual and the obvious. Occasionally, they may have raised their eyes to gaze on the summit of Parnassus. Mostly, they remained content with the surer profits to be earned by toiling on the lower slopes.[4]

There is a hint in this assessment of the commercial imperatives associated with changes in the field of journalism to which Newnes and *The Strand* were central. The magazine certainly exploited the common interest with great success. When, in late 1949, it was announced that it would cease publication with the January 1950 issue, American *Time* magazine responded with the claim that, in the years since its establishment, it had become 'a British institution'.[5]

The reflection model of periodical research has been subjected to considerable critical scrutiny in the recent historiography of the field, and in the introduction to this book. Nevertheless, *The Strand* serves to demonstrate that

---

3   Ibid., p.7.

4   Ibid., p.105.

5   *Time* as cited in Reginald Pound, op. cit., p.9.

some periodicals are more representative of 'reflection' than others which, actively engaging with or challenging their readers, are deliberately interactive, radical or creative. It has been argued, for instance, that in *Tit-Bits*, Newnes sought to establish an interactive and creative relationship with readers through editorials, correspondence columns, competitions and promotional schemes; a relationship that was based on a combination of marketing and social conscience. The aesthetic publications of the 1890s (*Yellow Book, Savoy*), to take another case, were specifically intended to provide a platform for advanced ideas and works that challenged Establishment views of literature and Royal Academy strictures concerning art. The concept of 'reflection' can, in this instance, be historicised to assess the character and appeal of *The Strand*.

In many respects, the 1890s was a period of considerable anxiety for the middle class, preoccupied with Britain's economic position in the world (under threat from competitors such as Germany and the U.S.), with the social and psychological effects of the Industrial Revolution, and with the failure of existing institutions to ameliorate the poverty that underpinned nineteenth-century progress.[6] A series of scientific discoveries and evolutionary theories undermined orthodox belief in creationism and unsettled religious faith. Newnes created *Sunday Strand*, a companion journal to *The Strand*, at the turn of the century in an attempt to counteract the damage sustained by late nineteenth century Christianity by providing religion with a culturally-adapted modern medium.[7] Middle-class anxieties found expression in the periodicals which, as Karl Beckson has noted, 'published articles in profusion with titles announcing the decline or decay of such phenomena as cricket, genius, war, classical quotations, romance, marriage, faith, bookselling, and even canine fidelity'.[8] *The Strand* offered a striking alternative to such pessimism and uncertainty, representing, in some sense, a contemporary alternative to the religious and moral certainty of the Victorian age. One reader, writing to *Time* in 1949, placed *The Strand* fondly alongside the Bible and *Pilgrim's Progress* as 'a major source of his youthful reading'.[9]

---

[6]   See, for instance, Henry George's *Poverty and Progress* and William Booth's *In Darkest England and the Way Out of It*. Many turned to the alternatives of socialism, as espoused by Morris, Blatchford and the Fabians. Edith Nesbit, who wrote hundreds of stories for *The Strand*, was a founding member of the Fabian Society, as was her husband, Hubert Bland.

[7]   The *Sunday Strand* (1900), into which *The Home Magazine* was incorporated in 1901, was a journal of popular religious news containing illustrated articles on clergymen of the day, Bible talks, religious stories and poems, hymns with music, and a range of philanthropic schemes. It included features on 'Great Religious Painters of the World' and 'Great Preachers of the World' and many other subjects. Missionary articles featured prominently, and the correspondence column, resembling a confessional, functioned as a mechanism for the provision of spiritual counsel. Through this magazine Newnes reached more people than his father did from the pulpit.

[8]   Karl Beckson, *London in the 1890s: A Cultural History*, New York and London: W.W. Norton and Co., 1992, p.xiv.

[9]   See Reginald Pound, op. cit., p.9.

Victorianism, traditionally associated with social and economic stability and confidence, was thus in retreat, and late Victorian cultural developments were habitually nominated 'new' and elevated to fashionable and modern status, even as they arose out of Victorianism. Such were the New Drama, New Woman, New Journalism, New Imperialism, New Criticism, New Hedonism and New Paganism. In fact, Newnes had been going to call *The Strand* by a name which captured its connection with a dynamic cultural climate and with the rise of the New Journalism: *New Magazine*. This period therefore represented a complex combination of two antithetical cultural trends: declining Victorianism and rising Modernism. And the success of *The Strand*, as George Newnes reflected in celebrating its first ten years, lay in the way in which it offered a synthesis of continuity and change, consolidating the experiences of a generation caught in flux:

> A new generation has grown up since that day in December, 1890, when NO. ONE, with its pale blue cover, now so familiar, first appeared on the bookstalls. What events have happened since then - what changes have come over the world, and, not least, over the world of literature and of periodicals and newspapers! Yet THE STRAND has not only survived these manifold and amazing changes, of most of which it was itself the cause, but it continues as popular as when it first made its modest bow to the public'[10]

Two more generations were to 'grow up with' *The Strand*. This magazine was innovative enough to be widely popular in the expanding literary marketplace (being 'the cause' of change). In Britain, according to its enterprising editor-publisher, *The Strand* was 'the pioneer of modern sixpenny magazines which aim at universal popularity'.[11] But it was also consistent enough, in its format and contents, and via the constant presence of an established editor-publisher, reputable Literary and Art Editors, and a contingent of proficient authors and illustrators, to offer a comforting sense of stability and continuity in a changing world (tenaciously 'surviving' change). The act of consumer choice was itself a means of regulating change, as Barbara Quinn Schmidt has pointed out. 'Feeling caught in massive change beyond their control', she has argued, 'Victorians found in magazines moments of stasis and choice which they could control and enjoy.' Moreover, the bound volumes of *The Strand* served as 'a decoration and a sign of social status', conferring on readers a reassuring sense of social distinction.[12]

---

[10] *Strand Magazine*, 20, 120 (December 1900) p.283. Formatting as per original. In this case, the bold lettering not only drew attention to the magazine's name, highlighting the words 'The Strand' as if in imitation of that thoroughfare's street sign, but emphasised its establishment ('NO. ONE') in a way that suggested its intimate connection with the new era.

[11] *Strand Magazine*, 34, 200 (October 1907), p.284.

[12] Barbara Quinn Schmidt, 'Novelists, Publishers and Fiction in Middle Class Magazines: 1860-1880', *Victorian Periodicals Review*, XVII, 9 (Winter 1984), p.142.

Crime fiction, a characteristic feature of *The Strand*, was central to the project of providing readers with a sense of security. Stephen Knight has argued that the success of the Sherlock Holmes stories, for instance, depended upon the writer's ability to order an uncertain world. After all, Doyle himself said of Holmes that 'his character admits of no light or shade'.[13] The scope of these stories was limited to bourgeois ideology. The crimes featured involved threats to tangible property. The reality of crime was avoided and criminals defined as such by their divergence from the correct ethical pathway of bourgeois morality. The impact of such fiction, according to Knight, was dependent upon its capacity to allay the anxieties of its readers: 'form and content together create the crucial realisation of a pleasing, comforting world view'.[14] Such a world view was crucial to the success of *The Strand*.

The appearance of *The Strand* coincided with the publication, in 1891, of George Gissing's remarkably popular *New Grub Street*. Gissing juxtaposed Reardon, the writer of literary conscience, with Jasper Milvain, the essentially mercenary (and untalented) literary man, bringing into focus the dialectic between artistic 'quality' and integrity, and the dictates of the modern marketplace in the process of literary production. In Gissing's time, Q.D. Leavis has argued, material success in the literary world became dependent upon connections with the press and publicity, and literature was becoming a commercial product, its production a trade.[15] To the educated middle class, 'to make a trade of an art' in this fashion meant compromising Victorian cultural and intellectual values, the very values that distinguished the discriminating middle class from the mass culture of the newly-educated and intellectually inferior. The creation of the Society of Authors in 1883, with Walter Besant as its spokesman, had represented the beginning of a new phase in the protracted and contested process by which writing became professionalised. And the status of writing as a profession remained problematic throughout the 1890s.

In the journalistic context, the debate focussed upon the relationship between 'quality' (or artistic) journalism and popular (or commercial) journalism. The idea of exclusivity was pitted against the commercially successful strategy of inclusivity. This period thus produced aesthetic publications such as the *Century Guild Hobby Horse*, *Yellow Book* and *Savoy*, which, in content, design, typography and material quality, were intended to suggest defiance of the mass-produced commercial magazines. On the other hand, it also produced publications such as *The Strand*, *Macmillan's Magazine* and *Cornhill Magazine*, which appealed to large readerships. Ultimately, being too highbrow meant that many of the aesthetic periodicals, their elite avant garde literary and artistic producers refusing to compromise with the petit bourgeoisie and determined to separate themselves from a mass readership, were doomed to

---

[13] Arthur Conan Doyle, *Memories and Adventures*, London: Greenhill, 1988, p.108.

[14] Stephen Knight, *Form and Ideology in Crime Fiction*, Bloomington: Indiana University Press, 1980, pp.1-3.

[15] Q.D. Leavis, 'Gissing and the English Novel', *Scrutiny*, VII, 1 (June 1938), p.75.

failure. *The Strand*, on the other hand, went on to survive two world wars, maintaining a high reputation, and boasting a range of literary and artistic contributors who were both commercially successful and professionally recognised. (Their qualifications were acknowledged within the pages of the magazine and in the remuneration they received for their work. They specialised in particular journalistic fields, after the fashion of the 'expert' of professional society. And they drew credibility from their occupational and social backgrounds.) It offered exclusive connections as well as popular appeal, 'solid' contents incorporated with innovative features, a 'high' tone and a good material quality.[16] *The Strand* thus represented a solution to the debate over literary production. It occupied the middle ground and was essentially middle-brow.

This chapter explores the ways in which *The Strand*'s reflective properties constituted the reinforcement of cultural security, class cohesion and literary compromise. This magazine offered a confirming, consolatory rigidity that was based on social and professional distinction, corporate identity, individual example, and commercial viability, and was comforting to a middle-class audience who, beset by anxiety, change and uncertainty, sought reassurance in its pages. At the same time, it represented a solution to the debate over literary and journalistic 'quality' and the crisis of literary succession, offering the unification of literary tradition and journalistic innovation, of commercialism and professionalism, and of inclusivity and exclusivity.

In establishing this illustrated monthly, Newnes was very much influenced by the American magazines *Harper's* and *Scribner's*. *The Strand*, he claimed in its one hundredth number, appeared at a time when 'British magazines were at a low ebb', and American magazines, 'smarter and livelier, more interesting, bright and cheerful', and heavily illustrated, were proving more popular than most British magazines.[17] Newnes decided that illustrations should be of paramount importance and the new publication formatted according to the principle of 'a picture on every page'. This plan had to be modified, because of the technical problems and expense involved, to allow for a picture at the opening of each issue. But the new half-tone process of photographic reproduction was experimented with from the first issue, and the reputations of many notable London photographic studios were enhanced through their association with *The Strand*. Cartoons appeared from the beginning, but were all reproduced 'by permission' from other publications until the first World War. Black-and-white illustration was a major feature of Newnes's magazine, and one of the keys to its popularity.

To some extent, *The Strand* revolutionised the market for magazines. Imitations followed thick and fast: the *Windsor Magazine* (Ward, Lock and Co.); *Pearson's Magazine* (from Arthur Pearson, who had also published the plagiaristic *Pearson's Weekly*); *Cassell's* (enlarged to *Strand* size and given a

---

[16] The first letter of *The Strand*'s first article was rendered as a decorative motif, linking it to the illuminated manuscript and the aesthetic periodical.

[17] *Strand Magazine*, 17, 100 (April 1899), p.364.

new look with an impressive array of author's names on the cover); *The London Magazine* (Harmsworth); and *Pall Mall Magazine* (financed by Astor).

In the earlier issues of the magazine, there was a considerable amount of material drawn from the writings of renowned European authors such as Tolstoy, Pushkin and Dumas, but as it developed the proportion of original literary material by British and American authors increased.[18] In fact, as Pound has noted, *The Strand* was designed to promote the art of short-story writing amongst British writers at a time when Continental and American proponents of the form predominated. The French writer Maupassant, for example, was generally recognised as a master of the art of short-story writing, and Newnes initially turned to the Continent for a good supply of short stories. *The Strand* went on to become something of a 'short-story magazine'. Newnes did not insist on the conventions of length (6,000 word minimum) that had governed the publication of English short stories. Thus, *The Times* assessed his contribution to English literature with the comment that 'he exerted a popular influence of great importance in that lively period of English story-telling which reached its height in the "nineties"'.[19] 'Just as *Punch* was the ultimate goal of the writer of humorous articles', David Jasen has noted in his biography of P.G. Wodehouse, 'so *The Strand* was that of the short-story writer'.[20] After 1910, Wodehouse wrote short stories exclusively for *The Strand* as far as publication in England was concerned.

Newnes was initially apprehensive about the sustainability of serials in magazines which appeared only monthly. But he used them with great success in *The Strand*. Children's serials, such as G.E. Farrow's 'The Escape of the Mullingong'(1904), and E. Nesbit's 'The Psammead'(1902) and 'The House of Arden'(1908) were very popular. Other early serials included Conan Doyle's 'The Hound of the Baskervilles', H.G. Wells' 'First Men in the Moon', W.W. Jacobs' 'A Master of Craft' and Rudyard Kipling's 'Puck of Pook's Hill'. 'The Hound of the Baskervilles' increased the magazine's circulation by 30,000.[21]

The Strand also pioneered the connected short story. Conan Doyle claimed that it was his idea to publish stories which employed the same character and yet were complete in themselves, in monthly instalments in a magazine. His rationale, he later claimed, was that 'the purchaser was always sure that he could relish the whole contents of the magazine', and yet could miss one number without losing all interest in the stories. This form, however, 'if it only engaged the attention of the reader, would bind the reader to that particular magazine'.[22] It was thus part

---

[18] Many of these stories had the advantage of being out of copyright.

[19] *The Times*, 14 December, 1949, as cited in Reginald Pound, op. cit., p.31.

[20] David A. Jasen, *P.G. Wodehouse: Portrait of a Master*, London: Garnstone Press, 1975, p.35.

[21] Reginald Pound, op. cit., p.74.

[22] Arthur Conan Doyle, op. cit., pp.95-96. There was some argument between Doyle and Phillips Oppenheim as to who exactly began this practice.

of a strategy which married narrative and commercial considerations. *The Strand Magazine* was the first to put Doyle's idea into practice, and it did so with great success.

Not merely a literary magazine, although many famous fiction writers were discovered or encouraged by the Literary Editor, Greenhough Smith, *The Strand* contained a good balance between stories and articles. Popular science and natural history articles proliferated. A series of 'Symposium' articles publicised the opinions of notable experts on various topics including sport, art, nature, education and fashion. They resembled the records of a debating society, and anticipated the panels of authorities that featured in later current affair radio and television programmes. A feature called 'Curiosities' that continued for many years in *The Strand* was probably a legacy of Newnes's editorial method in *Tit-Bits*.[23] 'Curiosities' however, was not always suitable to *The Strand*'s readership, and it was perhaps significant that it was relegated to the back pages of the magazine. 'The Queer Side of Things', the name of which had a colloquial appeal characteristically Newnesian, was similarly diverse in its contents and piecemeal in its format. This column made a regular feature of the sketch canvas of the history of certain objects: 'Children of a Thousand Years', 'Drinking Vessels of all Times', 'Boots and Shoes of All Ages', 'Head and Hair Curiosities', 'Some Historic Cradles'. It would thus seem to have had links with the contemporary public museum movement, and with the growth of anthropology. Newnes also introduced a 'Puzzle Page' in 1894.

The 'Portraits of Celebrities' series and its counterpart, 'Illustrated Interviews' (later succeeded by 'My Reminiscences'), were two of *The Strand*'s longest-running and most successful serials. They were crucial to its function as a medium of cultural security and class cohesion. 'Zig-zags at the Zoo', by Arthur Morrison with illustrations by J.A. Shepherd, was also extremely popular, running from July 1892 to August 1894. It was light-hearted and humorous in tone (drawing upon the pioneering works of children's literature and illustration produced by Lewis Carroll in the 1860s), and innovative and appealing in format. And it provided the inspiration for later authors such as Kenneth Graham and J.M. Barrie.

Advertising constituted a very important part of *The Strand*, filling 100 pages and representing over 250 advertisers per month, and Newnes employed an advertising manager to deal with the requirements of would-be space buyers. He was well aware of the importance of advertising and noted in 1907 that the volume of trade conducted through the magazine's advertising pages was such that 'if it were set forth in figures, would fairly stagger the imagination'.[24]

Newnes sold 300,000 copies of the first issue of *The Strand* at 6d. each (a fact which is indicative of his established reputation as a publisher, and, no doubt, his success in promoting this new magazine prior to its appearance). He was soon claiming that this was 'by far the most widely-circulating monthly in the

---

[23] It also resembled the 'Odds and Ends' column of *The Wide World Magazine*.

[24] *Strand Magazine*, 34, 200 (October 1907), p.288.

country'. By 1896, Newnes's magazine had a circulation of nearly 400,000, and it maintained this level of popularity into the twentieth century.[25] The audience of *The Strand Magazine* was diverse as well as large and included such well-known figures as Cardinal Manning and Queen Victoria. Sir Harry Johnson, the celebrated traveller, claimed that it had penetrated into the most remote parts of the world. Queen Margherita of Italy said that it was the only English periodical she read.[26] Sales in the U.S., initially poor, were increased markedly under the special American editorship of James Walter Smith and through the distribution network of the International News Company.

The vast majority of *Strand* readers, however, came from the upper and middle classes. They were encouraged to identify with the circle of *Strand* contributors and 'celebrities' who were drawn from their ranks. The middle class included white and blue-collar workers, and at the upper end, it merged with the fringes of 'Society'. In fact, 'Society', according to Harold Perkin, admitted 'anyone who possessed either power, political or economic, or the capacity to entertain, socially, culturally or intellectually'.[27] On these grounds, the authors and artists of *The Strand* earned the right to admission with every entertaining issue of the magazine.

The growth of railway travel contributed substantially to *The Strand*'s success. Newnes's magazine was a constant best-seller at the main line bookstalls, and most of the lesser ones.[28] Leaving Waterloo by boat train for Southampton on his way to the Cape in 1894, his day of departure chancing to coincide with the publication of the monthly number of *The Strand*, Sir Henry Lucy noted that 'every other person on the train had a copy'. He went on to remark on its popularity in 'all other parts of the world where the English race were settled', characterising it as a major British export:

> Among the ship's cargo was a bale of the magazine, and on the day after arrival I saw on the railway bookstall at Capetown a pile nearly as high as the Waterloo consignment, diminishing with equal rapidity.[29]

---

[25] *Strand Magazine*, 4, 24 (December 1892), p.598. *The Strand*'s circulation was estimated at 392,000 (including 60,000 to the U.S.) in 1896. See *Newsagents' Chronicle* (supplement to the *Publishers' Circular*), 8 August, 1896, p.8. And the *Publishers' Circular* listed *The Strand*, along with *Windsor Magazine* and *Pearson's Magazine*, as having circulation figures of 200,000-400,000 each. See *Publishers' Circular*, 22 October, 1898, p.479. See also Alvin Sullivan (ed.), *British Literary Magazines: The Victorian and Edwardian Age, 1837-1913*, Westport, Connecticut and London: Greenwood Press, 1984.

[26] Geraldine Beare (comp.), *Index to the Strand Magazine, 1894-1950*, Westport, Connecticut and London: Greenwood Press, 1982, p.xiii.

[27] Harold Perkin, Harold Perkin, *The Rise of Professional Society: England Since 1880*, London and New York: Routledge, 1989, p.74.

[28] Reginald Pound, op. cit., p.32.

[29] Henry Lucy, Henry Lucy, *Sixty Years in the Wilderness*, London: Smith, Elder, 1909, p.350. *The Strand* was also popular in Grenada, West Indies, where Lucy was given by a correspondent a sketch history of Grenada with a map as an acknowledgment of the pleasure derived from years of *Strand* reading.

The sheer visibility of *The Strand* guaranteed its reputation. It had a devoted readership, amongst both the upper and middle classes in Britain, and those who represented them in the empire. '*The Strand* became part of British life, from drawing-room to below stairs', wrote *Time* in 1949 when the decision to cease publication was announced, 'and colonials fondly regarded it as "a bit of London" in their far-off homes.'[30] It was these overseas readers of *The Strand* whom Newnes sought specifically to recognise in establishing *The Wide World Magazine*. Many of them, seeking to utilise their own particular experiences as exiled Englishmen to forge a connection with the comforting stability of the upper middle-class world of *The Strand*, sent accounts of those experiences to its editor. He responded by providing them with their own organ of identification: *The Wide World*.

Newnes established the image of *The Strand* in a variety of ways. The name '*Strand Magazine*' had been suggested to him by L.R.S. Tomalin whilst the two were walking on Wimbledon Common discussing Fleet St, the home of the newspaper press. Its significance, of course, lay partly in the proximity of Newnes's offices to The Strand, and the very first article in the first issue, entitled 'The Story of The Strand', emphasised this connection. The magazine's cover depicted Burleigh St, home to the *Strand* offices. It thus placed the House of Newnes firmly in the streetscape (*see Figure 7*).

Yet perhaps most importantly, The Strand was associated with a series of great names. As Walter Besant and G.E. Milton pointed out in a history of The Strand District, this was a neighbourhood with rich literary, theatrical and artistic associations.[31] Newnes had been exposed to such associations since he had moved the offices of *Tit-Bits* to Burleigh St in June 1886. There, he was surrounded by the offices of other publications (*The Globe*, the *Guardian*, *Church News*, the *Court Journal*), was neighbour to the printer William Oldhams, was a few yards away from the stage door of the Lyceum theatre, the scene of Sir Henry Irving's triumphs, and was placed opposite Exeter Hall, the focal point of the Evangelical controversy and the theatre of Fabian Society debates. The Adelphi precinct contained a terrace of several societies and institutions, at the centre of which was the Savage Club. John St contained the building specifically designed for the Society of Arts, the work of which was made public and visible in the 1890s by a series of circular tablets affixed to houses in London which had formerly been the houses of men eminent in literature, science or art. *The Strand Magazine* expanded the scope of these activities, chronicling the achievements of such men in various photographic and portrait series. And it nourished and guarded the reputations of new artists, authors and members of the 'intellectual class' of the period. Newnes thus

---

[30] Reginald Pound, op. cit., p.192.

[31] See Sir Walter Besant and G.E. Milton, *The Fascination of London: The Strand District*, London: Adam and Charles Black, 1903, pp 67-68, 76, 78, 98, 109.

established its claims to 'quality' by linking its contributors to a continuing literary tradition.

The Strand also drew on the social status and connections of its authors, editors, readers and subjects to establish its claims to 'quality' and guarantee its commercial appeal. Journalists gained a considerable degree of social acceptance in this period, appearing in a Royal Academy collection of celebrity portraits in 1881 (G.A. Sala, for instance, featured alongside Gladstone, Huxley, Browning and Irving) and in significant numbers in the *DNB* (established in 1882), and attaining membership of reputable and fashionable clubs such as the Athenaeum, Reform (especially Liberal journalists), Garrick, Savage and London Press Club (formed in 1890).[32] The circle of the professional journalist included the literary agent, who acted on commission for a variety of authors to negotiate publication of and payment for their work.[33] The literary agent functioned to separate literary men from the business side of their profession, softening their image as 'tradesmen'. Thus some journalists, according to Lucy Brown, 'probably a small minority, moved easily among actors, literary people, military experts, travellers, and the aristocracy in the general social vortex. From them they could enlarge and bring up to date their picture of the world.'[34] As a newspaper editor and proprietor, George Newnes entertained and maintained contact with a range of people, including H.H. Asquith, Herbert Gladstone, Henry Campbell-Bannerman, W.T. Stead, Seale Hayne and Arthur Conan Doyle.[35] His world view was informed by such connections. And as editor of *The Strand*, he played host (in a textual sense) to politicians (through 'From Behind the Speaker's Chair'), a range of 'celebrities' (government officials, artists, musicians, actor-managers and eminent professionals of all sorts appeared in 'Portraits of Celebrities' and 'Illustrated Interviews') and society women (who appeared in a portrait series entitled 'Celebrated Beauties' which was succeeded by 'Types of English Beauty').

The Strand received the benefit of the appearance and sanction of royalty. An early issue carried a full-page drawing with the caption 'The Queen's First Baby: Drawn and Etched by Her Majesty' (March 1891). It was succeeded by a sixteen-page article on the dolls of Victoria's infancy by Frances H. Low

---

[32] Lucy Brown, *Victorian News and Newspapers*, Oxford: Clarendon, 1985, p.128.

[33] Conan Doyle's 'man of business', as he called him, was A.P. Watt, one of the first literary agents to build up a successful and prosperous practice. He acted for some of the most successful authors, a number of whom wrote for *The Strand*. These included Kipling, A.D. Hope and Doyle.

[34] Lucy Brown, op. cit., p.129. Arthur Conan Doyle numbered amongst his acquaintances many 'Notable People', as he later reminisced in *Memories and Adventures*, including the Prince of Wales (later George V), President Roosevelt, Lord Balfour, H.H. Asquith, Lord Haldane, George Meredith, Rudyard Kipling, James Barrie, Henry Irving, Bernard Shaw, R.L.S. Tomalin, Grant Allen, James Payn and members of the Royal family. See Arthur Conan Doyle, op. cit., p.117.

[35] He lunched, however, according to Pound, four days a week with the same small group of business friends who gathered at the Hotel Cecil in the Strand. See Reginald Pound, op. cit., p.25.

(September 1892), read by the Queen in proof and published with her own footnotes, and many other articles in which she featured.[36] This was an unusual and striking example of the cooperation of royalty in a commercial publishing venture. It was a coup for Newnes. (And no doubt a successful public relations exercise for Victoria, who had withdrawn from public life after the death of Albert.) 'For *The Strand Magazine*', observed Pound, 'that august patronage was as good as the Royal Warrant.'[37] It was confirmation of the expanding power of journalism at a time when changes in technology and format were revolutionising the form. Just as advertisements within periodicals such as *The Strand* began to carry a stamp of royal approval as a technique of selling to the middle classes, so *The Strand* established its connection with royalty to enhance its appeal to a middle-class readership. Thus Newnes could claim that the tone (and indeed the connections) of his magazine were 'high' indeed. *The Strand* went on to publish articles on King Edward's unique collection of historic swords, and the Prince of Wales' travels in East Africa. Moreover, many members of British and European royal families featured in the 'Portraits of Celebrities' series.

This magazine was also associated with productivity and commercial success. Within the early issues of *The Strand*, Newnes sought to establish his own socio-economic status as a publisher, and the status of the journalistic profession in general. He presented a plethora of facts about technical and financial aspects of the publishing industry, about issues of production and distribution, and about the history, scope and output of his own publishing company.[38] Appearing at just the time at which Newnes was forming his publishing enterprises into a limited liability company, these articles were informed by the format of the commercial prospectus. In an exercise in public relations, Newnes invited London sightseers to visit his 'Machinery Hall' in the basement of the Southampton St building to watch *Tit-Bits* being printed at the then amazing speed of 24,000 copies per hour.[39] Advertising was also treated by Newnes in the two hundredth number of the magazine. *The Strand* was billed as 'one of the best advertising mediums in the world'. The 'amount of trade' that had been 'transacted through its pages', it was claimed, was vast. By the time the two hundredth number of the magazine was published, it had sold 79,363,000 copies (an average circulation of around 400,000 copies monthly). Thirty thousand pictures had been printed, and £100,000 spent on the literary contents

---

[36] These included 'The Queen's Hindustani Diary' (December 1892), 'The Queen's Yacht' (June 1894), 'The Queen's Stables' (June 1897) 'The Queen and Her Children' (June 1897), and 'The Queen as a Mountaineer (June 1898).

[37] Reginald Pound, op. cit., p.8.

[38] See, for example, 'Ourselves in Figure and Diagram', *Strand Magazine*, 14, 67 (July 1897), pp.37-42. At this point, Newnes's publications included *Tit-Bits*, *Strand Magazine*, *Musical Magazine*, *Woman's Life*, *The Hub*, *The Penny Library of Famous Books*, *British Boys*, *Navy and Army* and others.

[39] Reginald Pound, op. cit., p.53.

of the magazine, making the average cost of literary material £500 per issue.[40] Thus Newnes established his own professional credibility by establishing his company's commercial viability, adroitly drawing together the ideologies of professionalism and commercialism.

At the close of the century, at Westminster Abbey, Charles Gore, a future Bishop of Oxford, mourned the state of contemporary literature. The *Daily Mail* reported his speech:

> Our present-day literature is singularly without inspiration. There is no Carlyle to whom all men naturally turn to find some answer to their chaotic yearnings; there is no Tennyson to put into exquisite and melodious words the feelings of the educated. There is no prophet for the people.[41]

The problem of succession in the literary world was a cause of considerable concern to the late Victorian generation and was closely linked to the proliferation of periodical literature and the era of New Journalism. The arrangement of Queen Victoria editing an article for *The Strand* was an attempt to substitute social and political for literary and moral authority.

Yet Conan Doyle remembered the 1880s and 1890s as a time when, 'despite the general jeremiad in the London press about the extinction of English literature, and the assumed fact that there were no rising authors to take the place of those who were gone', despite the lack of a Dickens or Thackeray, there was:

> a most amazing crop, all coming up simultaneously ... so numerous and many-sided and with so high an average of achievement that I think they would match for varied excellence any similar harvest in our literary history.[42]

He named Kipling, James Stephenson Phillips, Grant Allen, J.M. Barrie, George Bernard Shaw, Marie Corelli, Stanley Weyman, A.D. Hope, Hall Caine and others, many of whom wrote for *The Strand*. (Significantly, he made no mention of writers like Hardy, James and Conrad who, whilst they are still remembered where Allen *et al.* have been largely forgotten, did not belong to the circles in which Conan Doyle moved.) Like Lucy, Conan Doyle characterised their combined output as a commodity ('crop', 'harvest'), measuring their contribution to British literary history using the terms associated with quantification and quality control in mass production ('so high an average of achievement'). His use of the term 'average' to describe their achievements is, in a very literal sense, further confirmation that their writing was, and was understood to be, middle-brow. These authors were a new generation, many of whom had honed their literary skills in writing for magazines.

---

[40] *Strand Magazine*, 34, 200 (October 1907), p.288.

[41] Charles Gore as cited in Reginald Pound, op. cit., p.59.

[42] Arthur Conan Doyle, op. cit., p.117.

The literary authority of *The Strand*'s contributors was guaranteed by their corporate identity and social homogeneity. Literary life often tended to assume the characteristics of coterie culture. Thus Doyle described a circle of literary men with whom he mixed in his early career as 'the group who centred around the new magazine, "The Idler"', and who 'met periodically at dinner'. The circle included Jerome K. Jerome (the editor), Robert Barr (the assistant editor, who later wrote for *The Strand*), George Burgin, J.M. Barrie, Israel Zangwill and many other 'rising men'. Such peer groups were clearly of considerable significance to their members, for Doyle was careful to point out, in language that suggested an analogy between his commitment to *The Strand* and the marriage contract, that he was '*not unfaithful* to *The Strand*'.[43] In a period in which the collective organisation of the professions was proceeding at a rapid rate, the 'intellectual class', embracing those who had formerly been named 'men of letters' and 'men of science', as well as university teachers and practitioners of the fine and performing arts (painters, sculptors, musicians, actors), organised themselves for intellectual and cultural, as well as professional purposes.[44] *The Strand* acted to consolidate and elevate the corporate identity of this class.

The authors and artists of *The Strand* met every month under the auspices of the '*Strand* Club', a kind of artistic and literary coterie, formed on the basis that each member should 'furnish either a story or a picture for the edification of the monthly gatherings'. Its meetings, attended by such men as E.W. Hornung, Max Pemberton, Sidney Sime and Max Beerbohm, were documented by Conan Doyle, in a series running from July 1905 to July 1907 entitled 'Chronicles of the *Strand* Club'. The series was a lively collection of anecdotes and short stories, and it served to reinforce the social and professional cohesion of the magazine's circle of contributors, and draw its upper middle-class readers into identification with them. A variety of 'symposia', paralleling the intercourse of the club, the debating society and the House of Commons itself (the debates of which were recorded in Henry Lucy's series 'From Behind the Speaker's Chair') served a similar purpose, but extended the circle of contributor-members to include a range of prominent men and women.

Newnes was probably influenced by the remarkably successful illustrated paper *Punch* (1841) in developing this aspect of *The Strand*. *Punch* men sometimes worked as a team, a strategy most evident in the Wednesday night *Punch* dinners at which members of the salaried staff met with the proprietor and printers around 'The Table' and decided the political cartoon of the ensuing week. Celebrated by Thackeray in his song, 'The Mahogany Tree', these gatherings were lively, witty and productive, and they brought authors and artists

---

[43] Ibid., p.118. My italics.

[44] The Society of Authors, for example, was founded in 1883 to defend the writer's property in his copyright. Between 1880 and the first World War, new qualifying associations, including chartered accountants, auctioneers, estate agents, company secretaries and town planners, were added to the twenty-seven existing ones (barristers, doctors, solicitors, architects, builders and others). Non-qualifying associations, such as the National Union of Teachers, representing salaried, employed professions, also grew. See Harold Perkin, op. cit., pp.85-86.

together in an atmosphere of mutuality. They were crucial to the image of *Punch*. Depicting the authors, artists and editors of *The Strand* as a social circle, and publishing the records of the meetings of the '*Strand* Club', Newnes may well have been drawing on such collaborative models. Furthermore, *Punch's* success was partly dependent upon the fact that it appeared to see things through the eyes of 'Mr Punch' himself. It was 'a point of view developed so personally', as Simon Houfe has pointed out, 'that people could identify with *his* views, and join *his* club, membership being the annual subscription to the magazine.'[45] Newnes himself cultivated this image. In *Tit-Bits*, 'The Editor' was a central and strongly-developed personality whose identity was almost inseparable from the image of the paper itself. In *The Strand*, the figure of the General Editor and publisher-proprietor loomed almost equally large, his established place in the publishing world underpinning the success of the magazine from the outset.

The Strand acted to consolidate the reputations of literary and artistic men and women by making a feature of the names of its contributors. New Journalism not only provided the writer with the material basis for his recognition as a professional, but represented him discursively as a popular public personality. The use of by-lines became a common technique in the competition for readers in the 1890s, furthering a process through which the tradition of anonymous journalism was gradually being eroded. And portraits of writers and pictures of their homes, such as those that featured in *The Strand's* 'Portraits of Celebrities' series, became a staple of magazines of the period. Journalism, like the music hall and the stage, created its celebrities.

In the early issues of *The Strand*, when translations of the works of Continental authors had formed a substantial part of the magazine's letterpress, each piece had been preceded by an introductory biographical rubric. The editor expanded upon the background and credentials of the author, as if introducing a speaker at a social function or club, thus nominating a European literary contingent for the *Strand* Club. 'It is a source of satisfaction', he wrote, with a hint of patronage, in a ceremonial address for the tenth year of *The Strand*, 'to know that ... *The Strand Magazine* has been able to create or enhance many reputations.' 'Many leading black-and-white artists', he continued, 'have actually found their first stepping stone in the pages of *The Strand*, and are now recognised as being at the head of their profession.'[46] Newnes's magazine was one of the first to include the names of its illustrators on the contents page. Such

---

[45] Simon Houfe, *The Dictionary of British Book Illustrators and Caricaturists, 1800-1914 with Introductory Chapters on the Rise and Progress of the Art*, Antique Collectors Club, 1978, p.57.

[46] *Strand Magazine*, 20, 120 (December 1900), p.283. Four thousand manuscripts were sent in to *The Strand* annually, of which about 18,000 were printed in the first ten years of the magazine, representing 600 authors. Many unused manuscripts were kept in stock by Greenhough Smith for emergency use. The illustrations for these numbered 17,000, 7,000 of which were original drawings and 10,000 photographs never before published. To illustrate the 900 odd short stories, twenty artists were kept constantly employed.

acknowledgments served to confirm the increasing professional status of magazine authors and illustrators in the literary world of the 1890s.

Newnes made an art of associating his publications with affective and social ties. In his celebratory birthday piece for the magazine's one hundredth number, he attempted to generate a kind of fraternal warmth, writing 'not in a boastful spirit, but with a feeling of friendship, loyalty and affection towards the "Good old *Strand*"' which, he was certain, was 'shared by many thousands of people'. Judging by the evidence provided by contemporary readers, it was. The General Editor acknowledged 'the ability, the faithfulness, and the loyalty' that Greenhough Smith and W.H.J. Boot had displayed towards the magazine.[47] There was also a strong affective element in Newnes's 'tenth year' address, presented as a greeting card 'To the Friends of *The Strand*, Old and New, Near and Far'. It listed many of the magazine's contributors ('patrons', as he called them), and served to emphasise the way in which *The Strand* operated to create a kind of upper middle-class social circle of contributors and readers who identified with the articles, biographical series, stories and illustrations of the magazine.[48] The magazine was their social space.

It is significant that Newnes chose the theme of a public reception to represent *The Strand*'s circle of contributors (*see Figure 8*):

> If we could imagine the Editor-in-Chief holding a public reception of his chief contributors, we should conjure up, as our artist has done, a scene of astonishing interest. The difficulty is to find what name of contemporary note is absent from the list, although the illustrator was unable, on account of space, to include more than fifty of our more prominent contributors.[49]

The occasion was the publication of the magazine's two hundredth number. The image evoked by the artist captured the essence of *The Strand*, depicting it as the site of a society social gathering, the company comprising the procession of figures mingling on the staircase, and the Editor-in-Chief acting as host.[50] Each issue of *The Strand* aggregately 'conjured up' such a scene. Newnes's magazine was offered as a forum for the maintenance of social and intellectual exchange and of the rituals of class solidarity.

George Newnes set the tone and format of the magazine, and was crucial to its image. The words 'Edited by George Newnes' were imprinted on the cover of every volume of *The Strand* up to 1910, although this was only really literally

---

[47] Again the word 'faithfulness', used by Doyle to emphasise his loyalty to the magazine, was used in connection with *The Strand*.

[48] *Strand Magazine*, 20, 120 (December 1900), pp.603-604.

[49] *Strand Magazine*, 34, 200 (October 1907), p.284.

[50] It is worth noting that the staircase in this picture bore a striking resemblance to that of the National Liberal Club, with which Newnes would have been intimately familiar. See *The National Liberal Club. A Description with Illustrations*, London: Political Committee of the National Liberal Club, 1894.

true until the late 1890s, when Greenhough Smith assumed more editorial responsibility. By this time, Newnes's other publications had begun to make more demands upon his time. The *Daily Courier* and *The Million* were both established in the mid-1890s, and although both were short-lived, a succession of new periodicals followed: *Country Life* (1897), *The Ladies' Field* (1898), *The Wide World Magazine* (1898) and *The Captain* (1899). Newnes continued to assume considerable editorial responsibility for *Tit-Bits*. Nevertheless, the link between George Newnes and *The Strand*, his most successful publication, was considerable. He wrote a number of articles for *The Strand*, including two travel narratives, and an account of the 'Southern Cross' Antarctic expedition, led by C.E. Borchgrevink, which he himself sponsored. He appeared in the series 'Portraits of Celebrities' and was thus associated with the circle of *Strand* contributors and 'celebrities' who composed the *Strand* Club.[51] In an article entitled 'A Description of the Offices of *The Strand Magazine*', 'large portraits of Mr Newnes' were reported as adorning all the offices of the magazine's editors, so that symbolically, as well as actually, Newnes oversaw the publication, maintaining a paternal, almost omnipotent presence.[52] His image - traveller, public benefactor, proprietor, 'celebrity' - was a guarantee of social and professional respectability and commercial viability.

H. Greenhough Smith was the Literary Editor of *The Strand* from 1891 to 1930, his continuing influence contributing to the consistency and familiarity of the magazine's contents. Smith was the son of an engineer, and was educated at Cambridge. He was therefore both a professional and an educated man. He spent his early years as a private tutor, then went into publishing after writing a number of novels. He frequented the Savage Club, and kept company with Eille Norwood (one of the best screen players of Sherlock Holmes), R.D. Blumenfeld (editor of the *Daily Express*) and Paul Verrall (a leading London orthopaedic surgeon) - much like the company he kept within the pages of *The Strand*. Formerly on the editorial staff of the *Temple Bar*, it was he who had first suggested the idea and general scheme of the magazine to Newnes. As Literary Editor of *The Strand*, he was prepared to encourage originality, but not at the expense of readability or of the magazine's good name. He thus maintained its commercial and literary viability, and safeguarded its social respectability.

Conan Doyle is now probably the best known of the *Strand* authors. Described by Greenhough Smith as 'the greatest short-story writer since Edgar Allen Poe', Doyle began his connection with the magazine when he submitted the manuscripts of two stories, entitled 'A Scandal in Bohemia' and 'The Red-Headed League', in late spring, 1891.[53] They were the first of the Sherlock Holmes stories. Newnes immediately made arrangements to secure the publishing rights for Conan Doyle's work. The first series of Holmes stories

---

[51] The editor-proprietor appeared in response to 'the repeatedly expressed wish of readers of *Tit-Bits* and *The Strand Magazine*'. See *Strand Magazine*, 4, 24 (December 1892), p.593.

[52] *Strand Magazine*, 4, 24 (December 1892), p.594.

[53] Reginald Pound, op. cit., p.41.

was to continue for three years and take *The Strand*'s circulation to new heights. Sidney Paget, who provided the illustrations for the Holmes stories, and supplied the deerstalker cap which was to define the public image of Sherlock Holmes, was also crucial to the creation of the Holmes fixation.[54] Conan Doyle also wrote a successful series on 'The Exploits of Brigadier Gerard', a variety of historical romances and later a number of articles on spiritualism for *The Strand*. And his literary reputation was welded to the commercial reputation of George Newnes, Ltd when he became a board member.

The death of Holmes at Reichenbach Falls, in 1899, met with the dismay of the public at large, as well as that of House of Newnes shareholders. The strength of the reading public's reaction to the news might be interpreted as proof that the Holmes stories, as Stephen Knight has argued, offered a comforting sense of security to readers. It was not until September 1903 that *The Strand* announced that Holmes was to reappear in a new series.[55] 'Readers have a vivid recollection of the time when Sherlock Holmes made his first appearance before the public', wrote the editor, conveying the assumption that a constant readership had been maintained, 'and of the *Adventures* which made his name a household word in every quarter of the world.' He went on, combining the art of advertisement with that of narrative expectation:

> The news of his death was received with regret as at the loss of a personal friend. Fortunately, the news, though based on circumstantial evidence which at the time seemed conclusive, turns out to be erroneous. How he escaped from his struggle with Moriarty at Reichenbach Falls, why he remained in hiding even from his friend Watson, how he made his reappearance, and the manner he signalised his return by one of the most remarkable of his exploits will be found in the first story of the New Series, beginning in the October Number.[56]

Conan Doyle received a flood of correspondence for the detective hero, as well as gifts for him and appeals for copies of his family tree and coat-of-arms. Holmes problems were debated in the newspapers. Doyle's detective gained a reputation overseas, on the Continent, and in the U.S., Australia and many other countries. In London, devotees queued outside one of the largest public libraries for the chance of reading the latest Holmes adventure. Demand for it was so high that the library's closing time was extended by half an hour on *Strand* publication day, usually the third Thursday in the month.[57] The Holmes stories represented

---

[54] Paget was trained at Heatherley's and the Royal Academy School, and employed the profile of one of his brothers as a model for the image of Sherlock Holmes.

[55] In the intervening years, 'Let's Keep Holmes Alive' clubs were formed in San Francisco, Chicago and Boston, and later in other cities and towns. The Baker Street Irregulars were formed in the U.S. to perpetuate the memory of Holmes, and they issued the *Baker Street Journal*.

[56] *Strand Magazine*, 26, 153 (September 1903), p.360.

[57] Reginald Pound, op. cit., pp.90-92.

an amalgamation of the author's narrative skill and his professional reputation, and they guaranteed the magazine's commercial success.

E.W. Hornung, Conan Doyle's brother-in-law, wrote a considerable number of short stories for *The Strand* including 'The Luckiest Man in the Colony' (1891) and the 'Stingaree' stories, a series set in an Australian context which appeared in 1904-1905. A prolific and popular author, he had travelled to Australia in 1884-1886, and tutored at Mossgiel station in the Riverina. A number of his stories were based on his experiences in the colony. Amongst his many short stories was the hugely successful 'Raffles' series, which featured the cricket-playing, gentleman-burglar, Raffles. Conan Doyle claimed that Raffles was 'a kind of inversion of Sherlock Holmes, Bunny playing Watson', and admired Hornung's skill at short-story writing. He was rather afraid of the dangerous potentialities of 'making the criminal a hero', a concern which echoed the moral insecurities of *Strand* readers.[58] Hornung's rogue-hero, however, succeeded in preserving ethical credibility by conforming to the social codes of public school gentlemanliness and loyalty. Even as the moral seriousness of the mid-Victorian generation was satirised, their codes of behaviour were ultimately employed to reinforce a consolatory sense of social order.

Doyle was also close friends with Grant Allen (1848-1899), another regular *Strand* contributor. Educated at Oxford, Allen began by writing serials and other stories for *Tit-Bits*. He went on to distinguish himself as a short-story writer of great talent, and as an outstanding interpreter of science to the general public. 'As a popular scientist', according to Conan Doyle, 'he stood alone.'[59] Allen was friends with such reputable men as Charles Darwin, T.H. Huxley, Herbert Spencer and Alfred Russel Wallace; an indication that 'popular' writers were integrated into an intellectually respectable social circle. He also created two female detectives - Miss Cayley and Hilda Wade - and these stories, like Arthur Morrison's Martin Hewitt detective stories, reflected the new acceptability and popularity of detective fiction amongst the middle class. When Allen died in 1899 leaving only a rough outline of the last episode of the Hilda Wade series, Doyle completed the chapter. Doyle's gesture, consistent with the image of fraternal solidarity and professional collaboration projected by *The Strand*, was interpreted by the magazine's editor as 'a beautiful and pathetic act of friendship which it is a pleasure to record'.[60]

Sir Henry Lucy (1845-1924) wrote an interesting and opinionated series on the proceedings and Members of Parliament, entitled 'From Behind the Speaker's Chair', which appeared continuously in *The Strand* from January 1893 to December 1902, then reappeared in 1911. Lucy had learned shorthand as a hobby, and thence used it to enter the journalistic profession, first as a reporter, and later as an editor and political columnist, writing for the *Gentleman's*

---

[58] Arthur Conan Doyle, op. cit., p.259.

[59] Ibid., pp 262-263. Allen's many publications included 'The Evolutionist at Large' (1883), 'Strange Stories' (1884) and 'Babylon' (1885).

[60] *Strand Magazine*, 19, 110 (March 1900), p.217.

Magazine, the *Pall Mall Gazette*, the *Observer* and *Punch*. (He was the author of the extremely popular 'Toby, MP' parliamentary diaries.) His career was representative of the way in which particular journalists came to specialise in niche areas of the field: for instance, parliamentary reporting, detective fiction, children's literature, or social commentary.

It was at one of the parliamentary dinner parties hosted by Seale Hayne that Newnes, sitting next to Henry Lucy and full of his plans for a new sixpenny monthly magazine, had recruited him as a political columnist.[61] The first series was illustrated by Francis Carruthers Gould, the second by E.T. Reed. When he accidentally wrote that the gift of a bishopric, whilst it was in the hands of the Prime Minister, was made from nominations made by the Bench of Bishops, Lucy received a mass of correspondence. 'I seem to have heard from all the rectories and vicarages in England', he observed.[62] This incident indicates that the middle-class, educated readership of *The Strand* included a large number of clergy.

Edith Nesbit wrote a vast number of stories for *The Strand*, and established a high reputation as a writer of children's stories.[63] She was commissioned to do a series of tales for the magazine in 1899, following the success of *The Story of the Treasure Seekers*. 'The Story of the Amulet', written in 1905-1906 for *The Strand*, and illustrated skilfully by H.R. Millar, was based on authentic material about ancient Egyptian magic derived from Babylonian texts, supplied to Nesbit by Dr Wallis Budge, keeper of the Egyptian and Assyrian Antiquities at the British Museum (1893-1924). Through these tales, Nesbit supplied thousands of children with their first glimpses of past civilisations, and her tales were staple fare for two generations of youth. Noel Coward, an enthusiastic reader of Nesbit's works as a child, used to save all his money to buy back numbers of *The Strand* for a penny from a secondhand bookshop on his way to school. He systematically saved a shilling at a time so as to get twelve numbers together, since he couldn't afford the bound volumes.[64]

Every set of Nesbit's stories was collected and turned into a book after serial publication, and she earnt considerable sums in royalties.[65] Yet she was so

---

[61] Although Lucy was initially hesitant to commit to a series of articles which relied on keeping in touch with Parliament but had to be at the printer's hands at least four weeks before publication, Newnes persisted. He managed to recruit Lucy, in spite of the latter demanding for the article what he thought would be a 'prohibitive price', winning him over with his 'cheery confidence' and pecuniary generosity. See Henry W. Lucy, op. cit., p.349. Lucy received £30 per article for the series. See Reginald Pound, op. cit., p.82.

[62] Henry Lucy, as cited in Reginald Pound, op. cit., p.83.

[63] Nesbit was a founding member of the Fabian Society, and numbered amongst her close friends and acquaintances Shaw, William Morris, Annie Besant, Charles Bradlaugh, Edward Carpenter, Mrs Pankhurst, Ramsay MacDonald, Graham Wallas, Bertrand Russell and H.G. Wells.

[64] Doris Langley Moore, *E. Nesbit. A Biography*, London: Ernest Benn, 1967, pp.226-227.

[65] 'Salome and the Head', for instance, was reprinted five years after its initial appearance by George Newnes as *The House with No Address*.

dependent on the income she received from the magazine that when the last instalment of 'The Wonderful Garden' appeared in November,1911 and was not immediately followed by another serial, she wrote to her brother in Australia:

> It was a great blow to me when, owing to the muddle-headedness of an agent, *The Strand* did without me last year. It made me very hard up, and added considerably to the worry of life.[66]

The Strand paid the highest prices of any contemporary magazine for its fiction, and it was Newnes's policy to pay authors for contributions on acceptance - a kind of professional courtesy. (Most publishing houses paid on publication.) Nesbit received a substantial £30 per story for her first series. W.W. Jacobs began on a payment of £49 12s. per story in 1898, but a year later his popularity was such that he received £400 for 'A Master Of Craft'. H.G. Wells received £83 6s. 4d. for his 'Mr Brasher's Treasure'. Conan Doyle received between £480 and £620 for each instalment of *The Hound of the Baskervilles*, depending on its length. From the mid-1890s, he never received less than £100 per thousand words from *The Strand*.[67] This sort of remuneration was a considerable increase on the one guinea prizes and payments that had been offered for contributions to *Tit-Bits*, and was proof of the professionalisation of the overlapping fields of literature and journalism.

W.W. Jacobs was another familiar name in *The Strand* in the first decade of the twentieth century. Jacobs wrote comic stories about dubious waterside characters, his work including serials such as 'The Lady of the Barge', 'At Sunwich Port' (1902) and 'Salthaven' (1908). He had worked for the Savings Department of the G.P.O. and written stories for other magazines unsuccessfully, until he sent two pieces to *The Million*, and was taken up by Greenhough Smith. From then on, all of his work was published in *The Strand* by arrangement, and he retired from the Post Office in 1899. Writing about Wapping (where his father was the manager of the South Devon Wharf) and Rotherhithe, Jacobs was the first of the 'local' writers who, at the turn of the century, were clearly associated with a particular geographical domain by the reading audience. In the same way, Israel Zangwill became associated with the London Jewry, and Arthur Morrison with the East End slums.

Many reputable authors contributed to the social and literary status of *The Strand*, and helped resolve the crisis of literary succession, at least in the minds of its readers. A.E.W. Mason's writing career spanned almost the entire publishing period of *The Strand*, and he wrote vast numbers of short stories, novels and plays. He enjoyed the life of an upper middle-class man of wealth, possessing a country home and a large circle of friends, maintaining membership of the Garrick Club, yachting frequently and travelling extensively. Like Newnes,

---

[66] Geraldine Beare, op. cit., p.xvii.

[67] Reginald Pound, op. cit., p.74.

he was a Liberal MP, entering the House of Commons when the Liberals were returned in 1906. Stanley Weyman wrote for *The Strand* from its first number, and was a master of the historical narrative. The son of a Shropshire solicitor, he was educated at Shrewsbury School and at Cambridge, and he gave up a career as a solicitor to pursue one in literature. Anthony Hope, the son of a rector, also gave up a career in law (as a successful barrister), and established himself as a novelist and playwright. That these men from professional and upper middle-class backgrounds chose to pursue literary careers was an indication of the increasing professional status attached to journalism. They were representative of a process through which the Victorian image of the writer as a prophet of the age was gradually eroded by a new type of writer: the expert practitioner of a particular 'branch' of literature, often a member of an exclusive literary coterie.

Other *Strand* authors included some of the most well-known names of the period in English literature: Rudyard Kipling, W. Somerset Maugham, P.G. Wodehouse, Max Pemberton ('the English Jules Verne'), Jerome K. Jerome ('the English Mark Twain'), H.G. Wells and Baroness Orczy (author of *The Scarlet Pimpernel*). Like Nesbit, Kipling wrote many stories and poems for children for *The Strand*, and children's literature was a popular feature of this diverse publication. P.G. Wodehouse began writing for *The Strand* in 1905 at a time when it was the chosen publication of many aspiring writers. He went on to write some two hundred stories for Newnes's magazine, keeping up his association with it for thirty-five years.

Graphic artists were prominent members of the *Strand* circle, their work remarkably innovative, their field increasingly professionalised, and their contributions crucial to the success of the illustrated magazine. The magazine was the black-and-white illustrator's natural outlet, and the weekly or monthly illustrated magazine was his (invariably it was a him) staple diet. The circulation of the magazine, once it became established (and initial costs were relatively low), varied little, and the magazine could offer continuous employment, whereas book publishing was regulated by the constraints of finance and speculative caution. Mason Jackson remarked in the 1880s that the *Illustrated London News*, like *Punch*, and *The Graphic* had served artists well in that 'their pages have always been open for young artists, and while they have helped forward struggling genius they have opened up new sources of enjoyment to the general public'.[68] *The Strand* continued this tradition, its pages offering permanent employment to some twenty illustrators and casual employment to hundreds more. It was a launchpad for many an illustrator's career. On the other hand, illustration had been crucial to *The Strand*'s success. 'We are glad', Newnes observed in the preamble to 'Artists of *The Strand Magazine*', 'to take this occasion to acknowledge our indebtedness to these gentlemen ... whose work has had so great a share in building up the popularity of *The Strand Magazine*.'[69]

---

[68] Mason Jackson, cited in Simon Houfe, op. cit., pp. 109-110.

[69] *Strand Magazine*, 10, 60 (December 1895), p. 786.

Industrialisation had given impetus to art and design in the nineteenth century, and to its dissemination through illustrated papers and cheap prints. From the chapbooks, broadsheets and illustrated ballads that were popular amongst the working classes, to Charles Knight's *Penny Magazine* (1832), which was liberally sprinkled with woodcuts, and the *Illustrated London News* (1842), which subordinated letterpress to illustration, illustration was a popular feature of many successful publications.[70] The main difficulties faced by early producers were ones of a technical variety. These publications stimulated greater visual sophistication amongst readers by exposing them to a variety of scenes and subjects. The pre-Raphaelite illustrators of the mid-nineteenth century, most of them formally trained, drew upon a more critical approach to the arts, and their work contributed substantially to the recognition of illustration as an authentic artistic form.[71] Artists began to be acknowledged on the contents pages of books. The 1860s brought an explosion in illustrations of contemporary life (as against the nostalgic medievalism of pre-Raphaelitism) both in magazines and novels. *Punch* or *The London Charivari*, established in 1841, invented the 'big cut' satirical print or 'comic'.[72] Newnes was to make extensive use of such satirical prints in 'The Queer Side of Things' and other features of *The Strand*, and in publications such as *The Million*.

Art Nouveau books and magazines such as *The English Illustrated Magazine* (1883), *The Butterfly* (1893), *The Studio* (1894), *The Quest* (1894–1896), *The Idler* (1892) and *Phil May's Illustrated Annuals* brought new recognition to illustrators, forged new links with the art schools, and stimulated the development of a new bohemian artistic culture.[73] The 1890s in particular produced a myriad of illustrated magazines. Newnes's publication *The Million* (1892) was one of these. The impact of the art and crafts movement, and of illustrated journalism in particular, was such that graphic art became the most popular and vital form of art in the period. *The Strand* was a cradle of the revolution in pictorial art. Newnes maintained three different types of printing machines for *The Strand*, including the rotary art press - the only one of its kind in Europe - capable of printing up to sixty-four illustrated pages at one revolution of the cylinders. It was also a medium for the professionalisation of the field of illustration.

This field was soon informally organised into a hierarchy. The artists of any magazine's staff, its special artists, and chief cartoonists, most of whom held special positions, were paid salaries or retainers, or maintained a privileged position in the magazine's pages, were at the pinnacle. Outside contributors who

---

[70] Simon Houfe, op. cit., p.50.

[71] They emphasised draughtsmanship and the organisation of space and detail.

[72] British caricature, it is worth noting, was heavily influenced by French naturalism and the comedy of manners. A number of *Strand* illustrators of the 1890s, such as Bernard Partridge and H.R. Millar, were influenced by the remarkable pen artists who emerged in Paris in the mid-1880s.

[73] See Simon Houfe, op. cit., p.167.

featured regularly but were not part of the inner coterie were next in the professional pyramid, and a collection of amateurs and 'hacks' formed the lower stratum. It was only in the 1880s and 1890s that illustrators gained pay conditions and status to equal those of their literary counterparts, and W.H.J. Boot, employed by Newnes as *The Strand Magazine*'s Art Editor, was the first to hold such a position. Boot, who remained at his post from 1891 to 1910, was a landscape painter and illustrator who had studied at the Derby School of Art, and then moved to London, devoting himself exclusively to illustration. He was Vice-President of the Royal British Academy during his years as Art Editor for *The Strand*, his dual roles an indication of the newly-established links between the traditional artistic establishment and the period's most dynamic artistic medium: the illustrated magazine.[74]

Magazines such as *The Strand* were less consciously artistic and employed cheaper processes of production than their aesthetic counterparts. Aesthetic periodicals, self-consciously artistic in style and middle class in appeal, were characterised by distinctive decoration, hand-made paper, beautiful type forms and carefully chosen subject matter, and they demanded a critical response from their readers.[75] Yet most of the artists of *The Strand* had professional training, many training and exhibiting at the Royal Academy. And the profession of illustration came to be characterised by a high degree of specialisation. H.R. Millar became known as the illustrator of fairy tales, J.A. Shepherd as 'one of the finest animal caricaturists, past or present', F.C. Gould for his parliamentary sketches, and J.F. Sullivan as 'a satirist and a humorist' of great note.

The Strand made its own contribution to fostering the art of black-and-white illustration in a unique way. Newnes devoted two rooms of the magazine's offices to a public art gallery in which original illustrations from *The Strand* and *The Million* were on display and sale. 'The Art Gallery', Newnes enthused, was 'a place open every day, all day, to the inspection of whomsoever may like to inspect.' It displayed the work of Sidney Paget, Phil May, Gordon Browne, Paul Hardy, H.R. Millar, J.A. Shepherd, J.F. Sullivan, J.L. Wimbush, W.B. Wollen, G.C. Haite, W. Stacey, Alfred Pearse and many other well-known illustrators:

> All these drawings are offered for sale, but whether a possible purchaser or not, the passer-by will not waste the time occupied by a look around these two pleasant rooms.[76]

---

[74] Boot's career spanned half a century of changes within the field of illustration, his first contributions being published in the first numbers of *The Graphic* (1870-1881), and his others in *Good Words, Illustrated London News, The Quiver, Boys Own Paper* and many other magazines. It was he who chose Sidney Paget to illustrate the Sherlock Holmes stories, though Doyle was in favour of Frank Wiles.

[75] They gained impetus from the aestheticism of Walter Pater and Oscar Wilde.

[76] *Strand Magazine*, 4, 24 (December 1892), p.597. The Harmsworths, always in competition with Newnes and resolving not to be outdone by him, made it known that the top floor of their new premises, Carmelite House, would be reserved for a permanent exhibition of contemporary art.

This was not merely a promotional scheme, but a cultural offering. Thus, Newnes posed as an art patron. In 1901, the Victoria and Albert Museum held a large exhibition of black-and-white drawings and represented on a national scale the extraordinary fertility and originality of magazine and book illustrators of the 1890s. Newnes had been representing them, through *The Strand* and 'The Art Gallery', throughout the 1890s. Boot, and his son, James Sidney, who succeeded him as Art Editor, introduced and encouraged many well-known illustrators, including Paget, Millar, Will Owen, Gordon Browne, W. Heath Robinson and G.H. Haite. (Haite designed the original *Strand* cover, and later helped to found the London Sketch Club.) These men became household names.

Full-size oil paintings of *Million* illustrations, on the other hand, actually became household items. They were distributed as prizes in the paper's many competitions. Mounted pictures sent to *The Million* in connection with the Christmas competition of 1893 were sent to hospitals, and many schools 'brightened' their walls with *Million* colour illustrations. One reader suggested that 'Millionaires who do not bind their favourite paper cut out the coloured pictures, mount them on cardboard, and, after they have been framed, send them to the local workhouse or hospital.'[77]

Black-and-white illustrators were central to *The Strand*'s identity, their names synonymous with the series which they illustrated. Just as the name Conan Doyle was inextricably linked to the Sherlock Holmes stories, so was that of Sidney Paget. Similarly, J.F. Sullivan was associated with 'The Queer Side of Things', W.B. Woollen with 'Brigadier Gerard', and J.A. Shepherd with 'Zig-Zags at the Zoo'. H.R. Millar illustrated the majority of Edith Nesbit's stories, working under difficult conditions. Nesbit was consistently behind with her manuscripts, and Millar frequently had to produce five or six detailed illustrations in a few days or working from a chapter precis. He also contributed many of the illustrations for the 'Stories for Children' series which appeared almost continuously in *The Strand* from 1891 to 1899, and then intermittently until 1917. *The Strand* was a pioneer in the field of children's literature and illustration, and W.S. Stacey was another who produced a large number of illustrations for a juvenile audience. He contributed to *The Strand* over the years from 1891 to 1906, as well as to a range of other magazines, including *Chums*, *The Temple Magazine*, *Cassell's Family Magazine*, *The Boys Own Paper*, *The Girls' Own Paper* and *The Wide World Magazine* (another Newnes publication).

In combination, the network of illustrators associated with *The Strand* presented a world view that was a reflection of contemporary conditions, and was shaped by new techniques and mediums of illustration, the emergence of a body of innovative, skilled and respected practitioners, and the development of a visually literate audience. The coupling of the illustrator-artist and the engraver-craftsman represented yet another solution to the problem of reconciling the

---

[77] *The Million*, 5, 129 (September 1894), p.300.

balance between artistic and commercial imperatives in popular journalism. Graphic art was both commercially profitable and professionally recognised. The work of the graphic artist represented a 'new', dynamic and innovative field of endeavour which had connections with the avant garde, and yet it also represented the cumulative developments of the century.

'Portraits of Celebrities' and 'Illustrated Interviews' were crucial to *The Strand*'s function as a medium of cultural security and class cohesion, and to its commercial success. 'Portraits of Celebrities' was a portrait gallery of eminent late Victorians and Edwardians at different times in their lives which began in the first issue of *The Strand* and ran for sixteen years. The first number featured Alfred Lord Tennyson, Professor John Blackie (a University professor, and 'at once the most learned and most popular of living Scotsmen', according to the columnist), the Reverend C.H. Spurgeon, Miss Ellen Terry, Henry Irving, Algernon Swinburne, Sir John Lubbock (a *Strand* contributor) and H. Rider Haggard. The series began with Lord Tennyson and ended with David Lloyd George. Public prominence was its watchword, and it conferred on *The Strand* much of its early popularity at a time when a photograph of a celebrity would have cost a shilling or more.

'Portraits of Celebrities' bore close links to the carte-de-visite form of commercial portrait reproduction, developed by the entrepreneurial French photographer André Disderi, that achieved widespread popularity in Britain in the 1860s. Multiple copies of identical tiny portrait cards, generated from a single negative print using new developing and printing techniques, had flooded the market. Nominated 'celebrity cartes', these portraits were sold through a variety of outlets including print shops, stationers, booksellers, fancy goods stores, novelty emporia and even via street vendors. 'Men of the cloth, scientists, artists, writers, singers, personalities of the stage and even prize fighters', according to Audrey Linkman, 'could all prove good money earners or "sure cards".'[78] The royal family headed the sales charts, with three to four million cartes of Victoria alone sold between 1860 and 1862 and over two million of the Prince and Princess of Wales following their marriage in 1863. It is significant then, that the *Strand* series 'Portraits of Celebrities' featured a positive plethora of royal models including Queen Victoria (in the first issue), Princess Marie of Edinburgh, Prince Ferdinand of Romania, the Prince of Wales, the Duchess of Teck and many more. Statesmen and politicians, realising the publicity potential of celebrity cartes, agreed to the publication of their portraits. Gladstone was regularly the most popular, selling a hundred to one of any other man of his set. He appeared in the second number of *The Strand*.

The purpose-designed photographic album developed in tandem with the carte, as the Victorian public began to collect and exchange portraits on a new

---

[78] Audrey Linkman, *The Victorians: Photographic Portraits*, London: Tauris Parke, 1993, pp.61-64, 67. The tradition of celebrity cards has been used by entrepreneurs throughout the twentieth century in the production of football and basketball cards, posters and stickers, and calendars, and in the propaganda of election campaigns.

scale, and it remained popular throughout the nineteenth century. Finishing his schooling and moving into an apprenticeship in the fancy goods trade in the 1860s, Newnes would have been well aware of the success of the carte. He would undoubtedly have seen it in the London stationers and newsagents that he frequented, and may well have sold it in his job as a commercial traveller. In the later nineteenth century, a succession of carte formats of varying dimensions were introduced in an attempt to revive the popularity of the format and stimulate the trade in portrait photography. [79] Newnes later harnessed the commercial potential of cheap portrait reproduction to ensure the success of *The Strand*, and employed the 'celebrity carte' and photographic album to reinforce the importance of upper and middle-class 'celebrities'.[80] In the twentieth century, when mass spectator sport was creating a new class of celebrity, Newnes was to exploit the popularity of the sporting hero in *C.B. Fry's Magazine*. He published full-page studio portraits of 'Famous Footballers' and 'Famous Cricketers'. Readers (or 'fans') of the sportsman-editor, C.B. Fry, were even offered free presentation photographs of C.B. Fry (cabinet size, on plate-sunk mounts, complete with Fry's facsimile signature).

The newspaper interview, which had been raised to prominence by Stead at the *Pall Mall Gazette*, was combined with photographic portraiture in 'Illustrated Interviews'. This series, allowing readers an intimate insight into the lives, habits and personalities of various prominent people, offered a rejoinder to concerns about the disjunction between the private lives of the middle and upper classes and the values which they advocated in public. It acted as a restorative tonic for readers. It was also representative of 'society journalism', a new journalistic prototype which arose out of New Journalism, with its emphasis on human interest stories, gossip and 'personal journalism' in general, and its aim of providing entertainment to a wide audience. 'The demand for such information is insatiable', wrote the author of 'Celebrities at Play', 'and the competition in the journalistic world so keen that the demand is supplied with as much detail as possible':

> To see the great unbend is, we have it on historic authority, a source of infinite amusement to the populace. If that was true in Macaulay's days, it is even less disputable in these, when a special journalism exists mainly to chronicle the small doings of the great, and every newspaper has a personal column.[81]

Newnes was to exploit this interest in 'seeing the great unbend' in a comprehensive manner in *C.B. Fry's Magazine*, with a series entitled 'Out of

[79] Ibid., p.77.

[80] Cassells pirated the idea, issuing 'Cassells Universal Portrait Gallery' from 1894. Each part, costing sixpence, contained twenty-four portraits of 'celebrities of the day', with autographs and brief biographical sketches. The first part, predictably, featured Queen Victoria, Mr and Mrs Gladstone, Adelina Patti, Henry Irving, Cecil Rhodes and others.

[81] *Strand Magazine*, 2, 8 (August 1891), p.155.

Harness'.[82] The *Strand* series featured actors and actresses, singers, composers, theatre managers, publishers, writers, artists, clerics, scholars, doctors, lawyers and others distinguished by their social or professional status (Cardinal Manning, Henry Irving, W.S Gilbert, Sir Augustus Harris, Madame Albani, Montagu Williams, Q.C., Sir George Lewis and George Newnes himself all featured), and they willingly joined the community of *The Strand* by lending photos, providing biographical details and obliging with interviews. Each interviewee boasted marks of esteem from influential members of their social set whom they had entertained, served, met or in some way impressed with their accomplishments. They were themselves carte collectors. Their entrance halls, libraries, consulting and entertaining rooms were bedecked with often autographed pictures of 'operatic stars and theatrical celebrities, city magnates, men eminent in the world of art and letters', and members of the British and European Royal families. This series thus reinforced the social reputation of *The Strand*, and implicitly extended its circle of influence.[83]

'Illustrated Interviews', 'Portraits of Celebrities', 'Artists of *The Strand*', 'Celebrities at Play' and many other *Strand* features may all be traced to a contemporary obsession with autobiography as a literary and narrative form (itself part of a democratic reaction against anonymous authority and a preoccupation of the self as it existed in time), and with deploying role-models (the 'gentleman' or 'self-made man', for example) as a means of assimilating, comprehending and directing change. Robin Gilmour has observed that the Victorians maintained a fascination with time because they were conscious of being its victims. Temporal awareness underpinned major contemporary discoveries in geology, evolution, biblical criticism, archaeology and anthropology. It was to be one of the key concerns of Newnes's *Wide World Magazine* (1898). It also resulted in the proliferation of the autobiographical form. The term 'autobiography', in fact, appeared only in the nineteenth century, although as a form of literature it had occurred from the earliest period, and significantly, the *Dictionary of National Biography*, designed and published by George Smith, was begun in 1882 with Sir Leslie Stephen as editor. *Who's Who* was also established in these years. 'Illustrated Interviews' was a version of these volumes.

The narratives of these series tended to be underpinned by certain social and ideological assumptions. Thus Cardinal Manning was found to practise a methodical life:

> I have a long, long day myself. At seven I get up, and
> oftentimes do not go to bed until half-past eleven - working all
> the time. My dinner is early, at 1:30, and tea comes round at

---

[82] Public interest even extended to the dogs, cats and other domestic pets owned by 'celebrities'. Sir Morrell Mackenzie's dog 'Moritz', Madame Albani's dog 'Chat' and many other animals were featured in 'Illustrated Interviews'.

[83] See, for instance, *Strand Magazine*, 3, 14 (February 1892), p.119.

> seven o'clock. Newspapers? I manage to get through some of
> the principal ones every day.

The world view of the Victorians, as Gilmour has argued, was dependent upon 'models of social harmony and personal conduct by means of which they could understand, control, and develop their rapidly changing world'.[84] *The Strand* performed just this function, offering readers a consolatory faith in the role-model.

Tit-Bits had been dependent upon commercial strategies and the creation of a kind of mass movement of 'loyal Tit-Bitites'. Hence, it was publicly represented by 'Tit-Bits' processions, sandwich boards, large advertising signs, banners and facsimile reproductions. It connected with its audience through promotional schemes, competitions, correspondence columns and editorial interjection. *The Strand* appealed to different instincts and a different audience. It was dependent upon consistently well-presented stories and articles, the encouragement of many authors and illustrators, the reputation of its editor-publisher and the stabilising effect of good, innovative management. Its reputation was established through its association with a part of London famous for its historical and literary associations, through reviews in the periodical press, through its commercial reputation, and through its links with esteemed authors and illustrators. And it connected with its readers through the serial story or short story, the black-and-white sketch, the biographical portrait or interview series, and the editorial 'address'.

The success of *The Strand* was also dependent upon the editor-publisher's editorial experience, and his creation of close affective and social ties with a circle of readers and contributors who identified very strongly with the articles, stories, illustrations and serials of the magazine. Appeals to 'loyalty' and 'friendship' were a common Newnesian ploy. But the readers of *The Strand* identified with the magazine because in doing so they were accepted into an exclusive social circle - the *Strand* club - consisting of 'a large circle of valued friends' (the authors, artists and patrons of the magazine);[85] of the leading lights of the upper and middle classes, from royalty to members of the professional classes, who endorsed the magazine and appeared in its pages; and of the editor himself, a leader in the publishing profession and model of the self-made entrepreneur, the host of the entertainment and the patron of the reader-contributor collective. *The Strand* was therefore depicted visually as an exclusive reception, whereas *Tit-Bits* had been represented in a double-page spread that depicted all aspects of production and distribution, and included readers, contributors, competitors and editors alike in a democratic collage. Thus *The Economist* berated the board of George Newnes, Ltd in 1949 for their decision to cease publication of the magazine:

---

[84] Robin Gilmour, *The Victorian Period: The Intellectual and Cultural Context of English Literature, 1830-1890*, London and New York: Longman, 1993, p.19.

[85] *Strand Magazine*, 17, 100 (April 1899), pp.363-364.

> A publishing house is a business enterprise whose projects must
> be financially sound, but it is also a trustee of the affections of
> the reading public in Britain and overseas, and of that public's
> standards of taste.[86]

The Strand's cultural role, it was emphasised, was at least as significant as its commercial viability.

Conan Doyle wrote to Greenhough Smith after returning from the Continent in the 1890s of the pervasive popularity of *The Strand*:

> Foreigners used to recognise the English by their check suits. I
> think they will soon learn to do it by their *Strand Magazines*.
> Everybody on the Channel boat, except the man at the wheel,
> was clutching one.[87]

Doyle's use of the word 'clutching' is suggestive. It hints at the kind of security that readers sought and obtained in *The Strand*. In a period of rapid change, *Strand* readers craved stability and entertainment. *The Strand*, going to press four weeks ahead of publication - five weeks by 1914 - showed no prescience of events. Despite a few articles discussing German activities in the decade before the first World War, *The Strand* maintained what Pound has called 'an editorial bias in favour of the timeless as against the timely'.[88] Its implication in the status quo represents a unique example of the way in which the reflection model of periodical literature is more consistent with the method and character of some periodicals than of others. It continued to confirm the familiar, and whilst it conducted a few investigations into such areas as child labour and the county courts, maintained an accent on entertainment. It thus went on to survive two world wars, despite the high rate of attrition amongst periodicals, outlasting all of its contemporaries and rivals; magazines such as *Pearson's Weekly*, *The Royal* and *Pall Mall*.

'Arriving on that propitious scene, partly by accident and perfectly matching its time', wrote Reginald Pound, '*The Strand Magazine* soon attained the status of a national institution.' Pound went on to elaborate upon the entrenched popularity of Newnes's magazine:

> Responsible and yet dégagé, developing its own ethos of dignity
> and popularity, it became as much a symbol of immutable
> British order as Bank holidays and the Changing of the Guard.[89]

---

86 *The Economist*, 17 December, 1949, as cited in Reginald Pound, op. cit., p.192.

87 Arthur Conan Doyle as cited in Reginald Pound, op. cit., p.63.

88 Reginald Pound, op. cit., p.64.

89 Ibid., p.9.

The Strand was a powerful cultural determinant. Its success lay in the fact that it was a timely and appealing response to the particular needs of its audience. *Tit-Bits* had been established at a time when the ranks of the lower middle-class were swelling, and democratisation, industrialisation, increasing literacy and an expanding communications network called for 'inclusive', interactive and entertaining journalism. And it was no accident that *The Wide World Magazine* appeared in the imperialist 1890s, confirming as it did the role of empire-builders and the nature of British and western identity, just as the Boer War threw the nation into controversy over imperialist policy (especially considering Newnes's Liberal-Imperialist associations). Appearing at a time when its middle and upper-class readers were beset by the forces of change and by anxiety over a variety of social problems, *The Strand* facilitated the consolidation of middle-class values, social status and cohesion, providing them with security, stability, a sense of 'immutable British order' and a 'pleasing comforting world view' (to recall Stephen Knight's description of the Sherlock Holmes stories). It was a medium for dealing with the cultural transition from the nineteenth century to the twentieth. In a period of crisis for established literary values and English literature, it offered a compromise between artistic quality and journalistic innovation, a combination of commercialism and professionalism, and thus a solution to the problem of literary succession: middle-brow literature. This magazine acted as a forum for the expression of developing artistic forms such as the connected short story, the detective story and black-and-white illustration, and it fostered and guarded the reputations of a new generation of talented and professional authors and artists. Its development reflected the continuing tensions between entrepreneurialism and professionalism in these years. Yet it did indeed become a 'national institution', and its popularity confirmed Newnes's genius as an editor and publisher, his success as an entrepreneur, and his status as an upper middle-class professional.

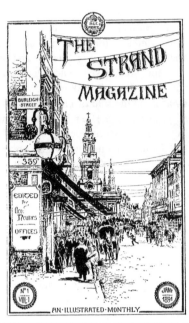

Figure 7. G.H. Haite's original cover drawing for The Strand Magazine *, depicting the intersection between The Strand and Burleigh St. This image became familiar to two generations of readers in every part of the English-speaking world.*

Figure 8. Illustration accompanying Newnes' editorial address for the two hundredth number of The Strand *(Strand Magazine, 34, 200 (August 1907), pp.286-287). Many notable contemporary writers are shown.*

Liberalism and Imperialism: Developing Formats and Expanding Horizons

Introduction to Part II

Newnes's next two publications, *The Westminster Gazette* (1893) and *The Wide World Magazine* (1898), emerged within a period of expansion (in terms of technology, travel and imperial ideology) and, for Liberals, political division. They engaged with a variety of political and cultural issues related to Liberalism and imperialism, and with ongoing debates about the New Journalism.

In Jules Verne's international best-seller *Around the World in Eighty Days* (1873), Fogg and Passeportout raced against time and conquered distance and space. This narrative of global travel was a mixture of fact and fantasy in which the masses who read the novel could participate vicariously. It projected the kind of world unity that the railroad, telephone, bicycle, aeroplane and cinema were to make possible in the ensuing decades. Verne's classic work, published when George Newnes was a teenager, avidly interested in popular literature of all kinds, no doubt made an impression on his youthful mind. He went on to establish a periodical that offered the same sense of conquered distance, and the same mixture of factual account and literary colour: *The Wide World Magazine*.

By the late nineteenth century, an expanding communications network, comprising postal, telephone and telegraphic services, a railway network and steamship routes, extended virtually world-wide, bringing people into closer proximity than ever before. The transport revolution and imperial expansion acted as a stimulus to travel, and organisers of mass travel such as Thomas Cook, Baedecker and Murray revolutionised the travel industry, making the world beyond Europe accessible to a considerably wider, if predominantly middle-class, market.[1] Ludgate Circus, where Thomas Cook was located, became the centre of a world of travel and the expansion of Cook's empire reflected the widening of the British world view. 'In their eagerness to provide for the ever-increasing number of their passengers and their needs,' Edmund Swinglehurst has observed, drawing upon 'Land of Hope and Glory' (from Elgar's *Coronation Ode*), 'the Cooks became involved in more and more enterprises, extending their organisation "wider still and wider" both geographically and in the range of its services.'[2] Half a million British tourists went abroad in the early 1890s. The number had grown to one million by the turn of the century. And overseas migration was continuing on an unprecedented scale, with 21.5 million English emigrating overseas between 1816 and 1914.[3]

The 1890s in Britain were, above all, an imperialist decade. The celebration of Queen Victoria's Jubilee in 1897 evoked the general popularity of the

---

[1]   See Edmund Swinglehurst, *The Romantic Journey: The Story of Thomas Cook and Victorian Travel*, London: Pica Editions, 1974; James Buzard, *The Beaten Track: European Tourism, Literature and the Ways to Culture, 1800-1918*, Oxford: Clarendon, 1993; Louis Turner and John Ash, *The Golden Hordes: International Tourism and the Pleasure Periphery*, London, 1975; Gilbert Sigaux, *History of Tourism*, London, 1966.

[2]   Edmund Swinglehurst, op. cit., p.147.

[3]   Ibid., p.138.

imperialist mission. The notion that 'the sun never sets on the British empire' flowed from a thousand pens. At the beginning of the twentieth century, Queen Victoria reigned over 400 million people, inhabiting over one-fifth of the globe. British missionaries continued to expand their activities in Africa, Asia and the Pacific. Britain became involved in a number of foreign conflicts, from the issue of Egyptian finances and the Fashoda crisis in the Upper Nile (a confrontation between British and French forces), through the Jameson Raid (1896) and the Boer War in southern Africa, to the Boxer Rebellion in China (1900). Other countries too, participated in imperial expansion. In the years between 1880 and 1914, Africa was divided up amongst the European nations. European domination extended over 11,500,000 square miles of which France had 4,238,000; Britain 3,495,000; Germany and Italy about 1,000,000 each; Belgium 800,000; Portugal 780,000; and Spain 75,000.[4] Acquisitions in Asia, though not quite as spatially extensive, were a manifestation of the same impulse for expansion. The United States annexed Hawaii, Puerto Rico, Guam and the Philippines in 1898, and the Canal Zone in 1903; acquired Cuba as a protectorate in 1901; and bought the Virgin Islands from Denmark in 1917. Imperialism, then, was fundamental to contemporary politics and popular consciousness, and was thus central to both *The Westminster Gazette* and *The Wide World Magazine*.

There were, in fact, substantial interconnections between New Journalism and late Victorian and Edwardian Liberalism, especially Liberal Imperialism. The decades preceding the First World War, as Michael Freeden has demonstrated, were ones in which Liberalism was revitalised in a manner which both preserved the continuity of a nineteenth-century liberal tradition and foreshadowed the development of the modern British welfare state.[5] 'New Liberals', belonging primarily to the professional middle class, their activites focussed within groups such as the Rainbow Circle, the Ethical Societies and others connected with the National Liberal Club and Settlement Movement, relied heavily on periodicals, and especially weeklies, as a means of mutual communication and influence. They concentrated their energies on social rather than political reform, advocating an approach which combined the rational pragmatism of utilitarianism, the fusion of nineteenth-century individualism and late Victorian socialism, the swing back from laissez-faire ideology to state intervention, and the spirit of English Idealism dominant at Oxford (where Arnold Toynbee pioneered the Settlement Movement at a time when J.A. Spender was studying there). And their debates focussed on old age pensions (first and foremost among the advanced measures recommended by liberals), unemployment, and later national insurance. The 'Liberal Imperialists' were closely associated with new Liberalism and shared a concern with Britain's international economic position and with defence and

---

[4]   Stephen Kern, *The Culture of Time and Space, 1880-1918*, Cambridge, Massachusetts: Harvard University Press, 1983, p.232.

[5]   Michael Freeden, *The New Liberalism: An Ideology of Social Reform*, Oxford: Clarendon Press, 1978, pp.1-2.

imperial questions, a strong interest in social reform and a belief in the importance of Temperance legislation.[6] Newnes was identified with Liberal Imperialism and was a strong supporter of collectivist social reform, as his editing of *Tit-Bits* had shown, and *The Westminster Gazette* echoed with the arguments and views associated with Liberal Imperialism and the reformulation of British Liberalism, with its new focus on social reform, state intervention, collectivism and 'national efficiency'.

The reader of *The Westminster* was confronted with a variety of issues relating to both domestic and foreign affairs, from internal divisions in the Liberal Party between Imperialists (representing a commitment to expansion) and 'Little Englanders' (representing 'Peace and Retrenchment'), to the perplexing question of British policy in South Africa.[7] Home Rule was one of the major preoccupations of political society and the political press. After two unsuccessful attempts to legislate Home Rule, the Liberals retreated from this commitment without disavowing it as a party. Liberal publicists in general maintained support for Home Rule, but in *The Westminster Gazette*, J.A. Spender preached revisionism. After three years in government, the Liberals suffered a crushing defeat at the polls in early 1896. They had governed for a short period of three years in a prolonged Conservative ascendancy, under the leadership of the 'Grand Old Man', William Gladstone, and after his retirement, Lord Rosebery. Imperialism seemed to offer the solution to a variety of political problems, enveloping the Irish question, and healing divisions within and between parties.[8]

Following the death of Queen Victoria in 1901 and the end of the Boer War, political attention turned towards social reform at home. Chamberlain's advocacy of Protection as the answer to German trade activity caused a split in the Conservative party, and was a political gift for Liberals. Many Liberal and some Conservative papers, including Newnes's *Westminster Gazette*, rallied together on the tariff question. In the lead-up to the general election of January 1906, they carefully played up the free trade issue, which represented a combination of popular appeal and the least potential for causing rupture in the Liberal ranks. Despite some remaining differences within the party, Liberalism was in revival, and the party achieved a sweeping victory at the polls.

---

[6] 'Liberal Imperialists' was a term used after 1898 to describe a group of prominent activists including Haldane, Asquith, Grey and Rosebery (its leader in the Lords), and a wider though only semi-coordinated body of men in British parliamentary politics who supported some of their arguments about policy and about the direction of liberalism, especially upon the issue of imperialism. See H.C.G. Matthew, *The Liberal Imperialists: The Ideas and Politics of a Post-Gladstonian Élite*, Oxford: Oxford University Press, 1973.

[7] This division was one which was to govern and plague Liberal politics until the free trade issue brought a natural resolution into party unity in the middle of the next decade. Spender, by this time editor of the *The Westminster Gazette*, felt that party divisions were 'unduly embittered by personal antagonisms which could not be explained to the public', and the paper came under fire for attempting a 'fictitious party unity'. See J.A. Spender, *Life, Journalism and Politics*, London: Cassell, 1927, vol.1, p.67.

[8] Imperialism and Home Rule were however, essentially incompatible, as L.R. Churchill had demonstrated in using imperialism to block the Home Rule Bill in 1885-1886.

The Westminster Gazette was a Liberal evening newspaper, owned by George Newnes and edited, from 1896, by J.A. Spender. At the beginning of the twentieth century there were three morning dailies (*Daily News*, *Daily Chronicle* and *Morning Leader*) and three metropolitan evening papers (*Westminster Gazette*, *Star* and *Echo*) which supported Liberalism to varying degrees. *The Westminster*, a penny paper, catered to the 'educated classes', whilst the *Star* and *Echo*, both halfpenny papers, appealed to a wider audience and made a speciality of sporting news. In December 1904, W.T. Stead described the London daily newspapers in the *Review of Reviews* as 'His Majesty's Public Councillors', categorising *The Westminster Gazette*, along with *The Times*, in the first rank. Both were political papers 'read by men of both parties'. Their reputations were high; out of all proportion to their modest circulations of 35,000 and 20,000 respectively.[9]

Between 1887 and 1889, the number of copies of the *PMG* taken by the National Liberal Club, of which Newnes was a member, rose from thirteen to twenty-six (as compared with four *Globes*, three *Stars* and one *Evening Standard*). When it was sold to W.W. Astor, thirty copies of *The Westminster Gazette* were substituted for it. Copies of Newnes's paper were distributed in the billiard room, smoking room, reading room, grill room and card room, suggesting, as Lucy Brown points out, that it represented 'a necessary priming of the evening's conversations'.[10] Spender conveyed the same impression of the paper's appeal and readership, observing that it 'gave the serious reader something to think about in his leisure hours - in the clubs when his working day was over, and at home in the evenings'.[11]

The Wide World Magazine was a sixpenny illustrated monthly 'true story magazine', dedicated to the journalistic exploration of the 'wide world'. Charles Dilke, travelling around the world in 1866, had found it both large and populated with Englishmen. He wrote a book entitled *Greater Britain* (1868) which became remarkably popular, and the idea of 'greater Britain' took off in fiction, popular magazines and the newspaper press. Imperialist fiction was in vogue in the nineties. Kipling's stories and poems told the story of the British overseas. And Henty pioneered the notion of narratorial trips involving the reader, who travelled 'To Natal With Buller' and 'To Pretoria With Roberts', or was imaginatively situated 'With Moore at Corunna', 'With Clive in India', or 'With Kitchener in the Soudan'.[12] It was this type of imaginative journey that *The Wide World Magazine* claimed to provide, with one notable improvement: its material was 'true', produced by the travellers themselves. It was founded at a time when a range of new periodicals, appearing in various western countries, were offering a global perspective to increasing numbers of readers. This was the age of the

---

[9]   W.T. Stead as cited in Lucy Brown, *Victorian News and Newspapers*, Oxford: Clarendon, 1985, p.1.

[10]   Lucy Brown, op. cit., p.110.

[11]   J.A. Spender, op. cit., vol. 2, p.134.

[12]   Published from the 1880s to 1900s, Henty's books carried these titles.

foreign correspondent and the 'special artist' in the newspaper press, and 'international news' was expanding in scope and diversifying in style. *The Wide World Magazine* added the personal angle, human interest element and visual component to international news, with a series of 'true narratives of extraordinary human endurance', accompanied by 'astounding photographs' that were printed using new techniques of photographic reproduction.

From a biographical perspective, *The Westminster Gazette* and *The Wide World Magazine* were associated with Newnes's own interests, experiences preoccupations and commitments, and with the experiments and successes of his early years in periodical publishing. Newnes was an MP for most of his working life, but he found the parliamentary machine, a far cry from his own constantly evolving and engrossing publishing business, a rather frustrating and oppressive one. 'Well may it be said', he remarked, 'that those who have only taken part in a few marathon races do not know what real pedestrianism means, unless they were also in [the 1892-95] Parliament.'[13] He thus expressed his devotion to the Liberal cause through his commitment to the liberal evening newspaper, *The Westminster Gazette*. *The Westminster* was established with the staff of the *Pall Mall Gazette* when that paper was bought by the American millionaire W.W. Astor in 1892, and it was announced that its politics would convert to Conservatism. The editor of *The Westminster*, E.T. Cook, claimed that the paper constituted the original publication under a new name. It was, in fact, a combination of journalistic continuity and innovation. It married traditional political journalism, which had a limited appeal (and was financially disastrous), with the kinds of popular journalistic techniques that were associated with the widely-circulating and profitable organs of the New Journalism. Newnes was anxious to make a contribution to the Liberal party, but political journalism was clearly unprofitable. He was not only a Liberal, but also a successful publisher and businessman. *The Westminster Gazette* represented an attempt to juggle business instincts and political loyalties.

Newnes also stepped into the breach, as he had done with *The Westminster* , when the Swansea Liberal paper the *Cambria Daily Leader* (a pioneer of the Welsh daily press) was in danger of being absorbed by its Conservative rival, the *Post*. He initially intimated that he did not want to buy the *Leader*, on both ideological and commercial grounds. He thought it undesirable that an MP should own the public prints of his own constituency, and he was unable to give adequate supervision to a business at Swansea. But he eventually agreed to buy it out of loyalty to the Liberal cause. 'He was too good a party man', Friederichs claimed, 'to let a Liberal organ, for want of what was to him an unimportant sum, fall into the hands of the Conservatives.'[14] No doubt his own local political prospects would not have been harmed by the decision.

---

[13] Hulda Friederichs, *The Life of Sir George Newnes, Bart*, London: Hodder and Stoughton, 1911, p.158.

[14] Ibid., p.170.

Country Life, appearing in January 1897, was owned in equal shares by Hudson and Kearns, and George Newnes, Ltd, and George Newnes was closely associated with its development.[15] The publishing and advertising was done from Newnes's office in Southampton St, although the paper itself was housed in Tavistock St. This magazine was an early and successful experiment in pictorial printing. The publisher's aim was to produce a weekly illustrated paper of the highest quality that would get the best possible results from half-tone blocks. And the first issue boasted that:

> The finest pictorial printing machinery available, which has been specially built in America for the production of the paper, has been imported and erected by Messrs Hudson and Kearns.[16]

Newnes learnt much from the experiment, and *The Wide World Magazine* and *The Ladies' Field*, both established in the following year, drew upon the production techniques developed through *Country Life*.

'As you follow the path leading to [Newnes's] place in the history of English literature', Friederichs observed, 'you see that every step is connected with the one preceding it; as one link in the long chain of his successes was finished, the next link was being forged, and joined adroitly and quite simply to the rest.'[17] Thus *The Strand* was founded through Newnes relinquishing the *Review of Reviews*. *The Wide World Magazine* was established in 1898 as a response to the accumulation of stories sent to the editor of *The Strand* by readers in remote parts of the world, claiming that they were factual accounts. It was an expression of Newnes's enthusiasm for the expansion of the communications network, the development of new technologies and the rise of internationalism, and of his patriotic zeal for the spread of Britons and other white, 'civilised', western peoples all over the globe. The phrase 'wide world' was a catchphrase at the turn of the century, and the magazine's motto, 'Truth is Stranger than Fiction', was also popular currency. *The Wide World* explored new spatial, temporal and imperialist perspectives, through a range of 'true stories of extraordinary human endurance' including travel, missionary and hunting tales, and through photographs, illustrations and maps.

This magazine also had a kind of biographical impetus, since Newnes had both travelled extensively in foreign lands himself, and invested politically (as a Liberal-Imperialist) and financially in geographical expansion. The Borchgrevink Antarctic Expedition, leaving Britain on 22 August, 1898, was sponsored by Newnes to the tune of £38,000. Borchgrevink named Lady Newnes Bay after Newnes's wife, and a promontory westward of Cape Washington was named

---

[15] When, in 1905, *Country Life* became a company in its own right, its directors were George Newnes and his son Frank Newnes, Edward Hudson and his son William Hudson.

[16] Bernard Darwin, *Fifty Years of Country Life*, London: Country Life Ltd, 1947, pp.14-15.

[17] Hulda Friederichs, op. cit., p.125.

Newnes Land 'after the generous Maecenas of the expedition, Sir George Newnes, Bart'.[18] Friederichs described Newnes's role in the expedition as an engagement with the heroic desire to explore what were literally the 'ends of the earth':

> [it represented] the generous endeavour to assist in discovering the secrets of the ends of the earth which the ages have passed like dreams and shadows, and on the barren soil and among the endless snowfields of which the conqueror man is now at last setting his footsteps.[19]

It was this spirit of discovery and high endeavour that animated *The Wide World*, which itself carried many narratives of polar exploration.

Newnes was also one of the principal directors of the British Commonwealth Oil Corporation, formed with a capital of £1.5 million to develop the oil shale industry in the Wolgan Valley, in the western Blue Mountains of New South Wales. *The Times* reported the plan in terms which echoed the rhetoric of entrepreneurialism with which Newnes was constantly associated, and the language of imperialism ('opening up') used in *The Wide World Magazine*:

> Seeing that the bulk of the money invested in the Commonwealth has been provided by British capitalists, it will be interesting to watch this opening up of the dormant sources of Australasian wealth.[20]

In 1906, the Company obtained leases in the Wolgan Valley, and built a rail-link from Newnes Junction to Newnes (the site of future operations in the Wolgan Valley). The town was named after George Newnes, and its story was one of economic development paralleling those which, focussed on many regions of the world but particularly on the U.S., filled the pages of *The Wide World Magazine*.

In a journalistic sense too, Newnes was committed to geographical expansion. *Under the Union Jack*, founded in November 1899 when the Boer War was gathering momentum, served as an explicit reminder of this. It was a twenty-four page, twopenny, weekly illustrated magazine which utilised extensive photographic material to mobilise support for British forces in South Africa, and keep the public informed about the events of the Boer War. And it acted as a focus for patriotic sentiment.[21]

---

[18] C.E. Borchgrevink, *First on the Antarctic Continent: Being an Account of the British Antarctic Expedition, 1898-1900* (intro. by Tore Gjelsvik), London: C. Hurst and Co., 1980, p.263 (first published in U.K. by George Newnes, Ltd, London, 1901).

[19] Hulda Friederichs, op. cit., p.218.

[20] *The Times*, 1 May, 1908, p.4.

[21] The opening editorial of *Under the Union Jack* captured the imperialist flavour of the magazine:

If *Tit-Bits*, *The Strand* and *The Million* were the products of an experimental, creative, building phase in George Newnes's periodical publishing career, then *The Westminster Gazette* and *The Wide World Magazine* were the inventions of a successful and accomplished publisher, and a well-informed, well-connected, well-travelled public man. Both were a result of the financial successes, journalistic techniques, and journalistic and political contacts forged in the previous ten years. *The Westminster* was an expression of Newnes's commitment to political Liberalism, and *The Wide World* an expression of his enthusiasm for imperialism and for the expansion of the geographical horizons of the British people. Yet neither was merely that. Each represented the introduction and application of new techniques, in combination with the continuation of established traditions, and the pioneering of new formats. And both, but particularly the more overtly 'political' and 'serious' *Westminster*, were embroiled in debates over the New Journalism which Newnes (and others) had been credited with inventing in the 1880s.

The war in South Africa is certainly the most important business Englishmen have been engaged in since the India Mutiny .... We are looking on at a tremendous drama that will group largely in the story of our imperial expansion .... It is the pulse of empire that is beating, and the future beckons us forward. Such things are not to be underrated, for we are the heirs of our history, and it is the past that points the way. (*Under the Union Jack*, 1, 1 (November 1899), p.3)

3

A Bold Stroke of Mingled Business and Benevolence

The Westminster Gazette (1893)

George Newnes argued in his autobiographical notes that *The Westminster Gazette*, the Liberal daily newspaper which he established in 1893, represented an attempt to exert 'influence' rather than a scheme to generate popularity and thus profits:

> There are two kinds of political papers; one which aims at a large circulation and large profits, and another which strives for influence amongst thoughtful people. The latter is what *The Westminster Gazette* has always been.[1]

There was an element of defensiveness, however, in Newnes's insistence on *The Westminster*'s non-commercial manifesto - its pretensions to being an influential 'journal of opinion'. Identified with the outstanding commercial success *Tit-Bits*, he was largely associated with 'popular' journalism. This was his first foray into daily political journalism. As a Liberal MP who was committed to his party, Newnes wished to make a contribution to the Liberal cause. Yet he was also a businessman and a successful publisher. *The Westminster Gazette* was developed according to its proprietor's need to balance political and commercial imperatives.

The political press was a feature of British journalism, and its nature and dynamics have been examined in a number of studies. Brewer has explored the close links between party politics and the press in the eighteenth century, and has shown that in the 1760s, politicians engaged in public controversy through pamphlets and contributions to the *Gazette* and *Public Advertiser*. Aspinall has surveyed the system prevailing in the succeeding period, in which press and politics were closely integrated through subsidies, pressure exerted upon editors,

---

[1]   George Newnes as cited in Hulda Friederichs, *The Life of Sir George Newnes, Bart*, London: Hodder and Stoughton, 1911, pp.240-241. *The Westminster Gazette* will generally be referred to here (for the sake of brevity and in line with some contemporary commentaries) as *The Westminster*.

the provision of exclusive news and advertising preferences.[2] Aspinall concluded his analysis in the middle of the century speculating that a consideration of nineteenth-century conditions and the increasing prosperity of the press would uncover a loosening of the links between the press and a parliamentary machine with bribes and threats at its disposal. Yet more recent studies by Alan Lee (*The Origins of the Popular Press*) and Stephen Koss (*The Rise and Fall of the Political Press in Britain*) have shown that on the contrary, political intervention continued and that, in the early twentieth century, Fleet St enjoyed unmatched political authority. Indeed, developments in New Journalism were closely connected with the various strands of late Victorian and Edwardian Liberalism, and journalists such as Spender played a key role in the formulation and mediation of Liberal social and political thought.

Koss has examined the remaining collection of newspapers with distinct political intentions and connections, evaluating journalism as political performance in its party political setting. He has shown that the connections between party politics and the press remained transparent and direct, with gradual alterations, well into the twentieth century. The political press promoted political causes and attended to the needs of electoral organisation. Papers such as *The Westminster Gazette* were deemed 'capable of rousing public conscience, facilitating (or retarding) the passage of legislation, and fuelling intra-party rivalries', readers and writers alike sustaining the traditional myth of the Fourth Estate.[3] With few alternatives to the press as a medium for propaganda, divisions in the Liberal and Conservative camps acting to increase journalistic intervention, and the emergence of the Labour Party acting as another restorative, the press maintained a pervasive influence.

Koss has comprehensively explored *The Westminster*'s partisan political and traditional aspects. Yet Newnes's paper also maintained strong links with the innovations of New Journalism, synthesising retrospective and modernising tendencies, and combining political views with popular techniques. And both its critics and apologists self-consciously problematised the combination, and reflected on the implications of the notion of journalistic independence. In the Edwardian period, as James Startt has shown, a symbiotic relationship existed between quality and popular journalism. 'Good journalism' and 'New Journalism', far from being incompatible, both benefited from this relationship. Newspapers of the period embodied the combination of 'political passion and journalistic skill'. These years, according to Startt, saw 'the triumph of the New Journalism as a constructive germination of the new and the old'.[4]

---

[2] John Brewer, *Party Ideology and Popular Politics at the Accession of George III*, and Arthur Aspinall, *Politics and the Press, C1780-1850*, as cited in Lucy Brown, *Victorian News and Newspapers*, Oxford: Clarendon, 1985, p.54.

[3] Stephen Koss, *The Rise and Fall of the Political Press in Britain*, Chapel Hill: University of North Carolina Press, 1984, pp.3-10.

[4] James D. Startt, 'Good Journalism in the Era of New Journalism: The British Press, 1902-1914', in Joel Wiener (ed.), *Papers for the Millions: The New Journalism in Britain, 1850s-1914*, New York: Greenwood Press, 1988, p.294, 275-298. *The Westminster Gazette,*

For all the value of his work, Koss has neglected the commercial and novel side of Newnes's paper. This chapter is an attempt to reinstate the 'popular' aspect of *The Westminster*, and to explore the intricate relationship that existed between 'good journalism' and New Journalism in the late nineteenth and early twentieth centuries: the distinctions (and points of contact) between 'commercial' and 'serious' ('popular' and 'quality') journalism. It seeks thus to add a new perspective to the historiography of New Journalism and the political press, and of contemporary British politics. And it serves to demonstrate the complex but interconnected nature of Newnes's world view, and the adaptability of his entrepreneurial skills. It will focus on a number of aspects of *The Westminster*: the eclectic complexity of the paper's textual form; the methods and features employed to promote the paper's 'influence'; the textual representation of the relationship between Newnes as a politically committed *and* commercially successful newspaper proprietor, and *The Westminster* as an organ of the partisan political press; and the ways in which the unruly synthesis between 'quality' and 'popular' elements was manifested in the paper's political narratives, and in the debates surrounding it. This newspaper was quintessentially a combination of 'political passion and journalistic skill' - the passion and skill of its proprietor, George Newnes, and of its staff.

The Westminster Gazette, a penny Liberal newspaper which ranged between eight and twelve pages over the thirty years of its publication, first appeared on 31 January, 1893. It was perhaps no coincidence that it appeared on this, the first day of the Home Rule session of 1893, since Newnes, then MP for the Newmarket division of Cambridgeshire, voted with Gladstone for Home Rule. 'Sir George was a keen politician', wrote H. Simonis in *The Street of Ink: An Intimate History of Journalism* (1917), 'and he stepped into the breach in consequence of the defection from Liberalism of the *Pall Mall Gazette*.'[5] He continued to direct and subsidise the publication for the next sixteen years, spending over £100,000 on its maintenance. *The Westminster* was certainly far from commercially successful (although the losses incurred by its publisher were not large compared with those borne by other proprietors of 'political' papers), a fact which must always underpin any discussion of its character.[6]

When Lord Astor bought the *PMG* in 1892 and turned it again into a Conservative organ, the editorial staff, including E.T. Cook and J.A. Spender, resigned. In a rescue operation for which he was highly praised Newnes founded *The Westminster Gazette*, employing Cook as Editor and Spender as Assistant

---

according to Startt, was one of a group of influential papers including *The Times, Daily Chronicle, Daily News, Daily Telegraph* and *Morning Post* that represented this creative synthesis.

   [5] H. Simonis, *The Street of Ink: An Intimate History of Journalism*, London: Cassell, 1917, p.99.

   [6] Viscount Cambrose, *British Newspapers and their Controllers*, London: Cassell, 1947, p.7. The *Tribune*, for instance, a Liberal journal started by Thomasson amidst the election of January 1906, lost somewhere between £200,000 and £600,000 in the two years before its demise. See Stephen Koss, op. cit., p.60.

Editor. 'I have heard that the PMG is to become a Unionist organ', he wrote to Cook on 8 October, 1892:

> If so, would you be disposed to enter into an arrangement to start another penny evening along the old lines of the PMG? A scheme of this kind has been running through my head, and I think would find favour with some of the leading men of the party.[7]

It clearly did find favour, and Newnes was rewarded in 1895 with a baronetcy. In 1896, when Cook resigned to edit the Liberal *Daily News*, Spender became the paper's editor, and he remained so until it became a morning journal in 1921.

This, then, was a paper that was associated with one of the period's most influential editors. Spender, an Oxford graduate like E.T. Cook, was an extremely prolific writing editor, contributing each day's front-page leader, as well as many thousands of special articles and book reviews. He was representative of a process, partly the product of the spirit of Liberal reformism dominant at Oxford and Cambridge, which saw graduates like him seriously pursuing journalism as a career from the 1860s onwards. They gravitated, however, to a relatively limited range of London newspapers and periodicals.[8] *The Westminster*'s three-paragraph front-page leader was one of its most characteristic and influential features, representing both the views of the editor and the political commitment of the proprietor. Spender claimed to have learnt much of the art of controversial writing from John Henry Newman. He recollected that an attempt to revamp *The Westminster*'s format by placing the leader on the second page provoked considerable outrage amongst readers.[9] But Newnes's paper also featured carefully sub-edited articles and literary material, and cartoons by F.C. Gould (another immensely popular feature).

The Westminster was an influential organ of 'cultivated Radicalism' according to contemporaries, despite its relatively small circulation of 20,000. Although there is little in the way of detailed information as to the paper's circulation, it is clear from the correspondence columns that the readers of *The Westminster* were mainly educated and middle class: 'City men', 'inveterate readers', commuters on trains or buses, people engaged in literary work, readers of the old *PMG*, men who perused the newspaper at their clubs or belonged to Liberal institutions on whose tables the publisher offered to place specimen

---

[7]   Newnes to Cook, as cited in J. Saxon Mills, *Sir Edward Cook, K.B.E.: A Biography*, London: Constable, 1921, p.127.

[8]   Spender began by contributing to the *Temple Bar*, *Truth* and *PMG* whilst still at Oxford. When he went to the *PMG* in 1892, he wrote that he had 'not only security of tenure, but the place which, of all others, had been most envied by the young Oxford men of my own time who dreamed of journalism'. In this context, his idealisation of Newnes as an employer who offered remarkable conditions and security to the staff of *The Westminster* is unsurprising.

[9]   J.A. Spender, *Life, Journalism and Politics*, London: Cassell, 1927, vol. 2, p.155.

copies. They lived, as the addresses given by correspondents indicated, in the well-off inner regions of London such as St John's Wood and The Strand. Members of the London County Council were typical of its readership. 'Your first issue seemed to be in the hands of nearly all the members of the London County Council to-day', observed one reader, 'and I saw more than one member scanning its contents in the Council Chamber during the sitting!'[10] The self-educated working-class reader occasionally joined the ranks. 'I wish, as a London artisan', wrote one such auto-didact, 'to welcome *The Westminster Gazette*. Its parent, the *PMG* [sic] was for years a source of instruction to me.[11]

In format, style and character, *The Westminster Gazette* reflected developments in the evening, Liberal and political presses, as well as representing a combination of 'popular' and 'quality' elements.[12] Like other newspapers of the period, it contained a substantial and increasing sporting component which included reports on golf, racing, and later field sports such as cricket and Rugby football.[13] It also offered City pages, a feature which, having evolved out of the mid-century business sections of London papers, was an integral part of the well-informed daily newspaper, with its own conventions of style and content.[14] *The Westminster*'s foreign news, like that of other metropolitan evening papers, was a compound of reports from Reuters and from the paper's own correspondent, and the comments of British political figures, and was particularly concentrated on Continental Europe.

As a Liberal paper, *The Westminster* also represented the traditions and innovations of the late nineteenth-century Liberal press. To a certain extent, George Newnes and Edward Lloyd (of *Lloyd's Weekly News*) were the beneficiaries of Liberal experiments in trustification through which the Liberal press had been built up by adventurers such as Labouchere and plutocrats such as Samuel Morley, Sir John Brunner and J.J. Coleman. They in turn were the forerunners of later publishing magnates such as Harmsworth and Pearson. 'For nearly two generations', Stephen Koss has observed, 'Liberal industrialists had vied with one another for the privilege of investing in newspaper enterprises.' These men generally boasted unexceptional origins and nonconformist backgrounds, and assumed newspaper obligations as 'an obvious way to render service and to secure social and political advancement'.[15]

---

[10] *Westminster Gazette*, 2 February, 1893, p.10.

[11] *Westminster Gazette*, 4 February, 1893, p.9.

[12] In the years between 1890 and 1914, the evening press of the capital consisted of four penny papers which catered to the 'educated classes' (*Westminster Gazette, Pall Mall Gazette, Globe* and *Evening Standard*) and two halfpenny papers which appealed to a wider audience and made a speciality of sporting news (*Evening News* and *Star*).

[13] *The Westminster* only published a record of results and odds. There were no tipsters in this paper, as Spender was careful to stress. See J.A. Spender, op. cit., vol. 2, p.152.

[14] The City pages contained impressive reports of share prices, commodity markets and other commercial concerns. By the 1890s, they had grown in range and sophistication.

[15] Stephen Koss, op. cit., p.42.

A Liberal MP in the House of Commons for twenty years, Newnes sought partly to gain the respect of party officials, as well as social prestige and influence in establishing this paper. He humbly described himself as 'a quiet member', though 'perhaps a useful one in many ways'.[16] His utility as the proprietor of *The Westminster* was largely extra-mural. Thus Newnes reminded Gladstone on 19 December, 1905 of his commitment to the Liberal cause in supporting *The Westminster Gazette*:

> For ten years I lost £10,000 per annum, and never asked any one of the party for any help ....
> I believe it is written that the Westminster Gazette has supplied an effective weapon to the Liberal party, and has been a powerful influence for the principles which we advocate. This could not have been achieved unless I had personally taken upon myself a great responsibility.[17]

He was not the only commercially successful publisher to seek political respectability through 'serious' political journalism. C.A. Pearson and Alfred Harmsworth (later Lord Northcliffe) engaged in similar campaigns.[18]

By the first decade of the twentieth century, wealthy Liberals such as Newnes, who had formerly served the party by subsidising the press, mostly preferred to realise their obligations by simple donation. This resulted in a spate of closures and amalgamations, and Liberal papers became a declining force in Fleet St, with *The Westminster Gazette* being the only Liberal paper to approach the influence of its Conservative rivals.[19] In 1905, Newnes was agreeing 'to subscribe largely to the Election Fund', possibly contemplating the sale of *The Westminster Gazette* which was to take place three years later.[20] Since 1893, though he never let Spender see that he was 'straining his fortunes', he had undertaken the financial support of the paper.[21] Newnes's decision to sell *The Westminster* may also have been partly a result of the improvement of his party's political fortunes. 'Liberal politicians', Spender later observed, equipped with a

---

[16] George Newnes to Herbert Gladstone, (19 December, 1905), Viscount Gladstone Papers, BL, Add. MS. 46063, f.227b.

[17] Ibid.

[18] Alfred Harmsworth owned the *Morning Advertiser*, *Daily Mail* and *Daily Mirror*, retained the *Southern Daily Mail* at Portsmouth as a souvenir of his candidacy there in 1895, and bid twice for *The Times* before obtaining it in 1908. He craved to be taken seriously, having obtained the title of Lord Northcliffe in 1905. (He had earlier complained that Newnes had been rewarded for his journalistic services to politics whilst he himself had remained unacknowledged.) And he sought, through *The Times* to impress his widening circle of social and political contacts. See Stephen Koss, op. cit., p.35.

[19] See Stephen Koss, op. cit., p.76.

[20] Newnes to Herbert Gladstone, (19 December, 1905). It wasn't until 1908 that, after various rumours about the state of his fortunes, he sold *The Westminster* to a Liberal syndicate headed by Sir Alfred Mond. It was later purchased by the Social Service Trust, which had merged with the Starmer-Morrell group. See Stephen Koss, op. cit., pp.41-43.

[21] J.A. Spender, op. cit., vol 2, p.41.

massive majority in the new Parliament, after the electoral victory of 1906, 'seemed to be in a position in which they were beyond the good or evil that newspapers could do, or the need of their assistance.'[22] Ironically, electoral victory seemed to signal the beginnings of the decline of Liberal political journalism. Newnes had supported *The Westminster* from 1893, when Gladstone was urging a largely reluctant party and Parliament to vote for Home Rule, thus dividing the party and undermining its political credibility, to 1908, when the party had once again settled into power after a convincing win at the polls in 1905-1906. His investment certainly represented the assumption of 'great personal responsibility' for the Liberal cause.

Yet unlike many other backbenchers who engaged in this form of political service, Newnes came to political journalism *through journalism* (and publishing) and not merely through politics. *The Westminster* was thus not merely a publication established in an attempt 'to amplify his public voice, to defend constituency interests, and generally to impress the party chiefs by his dedication'.[23] It developed out of experiences and connections other than political ones, and was almost as much a product of journalistic techniques pioneered by Newnes through experiments in New Journalism such as *Tit-Bits* and *The Strand* as it was a product of pure political fervour and ambition.

The interview, the parliamentary sketch, the black-and-white illustration: all of these were characteristic features of the New Journalism employed extensively in *The Strand* and transferred to *The Westminster*. And the promotional schemes and competitions for which Newnes had become well-known in connection with *Tit-Bits* were adapted with considerable success to the aims and audience of *The Westminster*. This paper may not have been 'popular' in the sense that its circulation was large, but it employed a variety of 'popular' techniques to arouse and maintain the interest of its reading community. 'Publisher's Announcements', a regular column from 1895, was a singular record of the publishing boom that had seen the success of a plethora of popular periodicals such as those that had enabled Newnes to fund *The Westminster*, and in fact featured advertisements for a range of Newnes's periodical publications.[24] This column is a symbol of the link, through Newnes's commercial profile as a publisher, between his 'political' and 'popular' publications.

There is compelling evidence, as Lucy Brown has noted, to suggest that journalists of the period were generally committed to the causes they espoused in their columns, and the staff of *The Westminster* represented a particularly clear case of this. Almost all of *The Westminster* staff were the 'old guard' from the *PMG*. Many of them stayed at *The Westminster* for the entire twenty-six years

---

[22] J.A. Spender, op. cit., vol. 1, p.134.

[23] Stephen Koss, op. cit., p.8.

[24] These included *Tit-Bits* (a fact that is significant given the debate over the readership of *Tit-Bits* and the orthodoxy that its audience, unlike that of *The Westminster*, was working class), *The Westminster Budget*, *The Wide World Magazine*, *The Strand*, *The Ladies' Field* and *Country Life*.

of Spender's editorship, probably as a result of a combination of factors which included the security offered by Newnes as an employer and the stability created by the continuous collaboration of proprietor and editor, as well as the staff's political commitment. The political and editorial consistency inherent in such an arrangement appears to confirm the persistence of traditional formats. Such consistency also constitutes a basic precondition for this exploration of the recurrent editorial preoccupations and distinctive journalistic characteristics of *The Westminster*. The coherence and organisation of the journalistic product certainly increased the editor or proprietor's ability to pursue effective journalistic campaigns.[25] Nevertheless, the staff of *The Westminster* were by no means lacking in connections with the innovations of New Journalism, nor limited to the narrowly political or the conventional.

F.C. Gould was assistant editor to Spender, an unusual choice given his lack of editorial experience, or indeed any experience in 'serious' political journalism. Gould had produced the political sketches that accompanied Henry Lucy's series, 'From Behind the Speaker's Chair', in *The Strand*. He was, according to Spender, 'a capable and keen politician, whose advice was worth seeking', and whose position enabled Spender to have leader and cartoon working in step. The partnership lasted until the First World War. Newnes allowed Gould a very free hand with his cartoons, and they were given considerable prominence in the paper.[26] Charles Geake was Spender's assistant leader-writer. A distinguished Cambridge mathematician and former Fellow of Clare College, he had a gift for storing up the past speeches of public men, and with *Westminster* 'Notes', according to Spender, 'supplied a whole generation of Liberal politicians with ammunition for the platform, and made himself a wholesome terror to the other side'. At the same time, he wrote light verse and rhyming impromptus (signed L.E.C.).[27] William Hill, later editor of the *Weekly Despatch* and *Tribune*, was the paper's news editor.

The more prominent contributors to *The Westminster* included Arthur Conan Doyle, P.F. Warner and Colonel A'Court Repington. Doyle was sent by *The Westminster* to Omdurman to obtain his first experience as a war correspondent in the campaign in which Kitchener became famous. He later wrote a pamphlet on the Boer War which was designed to promote sympathy for the British cause within Europe, and was remarkably successful. It was reprinted in *The Wide World*. Warner, who accompanied a number of English cricket teams to Australia, acted as a correspondent of the paper, writing popular articles on the sport. He later became the 'Athletic Editor' of Newnes's popular boys'

[25] See Lucy Brown, *Victorian News and Newspapers*, Oxford: Clarendon, 1985, pp.250-254. Brown has argued that even in the 1890s, incoming news was handled with little attempt at collation and organisation, and discrete items appeared in an uncompiled fashion rather than being shaped into a coherent body of reading. It was the genius of men like Harmsworth and Stead, according to Brown, that they deployed their paper's resources in a co-ordinated fashion in order to pursue effective journalistic campaigns.

[26] H. Simonis, op. cit., p.100.

[27] J.A. Spender, op. cit., vol 2, p.63.

magazine, *The Captain*. Colonel A'Court Repington was *The Westminster*'s military correspondent, and later became the military correspondent of *The Times*. The writers of *The Westminster*, then, represented a reasonably diverse range of journalistic perspectives and associations, some old and some new, some political and some 'popular'.

Political news was given prominence in the leader, suggesting that this journal retained some of the features of the political press, and highlighting the crucial role played by journalists such as Spender in Liberal parliamentary politics and in the populist mediation of 'new Liberal' ideas. *The Westminster*, wrote Spender, 'made politics its chief concern, and laid itself out to convert and persuade by its writing. Its readers bought it quite as much for its views as its news.'[28] The evening clubland papers, which included the *Pall Mall Gazette* and the *St James's Gazette*, as well as *The Westminster*, were especially geared towards the presentation of 'views', as parliamentary reporting declined in the newspaper press. They did not give the day's news as such, but represented the demand for more analysis than was provided by the morning papers, and more topical material than weekly or monthly periodicals offered to readers.

Spender made a practice of writing at least three leaders in succession (often four or five) on any subject which he felt to be particularly important, a method which went against the modernist trend of frequent changes in the subjects of principal leading articles, and contrasted starkly with the paragraphic technique of a popular paper such as *Tit-Bits*. The readers of a 'newspaper of opinion' (the politically-aware reading community), he suggested, did not want the same variety in their leading articles as they demanded in their news. 'This was what the serious reader wanted', he claimed, 'and my business was to provide it'. He went on to link narrative continuity to the newspaper's reputation for political sincerity:

> The psychological approaches to news and opinion are two different things; and if a newspaper takes up a subject with apparent earnestness and conviction and then drops it or only returns to it after many days, the reader is checked and disappointed.[29]

Thus the political potency of the paper was assumed to be a function of a traditional form of narrative continuity and editorial consistency. And readers of *The Westminster* were constantly reminded of the editor's consistency as Spender verified his case through insistent inter-referencing.[30]

---

[28]   Ibid., p.134.

[29]   Ibid., p.160.

[30]   This was particularly the case with his editorial treatment of important political issues such as the Boer War. Thus he recalled on 19 September, 1900: 'Inevitable, for our part, we have always held it to be from the moment that the first shot was fired, and our readers will bear us out that from the beginning of October last we have never hesitated to express that view, even when it brought us into collision with the Prime Minister himself.' See *Westminster Gazette*, 19 September, 1900, p.1.

Yet whilst its front page political leader connected *The Westminster* with older journalistic traditions and with political society, many other features of the paper were innovative and modernist. The editor's 'business' extended beyond the provision of the traditional political leader. The column which accompanied the front page leader was also an immensely popular feature. It often consisted of a biographical sketch, with the first issue featuring 'A Day in the Life of a Cabinet Minister', and being followed by sketches of the Foreign Secretary and the Colonial Secretary. This collection of sketches was succeeded by a series entitled 'Round the Courts', very much after the fashion of Henry Lucy's 'From Behind the Speaker's Chair' in *The Strand* or 'Peeps at Parliament' in *Punch*. The column featured F.C. Gould's popular 'Alice in Blunderland' series during the Khaki Election of 1900, as well as A.D. Hope's 'The Dolly Dialogues' - his first venture into literature. In *The Westminster*'s reporting of the Jameson Raid, Spender's leaders were invariably accompanied by illustrated biographical articles about key figures such as Dr Jameson and President Kruger.[31] Other contributors to this column included Grant Allen (a well-known popular writer who wrote for *The Strand*), W.T. Stead and Frederick Greenwood (both of whom were associated with the New Journalism), M.H. Spielmann and William Archer. This innovative feature functioned to give the paper individuality and link it to the modernising tendencies of the New Journalism.

Another feature which represented the modernising spirit of *The Westminster*'s proprietor was a series on 'Mems about Men of the Moment', sub-titled 'Transvaal Celebrities as Seen by a Uitlander'. The term 'Mems' was characteristic of a number of popular Newnes publications, as were the catchy alliteration and assonance of the title. And the series of biographical sketches of 'celebrities' was a phenomenon intimately associated with *The Strand*'s 'Portraits of Celebrities' feature.[32] Newnes's paper was also a pioneer in the publication of the serial in a daily newspaper. 'The Dictator', by Justin McCarthy, began in the first issue. The daily portions, however, were so much reduced in length by the demands of news space that the story dragged over many months and was published by Cassells in full and volume form before the daily parts were complete. The serial, the staple fodder of a popular monthly such as *The Strand*, was obviously inappropriate to a daily newspaper.

George Newnes brought illustrations to almost every form of periodical, and the daily newspaper was no exception. The directors of *The Westminster* prided themselves that it was the pioneer of illustrations in the evening press, containing in its early numbers 'a bevy of illustrations which have not been equalled since'.[33] Newnes's earlier attempt to establish the *Daily Courier*

---

[31] On 4 January, 1896, Spender's leader on the German Emperor's telegram to Kruger shared the front page with an illustrated article entitled 'About Dr Jameson. Personal Recollections and Anecdotes'. And on 6 January, W.T. Stead contributed a front page article entitled '"Dr Jim" of Berlin'.

[32] *Westminster Gazette*, 10 January, 1893, p.3.

[33] H. Simonis, op. cit., p.102.

reflected his belief in the demand for pictures, but the picture paper was only to gain popularity slightly later. F.C. Gould's cartoons and caricatures were integral to the impact and success of *The Westminster*, and through the many years of his association with the paper, Gould became very popular with its readers.

Gould's caricatures familiarised the public with the features of various actors on the political stage. The stage was exactly the image which he evoked in depicting the Khaki Election of 1900. He depicted the self-conscious posturing of Conservative politicians, attempting to manipulate the voting public as a kind of variety stage show or fancy dress ball dedicated to the theme of militaristic self-congratulation. The cartoon, entitled 'Dressing Up', sought to undercut the seriousness of the Conservative campaign by denuding its leaders (*see Figure 9*). 'The striking features of this General Election', one reader commented, 'have been brought into bold relief by the remarkable cartoons of Mr F.C. Gould.' This reader went on to draw the same theatrical parallel as this cartoon evoked:

> These able cartoons emphasise the fact that this is a Khaki Election under the control of Mr Chamberlain as the sole manager of the show.[34]

Thus black-and-white illustrations were deployed to support the political campaign, highlighting the heightened importance and popularity of the art as it gained impetus from new technological developments. Other political campaigns produced equally memorable images. Lord Rosebery appeared in various guises, one of the most famous of which was his depiction as the charwoman anxious to spring-clean the House of Lords, when reform to the bicameral system was the subject of hot debate. In November 1905, Gould produced a playful image on the tariff reform issue entitled 'A Nightmare Bunker' as *The Westminster* revelled in the prospect of Conservative electoral defeat (*see Figure 10*).[35]

Like other newspapers of the period, *The Westminster* contained a substantial sporting component, covering horseracing, rowing, rugby (Union), Association football, cricket, boxing, athletics, cycling and golf. Two full columns were regularly devoted to such subjects. Golf had recently been imported to England from Scotland, and the great golfer Horace Hutchinson wrote a weekly article on the sport for *The Westminster*. This paper, Spender claims, was the first to begin engaging well-known cricketers to write regularly on the game. P.F. Warner undertook this task for many years, and was later succeeded by A.G. Faulkner. The sportsman-author was to become a feature of popular periodical literature. In a series of transformations which reflected the increasing journalistic and commercial importance of such sporting experts, the sportsman-author was

---

[34] *Westminster Gazette*, 17 October, 1900, p.2.

[35] Yet such performances were not entirely free of the code of etiquette that restricted the editorial licence exercised by 'journalist-politicians' such as Spender. In a number of cartoons on the Boer War, for instance, Gould depicted Chamberlain as a dog. When he heard that it gave offence to Chamberlain, however, he immediately desisted. See J.A. Spender, op. cit., vol 2, p.95.

promoted to a sub-editorial post in Newnes's magazine *The Captain* (P.F.Warner wrote as *The Captain*'s 'Athletic Editor'), and ultimately appeared as the editor and figurehead of the popular sporting magazine. (C.B. Fry, who had begun as the Athletic Editor of *The Captain* later became the editor of another Newnes publication, *C.B. Fry's Magazine.*)

Journalistic competitions were developed with considerable success by Newnes in *Tit-Bits*, and deemed to be intimately associated with the commercial tendencies of the New Journalism. *The Westminster* offered a plethora of competitions. H.F. Fox, then a tutor of Brasenose College, Oxford, set weekly passages of English poetry to be translated into some Greek or Latin metre in a column which, according to Spender, 'brought *The Westminster* into touch with the public schools and schoolmasters, and caused lively debates in Oxford and Cambridge Common Rooms'.[36] And various literary competitions were conducted by Miss Royde Smith. Spender characterised Smith as a kind of schoolteacher task-mistress:

> [Readers] poured out prose and poetry to any model and in any metre; they produced epigrams and aphorisms by the thousand; they were as ready with parodies as with epitaphs, and gave equally when she asked for pathos or for bathos. She snubbed and cuffed them, and they took it lying down, and only promised to do better next time.[37]

Many of the competitors were young literary men, but some, such as Lord Curzon, who sent in entries on occasion, were more distinguished. Spender monitored the column to recruit contributors. Thus an educated body of ostensibly 'serious' readers was hooked by an innovative journalistic technique, adapted to suit their interests and skills.

Probably one of the most novel features of *The Westminster*, however, was its material character. Newnes chose green paper for his journal, and said it would be 'the most elastic' of evening papers, arranged so that it could be printed in any size from eight to twelve pages.[38] The proprietor anticipated that the readership of *The Westminster* would be such that it would appreciate a little sensationalism, though not of an aggressive sort nor so bluntly commercial as that employed for advertising *Tit-Bits*. He therefore sought something amusing but subtle such as would lend itself to dinner-table talk and to discussion amongst 'theorists and cranks and riders of hobby horses'. It must be 'of sufficient importance to interest seriously minded people'.[39]

The debate about *The Westminster*'s colour revealed much about the paper's readers. 'What floated *The Westminster Gazette* on to an indifferent world was of course, the sudden discovery of Sir George Newnes that green was

---

[36] Ibid., p.146.

[37] Ibid.

[38] H. Simonis, op. cit., p.162.

[39] Hulda Friederichs, op. cit., pp.225-226.

the best colour for the reading man', according to Harold Spender. 'A newspaper printed on green paper' he went on to declare, 'suddenly became an optical necessity, ocularly demonstrable.' Spender claimed that in this scheme, 'the newspaper proprietors learnt for the first time - Newnes before Harmsworth - that a newspaper can be sold like any other article, by tickling the public ear'.[40] Newnes, of course, had already learnt his lesson from *Tit-Bits*. *The Westminster*'s colour represented an innovative application of the techniques of commercialism to the apparently 'serious' political newspaper. This publication was as much an attempt to 'tickle the public ear', in a variety of ways, as a transparent expression of the proprietor's commitment to toeing the party line. In fact, the two were related. By popularising *The Westminster*, Newnes hoped both to increase circulation and to spread the party message more widely.

Special attention was drawn to *The Westminster*'s green colour in the editorials and even in the generally political leading article. And it was carefully explained that the tint was supposed to be less trying on the eyesight than any other. It would therefore save the eyes of its readers who, whether in train, drawing-room or study, would read it under artificial light. 'In consultation with an oculist of great experience', wrote the editor, 'we have decided to give a trial the tint of paper which the reader now has before him - the tint of the fields, the trees and the billiard table.' (The intended audience, it is clear, was possessed of leisure time.) In fact, a number of eminent oculists had actually preached the doctrine of the superiority of green paper over white as a background for print. 'Our only desire', reiterated the apparently benevolent editor, 'is to conform to the comfort and convenience of our readers.'[41]

In good liberal-democratic fashion, the editor canvassed readers' opinions on the innovation, so that the fate of the colour of *The Westminster* might be decided by a plebiscite. This, the publisher suggested, was an attempt at journalistic reform. Considerable public debate followed, and *The Westminster* offices were swamped with letters expressing opinions on either side. 'Clearly', wrote the *Weekly Sun*, a week after the appearance of *The Westminster*, 'Mr Newnes knew what he was about when he went in for this bold stroke of mingled business and benevolence.'[42] The combination was one that epitomised the spirit of the entire publication.

Many apparently entered into discussion on the subject of 'The Wearing of the Green' (the title of the editorial correspondence column, which made implicit reference to the Irish Question that occupied the early issues). The paper was dubbed the 'Sea-Green Incorruptible' (a phrase used by Carlyle in his *French Revolution* to describe Robespierre), in an extension of the political rhetoric in which the discussion was couched. The debate extended into the clubs, hotels and the House of Commons itself, and brought into focus a number of

---

[40] Harold Spender, *The Fire of Life. A Book of Memories*, London: Hodder and Stoughton, 1859, p.38.

[41] *Westminster Gazette*, 31 January, 1893, p.1.

[42] *Weekly Sun*, cited in *Westminster Gazette*, 6 February, 1893, p.11.

contemporary preoccupations: the modern condition of commuting, the issue of reading and light conditions in contemporary society, and the rhetoric of scientific experimentation.

'Evening papers', it was contended, were 'largely read by persons going home in badly lighted railway carriages, omnibuses, & c.' In such surroundings they were jolted around and subjected to bad light conditions.[43] Many readers put the 'experiment' to the test on their journey home from the city in the 'dim light' or 'semi-darkness' to which, as one reader complained 'most Railway Companies persist in consigning the travelling public at night'.[44] This was an age which saw the introduction of electric light. (Newnes was an early convert, and the house at Putney was converted to electricity in the early 1890s.) The spread of the newspaper-reading habit, especially a buy-your-own mentality, as Brown has pointed out, was partly related to improving lighting in houses and clubs.[45] 'The Westminster Gazette is an ornament to our club', wrote one club-going Liberal, 'and in the glare of the electric light its delicate green tint ... is as refreshing to the eye as the contents of the paper are to the mind of ... A LIBERAL.'[46] On the other hand, the green tint was credited with improving visibility in the 'bad light' of railway carriages, often lit with gas.

This was also an age interested in the idea of scientific experimentation and admiring of the rhetoric of science, and a number of readers engaged in the discussion by providing their own technical and scientific supporting evidence for the ocular benefits of green paper.[47] In the end, Prime Minister Gladstone's vote tipped the balance in favour of green, and The Westminster remained green from then on. Just as he had tapped into a range of contemporary preoccupations in promoting Tit-Bits and The Million, so Newnes appealed to a variety of potential readers in publicising The Westminster Gazette.

If this scheme was a manifestation of Newnes's adept application of the techniques of modern publicity to the old-fashioned 'journal of opinion', his influence was felt in a variety of ways in The Westminster. He was both a politically committed and commercially successful newspaper proprietor. His establishment of this paper was certainly a reflection of his political idealism (with Spender acting as a kind of proxy), and of his desire to serve the cause of Liberalism through partisan political journalism. Yet the way in which the figure of the proprietor was handled textually in The Westminster Gazette suggests that a new model of partisan journalism, complicated by concerns about the relationship between the promotional techniques of political and commercial journalism, and governed by strict rules of propriety, was developing at the turn of the century, a time when there was considerable public discussion of 'the

---

[43] Westminster Gazette, 31 January, 1893, p.1.

[44] Westminster Gazette, 1 February, 1893, p.9.

[45] Lucy Brown, op. cit., p.29.

[46] Westminster Gazette, 1 February, 1893, p.9.

[47] See, for example, Westminster Gazette, 1 February, 1893, p.9; and Westminster Gazette, 2 February, 1893, p.10.

problem of the Press' in relation to party politics. Newnes was rendered in discussions of the paper and the text itself not as a blindly loyal party man, but as a complex combination of the model employer, the independent journalist, the contemporary radical liberal, the beneficent 'Gentleman George' and the publishing entrepreneur, whose image as a partisan proprietor was hedged in by self-consciousness about the nature of contemporary political journalism. His identity was an ambiguous marriage of political loyalty and a self-reflexive form of journalistic independence.

In discussions about the alleged spread of corruption in the early decades of the twentieth century, as G.R. Searle has shown, 'the problem of the Press' and the issue of 'honours trafficking' between political parties and press barons attracted outspoken and continuing criticism.[48] Radical anti-Imperialists such as Hobson and Hirst believed that South African financiers and mineowners had manipulated the press in a way which partially caused the outbreak of the Second Boer War. Moreover, with the prospect of an increasingly commercially successful and therefore financially independent press, the circulation of which crossed barriers of class and party, political parties tended to confer titles on their supporters amongst newspaper proprietors as a method of press management. 'The problem of the Press' attracted even more attention after the Liberals' electoral victory in 1906, when the Conservative press attempted to discredit the Liberal Government by making personalised attacks on its wealthy members and supporters, inventing the label 'Radical Plutocrat'. Newnes was one such 'Radical Plutocrat', along with Pearson, Charles Solomon Henry, Sir John Brunner and Sir Alfred Mond. In this climate, the reticence with which Newnes was brought before readers of *The Westminster Gazette* and his decision to give up the paper in 1908 are hardly surprising.

Newspaper proprietors such as Newnes, as has been shown, were often MPs or men with political ambitions and affiliations which made them directly subject to various pressures from party whips. And editors frequently had these pressures transferred to them.[49] Newnes's relations with Spender, however, and with Cook before him, were particularly harmonious and supportive. Cook found Newnes a highly satisfactory proprietor who 'was content to reign as a constitutional monarch with as little interference as possible in the actual rule'.[50] Cook was notorious for his intolerant attitude towards proprietorial involvement, and Newnes was somewhat relieved when Spender became editor, and displayed more willingness for some collaboration. The two men met every fortnight to discuss *The Westminster*, and Spender described Newnes as a 'model employer'.

---

[48] G.R. Searle, *Corruption in British Politics, 1895-1930*, Oxford: Clarendon Press, 1987, pp.96-99, 128.

[49] At the *Daily News*, Gardiner found intolerable the 'niggling criticisms' levelled by Henry Cadbury, manager of his father's paper. The list of acrimonious relationships between editors and proprietors is endless.

[50] J. Saxon Mills, *Sir Edward Cook, K.B.E.: A Biography*, London: Constable, 1921, pp.153-154.

'The serious journalist', wrote Spender, in his testimony to Newnes in the paper, 'could have found no kinder or more forebearing employer than Sir George Newnes during the sixteen years that he was proprietor of *The Westminster Gazette.*' 'The *Westminster* staff', he concluded his piece, 'remember him gratefully as a kind, straightforward and warm-hearted man, who made it easy for them to do their best in the service of their newspaper.'[51] Whilst their praise was predictable, the language in which it was couched is revealing. Newnes was thus represented both as a patron of 'serious journalists', collaborating in their professional desire to 'service' their newspaper, and as a patron of Liberalism, promoting a desire to 'serve' the party through political journalism. Political loyalties and professional loyalties were intermixed in the image of *The Westminster* nourished by its producers.

Although there were several occasions on which Newnes was subjected to political pressure over Spender's writings in the *Westminster*, he invariably supported his editor, and granted him substantial editorial freedom. This may have been a result of a combination of factors in his journalistic career: his earlier disagreements with Stead over the *Review of Reviews*, his personal experience as an editor and a publisher, and his tendency, as was later manifest with *C.B. Fry's Magazine*, to choose an editor carefully and then leave him free to develop the publication. Newnes was thus in some sense the benevolent sponsor of independent journalism.

When Spender seemed to be fuelling the schism in the Liberal party by professing allegiance to Campbell-Bannerman after Rosebery's Chesterfield speech on South Africa, Newnes defended him against his many wrathful critics. Spender later described this period:

> My very good relations with Newnes, whom I was always careful not to take by surprise in any decision that I could foresee, carried me safely through, but he was genuinely distressed at the necessity which I saw for this particular decision and told me frankly that the strongest pressure was being put on him to secure its withdrawal.

Spender's comments were designed as much to demonstrate his own political principles and journalistic potency as Newnes's loyalty to him. Partisan this journal may have been, he insisted, but it was not confined to the dictates of the party powerbrokers:

> I was obliged to tell him that withdrawal would mean my retirement, and he very handsomely said that he would back my judgement against that of my critics.[52]

---

[51] *Westminster Gazette*, 13 June, 1910, p.3.

[52] J.A. Spender, op. cit., vol 2, p.107.

There was more than a hint of Newnes's sense of Spender's commercial and professional value as editor of *The Westminster*, mixed with a reverence for the notion of proprietorial independence, in his decision to 'back' him.

Within the text of *The Westminster* itself, there were relatively few points at which the proprietor of the paper made an appearance in some capacity. In January 1895, his name appeared in the New Year Honours list; in 1898, it was cited in connection with his sponsoring of the Borchgrevink Antarctic expedition; in 1900 his campaign in Swansea and election to Parliament were noted; and in 1910, a number of articles recorded his death and characterised his contributions to journalism and to politics. These instances of proprietorial prominence, within a long period in which Newnes was generally conspicuous by his absence from the pages of the paper, provide a sequence of passages through which to examine the self-image which Newnes projected as both proprietor and politician, and assess the extent to which *The Westminster* and its proprietor conform to the model of late nineteenth and early twentieth-century political journalism which Koss has described.

'Mr George Newnes, MP for the Newmarket Division of Cambridgeshire' appeared in the list of baronetcies issued on 1 January, 1895 (the same list that announced the appointment of Cecil Rhodes to the Privy Council). The paragraph read as follows:

> Sir George Newnes, says the *Daily News*, is widely known as the proprietor of *Tit-Bits*, the *Strand Magazine*, and *The Westminster Gazette*.[53]

This biographical sketch, unlike those of all of the other appointees, was an extract from another publication, albeit a Liberal journal. In this tactic there was a hint of the deliberate reticence with which the proprietor was brought before the readers of his own paper. His credibility was not to be compromised by his being written up in *The Westminster Gazette*.

In an article entitled 'Sir George Newnes's Antarctic Expedition' (August 1898) Newnes was represented essentially as the expedition's liberal and benevolent host. He had 'crammed the hold of the *Southern Cross*' with 'bounteous stores', and provided a sumptuous farewell luncheon party. The article resounded with references to the provisions made for the journey. Newnes's political Liberalism was neutralised, via a firmly informative style of reporting, to become a depoliticised form of liberalism more associated with the social ritual of entertaining. In *The Strand*'s account of the Borchgrevink Expedition, on the other hand, Newnes himself 'presided' as the narrator of the story. He assumed a literary identity, and supplied an adventure narrative, supplemented by novel photographs and featuring florid phrases.[54] The two publications demanded different images of the proprietor and different emphases,

[53] *Westminster Gazette*, 1 January, 1895, p.6.

[54] *Strand Magazine*, 18, 105 (September 1899), p.281.

and the contrast between them clarifies the complex nature of the late nineteenth-century political journal. *The Strand* was a popular monthly magazine which both reflected and promoted its editor-proprietor's journalistic career. *The Westminster*, on the other hand, was a *news*paper which, whilst it was designed to promote political Liberalism, was careful to stop short of promoting the political career of its Liberal proprietor.

Whilst his political career was not openly or actively promoted by the paper, Newnes's interests and views, as briefly reported along with those of other candidates in the lead-up to the election, were closely reflected in *The Westminster*. He was reported to be in favour of 'Disestablishment' (not surprising, given his Congregational background and Liberal affiliations), 'Home Rule All Round' (some measure of independent government in the colonies of Ireland, Wales and Scotland, with the maintenance of imperial links, as per Spender's editorial line in *The Westminster*),[55] 'Old-Age Pensions' (a significant preoccupation of *The Westminster* and of 'new Liberalism' in these years), 'Temperance Legislation' (strongly advocated by nonconformists within the Liberal Imperialist faction) and 'House of Lords Reform' (one of Spender's much-vaunted topics in the leaders of the paper).

In his electoral address, the proprietor of *The Westminster* expressed political views which marked him out as a Liberal Imperialist and signalled his affiliations with 'new' or radical liberalism, the nominated creed of the paper:

> I am very strongly in favour of Old-Age Pensions, and think that considering their promises in 1895, the Government have betrayed their trust in this matter, inasmuch as nothing has been done .... The question arises as to where the money is to come from, and I think that wise and thoughtful statesmanship can provide it without injustice, and at the same time prevent the deplorable fact of a large number of our industrial classes after spending their lives in labour, through no fault of their own ending their days in the workhouse.[56]

This was the Newnes behind *The Westminster*, which was staunch in its advocacy of old-age pensions, was concerned to review the Conservative government's performance in the past five years in great detail, and concentrated much criticism on the art of statesmanship.

The Westminster aspired to be 'as democratically socialist as Unionists can afford to be', according to W.T. Stead.[57] The Labour movement had no

---

[55] 'I am in favour of Home Rule for Ireland, Scotland, and for Wales, so that those who have the closest knowledge may be able to manage their own affairs', Newnes was reported as saying. 'But I am strongly opposed to anything in the nature of separation in these islands.' He was later to revoke this opinion, and solicit Campbell-Bannerman's support (in the paper) for dropping the Home Rule platform.

[56] *Westminster Gazette*, 29 September, 1900, p.8.

[57] *Westminster Gazette*, 7 February, 1893, p.3. Stead's words were echoed by Sir William Harcourt when, during the passage of the 1894 budget, in which death duties on real

major organs of its own and was therefore largely dependent upon the Liberal press. Thus the editor pledged to continue the interest devoted to the problem of the poor in the *Pall Mall Gazette*:

> The claims of Labour are now so loudly vocal that every man must listen whether he will or no .... The cause of Labour is in our belief bound up with the principles of Liberalism ... latter-day Liberalism is a frankly democratic force.[58]

These years saw a redefinition of Liberalism, fostered by writers such as T.H. Green, L.T. Hobhouse and J.A. Hobson, in which social reform and the principle of 'collectivism' became central.[59] Newnes participated in the development of the 'new Liberalism' through his sponsorship of *The Westminster Gazette*.

From 1902, *The Westminster* devoted some of its Christmas Fund to a scheme for pensioners. Weekly pensions of half-a-crown awarded by the paper numbered 83 by 1905. The scheme was consistent with the paper's political stance. Working at the head of a body of writers, some of them living in East London (some in settlement houses), and therefore with firsthand knowledge of social problems, Spender saw his staff as bringing 'a steady flow of criticism to bear on existing conditions, accompanied by proposals for their amendment'. *The Westminster*, according to Spender, who may well have been modelling himself upon W.T. Stead, contributed materially to the social reforms introduced by the Campbell-Bannerman and Asquith governments of 1906-1913. It did 'practical work' in the service of 'working people'.[60]

Spender's comments underline his role as a spokesperson for the kind of pragmatic and rational approach to social reform that was characteristic of 'new Liberalism'. Yet such a scheme also smacked of Newnes's engagement with the New Journalism and of his taste for 'true stories' - the *raison d'être* of *The Wide World Magazine*. 'More true tales that leave you with heartache and with a burning wish to help', wrote the editor, 'were told to us when we required an outline of an old man's or an old woman's life-story - and verified by us - than we had ever heard.'[61] As the paper's proprietor, Newnes played a political role in sponsoring campaigns for Liberal social reforms. Yet it was a role that was consistent with his editorial image as developed in *Tit-Bits* and *The Million*, in which he catered to the interests and preoccupations of the 'industrial classes'. There was a chain of connection, through themes such as social reform, between

---

and personal property were equalised, he claimed 'We are all socialists now.' The phrase was to become a catchcry of 'new Liberalism', epitomising the preoccupation of radical liberals with socialism, collectivism and the relationship between Liberalism and the Labour Movement.

[58] *Westminster Gazette*, 31 January, 1893, p.1.

[59] See A.V. Dicey, *Lectures on the Relationship Between Law and Public Opinion During the Nineteenth Century in England*, London: Macmillan, 1905.

[60] J.A. Spender, *Men and Things*, London: Cassell, 1937, p.63.

[61] *Westminster Gazette*, 27 November, 1905, pp.1-2.

Newnes's more popular, commercial publications, his public reputation and the overtly political *Westminster Gazette*.

If he was a figure of Liberal benevolence, Newnes also had the reputation of being a gentleman in politics. The electorate of Swansea dubbed him 'Gentleman George', and at Lynton he was written up as 'Sergeorge the Giver'. *The Westminster* offered a journalistic extension of his image as a liberal-democratic gentleman figure. At a series of campaign meetings, *The Westminster* recorded in 'Election News and Notes' in September 1900, under the sub-title 'One of the Welsh Battles', that Newnes 'besought his friends to fight the battle on political and social grounds and no other, in the most fair, manly and gentlemanly way'. It was the kind of entreaty that one might have expected from the editor of *The Captain*, R.S. Warren Bell, to his boy-readers as they prepared to enter a sporting contest. Indeed, *The Captain*, a broadly Liberal popular monthly, had been established only a year earlier. *The Westminster* both approximated Newnes's political views and made substantial reference to his experiments in New Journalism.

But by far the most revealing of these textual episodes of proprietorial prominence is the treatment of Newnes's death in 1910. Since he was no longer the proprietor of *The Westminster*, mentions of whom could be scrutinised for traces of self-promotion on his part or self-serving genuflection on the part of his employees, Newnes's death was loudly lamented in the paper. On 9 June, 1910, the day of his death, a 'Special Memoir' occupying a full page of the paper was published under the headline 'SIR GEORGE NEWNES. DEATH THIS MORNING AT LYNTON'. The following day, the first paragraph of 'Notes of the Day' was devoted to him. And on 13 June, Spender wrote a half-column eulogy to his old proprietor, beginning 'The serious journalist could have found no kinder or forebearing employer [sic] than Sir George Newnes during the sixteen years that he was the proprietor of *The Westminster Gazette*.'[62]

Eulogies were a professional courtesy. Yet into this sequence of paragraphs was woven a new and distinctive model of political journalism: a model characterised by the motif of journalistic propriety. The obituarist recounted the history of Newnes's association with *The Westminster* with an air of cultivated modesty, his depiction of Newnes's establishment of the paper as an act of 'gallantry' deliberately consistent with other textual images of the partisan proprietor.[63] Yet the self-consciousness with which this act of service was recorded was an indication that the relationship between the political journal and the political party (via the proprietor) was not uncomplicated by a concern with propriety and 'taste'. This concern pervaded the paper, and underpinned the reticence with which Newnes was written up in its pages. In this case, the writer sought neutrality in temporal distance:

---

[62] *Westminster Gazette*, 13 June, 1910, p.3.

[63] In this case, the gallantry involved service of the party, rather than service of a lady, as in the chivalric tradition. Newnes's Christian name was also, coincidentally, associated with gallantry, via the legend of St George, patron saint of England.

> That was as long ago as 1893 and, *without any breach of taste*, the fact may be referred to, even in these columns, that Sir George Newnes was generally regarded as having performed an act of the greatest service to the Liberal Party in coming forward with such spirit on this occasion.[64]

Partisan journalism this may have been, but, like chivalric romance, it was governed by strict rules of propriety, and even of textual concealment. The obituary concluded with an assessment of Newnes's political career:

> In the House of Commons Sir George did not play a very prominent part, though the great influence which he exercised outside the House was generally recognised by his fellow-members, and in his quiet, undemonstrative way he proved himself by no means a negligible quantity.[65]

Newnes's political substance lay in his extra-parliamentary journalistic connections, but these were screened here behind the silent assent of his fellow members, as they were concealed in the text of the paper, which, in its deliberate eschewal of the personal ('generally regarded', 'generally recognised') and its guarded reticence ('by no means ... negligible'), itself enacts the more impersonal 'quiet undemonstrativeness' it commends in Newnes. This was a new and subtly-rendered version of the partisan newspaper proprietor.

In 'Notes of the Day', Charles Geake depicted Newnes's death as the 'personal and intimate loss' of 'one with whose name *The Westminster Gazette* will always be associated'. The relationship between the proprietor and his staff was thus represented as a kind of familial bond in a way which combined naturally with modesty about the mention of the proprietor's name. Newnes's pseudo-relatives were engaged in protecting him, even in death, from charges of self-promotion, self-publicity and the brand-naming tactics of the developing ethos of commercialism. Alongside brief but commendatory testimonies to Newnes's character appeared a kind of disclaimer of the 'task of appreciation':

> We leave to other hands the task of appreciation; we are grateful for the many kind and generous things which are already being said elsewhere about him and his work.[66]

Thus the image of the grieving relative was merged with that of the decorous political journalist, with all his obligations of confidentiality and of editorial silence on sensitive matters. The motif of propriety was the very basis of a new model of political journalism, based on the old, but shaped by public discussion

---

[64] *Westminster Gazette*, 9 June, 1910, p.11. My italics.

[65] Ibid.

[66] *Westminster Gazette*, 10 June, 1910, p.2.

about 'the problem of the Press' in relation to corruption in British politics in the early years of the twentieth century.

The tension between 'serious journalism' and 'commercial enterprise' was most fully explored in Spender's eulogy to Newnes:

> In 1893, when he founded *The Westminster*, he was at the height of his fame as a pioneer of a new type of popular journalism, and there were not wanting those who predicted that he would either unduly 'popularise' or grow impatient of the time and effort required to establish a serious newspaper.

The distinction between 'popular journalism' and 'serious journalism' was thus established as a motif intimately connected with the publisher's public reputation. Contemporaries, it seems, tended to associate Newnes with the former. Spender, on the other hand, cited evidence of Newnes's promotion of *The Westminster*'s 'serious' and independent qualities (evidence which, at the same time, confirmed his own claims to impartiality):

> He recognised at once that if *The Westminster Gazette* was to succeed, it must be something more than a commercial enterprise, and he never at any time asked himself how a particular line of policy would affect the business prospects of the paper.[67]

Recalling the atmosphere of the months before the Boer War, when 'panic reigned in many newspaper offices and the staffs of various Liberal journals were suffering rapid changes', Spender praised his proprietor's resilience in the face of pressure from 'commercial men' and politicians alike, who assured him that *The Westminster*, on its then course, was steering straight for ruin. *The Westminster*, its editor implied, was impervious to the imperatives of commercialism and of partisanship alike. It represented independent opinion, he claimed, demonstrating in his sketch of Newnes a faith in the notion of the press as a 'Fourth Estate' that was characteristic of his time:

> He was equally cool a year or two later when the Liberal Party was threatened with a serious schism, and when, once more, he found himself assailed by eager politicians urging him to throw *The Westminster* into their scale. 'You will be doing best', he wrote to the editor on this occasion, 'when you are most in hot water, and you may rely on me to be well satisfied when that object is achieved'.[68]

This would appear to be a very different Newnes from the one who had pioneered and controlled *Tit-Bits*, *The Million* and *The Strand*, despite the

---

67 *Westminster Gazette*, 13 June, 1910, p.3.

68 Ibid.

thematic and journalistic connections between all of these periodicals. It was a very different publisher from the one who had separated from Stead and the *Review of Reviews*, out of a real terror of getting into 'hot water' in partnership with that unpredictable gentleman.[69] Yet it is also a very different Newnes from the one suggested by Stephen Koss's image of the mute benefactor of the Liberal political press, locked into a direct and transparent relationship to the party. The image of the proprietor projected by *The Westminster* was ambiguous, straddling the ground between partisan and commercial journalism, and oscillating between political potency and journalistic concealment. Newnes was *The Westminster*'s benefactor, but was not to be seen as a direct beneficiary of its capacity to create good publicity for Liberalism, nor as a blind supporter of party doctrine.

This is the key to understanding *The Westminster Gazette* and Newnes's position in relation to it. Newnes was a multi-faceted figure, his paper a liberal admixture of conventional political journalism and the modernising journalistic techniques for which its proprietor was well-known. 'Let me say a word first about George Newnes, whom I shall always remember with gratitude', wrote Spender in his autobiography:

> ... he had strong political convictions and a very real respect for
> the serious kind of journalism. When he started *The Westminster*
> it was freely predicted that he would want to make it a 'daily
> *Tit-Bits*'. Nothing was farther from his thoughts.

Spender too believed in *The Westminster*'s political mission:

> It was never in my mind that *The Westminster* could be anything
> but a political paper, and I knew that its appeal on other
> grounds must be limited by the fact that it was a serious political
> paper, expounding Liberal ideas.[70]

Yet when he appointed Spender as editor of the paper (an innovative decision in itself given Spender's comparatively youthful age of 33), Newnes observed to him that 'he had inquired into my work and found that I had done a good many things besides politics, and advised me not to lean too heavily on the political articles, but to give variety and brightness to the paper'. He wished *The Westminster*, according to Spender, 'to be a lively paper, but in its own way'. *The Westminster Gazette*, then, was a combination of serious political journalism and liveliness, variety and brightness.

If in one sense this was 'a serious political paper, expounding Liberal ideas', then it remains to examine the way in which the notion of 'serious political journalism' was explored and manifested in the text. The issue of 'independence' was central. The notion of the press as a 'Fourth Estate' or an

---

[69] See Newnes-Stead Correspondence, Churchill College Library, Cambridge.

[70] J.A. Spender, *Life, Journalism and Politics*, vol. 2, pp.52, 62.

independent mediator between state and people, as both James Curran and George Boyce have pointed out, was a pervasive myth which enabled the British press to stake its claim for a respectable place in British politics and society in the nineteenth century.[71] At the height of its power in the years 1880 to 1918 - the years of New Journalism - the British press seemed to act as an effective political watchdog, a fact which Stead constantly emphasised. In reality, as Brown has noted, there was a disjunction between the belief of journalists in their independence, and their actual dependence on party political backers such as Newnes and inextricable links with governmental institutions. As the twentieth century dawned, 'public interest' began to be championed over the partisan political interest of the press.

The transfer of the *PMG* to an unknown proprietor clearly illustrated the reality of journalistic dependence. Yet Cook wilfully chose to draw the opposite conclusion from the incident. In a haughtily general fashion, he maintained that the first number of *The Westminster* would:

> come as a useful demonstration of the fact that a newspaper staff, if it may be sold cannot be bought, and that though a political organ may be silenced for a little while, there is enough public spirit to ensure for it a speedy re-incarnation.

Newnes's obvious part in the operation was written out, or at least abstracted to become 'public spirit', in an attempt to elevate the independence of the new paper. In the following day's issue, the editor noted the good wishes received, from political supporters and opponents alike. He interpreted them:

> not only as a sign that they have confidence in our desire, in the future as in the past, to turn out a paper which, though strenuous in its advocacy of particular principles, shall be fair to all parties and interesting to all readers.[72]

Cook was, as it were, sold on the idea of the press as the champion of 'public interest'.

All the reinforcements were called in to support *The Westminster*'s case for an independent press, and discourse upon the responsibilities of the political journalist. W.T. Stead, writing on 'The Secret of Journalistic Power', harped on notions of 'fidelity to the lofty ideal of journalism', and juxtaposed an image of the old *PMG* as a paper associated with the cumulative weight of traditions, 'long years of struggle', and 'the memory of great deeds done for England and for the Empire' against a new ethos and language of consumerism in which the

---

[71] James Curran, 'The Press as an Agency of Social Control: An Historical Perspective', and George Boyce, 'The Fourth Estate: The Reappraisal of a Concept', in George Boyce, James Curran and Pauline Wingate (eds), *Newspaper History from the Seventeenth Century to the Present Day*, London: Constable, 1978, pp.21-30, 53-70.

[72] *Westminster Gazette*, 1 February, 1893, p.6.

newspaper represented 'merchandise' that could be bought and sold.[73] Frederick Greenwood claimed that journalists were 'not only politicians', but 'the only guardians of public morals'. The reconciliation of commercialism and partisan journalism, he argued, could only be achieved through independent criticism:

> We promise upright, outspoken, independent criticism, even though it be delivered weeping; which, for us, entirely settles the point of honour between the public who we profess to serve (whose pence, indeed, we take for the service), and the placemen and party managers whom we should scorn to call our directors in any form of programme, prospectus, or advertisement.[74]

Thus *The Westminster* pledged its 'most cordial support' to the Liberal government with whose principles it was in agreement. But at the same time, its editor maintained that its support would be 'independent', for 'no other kind of support is possible to an honest man, or acceptable to a wise one'.[75] This model of political journalism was precariously balanced, not least in its mediation between an aristocratic code of 'honour' and its economic dependence on the 'pence' of its 'public'.

Greenwood expanded upon the notion that the journalist's place was 'on a stage apart, between the official leaders of his party and the mass of those whose appointed generals they are'. Yet his description of the journalist's 'business', though infused with the language of the 'Fourth Estate' myth, betrays a sympathy with official circles:

> His business is to interpret between them as faithfully as perfect independence allows; with every consideration for the difficulties of government, every tenderness for unavoidable shortcomings, every willingness to make the best of well-meant if abortive or mistaken endeavour, but never forgetting that his duty is to the People whose guide he pretends to be. It is to them that his loyalty is due, and there lies his responsibility. It is a matter of contract.[76]

Greenwood's notion of the contract between the journalist and the People draws on both the legal contract and Rousseau's social contract. There is perhaps more in his 'pretends', however, than he meant there to be.

As Spender's recollections of his editorship of *The Westminster* amply demonstrate, there was a substantial amount of collaboration between politicians and journalists. Editors, Koss has argued, were recognised as party or factional spokesmen, 'allies of politicians' who enjoyed the confidences of such men, and in return 'defended their policies and safeguarded their secrets'. Spender, for

73 *Westminster Gazette*, 7 February, 1893, p.3.

74 *Westminster Gazette*, 1 February, 1893, pp.1-2.

75 *Westminster Gazette*, 31 January , 1893, p.1.

76 Ibid.

example, was 'an unofficial member of the Liberal Cabinet', according to Scott-James. And whilst Sir Edward Grey was Foreign Secretary, *The Westminster* was widely believed to be 'the organ of Sir Edward Grey', suggesting that it was a transparently partisan publication.[77] Spender denied this, commenting that Grey never asked him to write an article or prompted him to express a particular view. This may have been the case with 'foreign newspapers', but it was 'seldom true of English papers, and certainly was not true of *The Westminster*'.[78]

The very fact of his denial is an interesting case of a discursive shift in the meanings embedded in papers such as *The Westminster*, and their effort to constitute the public interest. In fact, it was the kind of access to confidential information alluded to by Scott-James which, according to Lucy Brown, was perceived by contemporaries to be the very basis of journalistic independence. Spender's defence of the paper represented a retrospective attempt to negotiate a model of partisan political journalism that was a synthesis of notions of journalistic independence, 'public interest' and an English Liberal tradition of free speech.

Access to 'inside news' could itself be a source of difficulty for the political journalist. Ministerial journalism, as Spender found in 1906 when the Liberals regained office, was particularly fraught with such problems. With many intimate friends in office in 1906, Spender expended much of his energy in criticism of and suggestions for draft Bills, and thus found it hard to gain a fresh journalistic perspective, since he was almost as much a party to the finished product as the Minister responsible for it. The notion of journalistic independence became much more complicated. 'If you go on like this', Stead warned him, 'you will cease to be an editor and become a departmental hack.' 'Whatever you do', he reiterated, 'don't let them draw your sting.'[79]

Discussions amongst journalists about the independence of the press and its devotion to the cause of 'public interest' can be linked to the ideology of 'national efficiency', itself part of a late nineteenth-century reaction against orthodox liberalism which sprang from anxiety about Britain's economic position (given the depression of the 1880s and 1890s) and Great Power status. Many contemporaries believed that parliamentary politics was paralysed by the party system and advocated a pragmatic and creative brand of administration, based on the imperial experience, as a means of achieving the goal of 'national efficiency'.[80]

Various incidents and issues in British political life became major narrative threads in *The Westminster*. The debate over Home Rule, the Jameson Raid

---

[77] Stephen Koss, op. cit., p.10; Scott-James, *Influence of the Press*, as cited in Stephen Koss, op. cit., p.10. See, for instance, J.A. Spender, *Life, Journalism and Politics*, vol. 2, pp.64-65.

[78] Ibid., p.170.

[79] Ibid., p.139.

[80] See G.R. Searle, *The Quest for National Efficiency: A Study in British Politics and Political Thought, 1899-1914*, Oxford: Basil Blackwell, 1971, pp.30-31.

(1896), the Boer War, Khaki Election and Mafeking (1899-1901), and the General Election of 1905 all represent interesting points of entry into the political and journalistic characteristics of *The Westminster Gazette*. *The Westminster* reported and analysed the passage of the Home Rule Bill in its early issues, for instance, in a way that brought into focus a number of what were to become its characteristic features. Cook published carefully-argued, balanced, rhetorical leaders, emphasising the privileged position of the political editor and his role as independent interpreter and political analyst. He published extracts from a range of London, Welsh, Irish, Scottish and provincial papers with diverse perspectives on Home Rule, presenting 'Some Tory Opinions', 'Some Unionist Opinions' and various other views. Designed to replicate the forum of democratic discussion and reinforce the paper's independence, this was a feature that was typical of *The Westminster*. It was a journalistic technique employed to emphasise a political moral: the moral of democratic freedom. The paper briefed its readers, keeping them constantly and comprehensively informed on the issues, debates and measures occupying Parliament in a way that reinforced the vitality of its own participation in the political process, and thus its loyalty as a serious political journal to the idea of 'public interest'.

The Jameson Raid, in December 1895, attracted considerable attention in *The Westminster*. Spender played up the dramatic immediacy and narrative excitement implicit in the uncertainty about the facts of the Raid, each day's issue constituting a new instalment in what was presented as a kind of serial of mysterious adventure. 'There is much in this morning's papers to confirm the impression', he wrote on 7 January, 'that Dr Jameson in crossing the frontier acted, not in accordance with any deep-laid plot and with the connivance of the Chartered Company, but on the spur of the moment.' It was, according to this report, 'in the belief that he was going to the rescue of men, women and children whose lives were actually at stake' that Dr Jameson acted as he did. The Jameson incident was a situation rich in journalistic potential, yet it was also rich in political significance.

In summarising his position, the editor highlighted the tension between narrative appeal, independent reporting and political caution:

> Our immediate object is only to bring out the atmosphere of
> doubt and confusion which still invests the whole circumstance
> of DR JAMESON'S sudden burst across the frontier, and
> therein to emphasise the necessity which all fair-minded men
> will feel to suspend judgement upon it.[81]

One reader at least was obviously convinced by *The Westminster*'s synthesis of journalistic and political technique. He praised the editor for remaining

---

[81] *Westminster Gazette*, 7 January, 1896, p.2.

circumspect, whilst 'everything was still obscure and many persons were jumping to false conclusions'.[82]

The Jameson Raid revealed deep and widening differences in the Liberal Party, and caused an escalation of tensions between Germany and Britain. In May 1898, Spender criticised Milner's enthusiasm for intervention in the Transvaal, arguing that a war against the Boers was 'a bad remedy and not to be thought of till others had been exhausted'. This line of argument brought criticism of Spender, *The Westminster Gazette* and its proprietor, George Newnes. 'The gravamen of the complaint was that *The Westminster* had said these things', according to Spender. He went on to add:

> The *Daily News* or the *Manchester Guardian* might have been expected to say them - they were Little Englanders and anti-Imperialists who would say anything - but *The Westminster* was supposed to be an organ of Liberal Imperialism, and the mouthpiece of Lord Rosebery, and if it could not be depended upon to back the offensive against the Boers, the Liberal Party was lost.

According to Spender, George Newnes, 'then, as many times later, greatly eased my burden by assuring me of his entire agreement'.[83] Though *The Westminster* was 'supposed to be an organ of Liberal Imperialism', it retained some of the qualities of the independence which continued to be a central motif in discussions about the press. In spite of their partisanship, Spender and Newnes remained committed to the ideals of editorial integrity and the autonomous social and political power of the press. *The Westminster* constituted the textual site in which political debate raged, and the paper's proprietor was something akin to a tolerant Speaker figure.

Throughout the Boer conflict, Spender continued to plead with readers to look beyond the war to post-war policy, and to bear in mind that the Boers would have to be integrated into the British Empire if South Africa was to prosper. He looked to reconciliation as the means of ensuring a lasting resolution to the issue. The *Westminster* was thus reproached for its defection from the Liberal-Imperialist faith. Yet Spender was also attacked by pro-Boers for rampant jingoism, because alongside these tempering remarks, he wrote strongly on behalf of vigorous military measures to bring about an early conclusion to the war and combat the optimism of the expectation that the hostilities would be 'over before Christmas' 1899.[84] There was more than a touch of pride in Spender's reminiscences of his staunch independence in this, the most bitterly contested internal political quarrel of these years. He was, however, the only

---

[82] *Westminster Gazette*, 10 January , 1896, p.2.

[83] J.A. Spender, *Life, Journalism and Politics*, vol. 2, p.88.

[84] Ibid., pp.91-92.

Liberal journalist to keep in touch with both sides throughout the quarrel, a fact which ensured his survival - and that of *The Westminster* - after the war.[85]

Spender aimed to keep the Liberal party strong and whole so that it could follow a conciliatory policy when the war ended in South Africa. He endeavoured to establish Liberal unity, the cherished aim of George Newnes and many other Liberals, pursuing what he referred to as 'the unheroic course of the "smoother"'.[86] His self-devised title was apt. The ways of the 'smoother' were to flavour the paper for many years. After the Czar's conference of January 1899, for instance, Spender wrote (wishfully) that the differences within the Liberal party were 'atmospheric and temperamental, not solid and practical', and the social questions of the day were large enough to 'provide bracing work for everybody'.[87] Thus did the political editor attempt to find common ground in candour, a kind of utilitarian faith in 'solid and practical matters', and in the 'bracing work' ethic of self-help ideology.

In fact it was a characteristic of the Liberal press of the early twentieth century, a time when it was somewhat depleted, that it attempted to minimise the differences in its own ranks, whilst emphasising the divisions in fiscal policy amongst Unionists. '*The Westminster Gazette*', as Stephen Koss has observed, 'was the most adept among the Liberal organs at papering over the cracks.'[88] It was significant that despite the huge electoral losses suffered by the Liberal party, George Newnes was returned in Swansea Town by a convincing margin with a marked swing to the Liberal candidate.[89] In this sense, *The Westminster* was very much a piece of partisan political journalism. The spirit of political debate was consistently and successfully harnessed to promote reconciliation within the Liberal ranks.

The relief of Mafeking in May 1900 was an event around which a variety of images of triumphant imperialism, frontier manliness, adventure and heroism clustered. These narrative motifs pervaded accounts of the incident in monthly publications such as Newnes's *Wide World Magazine* and his juvenile magazine *The Captain*. Yet they also complicated the treatment of Mafeking in *The Westminster*. 'The relief of this little town is clearly the relief of the whole British Empire from a great anxiety', began the editor, making the incident the focus of popular imperialist sentiment. He went on to gesture towards an exposition of British manliness and heroism:

> ... in the seven months of the siege [Baden-Powell] and his men
> have taught us lessons of patience and cheerfulness and courage
> which will not be forgotten by this generation of Englishmen.

---

[85] Both Cook, editor of the *Daily News*, and Massingham, editor of the *Chronicle*, later suffered for coming down on one side or the other.

[86] J.A. Spender, *Life, Journalism and Politics*, vol. 2, pp.102, 104, 105.

[87] *Westminster Gazette*, 28 January, 1899, p.1.

[88] Stephen Koss, op. cit., p.48.

[89] Newnes won the seat of Swansea Town from the Conservative member Sir J.T. Dillwyn-Llewelyn by 4,318 votes to 3,213. See *Westminster Gazette*, 3 October, 1900, p.9.

After an almost absent-minded lapse into imperial self-congratulation, there followed a narrative shift to the kind of thoughtful political analysis that was rather more typical of the political paper. (It is possible to talk of this narrative in terms of fleeting moments of editorial mood because Spender wrote the editorial leader, as he observed in his autobiography, in the allotted time of one and a quarter hours each day.) 'Let us, then', wrote the editor, 'do all honour to BADEN-POWELL and his gallant men, and then brace ourselves afresh to think about the situation which is before us':

> The ultimate aim and the only chance of final peace lies in a confederation of South Africa under British hegemony but consistent with the independence of the various States and governed in all common matters by Federal Parliament in which Dutch and British shall have perfectly equal rights according to their respective voting powers.[90]

The Westminster, as this example demonstrates, represented a combination of measured political analysis and popular journalistic technique.

In the lead-up to the Khaki Election, *The Westminster* published a series of front-page articles entitled 'British Statesmanship and South Africa, 1895-1900. A Study for Electors'. It was analytical, didactic and rather legalistic in style, and was employed by the editor to reinforce the political purpose of the independent press. 'It is a positive duty', read the first article, making reference to the myth of the 'Fourth Estate', 'to inquire most carefully into the causes which have involved us in this trouble.' With its party political focus on the government's deficiencies, however, the series resembled a campaign piece.

In the General Election of 1905, in which the Liberal party was to emerge from the divisions of the previous ten years to post a decisive electoral victory, the focal issue was that of fiscal policy. After years of attempting to heal divisions in the Liberal party, *The Westminster* revelled in the new narrative of Conservative disarray and disunity. Chamberlain and the Unionist party were lampooned in leader and caricature. In seeking to bolster Liberal claims to parliamentary power, Spender urged Liberals to participate in a new narrative of Liberal unity, and relegate the old narrative of division finally to the past:

> upon [Liberal leaders] falls the task of showing that they are united on their British and Irish policies and are determined not to fritter away their energies at this critical moment on any internecine quarrel.[91]

As the editor engaged in the art of political and journalistic prompting, so the proprietor engaged in the project in another form. On the very day that

---

[90] *Westminster Gazette*, 19 May, 1900, p.1.

[91] *Westminster Gazette*, 27 November, 1905, p.2.

Spender was issuing his plea to Liberal leaders, Newnes wrote to Henry Campbell-Bannerman soliciting a contribution to *The Westminster* and thus to Liberal unity. His letter has been quoted extensively by Stephen Koss to illustrate the links between proprietor and party politics. Admitting to having voted for both earlier Home Rule Bills, Newnes now pleaded the case for dropping the issue:

> It would greatly help Liberal candidates all over the country if you would say that whilst Ireland should be governed according to Irish ideas, and the full control of their own affairs should be left to the people of Ireland, you would not consent to separation between the two countries.

'If we can get these few words from you all will be well', he claimed. 'If not the old bogey which has kept us so long out of office will again arise.' He invoked the loyalty of *The Westminster Gazette* and himself to the Liberal cause, and raised the spectre of a party wrecked by separatism.[92] There clearly remained a substantial overlap between the fields of journalism and politics.[93]

Campbell-Bannerman evidently declined Newnes's invitation. On 29 November, Spender wrote:

> In the temporarily disturbed state of the atmosphere SIR HENRY CAMPBELL-BANNERMAN probably did wisely at the moment to 'add nothing' to his previous statement, whilst insisting that his opinions are rightly interpreted as 'very moderate.'

The invitation to 'add something' had come from Newnes; the interpretation of his opinions as 'moderate' and pragmatic had come from Spender on 27 November. Claiming that anything Campbell-Bannerman could say would be misinterpreted by the opposition, the editor had to resort to an allusion to journalistic confidentiality to establish the authority of his claims:

> We have, however, the evidence that we need that the essential unity of the Liberal Party and its ability to form a Government united on the Irish question as on other questions is solid.[94]

---

[92] Newnes to Campbell-Bannerman, 27 November, 1905, Campbell-Bannerman Papers, BL, Add. Ms. 41238, f.89b.

[93] Furthermore, Newnes's attempts to co-ordinate Liberal forces were not confined to journalistic endeavours, as is evident from a letter to Herbert Gladstone of 1903, requesting his presence at a rally in Swansea. See Newnes to Herbert Gladstone, 24 October, 1903, Viscount Gladstone Papers, BL, Add. Ms. 46061, f.31b. 'The Liberals of Swansea have asked me to invite you to be the principal speaker at a great demonstration in the Albert Hall of that town', wrote Newnes. 'Mr Chamberlain is to speak at Cardiff on the 20th and they want to have a counterblast the week after .... You will get such a reception as will be a sufficient answer to the singular insult which Chamberlain was guilty of at Newcastle.'

[94] *Westminster Gazette*, 29 November, 1905, p.1.

Asquith, on the other hand, obligingly provided fodder for the new narrative of Liberal unity and the disavowal of Home Rule.

> 'Everybody', as MR ASQUITH said last night, 'whether he desires the introduction of a Home Rule Bill or whether he does not, everyone who was acquainted with politics knows perfectly well that a great constitutional change such as that could not be carried in this country except by a distinct, definite, and irresistible movement of opinion.'[95]

It is possible that Newnes, a great friend of Asquith's, had prompted him to make this statement. His letter to Campbell-Bannerman contains the implication that he was actively canvassing such statements. Furthermore, Spender's language in *The Westminster* on the subject carries resonances of Newnes's letter, suggesting that the two had discussed the 'bogey' of Home Rule and entered into a mutual campaign to banish it from public discussion. Indeed, Liberal Imperialist strategies for the reconstruction of the party depended upon many Liberal Unionist defections and on minimising the inter-party bitterness that had arisen from the Gladstonian campaign for Home Rule. Rosebery and his followers believed that Home Rule must be removed from its previously central position in liberal ideology and seen in the general context of imperial devolution and as only one alternative in solutions to the Irish Question. 'The elector had ample guarantees' on the subject of a Liberal disinclination to push a Home Rule Bill before, wrote Spender, 'but he can no longer make that particular bogey his excuse for not supporting the Liberal Party on Free Trade'.[96] Thus there remained significant connections, behind the scenes, between political process and journalistic production in *The Westminster Gazette*, editor, proprietor, journalist and politician collectively participating in the creation of the text.

Newnes's death precipitated a re-evaluation of the character of *The Westminster* and of Newnes's investment in it. Ultimately, Newnes was represented in *The Westminster* itself as occupying the ground somewhere between Piers Brendon's idiosyncratic and independent nineteenth-century 'press baron' and the twentieth-century media magnate, the capitalist of the increasingly syndicated Liberal press, who had to relinquish much of the personal responsibility for his publications as his publishing enterprises expanded:

> He was not one of those proprietors who try to do the work of their editor ... and, in the agreement which he made, he yielded full political control - subject to the general lines of policy - without the slightest reserve. This did not mean that he withdrew from interest in the paper, or failed, when he thought fit, to

---

[95] Ibid.

[96] *Westminster Gazette*, 27 November, 1905, p.2.

express his opinions. For a period of ten years the editor lunched with him regularly every fortnight, and on these occasions every detail of the conduct of the paper - commercial or political - was fully discussed. He was a man of the shrewdest judgement, and the paper benefited greatly from his ideas and his criticisms.[97]

George Newnes has been viewed by the vast majority of historians (and some of his contemporaries) largely in the light of his connection with the successful weekly publication *Tit-Bits*. In this context he has been seen as a successful New Journalist with a gift for promotional schemes and for the commercial tactics of popular commercial journalism: the man who 'revolutionised popular journalism' and created the foundations of modern journalistic practice. *The Westminster Gazette* carries strong traces of this aspect of Newnes. Yet an examination of *The Westminster* also serves to highlight another side of Newnes's publishing career: his role and identity as a partisan newspaper proprietor, demonstrating his commitment to Liberalism by engaging in a tradition of political journalism that survived into the early twentieth century. The value of this study of the periodical publications of George Newnes lies in the way in which it highlights this dichotomy.

Stephen Koss has depicted *The Westminster Gazette* as a political journal which represented the persistent influence of the nineteenth-century partisan press, and its proprietor as a kind of Liberal retainer. Newnes was certainly dedicated to the Liberal cause, and *The Westminster* was designed to serve the party, voicing many of the views of Liberal Imperialist politicians and participating in the development of Liberal social and political thought. Yet he was also an experienced publisher of periodical publications and a successful businessman. He thus attempted to apply some of the 'popular' techniques of New Journalism in an effort to increase the political paper's popularity and attain profitability. *The Westminster* illustrates the symbiotic relationship that existed between quality and popular journalism in the Edwardian period, and the synthesis of new and old within New Journalism. In this paper, a new model of partisan political journalism was negotiated which revolved around the motif of journalistic propriety. Within this model, the image of the politically-affiliated proprietor reflected a balance between ideological control and financial investment. *The Westminster* constituted a marriage of political passion and journalistic skill; a fusion of the joint impulses to 'tickle the public ear' and 'toe the party line'; a combination of business and benevolence. Through this paper, Newnes played a significant role in the populist mediation of New Liberal and Liberal Imperialist ideas within a novel and innovative format.

---

[97] *Westminster Gazette*, 13 June, 1910, p.3.

*Figure 9. Political cartoon by F.C. Gould (*Westminster Gazette, *21 September 1900, p.3). A.J. Balfour checks himself in the mirror, whilst Lord Salisbury buttons his coat, and Joseph Chamberlain adjusts his boots. The image was designed to undercut the seriousness of the Conservative campaign to rally support as a patriotic party.*

*Figure 10. 'A Nightmare Bunker', by F.C. Gould (*Westminster Gazette, *18 November 1905, p.5). The issue of tariff reform split the Conservative party, and paved the way for a Liberal resurgence. The Liberal press devoted much attention to the issue.*

4

Expanding Human Consciousness Across the Globe

The Wide World Magazine (1898)

The Wide World Magazine was an illustrated sixpenny monthly magazine, established by Newnes in April, 1898. The Introduction to the first volume stated:

> It may be taken for granted that at no time in our history did we - the English-speaking peoples, that is - take such a quick, keen and intelligent interest, as at present, in the affairs of the Wide World. What is the result of this wonderful trend of the times? One result is that we demand almost hourly information from all parts of the Universe - literally from China to Peru. It is not our purpose in this Introduction to offer any explanation of this awakening. Rather do we offer *The Wide World Magazine*, feeling morally certain that its birth comes exactly at the right moment.[1]

The passage is crowded with the language of temporality and spatiality. 'History' and 'the present' or 'the times' are merged to produce an image of *The Wide World* as the very epitome of temporal efficiency, supplying the demand for 'almost hourly information about all parts of the Universe', and emerging at '*exactly* the right *moment*'. The magazine captured the enormous geographical scope of the wide world, spanning 'from China to Peru', and telescopically transported it into the confines of 'every home'. (It is worth noting that the language of marketing and exchange, encompassing terms such as 'supply', 'demand' and 'enterprise', creeps into the passage too, indicating the commercial imperatives underpinning this, like every other, Newnes project.)

A range of material developments, along with factors such as the introduction of standard time at the end of the nineteenth century, created new modes of viewing and experiencing time and space. This period saw the emergence of a new aesthetic and ethic which revolved around simultaneity and the spatially expanded and temporally thickened present. Contemporaries, according to Stephen Kern, 'joined in affirming the reality of a present that

---

[1]   *The Wide World Magazine*, 1, 1 (April 1898), Introduction. Henceforth, this magazine will be referenced as *Wide World Magazine*. In the text, the titles *The Wide World Magazine* and *The Wide World* are used interchangeably.

embraced the entire globe and included the halos of the past and future'.[2] *The Wide World* symbolised and explored the transformation in the dimensions of life and thought.

The cultural conversion identified by the publisher was offered, in this case, as a sort of quasi-religious phenomenon, amounting to a spiritual process of 'birth' or 'awakening'. The very cover of the magazine reinforced the symbolism of biological and spiritual renewal, depicting Britannia as a maternal figure, surrounded by a halo which appeared to represent the light of civilisation, an egg-like globe nestled beneath her (*see Figure 11*). The 'Chosen People' (the reading community) were, in this case, 'the English-speaking peoples' (those who could read Newnes's magazine, who included the Europeans whose stories appeared in English in *The Wide World*). They were, it would seem, assumed to be familiar with the quintessentially English Dr Johnson. Dr Johnson's *Vanity of Human Wishes* opens with the lines: 'Let observation with extensive view,/ Survey mankind from China to Peru'. It was they who had witnessed the revelation of geographical expansion.

The publisher continued to present the *The Wide World* in this vein:

> The enterprise is absolutely unique; and the Conductors conclude this 'foreword', in quiet assurance that *The Wide World Magazine* may safely be trusted to carry into every home, by means of the infallible camera and the responsible traveller, the almost incredible wonders of the Wide World.

In an extension of the image of the spread of Christianity and civilisation, *The Wide World Magazine* was imagined as a kind of bible, with the conductors of the magazine being responsible for the dissemination of the word 'into every home'. This was a new form of witnessing, dependent upon the kind of truth offered by scientific objectivity and moral responsibility: the testimonies provided by 'the infallible camera and the responsible traveller'. Such a version of the 'truth' underpinned nineteenth-century British imperialism, rooted in notions of British technological and moral superiority. And the cultural dynamics of imperialism were persistently to underscore the text of *The Wide World Magazine*.

The other major theme of the Introduction is that encompassed by the motto 'Truth is Stranger than Fiction'. This was to be the *raison d'être* of the magazine and its major selling point, and it became a catchcry of the period.

> There will be no fiction in the Magazine, but yet it will contain stories of weird adventure, more thrilling than any conceived by the novelist in his wildest flights. These will be the plain,

---

[2]   Stephen Kern, *The Culture of Time and Space, 1880-1918*, Cambridge, Massachusetts: Harvard University Press, 1983, p.88.

straightforward narratives of well-known travellers, explorers and others.[3]

The appeal of the material was thus in its authenticity, a quality that distinguished it from mere romantic fiction whilst it guaranteed its accessibility to an audience for whom the world represented an immense field of potential adventure and novel experience. At a time when empiricism was in the ascendant (aided by the 'infallible camera'), whilst fiction was proving immensely popular in the periodical press, and the content and formatting of foreign news in the press was being hotly debated, *The Wide World* employed a number of stock characters to provide readers with a range of perspectives on the 'wide world'.[4] These figures helped to make foreign news, yet they related their own personal stories, elaborating as they did so on the themes of time, space and empire that the publisher had introduced at the outset.

This chapter analyses the origins and format of *The Wide World*, suggesting that Newnes's magazine reflected new developments in literature and the periodical press and represented, most significantly, the revolution in photographic illustration and the invention of the 'true story magazine'. It argues that *The Wide World*'s popularity signified the popularisation of the 'world view' within British society at the turn of the century, the evolution of new attitudes to time and space, and the predominance of a culture of imperialism, its features resonating with new spatial, temporal and imperialist ideas. It sees both readers and writers as participating in a process of cultural assimilation of the periphery into British (and English-speaking) popular culture; the mental digestion or appropriation of the far-flung corners of the world. And it examines the ways in which Newnes's magazine brought the 'outposts of empire' and the ends of the earth into the homes of its readers through various narratorial personae who provided a range of perspectives on the 'wide world'.

'There has indeed, arisen a taste for exotic literature', Andrew Lang, the well-known reviewer, anthropologist and academic author, commented in 1891:

> people have become alive to the strangeness and fascination of the world beyond the bounds of Europe and the United States. But that is only because men of imagination and literary skill have been the new conquerors, the Corteses and Balboas of India, Africa, Australia, Japan and the isles of the southern seas. All such writers ... have ... seen new worlds for themselves; have gone out of the streets of the over-populated lands into the open air; have sailed and ridden, walked and hunted; have escaped from the fog and smoke of towns. New strength has come from

---

[3]   *Wide World Magazine*, 1, 1 (April 1898), Introduction.

[4]   A.C. Doyle's faked 'spirit photographs' were not to cast doubt on the infallibility of photographic evidence until slightly later.

> fresher air into their brains and blood; hence the novelty and
> buoyancy of the stories which they tell.[5]

'Novelty and buoyancy': the words exactly encapsulated the character of
The Wide World Magazine, in which extraordinary true stories, innovatively
presented, were offered up for the interest and entertainment of readers. This
magazine catered to the fascination of contemporary readers with the temporally
conjunctive and spatially enlarged 'world beyond the bounds of Europe and the
United States'; the 'wide world'. Its authors were in many ways 'conquerors'
who acquired and assimilated the world to the western imagination through the
rhetoric and ideology of imperialism.[6] Categories such as 'white', 'western',
'civilised' and 'European' were part of the language of identity and superiority
which structured British notions of the empire and the globe. And all of these
categories of identity contributed to the perspective created by *The Wide World*
despite the fact that the British section of its audience and contributors was by far
the most significant.[7]

Analysis of the nationalities of *Wide World* authors shows that almost two-
thirds of the contributions came from British writers.[8] There were also
contributions from Americans, Australians, Italians, Indians, French, Japanese,
Canadian, Germans and various other nationals, their participation reflecting the
international scope of the magazine. What distinguished *Wide World* authors,
and conferred authority on their tales, were their titles. They were Captains,
Lieutenants, Majors, Generals, Colonels, Marine Engineers, Commanders,
Admirals, Reverends, Doctors, and men with honorary titles (such as Sir Frank
Swettenham) or letters after their names (F.R.G.S., for instance). R.J.T. Bright
wrote as a lieutenant on 'Our Adventures in Unknown Uganda', in 1899. By
1901, he had been elevated to the rank of 'Brevet-Major' and was writing a more
substantial piece - a two-part series entitled 'A Summer Amongst the Upper Nile
Tribes'. Herbert Vivian and his wife, probably the magazine's most prolific early
contributors, wrote from France, Spain, Switzerland, Italy, Belgium and
Abyssinia, their contributions covering subjects such as processions and festivals,
hermits, nuns and lady bull-fighters, palm-groves and oyster-parks, and local

---

[5]   Andrew Lang as cited in Brian V. Street, *The Savage in Literature*, London:
Routledge and Kegan Paul, 1975, p. 11.

[6]   Lang's assessment also points up the way in which the assimilation process was
rooted in biology, environmental factors determining consciousness to some extent.

[7]   In fact the late nineteenth century witnessed the formation of the notion of 'the
West' as a cultural and imperial entity. Hence Kipling's lines in 'The Ballad of East and West'
(1889): 'Oh, East is East, and West is West, and never the twain shall meet.' After all,
Kipling's famous poem 'The White Man's Burden' was actually addressed to the Americans,
who had recently acquired the Philippines. Many of the stories in the *Wide World*
(approximately a third) were thus set in America and the magazine had a number of American
contributors.

[8]   This figure has been derived from a database analysis of the first forty numbers of
the magazine (volumes 1-7, 1898-1901).

personalities or legends.[9] They were representatives of the late nineteenth-century revolution in mass travel.

The Wide World's body of contributors were travellers, missionaries, hunters and exiles; representatives of European and western culture who had 'sailed and ridden, walked and hunted' in foreign lands. They had 'seen new worlds for themselves', taking empire at face value. And they explored the world, writing 'in the full glow of discovery and revelation'.[10] Hence the magazine's motto: 'Truth is Stranger than Fiction'. For these narrators, the world was full of high endeavour. The British, in particular saw themselves as the representatives of technological, political and cultural discovery. As Andrew Marr (chief political commentator for *The Independent* and author of *Ruling Britannia*) has observed: 'The British, in short, happened to other people.'[11]

The Wide World consisted of 'true stories' and 'astounding photographs'. It covered, according to the title page of each bound volume, 'adventure, travel, customs and sport'. Many of the narratives in the magazine were self-contained, but serials were also a feature. Maps, appearing at the front of each issue and within the text, were also characteristic. As the magazine's contents-maps showed, its geographical scope extended beyond European colonies to a vast range of locations, including the United States, the North Pole and many European countries themselves. And it boasted a vast range of narratives, from reports of technological development (American feats of engineering were particularly singled out for celebration), to accounts of the exploits of naturalists and collectors of various types of scientific specimens, and tales of maritime navigation and human survival in polar regions.

The stories presented in the pages of *The Wide World* took the reader imaginatively and the photographs visually to the furthest reaches of the 'wide world', and the accompanying maps placed these regions in their geographical context. Newnes, astute businessman that he was, correctly identified an immensely significant feature of the popular market and the popular mind, and the magazine was to have a long and illustrious career. In fact, the phrase 'wide world' became a catchphrase at the turn of the century, a variety of works incorporating it into their titles.[12] *The Wide World*'s readership included those of the middle and upper classes who had travelled or were living overseas and could thus identify with its narrators and their tales, and those who, lacking the means to travel, could explore the 'wide world' imaginatively through its pages.

---

[9]   See, for instance, Herbert Vivian's 'In the Footsteps of the Queen of Sheba', *Wide World Magazine*, 7, 39 (June 1901), pp.252-260.

[10]   Susanne Howe Nobbe, *Novels of Empire*, New York: Columbia University Press, 1949, pp.19-21.

[11]   *Independent Magazine*, 2 September, 1995, p.7. 'Now the world happens to Britain', he concluded, in a discussion of contemporary British culture, seeking to explain the sense amongst contemporary Britons that they are 'a forgotten people, a brushed-aside nation'.

[12]   *Wide World Adventure: True Narratives of Extraordinary Human Endurance* (1900), *Wide World Novellette* (periodical), *Wide World Reciter* (periodical), *Wide, Wide World* (1900), *Wide World Sea Adventures* (1901), *Wide World Atlas-Geographies* (1901).

Thus, an elderly clergyman on the Orient Express in Graham Greene's *Stamboul Train* tells his companions: 'I always read a *Wide World* when I travel.'[13]

Holbrook Jackson said of Kipling's stories that they read 'like tales told in a club', and the narratives of *The Wide World* follow exactly that tradition. In fact, its contributors actually formed themselves into the Wide World Club and corresponded with one another across the expanses of the world.[14] This magazine became the very definition of adventure. 'We were out for a ramble the other day', one authoress prefaced her story of a British colonel with whom she was acquainted, 'talking of India, adventures and *The Wide World*, which he carried under his arm':

> Anything strange happened to you Colonel Tyron? If so *do* tell me, and let me send it to *The Wide World Magazine*.[15]

Newnes himself was a traveller of some experience, visiting the United States and Jerusalem, motoring across England in every direction, cruising up the Nile and yachting in the Adriatic and Mediterranean, stopping in Norway, Corsica, Jaffa, Venice and the French and Italian Rivieras. He actually thought of writing a volume of yachting stories, and jotted down some notes, but hadn't the time to finish them. He did, however, write two travel narratives for *The Strand* in 1898, and these provide a valuable point of access to the spirit that animated *The Wide World Magazine*.[16]

In an article published in the very year that *The Wide World* was established, Newnes assessed his trip up the Nile from Cairo to Cataract. Travel, he suggested, as had Andrew Lang, could offer escape from the drab dirtiness of urban life. It could be physically invigorating and mentally stimulating. It also offered variety - the possibility of looking 'hour by hour, upon an ever-changing panorama'.[17] The panorama was most vivid in Cairo:

---

[13] Graham Greene as cited in Paul Fussell, *Abroad: British Literary Travelling Between the Wars*, New York and Oxford: Oxford University Press, 1980, p.61. Fussell makes an error in claiming that the *Wide World Magazine* began in 1917 (p.60).

[14] In the mid-1980s, an elderly Sikh gentleman contacted the offices of IPC Magazines (into which George Newnes, Ltd was incorporated in the 1950s), hoping that the company might hold some kind of register of the members of the Club. Members in Australia, Canada, the United States, India and other parts of the Empire and the world, he told the Company Secretary, had struck up correspondences through the organisational mechanisms of the club, and he wished to get in touch with some of those with whom he had shared a great bond and spirit (interview with IPC Company Secretary, John Gore).

[15] *Wide World Magazine*, 3, 18 (September 1899), p.580.

[16] See George Newnes, 'From Cairo to Cataract', *Strand Magazine*, 15, 87 (March 1897), pp.305-316; 'A Journey to Jerusalem', *Strand Magazine*, 15, 87 (April 1898), pp.436-442.

[17] George Newnes, 'From Cairo to Cataract', p.316.

> The hours slip rapidly by amid the varying scenes. Nobody is
> ever bored in Cairo. It seems as if every nation on earth has sent
> its quota to form the general kaleidoscope.[18]

Just as Cairo represented, for Newnes, the geographical site at which the kaleidoscopic effect was manifested, so his magazine represented the textual site at which a multiplicity of images, scenes, peoples, countries and ideas were explored. For Newnes, the effect was intimately associated with time (both the terms he used to indicate variety - 'ever-changing panorama' and 'kaleidoscope' - are coupled with the mention of 'hours'), and with the enormous geographical and cultural scope of the world. *The Wide World* was an expression of the kaleidoscopic possibilities offered by the far corners of the earth within a newly expanded sense of time and space.

In fact, in his two travel tales written for *The Strand*, Newnes introduced many of the themes which were to thread through the narratives of *The Wide World*. Racism, typical of the period and of *Wide World* narratives, flavoured the traveller's engagement with his surroundings. And the assumptions of a socially segregated society produced a perspective within which the native population represented a servant class. Newnes's long monograph on the dragoman employed by his party to accompany them on their trip up the Nile reinforced such a view. The dragoman's construction as the ideal manservant characterised the depiction of native races in *The Wide World* in a manner that reinforced their inferiority and subservience.[19]

Newnes made a conscious effort to distinguish his perspective as a 'traveller' from that of the mere 'tourist', representing it as authentic, fresh and disinterestedly objective. He thus expressed a dichotomy that had evolved during the nineteenth century, stimulated by the development of mass tourism in the century's latter half.[20] 'I recommend that all travellers on the Nile, who charter their own private steamers, visit some of those places where Cook's tourist boats do not stop' he wrote, portraying Thomas Cook as the manufacturer of the tourist. 'There you see the real Eastern life, untouched by European invasion, and the curiosity you arouse in them and they arouse in you is mutually interesting.' He himself went to places 'unknown to the usual tourist'.[21]

Newnes depicted himself as a traveller with a conscience and an understanding of the environment through which he moved. Bemoaning the demand for 'backsheesh' in Egypt, and the fact that 'British and American tourists by their lavishness have made the natives dissatisfied with less than half a

---

[18] Ibid.

[19] He was likened to 'admirable Crichton', who 'was supposed to know everything and do everything'.

[20] James Buzard has argued that the practice of 'travel' acquired a special meaning in the nineteenth century through a process of cultural stereotyping in which the traveller was defined in opposition to the tourist. See James Buzard, *The Beaten Track: European Tourism, Literature and the Ways to Culture, 1800-1918*, Oxford: Clarendon, 1993.

[21] George Newnes, 'From Cairo to Cataract', p.311.

piastre' (1 1/4d.), he claimed that 'the best way is to pay only for services rendered, and thus discourage this tiresome and demoralising wholesale beggary'.[22] This was the language of the debate over English Poor Law reform. *Wide World* narrators typically saw themselves as engaging in an authentic process of 'exploration' and 'discovery' in 'remote regions' (James Buzard's 'off the beaten track'). Unlike the conventional 'tourist' locations on the Continent, these places offered infinite space for the creative expression of an authentic, dynamic and heroic self-image. The notion of authenticity, moreover, was central to the appeal of the magazine.

Whilst Newnes revealed himself to be aware of the transformative effects of 'European invasion', his own engagement with his surroundings was underpinned by imperial ideology. His sense of horror at the 'depravity' and 'degradation' which he witnessed at the Fish Market in Cairo, for instance, was heightened by the fact that this was 'a country under British rule'. At the same time, he found comfort in his faith in British imperialism:

> It is only fair to say, that since the British occupation, much has been done to sweep away these vice spots, and doubtless more will be accomplished in the future.[23]

Newnes and his party also gave provisions, in the form of dates, oranges, bread, cheese and cigarettes to the workmen and soldiers engaged in the building of the Berber portion of the railway line. They thus constructed themselves as representatives of a benevolent kind of British imperialism.[24] Similarly, many of the travel narratives of *The Wide World* were underpinned by a belief in imperialism and 'civilised' values.

In introducing his first travel narrative in *The Strand*, Newnes defined it against a tradition of travel writing that was becoming outdated:

> This is not an attempt to describe the archaeological and historic wonders that abound in the land of the Pharoahs. That work has been done so often and so well, that further effort would probably result in mere repetition.[25]

Such 'work', linked to the tradition of the eighteenth and early nineteenth-century Grand Tour, and associated with an educated class seeking to hone their literary skills and confirm their social status, was governed by generic convention and generally divested of the personalised reactions of the authors themselves.[26]

---

[22] Ibid., p.314.

[23] Ibid., p.308.

[24] Ibid., p.311

[25] Ibid., p.305.

[26] See Charles L. Batten, Jr, *Pleasurable Instruction: Form and Convention in Eighteenth Century Travel Literature*, Berkeley: University of California Press, 1978, pp.117-119. In a novel which captured the dryly humorous spirit of the *fin de siècle*, Samuel Butler satirised George Pontifex's conventionally eloquent and falsely rapturous descriptions of his

Newnes characterised it neatly through his use of the conventionally expectation-raising phrase 'land of the Pharoahs', and through the mention and linguistic enactment of literary repetition ('so often and so well').

Travel narratives of the late nineteenth century, on the other hand, tended to be rather autobiographical, containing a substantial element of personal reaction and anecdote, and designed largely to provide entertainment. Thus, Newnes went on to characterise his own narrative as 'an account of the experiences of six Britishers who spent about a month on the glorious Nile'. 'What they saw and what they did', he modestly suggested, 'may be of interest to those who have never traversed those regions, and it will revive pleasant memories perhaps in those who know them well.'[27] It was this approach that *The Wide World* represented. Newnes's magazine consisted of 'plain, straightforward narratives' which stimulated the imaginations of the untravelled and the empathy of those for whom travel was within the realms of experience. Its success depended on heroic individual action and entertaining originality. Its narratives represented a new, less stylised, more accessible style of literary performance and an expansion in the geographical field covered by authors for whom travel was no longer limited to the Continent. And its character reflected new developments in literature, periodical publishing and printing technology.

The expansion of England overseas had worked its way into literature in the nineteenth century, shaping the novel, popular magazines and the newspaper press. Imperialist fiction such as that produced by Rudyard Kipling, G.A. Henty, Bertram Mitford and Rider Haggard, written in the journalistic style, was in vogue in the nineties.[28] Kipling's soldier songs and stories, in particular, captured the market, as his writing resonated with his own generation's experience of the partition of Africa, South-East Asia and the Pacific; a generation that had seen the last corners of the earth revealed to them and had been involved in the establishment of a comprehensive world system of communication and commerce. This generation saw themselves as 'the makers of the world as it was at the turn of the century', and saw the story of the British in this, the age of Kitchener, Rhodes, Milner and others, as 'the story of the British overseas'.[29] Kipling's stories and poems represented an acknowledgment of the importance of the Briton living in the 'outpost of empire'; 'the elemental Britisher who has made some utmost end of [the world] his own', to use E.W.

---

his travel on the Continent: 'The first glimpse of Mont Blanc threw Mr Pontifex into a conventional ecstasy.' See Samuel Butler, *The Way of all Flesh*, London: Signet, 1903, p.16.

[27] George Newnes, 'From Cairo to Cataract', p.305.

[28] In Henty's novel *With Kitchener in the Soudan*, for instance, Gregory Hilliard describes his efforts at short-story writing whilst in Egypt, commenting that 'editors of magazines like a succession of tales of that kind'. See G.A. Henty, *With Kitchener in the Soudan*, London: Blackie, 1903, p.22.

[29] Charles Carrington, *Rudyard Kipling: His Life and Work*, London: Macmillan, 1978, pp.393-398.

Hornung's phrase.[30] This was exactly the sort of person who contributed to *The Wide World Magazine*, and guaranteed its popularity.

The hero in H.G. Wells' novel on Edwardian life, *The New Machiavelli*, claimed of Kipling that he 'helped to broaden my geographical sense immensely'.[31] The American magazine *National Geographic*, founded in 1889, sought specifically to disseminate geographical information. Beginning as a technical, scientific journal, scholarly in style, and limited in circulation, it had developed a popular, entertaining style by the turn of the century, using many eye-witness accounts and photographic reproductions. According to the editors of Time-Life Books, 'the magazine soon had swarms of photographers circling the globe to bring back for stay-at-homes pictures of exotic lands and cultures'.[32] A range of new periodicals, published in various countries, represented a similar project. These included *Annales de géographie* (1891), *The Geographical Journal* (1893) and *Geographische Zeitschrift* (1895). Among magazines which offered the global perspective to the wider audience, *The Wide World Magazine* (1898) was the outstanding British version, shaped by the man and the hour.

The scope of 'international news' in the press expanded as Reuters, the Press Association and various other international news agencies extended their networks of correspondents and 'special artists' across the world, and the demand for imperial and foreign news increased.[33] The content of international news became a subject associated with the continuing debate over 'popular journalism'. 'As to the great majority of the uneducated and unintelligent classes', wrote Moberly Bell in 1903:

> ... people of this sort don't want news unless it is something that they can imagine happening to themselves .... As to a place where they have never been and know no one who has ever been there - nothing can interest them about it .... Feeble jokes, tit-bits of sorts, is what they want and can get for a halfpenny or penny already.[34]

[30] E.W. Hornung, *The Thousandth Woman*, London: George E. Harrap, 1924, p.10.

[31] H.G. Wells as cited in Charles Carrington, op. cit., p.409.

[32] *Photojournalism*, Life Library of Photography, Time-Life International, 1971, p.16.

[33] The 'Special Artist' developed into a particular breed: adventurous, resourceful, flamboyant, quick at sketching, and possessing considerable social and journalistic status. G.A. Henty was a 'Special' for the *Illustrated London News* in the Abyssinia expedition of 1867. And C.J. Staniland, who produced many of the illustrations in *The Wide World*, was a 'Special' on the Franco-German front in the Crimean campaign. See Simon Houfe, *The Dictionary of British Book Illustrators and Caricaturists, 1800-1914 with Introductory Chapters on the Rise and Progress of the Art*, Antique Collectors Club, 1978, pp.137-140.

[34] Moberly Bell, *Life and Letters of Moberly Bell*, as cited in Michael Palmer, 'The British Press and International News, 1851-99', in George Boyce, James Curran and Pauline Wingate (eds), *Newspaper History from the Seventeenth Century to the Present Day*, London: Constable, 1978, p.216.

The reference to 'tit-bits' available for a penny was clearly a dig at *Tit-Bits*. In response to competition from Dalziels, a new international agency, Reuters and the Press Association created a supplementary foreign service, providing news in which the human interest element and personal angle were dominant. In the context of developments in popular journalism, as Michael Palmer has observed, there occurred 'a heightening in the tension between accuracy as against rapidity and colour'.[35] If such a tension was beyond the scope of *Tit-Bits*, it was the very substance of *The Wide World*, in which Newnes sought to reconcile these two elements by combining them in stories which reflected the motto 'Truth is Stranger than Fiction'.

The Wide World, as the editor was careful to point out, provided both 'instruction and entertainment', enacting, in this respect, a long-established literary ideal of 'high culture'.[36] Of the 'Odds and Ends' section he remarked:

> And you cannot help acquiring valuable knowledge as you glance at these photos, and read the brief description accompanying each - knowledge more accurate and practical than that contained in academical text-books.[37]

The first-person narratives published in this magazine enabled its readers to imagine the incidents related 'happening to themselves', by transporting them to all corners of the earth through the authentic anecdote and the novel photograph. Newnes's magazine provided material that was practical, as opposed to 'intellectual' or academic, but was also *accurate*.

Photography revolutionised magazine illustration in the 1890s. The Kodak camera gained remarkable popularity, photography clubs sprang up everywhere, and a number of photographic societies were formed. And photographic illustration was central to the establishment and success of *The Wide World Magazine*, as illustration was characteristic of many of Newnes's magazines. Magazines such as the *Illustrated London News* in Britain and *Frank Leslie's Illustrated Paper* in the U.S. had been devoting a substantial amount of space to pictures since the mid-nineteenth century. It was only in the 1890s, however, that the transition to widespread use of half-tone photographic reproduction made possible the detailed rendering of high-contrast pictures such as those appearing in *The Wide World*.[38] In Newnes's magazine, photographs were celebrated as a

---

[35] Michael Palmer, 'The British Press', in George Boyce, James Curran and Pauline Wingate (eds), op. cit., p.215.

[36] *Wide World Magazine*, 5, 26 (May 1900), p.218.

[37] *Wide World Magazine*, 4, 24 (March 1900), p.747.

[38] Despite the fact that technological developments in the U.S. had made the reproduction of photos in half-tone by lithographic printing process possible by 1880, a successful campaign by newspaper artists and hand engravers delayed the introduction of half-tone reproduction. See R. Smith Schuneman 'Art of Photography: A Question for Newspaper Editors of the 1890s', *Journalism Quarterly*, 42, 1 (Winter 1965), pp.43-52, and Robert S. Kahn, 'Magazine Photography Begins', *Journalism Quarterly*, 42, 1 (Winter 1965), pp.53-59. Amongst the large-circulation newspapers the New York *Daily Graphic* was the first

novel form of recording posterity, and a feature of the magazine that brought ideas 'to the minds of the untravelled' with compelling force. They also represented scientific 'evidence', and were used as a tool of scientific or social investigation. Missionaries, anthropologists and criminologists all employed photography in the accumulation of objective data, and 'notebook and camera' became the essential equipment of the traveller in *The Wide World*.[39]

Just as Newnes took part in the development of photographic reproduction in periodical publishing, so he was at the forefront in developing the 'true story magazine'. He pioneered a formula that was later taken up by the American publishing giant Bernarr Macfadden in the 1920s. Macfadden, who like Newnes established a vast array of magazines which sustained large circulations and amassed him a considerable fortune, established a magazine entitled *True Story* in 1919. It was one of the early 'confession magazines', and its success prompted many publishers to emulate it. Macfadden had visited Britain in 1899 and it is quite possible that he had been impressed with George Newnes's new monthly publication, *The Wide World Magazine*, which was attracting a good deal of publicity with the de Rougemont series at the time. Macfadden insisted, in the opening number of *True Story*, on Newnes's motto that 'Truth is Stranger than Fiction'. The article was entitled 'Why the True-Story Magazine is Different'. In publishing *The Wide World Magazine* Newnes was thus, in some sense, the originator of the 'confession magazine' or 'true story magazine' genre that was to gain immense popularity in the 1930s.[40] And one contributor commented that the publisher of *The Wide World* deserved praise for filling the void in modern literature by supplying 'that class of history which has for so long past been received by the unbelievers with howls of derision as mere "traveller's tales"'.[41]

In one instance, Newnes's magazine actually became famous for the inauthenticity of one of its narratives. In its early days it serialised Louis de Rougemont's incredible and exciting account of his adventures in Northern Australia, stranded, Robinson Crusoe-like, on a desert island for two and a half years, and living with a 'cannibal tribe' of Aborigines. The series was entitled

---

successfully to demonstrate half-tone engraving in 1873, and the London *Daily Mail* published its first photographic engravings in 1904.

[39] See, for instance, an exposé entitled 'How the Opium Fiends were Fought with a Camera', *Wide World Magazine*, 5, 26 (May 1900), pp.187-191.

[40] Like Newnes, Macfadden called for extensive reader commentary and criticism (as well as manuscripts), offered prizes for contributions and made extensive use of pictures. Appearing in an age in which commercially networked radio was developing rapidly, *True Story* spawned the human interest radio programme. In 1928, Macfadden introduced 'True Story Hour', introducing Mary and Bob, 'radio tourists' who travelled America 'seeing life' and collecting 'true stories'. The programme was advertised in language that closely reflected Newnes's descriptions of *Wide World*. See *True Story*, January 1930.

[41] *Wide World Magazine*, 4, 21 (January 1900), p.385. The editor reinforced the point, commenting about one narrative: 'Remember, this is the evidence of a responsible expert, given before a Government Commission, and not a mere squatter's yarn.' See *Wide World Magazine*, 1, 2 (May 1898), p.125.

'The Adventures of Louis de Rougemont', and was illustrated by the celebrated artist Alfred Pearse. It ran for seven months in the first year of the magazine. De Rougemont was taken up as a national hero, his account of his experiences in 'the wilds of unexplored Australia' meeting with unparalleled enthusiasm in Britain. Readers of the series sent thousands of letters to the *Wide World* narrator. De Rougemont's narrative was authenticated by British scientific organisations such as the British Association and the Royal Geographical Society, to whom he presented a number of papers. It thus entailed something of a crisis for readers when De Rougemont, his stories becoming more and more far-fetched, was shown to be a fraud, or at the very least to have 'exaggerated' his experiences. The solution to this crisis of authenticity? De Rougemont's narrative was validated as extremely *good fiction*, exciting 'the deepest interest'.[42] Thus objectivity and authenticity were written off in favour of the appeal of the story; 'reality' was subordinated to 'fiction'. 'Rapidity and colour' served, for the moment, to rescue the popularity of the magazine.[43]

The late nineteenth century brought new modes of thinking about time and space, the material foundation for which lay in technological innovations including the telephone, wireless, telegraph, x-ray, high-speed rotary press, cinema, bicycle, automobile and aeroplane. As early as 1889, Lord Salisbury commented on the simultaneity of experience made possible by the telegraph, which had 'combined together almost at one moment ... the opinions of the whole intelligent world with respect to everything that is passing at that time upon the face of the globe'.[44] In *The Strand*, Arthur Mee, subsequently editor of *The Children's Encyclopaedia*, reported on a system of telephony in Budapest, in which subscribers could be switched on to concerts and news services. He foreshadowed an escalation in the scale of such operations. The air of excited anticipation that characterised the article, and the ideas and language contained in it, mirrored the tone, contents and language of *The Wide World*, launched in the same year: 'Who dare to say that in twenty years the electric miracle will not bring all the corners of the earth to our own fireside?'[45] The cinema, discovered between 1893 and 1896, had a far-reaching impact because it could bring together an unprecedented variety of images and arrange them coherently into a unified whole. A number of early film-makers employed contrast editing or intercutting, splicing open a moment to insert a number of simultaneous activities or scenes. Stephen Kern has summarised the psychological effects of these

[42] *Wide World Magazine*, 2, 12 (March 1899), p.643.

[43] The incident was widely publicised, and became an accepted item of cultural reference. See, for example, Beth Ellis, *An English Girl's First Impressions of Burma*, London: Simpkin, Marshall, Hamilton, Kent and Co., 1899, p.246. Newnes's Arctic expedition was partly designed to counter the damage his reputation had sustained in the de Rougemont episode, by providing *The Wide World* with unimpeachable material.

[44] Speech printed in *The Electrician*, 8 November, 1889, as cited in Kern, op. cit., p.68.

[45] *Strand Magazine*, 18, 108 (December 1899).

developments in the phrase 'human consciousness expanded across space'.[46] It might have been specifically intended to describe *The Wide World*.

Cultural developments such as the stream-of-consciousness novel, psychoanalysis, cubism, philosophical perspectivism, Futurism, simultaneous poetry, geopolitical theory and internationalism shaped consciousness directly. And whilst *The Wide World* preceded many of these movements, it was, like them, associated with a cultural climate within which Victorian models of linear development and single authority were rejected in favour of a democratically modern outlook on social, temporal and spatial organisation. Various writers produced versions of simultaneous poetry and debated the new form. Henri-Martin Barzun, for instance, wrote a poem about the unification of the world by wireless. Writing in 1904, Paul Claudel observed that the morning newspaper gave a sense of 'the present in its totality'.[47] The highpoint of simultaneous literature was *Ulysses*, serialised in the *Little Review* from 1918, in which James Joyce, deeply impressed by cinematic montage, used various techniques to create an impression of simultaneous activity. He argued that only simultaneous poetry could capture the democratic character and multiplicity of modern life: 'multiple lyricism must render the multiplicity of modern life'.[48] In the first quarter of the nineteenth century, a number of writers, including Proust, Virginia Woolf, Gertrude Stein, Joyce and Nietzsche, went on to describe and render a temporally expanded or thickened, and experientially heightened present in response to such debates. *The Wide World Magazine*, with few dates to locate its narratives temporally, a catalogue of contemporary experience condensed into each single issue or volume, and a manifesto, according to the publisher, to compress 'history' and 'the present' into a heightened moment of 'awakening' akin to Pater's aesthetic 'moments as they pass', was emblematic of just such a temporally thickened present.

Newnes's magazine was a kind of textually manufactured version of simultaneous action and a temporally thickened and spatially eclectic present, in which the reader was presented with a diverse set of temporal, cultural and geographical settings. Out of these, the publisher created a single issue in an attempt to bring order to heterogeneity. In a conceptual shift from the rules of perspective that had governed the rendering of space in painting for upwards of 400 years, the Impressionist and Cubist painters of the period used multiple perspective to create radical treatments of space that resembled the techniques of the cinema. In the same way, the narrators and photographers of *The Wide World Magazine* displayed various degrees and types of imaginative engagement with their subject matter, applying a multiplicity of perspectives - western, European, British, 'civilised'; 'scientific', ethnographic, administrative; traveller

---

[46] Stephen Kern, op. cit., p.34.

[47] Max Nordau, *Degeneration*, 1892 as cited in Stephen Kern, op. cit., p.70; Paul Claudel, 'Connaissance du temps', in *Fou-Tcheou* (1904), as cited in Stephen Kern, op. cit., p.70.

[48] Stephen Kern, op. cit., p.72.

or tourist, missionary, hunter or exile - to the hierarchy of geographical and cultural spaces made available by nineteenth-century technological progress and late nineteenth-century imperialism.

The 'Odds and Ends' section at the end of each issue of *The Wide World* represented the visual and imaginative fusion of distant events. It consisted of a series of photos accompanied by commentary, and ranged over all areas of the world. This feature actually appeared to diminish distance and compress time through a series of rapid narrative and photographic shifts from one location to the next. The effect resembled that produced by a kaleidoscope, by the quick cut of the developing cinema, or by the simultaneous poetry of writers such as Blaise Cendrars.[49] The 'Odds and Ends' rubric united action at many separate places by stringing it together in a series of barely separated titles, much as James Joyce was to create the impression of unifying disparate events or settings in *Ulysses* by employing a series of run-on phrases, separated only by simple conjunctives. One example from *The Wide World* in 1900 may serve to illustrate this technique (*see Figure 12*):

> An Ambulance in the Backwoods - What a Cyclone Did - Religious Fervour in Mexico - Tea-Picking in Assam - A River Festival on the Irawaddy - Life in Tahiti - The Sacred Monkey Temple - Love-Making in Havana - The New Zealand Rabbit Inspector, etc.[50]

The reader of Newnes's magazine was transported from one location and situation to the next in an imaginative version of travel or a textual version of cinematic montage. The scope and variety of the images which 'generally reach us in thousands from remote countries', the editor emphasised, 'enable the home-stayer to do his sightseeing by his own fire-side.'[51] The magazine thus represented the exotic domesticated, 'remote countries' being assimilated to 'hearth and home' through the medium of the ground-breaking journalist or photographer.

The 'contents-map', an innovative feature which rapidly became a symbol of *The Wide World*, was introduced in 1899. It consisted of a world map on which were pinpointed the locations of the various stories recounted therein, and appeared at the front of each issue initially, but was later transferred to the back page. This feature was a visual enactment of the new temporal dimension of simultaneity and thus manifested a developing sense of temporal awareness. The

---

[49] Cendrars published what he described as the 'First Simultaneous Book' in 1913: a poem describing his journey from Moscow to Harbin on the Trans-Siberian railway in 1904, alongside a map showing the route and an illustration made up of 'simultaneous' colours. It was designed to create an impression of the journey as a whole. And the poem toyed with chronology by uniting remote ages, compressed time, and edited out spatial separation to break down the divisiveness of distance.

[50] *Wide World Magazine*, 5, 29 (August 1900), p.553.

[51] *Wide World Magazine*, 3, 18 (September 1899), p.666.

maps placed the scenes of *Wide World* narratives in their geographical context, fostering the development of spatial perception. The reference labels (paraphrased versions of the titles of the stories) demonstrated the way in which innovative publishers such as Newnes had perfected the art of titillating the readers' interest with snappy titles (*see Figure 13*).

Cartographic illustration was, in fact, rare in British and American newspapers until photographic engraving decreased the cost of preparing illustrations and diagrams for the popular press in the 1890s. But it became a feature of the foreign news of the Harmsworth press in the early twentieth century. Thus geography gained a place in the New Journalism.[52] Indeed, the nineteenth century saw the emergence of the modern discipline of geography and the diffusion of geographical knowledge through geographical societies, periodicals devoted to academic geography, and by the end of the century, through the new comprehensive schools, universities and the popular press. For example, the illustrated school atlas came to popularity in the 1890s.[53] And at the instigation of the Royal Geographical Society some geographical education began at Oxford, where H.J. Mackinder was appointed reader in 1887, and Cambridge, where the first lecturers were appointed in 1888. In 1904, an International Committee for the Map of the World was founded: a reflection of the growth of internationalism and the cultural significance of geography and cartography in the period. Through the printed map, *The Wide World* extended the geographical horizons of its readers, and participated in the 'expansion of human consciousness across the globe'. It attempted, like the contemporaneous *National Geographic* but in a different manner, 'to popularise the science of geography' and take 'this great world of ours' into 'the homes of the people'.[54]

At a linguistic level, the distant and diverse scenes of the 'wide world' were assimilated to the experience of the readers of *The Wide World* through simile. Familiar comparisons were frequently used: the bridge at Chao-Chow-Fu in China was 'like old London Bridge'; a memorial arch was 'the nearest Chinese

[52] The historiography of map journalism is still remarkably thin. The five-volume Library of Congress *Bibliography of Cartography*, covering the period 1875-1972, listed a single study of news maps: Walter Ristow's 1957 essay on maps of the second World War and the Cold War in daily newspapers and weekly news magazines. See 'Journalistic Cartography', *Surveying and Mapping*, 17, 4 (October 1957), pp.369-390. The few recent studies to explore the field of map journalism have included Mark Monmonier's *Maps with the News*, Chicago: University of Chicago Press, 1989; David Jolly's two-part study, *Maps of America in Periodicals before 1800*, Brookline, Massachusetts: D.C. Jolly, 1989; and a few relevant articles. See, for instance, Paul Bimal Kanti, 'Maps on Journal Covers', *Geography*, 76 (January 1990), pp.52-57 and W.G.V. Balchin, 'Media Map Watch', *The Geographical Magazine*, 57 (August 1985), pp.408-409.

[53] Frye's *Complete Geography* (an illustrated atlas with an impressive collection of illustrations, mainly supplied from the Gardiner collection of photographs belonging to the Geography Department of Harvard University), appeared in the U.S. in 1895. It was reproduced in a modified form in England as A.J. Herbertson's *Illustrated School Geography*, London: Edward Arnold, 1898.

[54] Bernard Block, 'Romance and High Purpose: *The National Geographic*', *Wilson Library Bulletin* (January 1984), p.334.

approach to a European triumphal arch'. Such allusions, applied within a global perspective, were part of the language of internationalism and of the spatial revolution that had so deeply affected contemporary culture. One narrator, for instance, likened 'the system of "smokes" by which the black fellows signal intelligence to other natives hundreds of miles distant in the space of a very few hours' in the Australian desert to Marconi's wireless telegraphy.[55] Marinetti insisted in a manifesto of 1912 that the modern writer must create a new language making extensive use of analogy, since in the new technologically-transformed world in which distant, seemingly diverse things could be rapidly assembled together, everything must bear an analogical connection to something else.[56] Many *Wide World* narrators showed themselves to be versed in the new language.

Geopolitics, a branch of social science that emphasised the connection between the size and geographical location of states and their politics and history, and developed alongside imperial expansion in the late nineteenth century, placed a new emphasis on the notion of distance. A variety of writers, from Friederich Ratzel (who pioneered modern systematic geopolitics in Germany) to Halford J. Mackinder (Reader in Geography at Oxford and Director of the London School of Economics) espoused theories of geopolitics. Some saw the global perspective as a force for peace and community,[57] and others as a cause of war, but all shared the notion that the world was becoming smaller and more unified. William Gladstone, for instance, remarked that 'each train that passes a frontier weaves the web of the human federation'.[58] One *Wide World* narrator, writing from an ethnographical perspective, represented the global perspective in similarly optimistic terms as 'the transition and fusion of opposite races'. He foresaw the development of the kind of global village anticipated by many who detected a growing sense of community, unity and collaboration in the diminution of distances between people and nations and the extension of experience beyond traditional horizons:

> To the historian of the twenty-first century one of the most remarkable phases of the Victorian age will be the awakening of native races by contact with civilised man .... In a few generations the very natives themselves will have ceased to exist as a separate people, just as the Picts and Britons, from whom most Englishmen could claim descent, merged their blood with that of their Roman and Saxon and Norman invaders to form

---

[55] *Wide World Magazine*, 16, 94 (January 1906), p.361.

[56] Filippo Marinetti, 'Technical Manual of Futurist Literature' (1912), as cited in Stephen Kern, op. cit., p.219.

[57] Hopes for international cooperation ran high when forty-five nations sent representatives to the Second International Conference at the Hague in 1907. In fact, the number of international committees grew at a rapid rate after the turn of the century, 119 being formed between 1900 and 1909, and 112 more in the next five years before the war. See Stephen Kern, op. cit., p.232.

[58] William Gladstone as cited in Stephen Kern, op. cit., p.229.

> the English people to-day. The eating up of nations is as old as
> the human race, and the romance of the assimilating stages
> comes with time.[59]

Despite the references to the civilising mission, it was a view that emphasised
international and racial unity. Cannibalism ('the eating up of nations') itself
became a form of civilisation, ultimately transformed by time into 'romance'.

Internationalism, however, was also associated with imperialism and led to
conflict. 'Internationalism and imperialism', as Stephen Kern has observed,
'coiled around the staff of new technology and around one another like the
snakes of a caduceus.'[60] The language and literature of geopolitics fed into a
growing culture of internationalism. Yet geopolitics also devised the notion that
was to become the ethical imperative of imperialism - that 'big is good'. In
Britain, various writers articulated the popularity of expansion: J.R. Seeley in *The
Expansion of England* (1883), James Froude in *Oceania* (1885) and Sir Charles
Dilke with an imperialist tract of 1890 that followed the tradition he had
pioneered in *Greater Britain* (1868). All of these imperialist apologists shared
the same imagery and rhetoric, because they shared a commitment to the idea that
size was essential to national strength, prosperity and hope for future generations.
It was an idea that was embedded in the historical consciousness of European
peoples, and its distinctive manifestation in the late nineteenth century was
materially and intellectually dependent upon the new technology that had unified
distant places with a system of efficient communication and transportation.

The Wide World was a manifestation of imperial ideology. Through the
association of its title with both an imperialistic national creed (via the anthem,
'Land of Hope and Glory') and with individual moral progress (via that work so
immensely popular in Victorian times, *Pilgrim's Progress*), it symbolised the
link between the civilised individual representative of Britain (or the western
world) and a powerful, progressive nation.[61] It represented an acknowledgment
of the latent potentialities of the entire globe - 'the consistency and density of
continuous enterprise' which Edward Said has identified as a product of the
move toward empire.[62]

In *Culture and Imperialism*, Said has argued that European writing on
Africa, India, parts of the Far East, Australia and the Caribbean constituted a
'structure of attitude and reference', and was part of a European effort to rule
distant lands and peoples. Stories, according to Said, are the basis for the
negotiation of power relations, and there is thus a crucial connection between

---

[59] *Wide World Magazine*, 3, 16 (July 1899), p.376.

[60] Stephen Kern, op. cit., p.232.

[61] 'Land of Hope and Glory, Mother of the Free,/ How shall we extol thee, who are
born of thee?/ *Wider still and wider shall thy bounds be set;*/ God who made thee mighty, make
thee mightier yet' (A.C. Benson, written for Elgar's *Coronation Ode*, 1902). 'As I walked
through the wilderness of this world' (John Bunyan, *The Pilgrim's Progress* (1678), opening
lines).

[62] Edward Said, *Culture and Imperialism*, London: Vintage, 1994, p.9.

imperial literature and imperial politics; between the cultural and political spheres. 'There is a convergence', argues Said, 'between the great geographical scope of empires, especially the British one, and universalising cultural discourses.'[63] Patrick Brantlinger has traced a similar connection between the expansion of empire in the Victorian period, and the development of imperial ideology through various narrative forms of discourse - adventure tales, travelogues and histories.[64] *The Wide World* represented this very connection, engaging in a process of cultural and ideological assimilation of the periphery that paralleled geographical expansion and drew on the language of imperialism.

'Exploration', 'penetration' and geographical inquiry were common themes in the stories of *The Wide World*. Such concepts were enlisted in the process of asserting white racial supremacy and arguing the moral necessity of 'knowing' and 'civilising' continents such as Africa. The 'dark continent' of Africa was 'opened up' by British 'missionary pioneers'. 'Wild and little-known regions' were 'penetrated into'. One narrator related how priests of the Greek Church 'penetrated far into the interior' of Alaska, and 'through the influence of their teachings paved the way for the peaceful entry of the dominant race', acting as substitutes for John the Baptist.[65] Another concluded his narrative of exploration with a celebration of British imperialism:

> I have been told by some people that it was foolish to venture into an unknown country, inhabited by savage tribes, without an adequate escort of armed men. The only answer I can give to this is that if all explorers had gone on this principle, our present knowledge of the world would be practically limited by the borders of civilised countries, and many nations who now enjoy the protection and civilisation of the British flag would still be living in a state of savage warfare and slavery.[66]

The rhetoric of the civilising mission was repeatedly employed in *The Wide World* narratives to lend moral and intellectual authority to the process of expansion. Acts of geographical exploration and discovery were linguistically associated with white racial dominance (and with male sexual dominance). The language of geographical expansion was transparently the language of power.

Yet other cultures were often resistant to assimilation. White notions of justice and the rule of law prevailed in one story, set in the U.S., about the punishment of two Indians - 'Head Chief and Young Mule' - for the 'deliberate murder' of a white man. The story ended with the mother of Young Mule shaking hands with the white Inspector, followed by all of the Council of Indians. This ritual apparently signalled reconciliation. But even as it was performed, the

---

[63]   Ibid., p.130.

[64]   Patrick Brantlinger, *Rule of Darkness: British Literature and Imperialism, 1830-1914*, London: Cornell University Press, 1988.

[65]   *Wide World Magazine*, 3, 17 (August 1899), p.424.

[66]   *Wide World Magazine*, 2, 8 (November 1898), p.208.

native Indians revealed the irreconcilability of Indian notions of 'compensation' with western notions of punishment, saying the Inspector 'only did his duty, but that they could not understand why two Cheyennes should die for one white man' when they had offered thirty ponies in compensation for the death of the white man.[67] Imperial expansion, as it was represented in *The Wide World*, was not without cultural resistance.

Racial contact was often described in terms that belonged to the relatively new sciences of anthropology and ethnography. These disciplines stimulated the codification of racial difference and developed categories such as 'primitive', 'savage', 'degenerate', 'natural' and 'unnatural'; categories through which *Wide World* narrators articulated and confronted racial difference. Colonial schools were founded in Britain, France and Germany in the 1890s, and they featured new studies in ethnology, linguistics and folklore as training for colonial service. *The Wide World Magazine* told the story of various Britons and other Europeans who went and lived amongst native tribes and provided descriptions of their habits and cultures. Two young Oxford graduates, for example, went to live 'Among the Head-Hunters of Lushai', and another narrator 'Among the Pigmies'. Very physical descriptions of native peoples were common, the Zulus, for example, boasting 'great thighs and biceps', and Lushai women possessing 'calves of the legs to an enormous size'. 'Hairy, of forbidding aspect, and greatly emaciated', wrote one author of the aborigine pictured within his narrative, making reference to Social Darwinism, 'he is a fair type of the low order of human beings known as the Australian desert aborigines'.[68]

The articulation of racial difference in *The Wide World* was structured by a vocabulary of racism. The individual characteristics of native peoples tended to be subsumed within a language that nominated entire races as 'wild savages', 'unruly hordes', 'primitive' or 'uncivilised' peoples. In one narrative about the transporting of pilgrims to Mecca, the pilgrims are described variously as 'an aggressive lot of fanatics', a 'cantankerous congregation', a 'screeching, turbulent mob of Mecca-bound pilgrims', and a 'horde of half-crazy fanatics'. The narrator emphasises the lack of reason or self-restraint shown by the pilgrims when the ship runs into trouble, and the incongruity between the supposed motive for the pilgrims' journey and the intemperate, animalistic, instinctively self-preservational nature of their behaviour. Their moral weakness (which is implied to be racial) contrasts with the self-possessed heroism and 'determined appearance' of the ship's captain, who remains 'at his post on the bridge, directing operations', the very epitome of order, efficiency, resolution and vigour, and a fine representative of the sturdy British race. One 'grand old Arab sheik' is presented as a more dignified figure, 'offering supplications to Allah for the safety of himself and his fellow co-religionists'. But his dignity is signally destroyed when he refuses to be shifted from his dangerous position on the bridge, and is 'hurled down amongst the pilgrims, upon whom he descended

---

67 *Wide World Magazine*, 4, 21 (December 1899), pp.389-393.
68 *Wide World Magazine*, 16, 94 (January 1906), p.361.

with such force as almost to break the necks of two or three particularly vociferous Goanese merchants'.[69]

Yet some of the narrators of *The Wide World Magazine* depicted native peoples in a fashion articulated by Kipling in 'The White Man's Burden' (1899). He describes those under American rule as 'Your new-caught, sullen peoples,/ Half devil and half child.'[70] Thus, in one narrative entitled 'What I Saw at the Snake Dance', genuine affection and admiration for the native Moki Indians is mixed with a kind of compassionate and arrogant condescension: 'Look at them approach with dignity and seriousness .... We may lament their benighted condition, but we must respect their earnest prayers .... Look at the earnest faces of these poor savages as they pray.'[71]

Heroism, such as that demonstrated by the British sea captain, seems to be the defining characteristic of the European narrators and protagonists of *The Wide World*. But if heroism might appear to be a European monopoly, the narrator of one tale suggests otherwise by opening his narrative with the comment:

> The following story will show that deeds of bravery are not restricted to Europeans. In our self conceit we are apt to think that this is so, although even races which we consider untutored and barbarous perform from time to time astonishing acts of heroism. Most of these deeds - as distinguished from those of Europeans - pass unnoticed and unrecorded, and it is only now and then that we accidentally hear of an isolated case.[72]

Yet whilst the opening comments seem to establish the case for native heroism, the suggestion that these acts occur only 'from time to time' makes such heroism tenuous. At the same time, the native watchman's account of his adventures is sullied by 'profuse and flowery metaphor', whilst by contrast, the British narrator translates the story into 'plain, straightforward narrative', his prosaic self-discipline a reflection of his heroic brand of self-possession. True heroism, then, was essentially the preserve of the white, western man. And the evidence that he possessed this quality lay in his telling of his story, his civilised 'noticing' and 'recording' of a more barbarous kind of heroism which would otherwise have remained uncommemorated and accidental, 'life' rather than 'art'.

The 'expansion of human consciousness across the globe' was achieved in *The Wide World Magazine* through various mediators of the revolution in the dimensions of geographical, ideological and journalistic space who brought a range of perspectives to the wide world. 'All the world's a stage', wrote

[69] *Wide World Magazine*, 1, 2 (May 1898), p.153.

[70] Rudyard Kipling, *Selected Poetry* (ed. Craig Raine), Harmondsworth: Penguin, 1992, p.127.

[71] *Wide World Magazine*, 1, 2 (May 1898), pp.266-270.

[72] *Wide World Magazine*, 4, 21 (December 1899), p.372.

Shakespeare in *As You Like It*, 'and all the men and women merely players.'[73] The world, it appeared from this magazine, was a world populated by a network of Britons, Europeans and other emissaries of the West, and the text constituted a kind of roll of honour. The photographs, according to the editor, were collected by 'travellers, explorers, missionaries, tourists, naval and military officers, Government officials, and many others who "see the world", for reasons of pleasure, profit, or profession'.[74] The key players in the narratives of *The Wide World* were travellers, missionaries, hunters and exiles. Apollinaire had invented Baron d'Ormesan, a film director whose ability to appear simultaneously in a multitude of places around the world embodied the techniques of the cinema. The Baron died in 820 places simultaneously. *The Wide World*, with its cast of stock characters who related stories from all corners of the world within a single issue and thus created the illusion of being in many settings at once, produced a similar effect. And its narrator-players explored new ways of experiencing time and space, the multiple dimensions of imperial ideology (from methods of 'territorialisation', through the rhetoric and evidence of racial contact, to images of frontier manliness, and the literature of the 'victims of Mahdism'), the techniques of 'popular' journalism, and issues of gender stereotyping and its subversion.

The traveller was one character who claimed the 'wide world' as his theatre of action and interpreted it for readers. (This character was generally male, although occasionally female.) The term 'globetrotter' was part of a new jargon used to describe a type of traveller that was appearing in increasing numbers. The transport revolution made many new forms of travel available to contemporary adventurers, and accounts of circumnavigational, trans-Atlantic, cross-Continental and arctic travel abounded in *The Wide World*. 'Across Europe Without a Passport' (1899), 'Round the World on Wheels'(1899), 'My Attempt to Reach the North Pole'(1900), 'Twelve Thousand Miles AWheel [sic] in India' (1901), 'Across America in an Automobile' (1904), and 'Across the Great Thirst Land [Australia]' (1906) were but a few of these. Half a million British tourists went abroad in the early 1890s, and the number had grown to one million by the turn of the century. Both hunting and mountain-climbing, taking their devotees to distant venues, were heroic and popular pastimes.[75]

Travelling and exploring were, in many cases, conflated in *The Wide World*, 'the traveller' taking on the heroic, inquisitive, acquisitive character of the explorer and the agent of imperial expansion. The identity of the *Wide World* traveller-explorer was integrally associated with a particular type of engagement with Nature - scientific, exploitative, mastering and modernising - and with the

---

73   William Shakespeare, *As You Like It*, II. vii. 139.

74   *Wide World Magazine*, 4, 22 (January 1900), p.522.

75   *Wide World Magazine* picked up on the enthusiasm for mountain-climbing which Newnes had witnessed as a youth in the 1850s and 1860s: the so-called 'golden age' of mountain-climbing as a sport. See Bruce Haley, *The Healthy Body and Victorian Culture*, Cambridge, Massachusetts; Harvard University Press, 1978, p.132.

conquering of distance. The traveller made 'uncharted' and 'untravelled' territory accessible and knowable by means of exploration, surveying, the collection of botanical specimens and the discovery of territories and rivers. His identity thus consisted in the pursuit of scientific and geographical knowledge, and the ability to overcome the challenges of distance through technological superiority. Notably, his technological superiority was transformed into a brand of moral and physical superiority that took the form of endurance, self-discipline and sportsmanship. He was thus a vehicle of 'progress' and 'civilisation' (the keys to European economic and cultural hegemony). Whilst Europeans were represented as expanding their geographical horizons, native peoples were often characterised by their insular parochialism and 'ignorance of anything outside of their own native lands'.[76] The spirit of the geopolitical ethic that 'big is good' and of the transformation of space had obviously not penetrated the consciousness of native peoples. And such deficiencies in the spirit of geographical inquiry, it was implied, represented a justification for European imperialism.

If the male traveller made unfamiliar space familiar by mapping, surveying, and the combination of 'adventure and geography', then females, as they were represented in *The Wide World*, tended to 'territorialise' by introducing the symbols and effects of domesticated civilisation (pets, pictures, furniture and beds), setting up house and training native peoples as servants.[77] Thus one narrative, entitled 'My Housekeeping Troubles in East Africa', was summarised as follows: 'How she beautified her mud hut; the mysterious tragedy of the bottles of port; training savages as servants; famine experiences; queer pets.'[78] Such matters of domestic management would have interested the readers of *The Ladies' Field*, established by Newnes in the same year as *The Wide World Magazine*. In *The Wide World*, the 'ladies' field' was expanded to incorporate geographically and culturally remote regions and foreign experiences.

A significant number of missionaries also took part in *The Wide World*'s project to 'expand human consciousness across the globe', to assimilate the periphery to the centre and to 'weave the web of human federation', as Gladstone put it, through the civilising mission. In fact, the title of the magazine recalled the enthusiastic fervour of religious witnessing, via its connection with the Book of Common Prayer: 'The heavens declare the glory of God .... Their sound is gone out into all lands: Their words into the ends of the world.' Frederick Burns celebrated the work of the missionaries in a series entitled 'The Romance of the Mission Field'.[79] Missionaries were represented as agents for the creation of a

---

76 *Wide World Magazine*, 4, 21 (December 1899), p.345.

77 'Territorialisation' is the term that Eric Leeds has used to describe the process by which a 'mobile ethnicity - a transportable structure of human relations and identities - is grounded in a site'. See Eric Leed, *The Mind of the Traveller: From Gilgamesh to Global Tourism*, New York: Basic Books, 1991, p.18.

78 *Wide World Magazine*, 5, 28 (July 1900), p.389.

79 *Wide World Magazine*, 1, 2-6 (May-September 1898).

cinematic montage, collaborating in fusing distant places in the vision of *The Wide World*'s readership. Readers were thus presented with volumes 'full of graphic descriptions and photographs taken by the missionaries themselves, illustrating the wonderful sights seen by these devoted men, who pass their lives in remote regions'.[80]

The series was offered as an alternative to missionary publications (which were seen as epitomising evangelical and utilitarian attitudes to reading) in an attempt to lure readers who desired literature that was entertaining:

> You all know what a missionary is; but not all of you read missionary publications, having a leaning, perhaps to more frivolous and light reading generally. Nevertheless, it cannot be denied that missionaries are brought into daily contact with much that is quaint and picturesque, and had they only time to devote themselves to literature, they might well give to the world some of the most thrilling romances and extraordinary stories that were ever published.[81]

Once again, the issue of the demoralising effects of 'popular' literature reared its ugly head. And once again, the combination of truth and literary colour was presented as the solution to the problem. It was a solution that was driven home by the editor, who characterised the information provided for *The Wide World* by the Church Missionary Society as 'missionary tit-bits': a reference to Newnes's most famous popular publication.

The nature of British missionary endeavour and the rhetoric of the 'civilising mission' have been key themes of post-colonial history. As Catherine Hall has pointed out, the British recognised themselves *in relation* to other races. In describing, characterising and defining others, they described, characterised and defined themselves, 'constructing their own identities and writing their own histories' through their interventions in other cultures.[82] The missionaries of the *Wide World* saw themselves self-consciously as workers, influenced by the spirit of industry that Samuel Smiles had popularised in his influential work, *Self-Help* (1859).[83] Thus they were depicted as active and energetic men and women, prepared to undertake any task which presented itself, their activities spanning the gamut of civilised activity. 'For be it remembered', wrote Burns, 'our missionaries have to work. They may even have to make bricks occasionally, design churches, shoot alligators, adjudicate in disputes.' Medical and surgical

---

[80] *Wide World Magazine*, 1, 2 (May 1898), p.171.

[81] *Wide World Magazine*, 1, 2 (May 1898), p.171. See also 1, 6 (September 1898), p.476.

[82] Catherine Hall, *White, Male and Middle Class*, Cambridge: Polity Press, 1992, p.209.

[83] 'The spirit of self-help' wrote Smiles, 'as exhibited in the energetic action of individuals, has in all times been a marked feature of the English character, and furnishes the true measure of our power as a nation.' See Samuel Smiles, *Self-Help, With Illustrations of Character and Conduct*, London: The World Library, 1859, p.18.

knowledge, too, were 'all but indispensable in the missionary field'.[84] Missionary endeavour, as Kipling had shown, constituted 'The White Man's Burden', and was the mark of a morally responsible and advanced nation. It was often motivated by benevolence, and was not without sacrifice.

Just as the cinema and the modern stage brought together disparate images to capture the qualities of simultaneity, unity and synthesis that were associated with new ways of thinking about time and space, so *The Wide World* captured a distinctively contemporary experience of the world by representing the commingling of different cultures in photographic spreads. It was a project that produced images of dissonance, as well as images of synthesis. In one such instance, the middle-class breakfast parlour was reconstructed in the wilds of West Africa, the missionaries performing the rituals of civilised society as a crowd of natives looked on:

> portable chairs and a table have been unfolded, tea made, and
> some tinned provisions laid out in quite a cosy manner .... A
> crowd assembles to watch the *oyinbo* at his *alfresco* meal.[85]

The interest of the villagers on this particular occasion has been greatly increased by the presence of an English lady - a rarity in the interior of West Africa (*see Figure 14*). The image of fusion in the photograph is overlaid with the arrogance of European imperialism, as the missionaries set themselves up centre-stage as role-models of civilised behaviour, and cast the native peoples as passive recipients of the lesson. And one native has been enlisted as a servant in a manner that reinforces European domination. Conrad's accountant in *Heart of Darkness* is not too far away, working away at his books and employing a native laundress to ensure the cleanliness of his collars, in the midst of an impenetrable 'heart of darkness'.[86]

Evidence of the synthesis of different cultures in *The Wide World* largely consisted of accounts or photographs of imitative behaviour, in which native peoples cooperated in a process by which British missionaries almost narcissistically fashioned them in the image of the civilised European. In a narrative of 1905, for instance, the Prime Minister of Toro (Upper Nile) was depicted in his office, seated on one of two upholstered chairs of which he was 'the proud possessor', his Yost typewriter and clock on his desk. Adorning his walls, significantly, were 'pages cut from *The Wide World Magazine* and *The Strand*'. These 'touches of civilisation' within 'heathen surroundings', it was implied, were symbolic of the Prime Minister's voluntary submission to colonial rule: 'This enlightened official has done noble service for the British flag.'[87]

---

[84] *Wide World Magazine*, 1, 2 (May 1898), p.172.

[85] *Wide World Magazine*, 1, 3 (June 1898), p.258.

[86] Joseph Conrad, 'Heart of Darkness' in *Youth: A Narrative and Two Other Stories*, London: Gresham, 1925.

[87] *Wide World Magazine*, 16, 92 (November 1905), p.134.

This native thus appeared in the guise of the British statesman-administrator. In another image the native assumed the outward appearance of the British missionary (*see Figure 15*). Such images were invariably underpinned by the power relations implicit in imperial ideology.

Women, too, worked overseas as missionaries, and their stories featured in *The Wide World*. E.M. Lee, for example, wrote two articles entitled 'My Experiences as a Lady Missionary in China'. The geographical extension of the empire allowed many women potential knowledge of and contact with their 'sisters' in other lands. Contact took many forms and the female missionary was a many-faceted and not uncontradictory figure.[88] Beneath all forms of contact, however, the identity of the female missionary of *The Wide World* was firmly that of the coloniser. Despite her self-consciousness about cultural stereotyping (partly a product of a more general lack of self-confidence as a female interlocutor in what was a predominantly male travel discourse), and her sensitivity to and genuinely sympathetic engagement with native Chinese women, Lee ultimately presented herself in a traditional and gendered role, as schoolmistress, social facilitator and maternal figure.[89] A growing mass of post-colonial women's history has addressed the question of how gender mediated the experiences of European travellers to empire.[90]

The 'famous hunter' was one of the most common representatives of western civilisation found in this magazine in a period in which, as John Mackenzie has demonstrated, hunting was an extremely popular theme. Images of the hunter proliferated: in the pioneering and adventure tradition in juvenile literature, in a veritable plethora of hunting stories and publications, in popular visual imagery of the Hunt (adorning tins, packages, plates, textiles and furniture) and in the rhetoric associated with various youth organisations such as Baden Powell's Boy Scout movement.[91] The publication of Baden Powell's *Scouting For Boys* (1908), one of the twentieth century's best-sellers, marked the climax of a process in which images of frontier manliness, from a dispersed and varied set of imperial environments, were assembled in a variety of popular cultural forms. *The Wide World Magazine*, boasting a host of images of the hunter derived from a range of imperial settings, exemplified this process.

---

[88] Vron Ware has argued that the empire 'provided both a physical and an ideological space in which the different meanings of femininity could be explored or contested'. See Vron Ware, *Beyond the Pale: White Women, Racism and History*, London and New York: Verso, 1992, p.120.

[89] *Wide World Magazine*, 7, 39 (June 1901), p.232.

[90] See, for example, Susan L. Blake, 'A Woman's Trek: What Difference Does Gender Make?' in Nupur Chaudri and Margaret Strobel (eds), *Western Women and Imperialism: Complicity and Resistance*, Bloomington: Indiana University Press, 1992, p.32. Implicit in Blake's question is a hope that women, colonised themselves by gender, might recognise and oppose colonisation based on race.

[91] John M. Mackenzie, 'The Imperial Pioneer and Hunter and the British Masculine Stereotype in Late Victorian and Edwardian Times' in John M. Mackenzie (ed.), *Imperialism and Popular Culture*, Manchester: Manchester University Press, 1984.

The big-game hunters of *The Wide World*, most often military men on leave, were represented as figures of potent masculinity. Colonel Colenbrander, for instance, 'the famous South African hunter and warrior' was described as 'the finest horseman ... the finest shot ... a mighty hunter, a fighting man and a trader', a figure who had played 'a man's part in the recent campaign'. (He was a version of Nimrod, 'the mighty hunter' of Genesis.) Colenbrander was 'in the pink of condition and as tough as a whipcord'. This version of manliness was shown to be characteristic of the British overseas and crucial to their imperial strength. 'For empire-building, as for all her work', wrote one narrator, 'England wants the best of her sons, and it must be admitted that she generally manages to get them.'[92]

The story of Colonel Colenbrander ended with the Zulu nation (a people revered by Europeans themselves for their fighting ability) uniting in allegiance to the hero who had proven himself in battle against marauding neighbouring tribes:

> And thenceforward there was not a man of the nation who would not gladly volunteer to follow him to death; for among a people who worship force he had been fiercely tried - and proven.[93]

The narrator, offering a moral tale and a Christian hero, drew on biblical language and rhythms, and employed the terms of the marriage service to reinforce the almost connubial sense of unity inspired by the manly imperial hunter. The great late nineteenth-century German historian Treitschke saw hunting as the means by which 'virile' nations expressed their capacity to dominate. Assumptions about male sexual dominance, implicit in Treitschke's explanation of imperial strength, also underpinned the language of geographical 'penetration' which characterised *Wide World* narratives.

The hunt was seen as off-limits to women, so that the symbolic power of the woman who did participate lay largely in her engagement with notions of female emancipation and her subversion of female stereotypes. The female hunter of a narrative of 1900, entitled 'A Lady Ibex-Hunter in Baltistan', was obliged to 'dress like a man'. She displayed considerable self-consciousness about challenging stereotypes of femininity - pity for all slaughtered animals, for instance - and ultimately subordinated her own success to that of her husband, with due deference to his superiority in shooting from a much greater distance than herself. By 1910, however, the subversion of female stereotypes was much more blatant and deliberate, and *The Wide World* was printing pictures that clearly symbolised female emancipation from the gender stereotype (*see Figure 16*).

---

[92] *Wide World Magazine*, 16, 93 (December 1905), p.253.

[93] *Wide World Magazine*, 4, 21 (December 1899), p.263.

For Baden Powell, hunting represented the essence of the pioneering spirit and the means of preparing peace scouts for war. The narrators of Newnes's magazine closely resembled the 'peace scouts' described in *Scouting for Boys*:

> These are the frontiersmen of all parts of our Empire. The 'trappers' of North America, hunters of Central Africa, the British pioneers, explorers, and missionaries over Asia and all the wild parts of the world, the bushmen and drovers of Australia, the constabulary of North-West Canada and of South Africa - all are peace scouts, real *men* in every sense of the word, and thoroughly up on scoutcraft, i.e. they understand living out in the jungles, and they can find their way anywhere, are able to read meaning from the smallest signs and foot-tracks; they know how to look after their health when far away from any doctors, are strong and plucky, and ready to face any danger, and always keen to help each other. They are accustomed to take their lives in their hands, and to fling them down without hesitation if they can help their country by doing so.[94]

Hunting was transformed from an economic activity and a pioneering system associated with survival into an elite ritual associated with an elaborate system of etiquette. This code, characteristic of the way in which *Wide World* narrators described and defined themselves, was used to represent the empire as a moral training ground for the imperial elite and the Hunt as a system of military preparation for war.

'During one of my shooting excursions from Lake Baringo I picked up the tracks of a lion.' Thus began one tale by Major P.H. Powell-Cotton, published in 1904.[95] And there were many more like it. The sporting hunter's main motive was the acquisition of trophies and specimens, whereas the primitive hunter, whom he usually used as an auxiliary, hunted for survival and for economic reasons. Sporting etiquette was complex but widely accepted and articulated. The hunters of these narratives emphasised notions of 'sportsmanship', of testing the nerve and courage of the sportsman and of giving the game a chance of life.[96] The sporting hunter of the *Wide World* shot to kill and not to wound, often

---

[94] R.S.S. Baden-Powell, *Scouting for Boys: A Handbook for Instruction in Good Citizenship*, London: Horace Cox, 1908.

[95] *Wide World Magazine*, 12, 71 (February 1904), p.457.

[96] It is significant, in this context, that the skills of the native Indian who appeared in one of the narratives (keen eyesight, for example) though admired by the white hunter, were undermined by his tendency to exhibit 'an uncontrollable excitability in the presence of big-game, which is incomprehensible to the white man'. The white man, by contrast, was depicted as self-controlled and level-headed; characteristics which subtly reinforced his right to imperial domination. See *Wide World Magazine*, 5, 25 (April 1900), p.101. The many narratives of redemption, in which British officials were called upon to exercise their superior hunting skills to save helpless native villagers from the depredations of savage tigers and other wild animals, also reinforced the ideology of British imperialism. See, for instance, a narrative entitled 'The Man-Eater of Lalpur-Arani', *Wide World Magazine*, 12, 70 (January 1904), pp.330-334.

aiming for a 'brain shot', and being obliged by the sporting code to track an animal to finish it off if he had inflicted a non-mortal wound. He always hunted alone, never impinged on a rival's territory, and exhibited supreme skill at 'woodcraft' and 'marksmanship'. Thus one *Wide World* narrator described 'pig-sticking in India' with an insistently rhetorical emphasis on the ideal of frontier self-sufficiency:

> ... there never can be, and never will be any sport equal to [pig-sticking] in any part of the globe. Here you do your own hunting. The eventual death of the pig depends upon your own skill, your own horsemanship, knowledge of the country, of the pig and his ways, your prowess with the spear, and courage to use it properly .... 'Tis you and you only who are responsible for the kill.[97]

The magazine's title conjured up the Olympic Ode, recently written by the Oxford professor G.S. Robertson, and the hunter represented the spirit of sporting combat, and (via the emphasis of Treitschke's thesis) national competition.[98]

Wide World narratives provided British administrators, military officers and those otherwise 'populating the globe' on behalf of European nations with a source of identity and connection with 'Home'. Kipling wrote of the imperial mission as an altruistic kind of voluntary exile.[99] The state of exile was particularly associated, according to Susanne Howe Nobbe, with the British living in India, whom she describes as 'self-consciously rulers in an alien world'.[100] While Africa represented a new frontier and was associated with the hunter and the explorer-hero, India was often associated with the experience of exile, its larger outposts (like Kipling's Simla) containing replicas of London.

This experience tended to be associated with the replication of familiar patterns and symbols of 'civilised' life. Thus the narratives of *The Wide World* convey a sense that 'first-rate safety bicycles', the tents of Europeans, the flags of European nations and the inevitable Kodak were to be found in the remotest corners of the earth. They were emblematic of a kind of internationalism that made Europe its source point, and a kind of transplantation that bred an exaggerated sense of European unity. One authoress, describing her trek into British South Africa in 1905, rendered a settler's farm according to the nostalgic English rural ideal. The country was 'well-watered'. The house was surrounded

---

[97] *Wide World Magazine*, 7, 40 (July 1901), p.385.

[98] 'Lo, from the wide world manifold we come-/From England's hearths and homes draw hither some,/Children of sires who, in days gone by,/Warred for thy liberty.' See Gary Lester, *Australians at the Olympics*, Melbourne: Kingfisher Books, 1984, p.16.

[99] 'Take up the White Man's Burden-/ Send forth the best ye breed-/ Go bind your sons to exile/ To serve your captives' need'. See Rudyard Kipling, 'Take up the White Man's Burden', in *Selected Poetry*, op. cit., p.127.

[100] Susanne Howe Nobbe, *Novels of Empire*, New York: Columbia University Press, 1949, p.36.

by 'beautiful peach woods' in which fruit grew 'in profusion', and by 'quite English-looking meadows of buttercups and daisies'. The porch was 'cheerfully lit'. And in the stream nearby, two children with 'uncovered heads of curly flaxen hair' and 'joyous voices' played. Even the farm's name, 'Peach Dale Farm', carried an excessive sense of the idyllic rural scene.[101] This was a version of nineteenth-century pastoral transported to a corner of a foreign land that was forever England.

The most preoccupying and problematic region of British involvement in the 1880s and 1890s was Egypt and the Soudan, and this region was the focus of a *Wide World* theme of reverse political exile. The success of Kitchener's expedition in the Soudan meant liberation for a number of European political prisoners, and *The Wide World* published a continuing literature by the 'victims of Mahdism', men like Father Ohrwalder, Neufeld, Slatin and Bekarelli, who had been imprisoned by the Mahdi some twelve years earlier. Bekarelli, for example, whose account appeared under the religiously suggestive title 'The Sufferings of Bekarelli, the Greek', described the terrors of being forced to institute a harem and to swear allegiance to Mahdist religion and law, and of having fortunes earned by dint of labour and exile in this foreign country requisitioned by the Mahdi.

Yet these narratives served to confirm the resilience of European identity and Christian values in the face of the oppressive, destructive, tyrannical forces of Mahdism. Internationalism and unity may have been the order of the day, but they were not to be achieved at the expense of *European* culture. European captives depicted themselves as Christian martyrs. Bekarelli, for instance, constructed his confrontation with Mahdism in the following terms: 'It is not well to meet with the Evil One, but when you do, you can only cross yourself.'[102] Yet these stories of long and arduous exile also represented a tension in the identity of British and European exiles overseas. Men such as these had been sacrificed - 'left helpless', to use Bekarelli's words - by the very governments with whom their cultural and political identities were bound up. For them, distance was exaggerated rather than diminished. Their sufferings were thus inherently problematic as far as the European imperialist was concerned, since they represented, in some sense, the vulnerability of European nationals in foreign lands and the tenuousness of the foreign presence in the Soudan.

Neufeld's ten-part narrative, entitled 'In the Khalifa's Clutches; or My Twelve Years in Captivity', was introduced by the proprietor of *The Wide World Magazine*, George Newnes himself, and so bore Newnes's endorsement. Newnes had become acquainted with Neufeld in Cairo, meeting with him both prior to his trip up the Nile, and at the trip's conclusion. He introduced the exile, in a phrase that quite aptly evoked the spirit of theatrical performance, to 'make his bow to the British public' by telling the story of his suffering at the hands of

---

[101] *Wide World Magazine*, 16, 93 (December 1905), pp.289, 294.

[102] *Wide World Magazine*, 5, 25 (April 1900), p.5.

the Mahdi.[103] In this case, the process of writing was, Newnes suggested, a therapeutic process essential to Neufeld's reintegration into 'civilisation'. *The Wide World* transformed geographical remoteness into cultural connection through the 'true story'.[104]

Neufeld's account was almost a rewrite of the Bible, complete with stonings, prisoners of the recalcitrant Mahdi 'walled up' in 'living tombs', and countless references to Christianity as the source of the narrator-hero's inner strength, moral fortitude and identity. Neufeld was 'spurned and shunned as the incarnation of everything despicable in a man' by his 'own people' when, liberated from Omdurman, he was accused of being a traitor to Britain by voluntarily aiding the Mahdist war effort. As the pseudo-biblical narrative of *The Wide World* proceeded, however, he was recast as a martyr-hero in the Gordon mould, undergoing a kind of discursive conversion reminiscent of Saul's transformation. Neufeld's identity, poignantly expressed in the face of physical and mental torture, was bound up with his European blood, fighting spirit, whiteness and Christianity. His ultimate source of self-definition, faced with death, was 'pride in his race' as 'a European - a Prussian - a man who had fought with the British troops in what turned out to be the "too late" expedition for the rescue of Gordon ... a white man, and a Christian'.[105] Neufeld depicted his release, in terms that carried a sense of his essential identification with Europe, as a return to 'civilisation and liberty'.

Gordon was the ultimate 'martyr-hero' in whose image the exiled and released narrators of *The Wide World* cast themselves. Christ-like, the figure of Gordon was resurrected and paid reverence as the captives of Egypt were liberated, feeding the huge demand in England for eulogies of the 'martyred hero'. 'The British nation', one narrator claimed, 'may be said to have breathed again as they read how their martyred hero had at last been avenged.'[106] In Neufeld's narrative, Gordon was rendered as a 'soldier and lion-hearted man', a man who died a 'magnificent death' when, 'half raising his sword to strike, he fell dead with his face to Heaven'. He was depicted in an extremely loaded image, which, in a manner inconsistent with the narrative, showed him with a revolver rather than a sword. *The Wide World* thus demonstrated the way in which the mythology of Gordon's life and death became riddled with contradictions and inconsistencies. At any rate, Gordon was certainly fodder for the rhetoric and ideology of imperialism. If Nelson had been the embodiment of British naval

---

[103] 'Personal Impressions of the Author, by Sir George Newnes, Bart', *Wide World Magazine*, 3, 15 (June 1899), p.227.

[104] Newnes advised Neufeld to ignore 'improper and illegal threats' from the War Office that he 'was not to be allowed to publish his story except through certain people who had subscribed to the fund for the relief of prisoners at Omdurman', and urged him to accept Chapman and Hall's offer to publish his book. The 'true narrative' of *The Wide World*, it was implied, was an expression of the democratic freedoms that characterised civilised societies. See *Wide World Magazine*, 3, 15 (June 1899), p.227.

[105] *Wide World Magazine*, 4, 19 (October 1899), p.11.

[106] *Wide World Magazine*, 4, 21 (December 1899), p.227.

supremacy, Gordon was the embodiment of British military and imperial strength. Such, then, were the players on the stage of the 'wide world' as they were rendered in Newnes's magazine, and such their sources of reference.

In 1901, H.G. Wells observed that 'the world grows smaller and smaller, the telegraph and telephone go everywhere, wireless telegraphy opens wider and wider possibilities to the imagination'.[107] His observation echoed the very language of *The Wide World Magazine* and described the material and cultural conditions that inspired its 'birth' and guaranteed its success. 'It may be taken for granted that at no time in our history did we - the English-speaking peoples, that is - take such a quick, keen, and intelligent interest, as at present, in the affairs of the Wide World.' With these words, the publisher had introduced *The Wide World* three years earlier, in April 1898. This was an entertaining and visually innovative monthly publication that employed 'true stories', laced with 'rapidity and colour', and a range of photographs, from a cast of characters inhabiting diverse global settings, to capture a view of the world that was a liberal mixture of internationalism and imperialism. It mediated between the world of scientific fact and the exotic world of late nineteenth and early twentieth-century fiction.

---

[107] H.G. Wells as cited in Stephen Kern, op. cit., p.229.

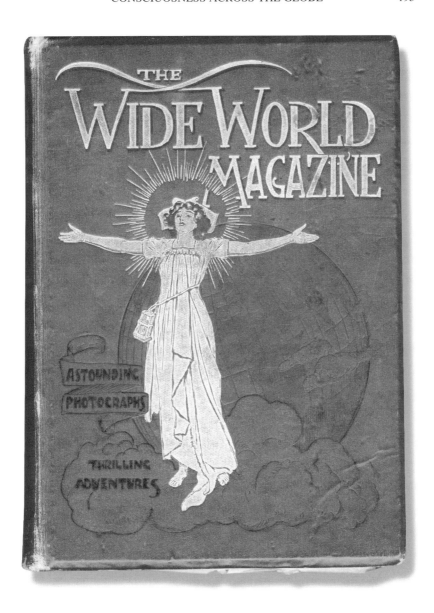

Figure 11. The cover of the bound volume of The Wide World Magazine. *The image carries multiple meanings. Through the use of gilt detailing, Britannia is rendered both as a symbol of wealth and as an almost angelic figure; illuminated and illuminative. She welcomes 'the wide world' with open arms, but appears at the same time to lay herself out, Christ-like, as a sacrifice to it.*

Odds and Ends.

An Ambulance in the Backwoods—What a Cyclone Did—Religious Fervour in Mexico—Tea-Picking in Assam—A River Festival on the Irawaddy—Life in Tahiti—The Sacred Monkey Temple—Love-Making in Havana—The New Zealand Rabbit Inspector, etc.

I.—THIS IS THE KIND OF AMBULANCE USED IN THE BACKWOODS OF SOUTHERN CANADA WHEN A
From a] " LOGGER" MEETS WITH AN ACCIDENT. [*Photo.*

reaches the settlement a hearse. In nearly every case, however, the patients, inured as they are to hardships, survive the rough travelling and retain life-long memories of their novel ride. The horse which draws this ambulance is the regular "tote horse" used for hauling supplies to camp. The casks are used simply because they are the most handy things to be found in a lumber camp, all the grain and other provisions being brought to camp in these receptacles.

 HEN a backwoodsman is injured or taken ill in a distant logging camp in Southern Canada he is carried to the nearest settlement for nursing and medical attendance in one of the peculiar ambulances which we show here. As will be seen, it consists of nothing more than a barrel and a rough sledge. The cask is firmly lashed to the sledge, and partly filled with heated stones and loose hay. Then the invalid,

Our next photo. was taken on the Meagavaram Mentupet Railway, about eight miles south of Tiruvallur Junction in the Tanjore District of the Madras Presidency. A violent cyclone was raging, and the driver, seeing some fallen trees on the line in front, stopped the train, which was then blown completely over by one terrific gust. There were about fifty passengers in the train, which consisted of thirteen vehicles, but fortunately no one was seriously hurt. The

*Figure 12. 'Odds and Ends' (*Wide World Magazine*, 5, 29 (August 1900), p.553). This feature offered a photographic and textual version of cinematic montage.*

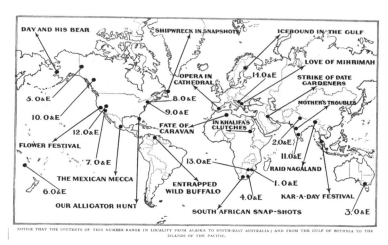

Figure 13. Wide World *contents-map (*Wide World Magazine*, 4, 23 (February 1900), p.529). The captions accompanying the contents-map varied. This one points to the geographical scope of the magazine and linguistically reinforces the notion of simultaneity by leaping from one continent to another in a single phrase.*

A HALT FOR BREAKFAST IN WEST AFRICA.

*Figure 14 'A Halt for Breakfast in West Africa' (*Wide World Magazine, *1, 3 (June 1898), p.258). The curious ritual of the English breakfast is projected onto a very foreign backdrop.*

A SOLOMON ISLANDER IMITATING A MISSIONARY IN THE
From a]   HOPE OF ACQUIRING HIS VIRTUES.   [*Photo.*

*Figure 15. 'A Solomon Islander Imitating a Missionary in the Hope of Acquiring his Virtues' (*Wide World Magazine, *4, 20 (November 1899), p.112).*
Many photographs and narratives exemplified the attempt by British missionaries to model native peoples in their own image, but perhaps none more clearly than this photograph and its dryly revealing caption.

*Figure 16. 'How I Shot My First Elephant' (*Wide World Magazine, *25, 147 (June 1910), p.225). This picture represents a blunt rejection of gender stereotypes. The female hunter and her native companion appear to have been superimposed upon the dead elephant's back.*

Specialisation and Diversification: Targeting Niche Audiences and Exploiting a Segmented Market

Introduction to Part III

Over the course of the nineteenth century, the total population of Britain had increased from 10 to 40 million, and the urban population had increased from 30 per cent to 80 per cent of the total.[1] By 1900, the majority of Britons lived in six major conurbations which constituted vast concentrations of consumers linked by greatly improved networks of communication, distribution and transportation. All of these developments contributed to the growth of a large and concentrated reading audience.

For publishers such as Newnes, these conditions created the need for the inter-related processes of specialisation and diversification. They saw the financial advantages of directing their titles at specific sections of the audience in order to attract the business of advertisers, and catering to a variety of interest, social and professional groups in order to exploit the full extent of the market and maintain high circulation levels. In fact, David Shumway has suggested that in the 1890s in particular, magazine editors and advertisers exuded great confidence in their ability to appeal to and shape the needs of their audience, indulging heavily in 'boosterism'.[2] Magazines began to be targeted positively towards specific classifications such as female readers of various types, juvenile readers, and those with special interest areas such as art, music, science, travel and sport. The key to success was to compartmentalise and specialise. Even within particular segments such as the market for women's periodicals, publishers targeted sub-groups such as the young, the middle-aged, working girls, Society women or housewives. Some niche markets which Newnes successfully exploited were the women's market (with *The Ladies' Field*) and the juvenile market (with *The Captain*).

In launching these two new periodicals, Newnes was guided by contemporary cultural conditions. The Society woman, cultured and fashionable, played a central role in maintaining the fabric of social life, and the traditional nineteenth-century 'ladies' paper' nourished her preoccupation with the rules and fashions of Society. By the end of the century, however, the 'New Woman', socially liberated, politically vocal, economically independent and increasingly prominent in public life, was emerging to challenge the conventions upheld by the 'woman of culture'. Gender roles were increasingly contested. Employment opportunities were increasing, and considerable numbers of women were finding new roles as teachers, nurses, typists, telephonists and clerks, and in the burgeoning retail trade. As Britain developed into a consumer society and both the supply of goods and the volume of potential purchasing power at the disposal of the British consumer grew, producers increasingly targeted those groups whose purchasing power was growing most visibly. Female consumers

---

[1]   E.J. Hobsbawm, *Industry and Empire*, London: Penguin, 1968, Figures 1 and 13.

[2]   David Shumway, 'Objectivity, Bias, Censorship', in Richard Ohmann (ed.), *Making and Selling Culture*, Hanover and London: Wesleyan University Press, 1996, p.241.

represented one of these groups. Although women retained their traditional responsibility for the purchase of food, family clothing and small household goods, they acquired some say in the purchase of consumer durables and a significant role in the purchase of consumer goods produced by the beauty, fashion and medical industries.[3] Periodical publishers, heavily dependent upon advertising revenue to finance new publications, offered increasing space to such industries for their marketing initiatives. Women thus constituted an important and increasingly diverse segment of the market for magazines.

Juveniles represented another potential source of readership. Victorian and Edwardian children, according to James Walvin, 'personified the population explosion which was the central force in British history from the eighteenth century onwards'.[4] In 1901, the proportion of the expanding British population aged between 5 and 19 years was approximately 31 per cent.[5] They also represented, to many contemporaries, a significant social problem. Youth culture, the distinctive psychology of the newly-categorised 'adolescent', and the problems associated with urban youth were all themes of an ongoing public debate. The ideology of the public schools, particularly the cult of athleticism, exerted a strong influence on middle-class culture, and was a pervasive feature of the boys' penny weekly magazine. Sporting culture, an important component of the process by which juvenile periodicals appealed to readers, could also be harnessed to attract a cross-section of the population to the periodical press, and Newnes was to exploit the market for sporting papers in the early twentieth century, with *C.B. Fry's Magazine*. C.B. Fry, one of the period's most prolific sportsmen, was the prototype of the twentieth-century sportsman-editor, his authority as a sportsman strenuously marketed to readers through Newnes's magazine.[6]

Developments in journalism were inextricably linked to the expansion of the advertising industry, as Terence Nevett has demonstrated. The increasingly specialised press became a more flexible instrument for the advertiser, who could isolate particular segments of the population or particular interest groups by using appropriately-targeted magazines. Thus, Clarence Moran wrote in 1905:

> Every rank of society, from the highest to the lowest, reads newspapers .... There is, in fact, no class of consumers which

---

[3]   See John Benson, *The Rise of Consumer Society, 1880-1980*, London and New York: Longman, 1994, p.61.

[4]   James Walvin, *A Child's World: A Social History of English Childhood, 1800-1914*, Harmondsworth: Penguin, 1982, p.18.

[5]   See E.J. Hobsbawm, op. cit., Figure 2. Walvin gives a slightly different measure, showing that the proportion of those aged 14 and under in 1901 was 32.4 per cent. See James Walvin, op. cit., p.19.

[6]   See Kate Jackson, 'C.B. Fry: The Sportsman-Editor', in *Victorian Periodicals Review* (Winter 2000).

cannot be affected through the medium of some section or other of the press.[7]

Moran applied the descriptive terms of both pre-industrial hierarchical society (the language of 'rank' and 'degree') and industrial class society ('class of consumers') to a social structure in which the consumer represented the basic unit. He thus demonstrated the extent to which the divisions created by purchasing power, as against (or in addition to) social rank or class, assumed increasing importance as Britain developed into a modern consumer society. Advertisers and newspaper proprietors became locked in a relationship of mutual dependence, their interests in close alliance. Magazine formats reflected this alliance and publications such as *The Ladies' Field* and *C.B. Fry's Magazine* characteristically sustained a transparent connection between advertising and letterpress.

Newnes devoted increasing space to advertising copy, employing advertising revenue to finance new publications. And George Newnes, Ltd advertised its periodicals as a group, emphasising their wide market coverage as a means of attracting advertisers. 'Their advertisement revenue was very large indeed', read the report of the tenth Annual General Meeting of the company, in August 1907, 'this was greatly owing to the fact that the company's publications were known to circulate among people who had money to spend'.[8] The diversity of Newnes's publishing operations meant that he could utilise the pages of one periodical to advertise or sell another similarly targeted publication, and therefore make the most of readership continuities. In the advertising pages of *The Ladies' Field*, for instance, *Country Life*, *The Wide World Magazine*, *The Strand Magazine*, *Navy and Army Illustrated* and various other publications of the House of Newnes, all aimed at readers of a similar social class, appeared side-by-side in attractive full-page advertisements.[9] And winners of consolation prizes in *Captain* competitions were offered their choice of a volume of *The Captain*, *The Strand*, *Sunday Strand*, or *The Wide World Magazine*. The first number of *The Ladies' Field* preceded *The Wide World* by only four days, and carried a half-page advertisement for its sibling publication: 'A NEW SIXPENNY MONTHLY ON ENTIRELY NEW LINES AND BEAUTIFULLY ILLUSTRATED.'[10] The name of the publisher, George Newnes, Ltd, framed the advertisement, featuring at both the top and bottom of the page. George Newnes

---

[7]   Clarence Moran as cited in T.R. Nevett, *Advertising in Britain*, London: Heinemann, 1982, p.86.

[8]   *The Times*, 10 August, 1907, p.14.

[9]   It is worth noting that for the Press Fete to aid the London Hospital held at the Hotel Cecil in June 1898, *The Ladies' Field*, *The Strand Magazine* and *Country Life* hosted a joint stall, readers of these magazines volunteering to staff it. Presumably such readers shared an interest in philanthropy, and the stalls hosts (Newnes's readers) included the Duchess of Newcastle, the Marchioness of Zetland and Lady Edward Spencer Churchill. See *The Ladies' Field*, 2, 18 June, 1898, p.3.

[10] *The Ladies' Field*, 1, 11 June, 1898, p.xii. Format as per original.

was thus everpresent on the scene constituted by his various publications, through advertising.

The segmentation of the reading market was reflected in the number and type of titles appearing on the periodical scene. In the twenty years from 1880 to 1900 there was a significant expansion of the market for women's magazines. Forty-eight new titles appeared.[11] The latter part of the nineteenth century was also one in which there was substantial exploitation of the juvenile market. In the period 1866 to 1914, over 500 periodicals for children and young people came into existence; some short-lived, but many long-lasting.[12] The sporting paper developed in a similar fashion. First appearing in 1822 and taken over by *Sporting Life* in 1886, *Bell's Life in London* was the forerunner of and part-model for many later sporting papers. It was issued on Sunday and catered to a gentleman class of readers. By the 1880s, three or four specialist papers existed and a flourishing weekly sporting press included such publications as *The Field* and *Athletic News*. The specialist sporting press was gradually undermined as the daily and Sunday press devoted more space to sporting news and covered an increasing range of sports. George Newnes catered to all of these segments of the market with a variety of weekly and monthly publications. Of these, two successful magazines will be examined: *The Ladies' Field* (1898), a weekly illustrated journal for Society and middle-class women, and *The Captain* (1899), a monthly illustrated magazine 'for Boys and "Old Boys"'.

The Ladies' Field, appearing in March 1898, represented Newnes's expansion into the increasingly lucrative female market. Newnes had emphasised the importance of female readers to the New Journalism within his account of the origins of *Tit-Bits*. The idea for *Tit-Bits*, he explained, came to him whilst he read a 'tit-bit' from the newspaper aloud to his wife. *Tit-Bits* was inspired by her enjoyment.[13] Now Newnes placed periodicals for women at the forefront of his publishing business. *Woman's Life*, a penny weekly publication aimed at a middle-class female audience, was established by Newnes in 1895, and rapidly reached a circulation of 200,000.[14] *The Ladies' Field* was conceived as its more

---

[11] Diana Dixon, 'Children and the Press, 1866-1914', in Michael Harris and Alan Lee (eds), *The Press in English Society from the Seventeenth to Nineteenth Centuries*, London: Associated University Presses, 1986, p.14.

[12] Ibid., p.133.

[13] See Hulda Friederichs, *The Life of Sir George Newnes, Bart*, London: Hodder and Stoughton, 1911, p.55. The female reader was also used to advertise *Tit-Bits*: 'I like it. My wife likes it....' And Newnes's brother-in-law, James Hillyard, invoked Mrs Newnes (his sister) as an example of the paper's morally pure readership, in an attempt to persuade a newsvendor in Newcastle to take it in. According to Margaret Beetham, many of the features of the New Journalism were linked to the feminisation of the press. See Margaret Beetham, *A Magazine of Her Own? Domesticity and Desire in the Woman's Magazine, 1800-1914*, London and New York: Routledge, 1996.

[14] This magazine was edited by Galloway Fraser, who later (1904) assumed editorship of *Tit-Bits*. It continued publication until 1934 when it was revamped as *Woman's Own*, a title that dominated the market in the mid-twentieth century. It has not been examined here for reasons of space.

up-market companion. It was a sixpenny weekly magazine, beautifully illustrated and produced, with an emphasis on fashion, advertising and advice columns, and was designed to appeal, so the editor indicated, to 'cultured women, both at home and abroad'. Such a woman was Lady Newnes, who occupied herself with entertaining, gardening and philanthropic and public duties. Yet the 'cultured woman', as she was reflected back from the magazine's pages, was not unaffected by the various alternative images of femininity that were rapidly becoming available to her. Various images, both verbal and visual, were invoked in an attempt to maximise the magazine's circulation within the female niche market it was designed to capture, and in an effort to define and negotiate 'the ladies' field', in a period which saw many changes to traditional gender roles and to British culture.[15]

In 1899, Newnes made a play for the juvenile market, introducing a magazine called *The Captain*. Like Cassell's *Chums* (1892), *The Captain* was clearly aimed at middle-class, public school boys, and those who identified with them. It both appealed to boy (and girl) readers and met with the approval of their parents.[16] 'Captain' was a term of address associated with the newsvendors on the streets in the 1890s, although it also had military and sporting connotations. W.E. Henley, whose poems, drawing significantly upon the ideology of the English public school, were widely popular at the end of the century, had published a poem in 1888 with which Newnes was no doubt familiar. 'It matters not how strait the gate,' it read, 'how charged with punishments the scroll,/ I am the master of my fate:/ I am the captain of my soul.'[17] Established amidst concern about a range of issues relating to contemporary youth, *The Captain* deployed a variety of mentors and role-models who embodied the spirit of Henley's verse, and encouraged juvenile readers to take a responsible attitude towards 'mastering their fates' and 'captaining their souls'. In the first decade of the twentieth century, Newnes's magazine particularly addressed itself to the need for military recruits and imperial administrators, emphasising the current phase of aggressive imperialism in which Britain was engaged.[18]

C.B. Fry was so successful as a sportsman-editor figure in *The Captain* that a new magazine, devoted entirely to the sporting and outdoor theme and

---

[15] The 1890s, for instance, had seen women officially accepted into political society in an international context. New Zealand was the first nation to accord women over the age of 21 the vote, in 1893.

[16] Newnes clearly understood the appeal of the magazine, demonstrating this in writing an article for the series on 'What I Wanted to Be'. He employed a narrative style, making reference to the popular public school story, and opening his piece in the manner of a schoolboy addressing a master: 'You ask me, Mr Editor, to say what, as a boy, I wanted to be when I became a man.' But he also addressed himself to the parents of the juvenile reader, offering them humorous advice on the issue of finding suitable employment for their sons. See *Captain*, 1, 5 (August 1899), p.492.

[17] W.E. Henley, 'Invictus: In Memoriam R.T.H.B.' (1888).

[18] In 1898, Britain had obtained a 99-year lease on Hong Kong. In 1899, the British went to war against the Boers in South Africa. And 1900 saw the Boxer Rebellion in Peking, which led to the consolidation of European power in China.

edited by Fry, was introduced by Newnes in 1904. *C.B. Fry's Magazine*, an illustrated sixpenny monthly which featured articles and stories about a variety of sports, as well as competitions, serials, advertising and illustrations, constituted a redefinition of the mid-nineteenth-century sporting paper - a low, sensational type of publication written in a racy style. Newnes transformed the sporting paper into a respectable and wide-ranging journal. The gospel of the magazine was 'the moral value of games', and it treated sport and outdoor activity as a serious national and moral issue. It claimed to be 'a popular magazine of outdoor life, a magazine of general interest, readable by everyone, carrying fresh air and outdoor life into the home'. As *The Wide World* brought the life of the traveller, explorer, adventurer, missionary and exile into the homes of the people, so *Fry's* brought them 'fresh air and outdoor life'. And as *Tit-Bits* had aimed to capture the interest of the newly-educated popular masses by providing material that was interesting and entertaining, so *Fry's* was pitched at the twentieth-century masses, obsessive followers of mass spectator sports such as football, cricket and racing. In an era in which the rhetoric of 'expertise' was pervasive and specialisation and professionalisation were on the increase, it was a task that required the participation of 'experts' and 'authorities'. Thus, like *The Ladies' Field* and *The Captain*, *C.B. Fry's Magazine* was a result of the editorial collaboration of various 'experts'.

Both *The Captain* and *C.B. Fry's Magazine* were infused with the spirit of muscular Christianity, and with Newnes's enthusiasm for outdoor sports and physical activity. Newnes was not only a very industrious worker but a keen sportsman, and he was fond of describing himself as one who 'worked hard and played hard'. He might well have been included in *Fry's Magazine*'s long-running series on 'Outdoor Men'(men who combined a prominent career in public life with excellence in the sporting field). He played cricket at the Shireland School in Birmingham, where he earned the nickname 'Not-Out Newnes'. He loved both motoring and walking. He played golf at Wimbledon Common on Saturdays. He was also concerned to keep up the standard of the game, and to this end took an interest in its professional side, organising many matches in Putney and elsewhere. Newnes was similarly devoted to tennis, and Wildcroft (his house on Putney Heath) had a covered court on which the game could be played in all weathers. He owned an excellent yacht and expressed a willingness on many occasions to nominate as a challenger for the America Cup [sic]. Newnes's devotion to outdoor activity was reflected in his donations to the community of Lynton: a public park, a bowling green and a cricket field and clubhouse.

Whilst Newnes's spirit and assumptions imbued these new magazines, he had little to do with their ongoing production. 'Sir George liked starting something new', C.B. Fry later wrote of the entrepreneurial publisher:

> He was by temperament a projector and a promoter. He liked to
> settle the essential aim of a publication, to find someone who he
> believed could carry out the idea, and to leave the rest to him.

He never interfered in the details of a publication once it had been launched.[19]

As Newnes moved into the last decade of his career as a periodical publisher, he acquired some of the characteristics of Piers Brendon's 'media magnate' - the remotely controlling financier of twentieth-century corporate capitalism. Yet he continued to play a significant role in establishing and shaping the many new, specifically-targeted periodicals which he developed in the twentieth century. His world view was imprinted upon these publications. *The Ladies' Field* and *The Captain* represented the convergence of culture and profit. Through them, George Newnes addressed the varied experiences, preoccupations, anxieties and needs of contemporary readers, whilst exploiting the characteristics of particular social and consumer groups in the ongoing mission to increase profits.

---

[19] C.B. Fry, *Life Worth Living: Some Phases of an Englishman*, London: Eyre and Spottiswoode, 1939, p.156.

5

Femininity, Consumption, Class and Culture in the Ladies' Paper

The Ladies' Field (1898)

The Ladies' Field was a sixpenny illustrated weekly magazine, its format derived from the nineteenth-century ladies' paper. It featured Court and Society news, reviews of musical, artistic, theatrical and sporting events, reports on recent and forthcoming marriages and at least one serial story; and it emphasised fashion, etiquette and social ritual. Domestic interests had long been central to the profitable women's magazine. 'At one time fashion plates and articles, cookery recipes, household advice, domestic difficulties, needlework designs and accounts of charitable undertakings formed what one may call the stock-in-trade of the [woman's] paper', one of its editors commented in introducing a new feature in February 1899, and such subjects 'must always find a place in any paper that caters for women'. But by the 1890s, the field was expanding rapidly. 'Glorified domesticity', observed the same writer, 'excellent, nay, even necessary, as it is in forming the solid background of the paper, is not in itself sufficient today.'[1] Newnes had utilised the appeal of this theme with *Woman's Life* (1895). With *The Ladies' Field*, he attempted to exploit the most successful features of the more democratically inclusive middle-class woman's domestic magazine whilst retaining links with the exclusive and up-market ladies' paper.

The features of *The Ladies' Field* were designed to 'keep pace with the endless requirements and interests of those on whom it relie[d] for support'. After all, women's cultural horizons were expanding, their role in society increasingly contested. And the woman's paper must rise to meet new demands:

> In every direction newer and fuller life is opening out before women, and the woman's paper, therefore, to justify its existence and hold its own amid the competition of the brilliant journalism provided by the daily Press, must be ever prepared for development as the demand arises. At one moment the professional woman has to be considered, and articles arranged to bring her in touch with all the information likely to be of use to her, new openings have to be gone into and examined, reports and statistics have to be digested and mastered, experiences have

---

[1]   *The Ladies' Field*, 4, 25 February, 1899, p.519.

to be exchanged, and facts have to be tabulated. Then there is
the woman of sporting and athletic tastes to be provided for.

Yet it must also cater for less radical tastes, offering 'literary articles, reviews, art
and musical criticisms, the intellectual and scientific *causerie* of the moment, and
much else of the same strain'. Finally:

> it must be as good as possible of its kind, well arranged and well
> written, bearing the hall-mark of culture and refinement.[2]

The Ladies' Field sought to appeal to the increasingly independent,
consumerist and professionalised modern woman whilst maintaining a
sympathetic relationship with the woman with domestic preoccupations and the
more socially conservative 'woman of culture' (a term used by the editor to effect
a blurring of class distinctions). It actually attracted a readership that, in social
terms, was clearly middle class and upper middle class. Those genuinely in upper
Society would not have required such instruction as it provided regarding social
conventions.

In historical and cultural terms, *The Ladies' Field* functioned at the
intersection of many different economies: public discourse, commercialism, class
ideology and cultural change. This is the key to its complexity as a text. The
meaning and format of the woman's magazine itself was constantly evolving as a
result of cultural negotiation and journalistic innovation. And female identity was
constantly being re-defined and re-invented. The header illustrations in *The
Ladies' Field*, utilising a series of images of femininity from various periods and
contexts, reinforced the historical development of a gendered identity. The
evolution of this magazine was thus intertwined with the changing meaning of
womanhood, the rise of a culture of consumption, shifts in the ideology and
reality of class structure, and the incursions of a radical, material, bourgeois
culture into the traditional practices of 'high culture'.

The women's press had remained an upper-class institution until the
middle of the nineteenth century when Samuel Beeton realised the untapped
potential of the middle-class market and established *The Englishwoman's
Domestic Magazine* (1852), issued monthly at the cheap price of twopence.
Dedicated to 'the improvement of the intellect, the cultivation of morals and the
cherishing of domestic management', this magazine contained all of those
features which *The Ladies' Field* nominated 'the stock-in-trade of the woman's
paper'. A column in which Beeton offered advice on courtship and marriage
issues, entitled 'Cupid's Advice Bag', prefigured the later development of the
personal problem page. Domestic life, motherhood and household management
were *The Englishwoman's Domestic Magazine*'s main editorial concerns, and
they were concerns which continued to preoccupy the publishers of women's
magazines into the twentieth century. The last two decades of the nineteenth

---

2   *The Ladies' Field*, 4, 25 February, 1899, p.519.

century saw a vast expansion in publishing for women, and forty-eight new publications appeared.[3] Many of the new titles, such as *Hearth and Home* (1891) and *Home Companion* (1897), reflected the preoccupation with what *The Ladies' Field* called 'glorified domesticity'.[4]

At least ten of the new titles, including *The Lady* (1885) and *The Gentlewoman* (1890), were Society journals. Like Beeton's other magazine, *The Queen* (1861), they espoused traditional values and were concerned with high fashion and high society.[5] *The Ladies' Field* (1898) was essentially a 'Society magazine', lavishly illustrated and well produced. The formula for the 'Society magazine' or 'ladies' paper' included extensive reporting on Court and Society functions throughout Britain and overseas, coverage of the arts, music and theatre, and commentaries on sport. The Society column, addressing Scotland and Ireland as well as England and featuring paragraphs on the latest 'Drawing Rooms', the hunting field, marriages and other aspects of the upper-class social scene, was central. It tended to function as a mechanism of communication amongst the 'upper ten thousand'. In *The Ladies' Field*, columns such as 'The Ladies' Field', 'Court News', 'Society at Home and Abroad', 'Irish Notes' and 'In Hymen's Realms' were representative of this component of the formula.[6]

Late Victorian and Edwardian social life was closely circumscribed by ritual and by a formal and intricate social code which acted to promote upper class cohesion and defend the boundaries of the 'best circles'. And advice on etiquette was an increasingly standard feature of up-market women's magazines. Card-leaving, a complicated and socially significant procedure, occasioned the most number of inquiries. 'Contessa' (an appropriately dignified pseudonym which drew upon a contemporary sense of Italy as the centre of 'civilisation') answered the queries of readers of *The Ladies' Field* regarding such rituals in a column entitled 'Manners and Customs'. Her presence underlines the sense that Newnes's magazine was aimed at the nouveau riche and those who aspired towards middle-class status yet required instruction in the rites of Society. Such columns ultimately undermined Society by making its codes available to the middle classes.

In fact, *The Ladies' Field* contained many correspondence columns, through which a network of specialist and sympathetic sub-editors engaged readers in an ongoing exchange regarding questions of dress, appearance, health, entertaining, etiquette and work, exploring the notion of feminine space and offering a multi-faceted image of femininity. 'Menage and Means', 'The

---

3   Cynthia White, *Women's Magazines, 1693-1968*, London: Michael Joseph, 1970, p.58.

4   See Brian Braithwaite, *Women's Magazines: The First 300 Years*, London: Peter Owen, 1995, pp.12-13, 19-20.

5   Edited by Frederick Greenwood, *The Queen* was comprised of sixteen folio pages, and contained reports on events of the day, needlework designs, fashion articles (written by Isabella Beeton), engravings of fine art subjects, literary topics, gossip, society intelligence and details of public entertainments.

6   Hymen was the Greek god of marriage.

Boudoir', 'Manners and Customs', 'Illustrated Dress Advice' and 'Art in the House' were but a few.[7] The emergence of the 'New Woman', who threw off the security of parental protection and dominance yet required some other form of support and guidance, created a need for new counsellors and new friends. The complexity of social and economic life, increasing as industrialisation and commercialisation disrupted traditional patterns of social formation and made a range of new services, products and opportunities available to women, further fuelled the need for advisors. In a range of magazine competitions, women were encouraged to devote their energies to creating a plethora of useful objects: napkins, album covers, handkerchiefs and many more. The pin-cushion, according to Irene Dancyger, featured prominently.[8] Competitions were a regular feature of *The Ladies' Field*. Many Society magazines also provided features especially written for children. *The Ladies' Field*'s children's page was entitled 'The Children's Hour'.[9]

Dress and appearance had entered the up-market woman's magazine as 'fashion' as early as the late eighteenth century, in the form of reports on what was being worn by court ladies in London and Paris. Fashion coverage continued to be a staple of the genre throughout the nineteenth and twentieth centuries, increasing as the fashion trade expanded rapidly on both sides of the English Channel in the late nineteenth century.[10] Fashion intelligence and shopping tips were perhaps the most prominent feature of *The Ladies' Field*, and illustrations and commentaries on these subjects filled the columns of features such as 'Vanity's Visions', 'Society at Home and Abroad' and 'Saunters Through the Shops'. Contemporary reviews of the magazine, utilising the language of the fashion pages to describe the quality of its production, reflected the importance of this component. The *Midland Weekly Herald*, for instance, observed that *The Ladies' Field* was 'got up in the very highest style'. And *The Observer* claimed that: 'In the advance number, this famous publishing house had surpassed itself - literary contents, illustrations, and general get up are each of the highest order.'[11]

---

[7]   The problem page, a department which became the most characteristic feature of women's magazines in the twentieth century, was never included in the 'Society' journal. The personal problems of the upper classes were not, it might be concluded, deemed suitable for public consumption. Nor was it helpful to the public image of this class to discuss private problems which, under the impetus of 'Society journalism' and 'New Journalism', were already attracting some unwanted publicity.

[8]   Irene Dancyger, *A World of Women: An Illustrated History of Women's Magazines*, Dublin: Gill and Macmillan, 1978, p.76.

[9]   *The Million*'s children's feature, abandoned three years earlier, had borne the same title.

[10]   This development was emphasised by the establishment of an English edition of France's reigning fashion journal, *Le Moniteur de la Mode*, an expensive, glossy magazine of thirty-two years standing. One British fashion journal, *The Ladies' Gazette of Fashion*, made the change from monthly to weekly publication to cater for the growing demand for fashion intelligence.

[11]   *The Ladies' Field*, 1, 2 April, 1898, p.96.

From the mid-nineteenth century, there had been a close connection between the Paris art world and that of fashion illustration, and the fashion plates in *The Ladies' Field*, as well as its cover illustrations, reflected this connection. They consisted of well-produced black-and-white images of graceful women, set against socially significant but not overly intrusive backgrounds, and entered deeply into the ideologies of class, gender and consumer culture. Black-and-white work, in vogue in the art world, had become increasingly popular by the turn of the century. It had the advantage of being easier and cheaper to produce in magazines and newspapers.[12] Beauty culture too began to have a recognised place in late nineteenth-century society and much advice and advertising was concentrated on personal care and beauty.

Advertising was also a prominent feature of *The Ladies' Field*, accounting for almost half of each issue. Advertisements, once relegated to the back pages and covers of magazines, were now interspersed through them, and even attracted enthusiastic comment:

> Advertisements nowadays are so attractive .... It is impossible to glance through the advertising pages of a paper like *Ladies' Field* without being struck by the differences in the methods by which different men of fine business capacity and long experience set to work to bring about the same, or similar results.[13]

This was a far cry from Newnes's early agonising over the decision to place advertisements on the cover of *Tit-Bits*. Advertising was crucial to *The Ladies' Field*, underpinning its financial success, influencing its visual impact, and overlaying its definitions of femininity.

As print technology developed and the visual became a central component of the advertiser's new discourse, advertisers stressed the relationship between advertising and High Art (and thus between commercialism and 'high culture'). Poster art assumed a new importance in the 1880s and 1890s, and the first poster exhibition, featuring the work of well-known artists such as Beardsley, was held in London in 1894. Advertisers in *The Ladies' Field* harnessed the power of new techniques, often making visual and verbal references to classical art to underline the value of their products. An advertisement for Vogeler's Curative Compound, for instance, invoked a conventional classical image of voluptuous maternal vitality in the form of a reproduction oil painting entitled 'Health's Messenger'. Classicism, as this example demonstrates, also provided an acceptable model for

---

[12] Many of the most popular French magazines issued international co-editions, and many French fashion illustrators supplied fashion plates to English magazines. George Pilitelle was one of the most popular illustrators. His work was slightly art nouveau in character, and he was credited with the invention of the 'seven foot beauty with the ten inch waist'. See Madeline Ginsburg, *An Introduction to Fashion Illustration*, London: Victoria and Albert Museum (Pitman/Compton), 1980, p.11.

[13] *The Ladies' Field*, 48, 19 March, 1910, p.129.

the representation of the eroticised, scantily-clad female figure in the advertising pages, where such an image would have been unacceptable as an illustration to the editorial text. Column headers too employed art nouveau principles of design (*see Figure 17*). And the many photographs that appeared in the magazine all bore the name of Hudson and Kearns, the co-producers of *Country Life*. Newnes employed an Art Editor for *The Ladies' Field*, as he had for *The Strand*.[14]

In fact, *The Ladies' Field* was one of a crop of new magazines for women which appeared in the 1890s. Newnes, Harmsworth and Pearson, with their multiple publications and aggressive marketing strategies, launched many titles in the struggle for this niche market. Harmsworth established *Forget-Me-Not* (1891), *Home Sweet Home* (1893) and *Home Chat* (1895). Pearson bid for the market in penny domestic magazines with *Home Notes* (1894), and Newnes with *Woman's Life* (1895). Newnes then launched *The Ladies' Field* in March 1898, a magazine which continued until March 1922, when it briefly became *Ladies' Field Fashions* (a title that was significant given the fashion component of the magazine), and was then incorporated with *Home Magazine* in 1928.

The title 'Ladies' Field' carried an air of social exclusivity, by contrast with the title 'Woman's Life' which was a cross-class magazine. The term 'lady' denoted an upper-class woman, and the word 'field' bespoke aristocratic as well as sporting connections. Yet the latter word also evoked the field of battle, its ambiguity representing the competing possibilities available to the Society woman: aristocratic, country life or female militancy. The 'ladies' field' constituted the territory on which 'femininity' was contested. Moreover, the internal column titles of *The Ladies' Field* conjured up a number of competing images of femininity. 'In My Lady's Garden' (a title that evoked the terms, conditions and activities of upper-class existence) appeared alongside 'Women Workers' (a title with a distinctly democratic ring). The words 'lady' and 'woman' were volleyed back and forth in the women's press of the 1880s and 1890s, indicating the centrality of class to both the discourses of femininity and those of New Journalism. Oscar Wilde's refusal to edit *Lady's World* unless Cassell's agreed to change its title to *Woman's World* was but one famous example of a general process by which 'woman' became a positive term for 'all classes'.[15]

The Ladies' Field, along with *Country Life*, Friederichs claimed, was to be found in almost every country house in the United Kingdom.[16] This would put its circulation in the hundreds of thousands, although other 'ladies' papers' recorded substantially smaller circulations.[17] Its weekly price of sixpence put it

---

[14] Leslie Wilson was *The Ladies' Field*'s Art Editor.

[15] At the lower end of the market, the 'penny dreadfuls' frequently bore deceptively genteel titles such as *My Lady's Novelette* and *The Lady's Own Novelette*, a practice deplored by the established women's press.

[16] Hulda Friederichs, *The Life of Sir George Newnes, Bart*, London: Hodder and Stoughton, 1911, p.132.

[17] *The Lady*, for instance, recorded a weekly sale of 17,687 in 1895, and 27,949 in 1905. See Cynthia White, op. cit., p.68.

beyond the reach of the lower and lower middle classes, and its contents suggested that it was aimed at a largely metropolitan, upper middle-class audience. This magazine was directed at a readership with high social aspirations and a considerable amount of spending power, interested in court news, fashion, philanthropy, travel, entertaining, and increasingly in work and even political and industrial issues. It circulated outside Britain in Paris, the United States, Canada, Australia, Capetown and India, conferring the news of British Society upon a substantial readership, and could be obtained at all W.H. Smith bookstalls as well as ordered at selected newsagents.[18]

This chapter will demonstrate, in the first instance, the ways in which the fashion and advertising components of *The Ladies' Field* represented a combination of traditional and novel journalistic techniques, class and gender signification and consumer culture. Secondly, it will examine the ways in which feminine space was explored and femininity defined variously, in the correspondence columns and editorials, in terms of intimacy, class ideology, the rhetoric of 'expertise', consumption and social ritual. Finally, it will interrogate the different images of femininity negotiated in the magazine, arguing that *The Ladies' Field* was the site at which all of these images were interwoven in an attempt to widen the appeal of the magazine, ensuring that it held its own and turned a profit against the fierce competition that characterised the field of women's magazines.

Fashion had always been a major component of women's magazines, and was central to the construction of the Society lady, for whom every cap, bow, streamer, ruffle, fringe, bustle, glove, and especially every item of jewellery, was symbolic, within an elaborate female dress code. The preoccupation of Society journals with dress and fashion prompted Oscar Wilde to observe that the 'lady's world' was defined by papers such as the *Queen* and *Lady's Pictorial* exclusively in terms of 'mere millinery and trimmings'.[19] Newnes encouraged his editors to exploit fashionable society's preoccupation with dress and appearance in *The Ladies' Field*. Features and correspondence columns on matters of fashion multiplied as styles became more complicated and changed more and more rapidly. The demand for such columns intensified under the impact of industrialisation and social mobility, as a new class of female consumers emerged: women with money to spend but little understanding of Society's dynamics. For such women, magazines like *The Ladies' Field* provided an indispensable guide to the established rules of dress, taste and decorum, offering access to upper-class social status.

Yet as women's magazines evolved in the late nineteenth century, they increasingly presented an image of femininity that was less related to the conventions of class society than to a modern culture of consumption. Each issue of *The Ladies' Field* featured literally hundreds of advertisements for all manner

---

[18] *The Ladies' Field*, 4, 7 January, 1899, p.146.

[19] Simon Nowell-Smith, *The House of Cassell, 1848-1958*, London: Cassell, 1958, p.253.

of fashion accessories from dresses to bustles, knickerbockers and corsets, a multitude of beauty products from skin restorers to hair dyes and fragrances and a variety of consumer goods. Advertising revenue played a material role in underpinning the financial success of such publications. But it also had an ideological and symbolic importance in defining and positioning the female reader as a consumer of commodities. Through women's magazines, Janice Winship has argued, women were 'caught up in defining their own femininity, inextricably, through consumption'.[20]

The Ladies' Field helped to create a bourgeois commodity culture within which women were defined as 'shoppers'. Commodities, both those useful to the physical construction of femininity such as dresses, corsets, hairpieces and beauty products, and those related to her social and economic role as domestic provider, were increasingly represented as essential to the work of being feminine. The consumer was reflected back from the pages of the woman's magazine in the advertising's recurrent images of the female body, constructed out of commodities such as corsets, hair dyes, hats and shoes.[21] Moreover, the new urban department stores (Peter Robinson, John Lewis, and Dickins and Jones), catering for the upper and middle classes and featuring elaborate window displays, were depicted in *The Ladies' Field* as the woman's realm. This magazine thus offered an image of femininity that revolved around consumption.

Margaret Beetham has implied that the new woman of advertising culture, identified with 'the pleasures of consumption', was a disempowered and rather frivolous figure by contrast with the New Woman, who demanded access to paid employment and productive labour.[22] Yet the advertising sections of *The Ladies' Field* evoked a number of competing images of the feminine consumer in which she was seen, by extrapolation, to be actively engaged in a variety of activities in which cultural change and consumerism were both significant factors. She was variously represented as a creature of fashion, domestic provider, mother, sporting figure and as a paid worker. Advertisements for various types of furnishings - chair coverings, pianos, curtains, rugs, bookshelves, dressers - bespoke the increasing power wielded by women in the purchase of large household objects. Advertisements for 'Eton suits' evoked the contemporary woman's maternal role. Advertisements for specialised clothing - 'specially light weights for tropical wear', bicycle wear, hunting skirts, shooting wear, waterproof skirts, fishing boots, yachting and boating clothes, golf apparel, 'Travelling, Cycling, Tourist, Seaside and General Wear; to suit all purses, all climates, at all seasons' - conjured up the New Woman, engaged in an ever-growing number of sports and activities. And advertisements for new goods such as typewriters were

---

[20] Janice Winship, *Inside Women's Magazines*, as cited in John Storey, *An Introductory Guide to Cultural Theory and Popular Culture*, New York: Harvester Wheatsheaf, 1993, p.147.

[21] See Margaret Beetham, *A Magazine of Her Own? Domesticity and Desire in the Woman's Magazine, 1800-1914*, London and New York: Routledge, 1996, pp.8, 150.

[22] Ibid., p.150.

suggestive of women's entrance into the field of paid employment in areas such as the clerical occupations.

The marriage of culture and consumption continued to pervade *The Ladies' Field*, to the point of influencing its formal properties. What was most striking about Newnes's magazine was that it was such a well-integrated piece of journalism. Support for advertisers became increasingly direct, encompassing editorial mentions and recommendations. In his study of the cultural industry, *L'esprit du Temps*, Edgar Morin uses the term 'syncretism' to describe the homogeneity that he sees as typical of women's magazines.[23] And Clothilde de Stasio has shown that in the late Victorian *Woman*, information, advice and gossip columns, advertising and serials blended into an homogenous whole. Serials often turned out to be 'an advice column camouflaged as a story'. Advertising dealt with the main concerns of the magazine: food, health products, upholstery, clothes, cosmetics.[24]

In *The Ladies' Field*, advertisers often employed the newest techniques of journalistic copy: sensationalist banner headlines, striking black-and-white illustrations, attention-grabbing, bold type-face and personal appeals to readers. The full-page advertisement remained a staple of up-market papers such as *The Ladies' Field*, whereas cheaper papers began to carry pages which mixed editorial copy and advertising. Yet the physical and visual blurring of the boundaries between advertising and editorial copy meant that even in this magazine advertisements were sometimes virtually indistinguishable from the letterpress. Advertisements began to be placed strategically in relation to editorial matter so that a 'puff' for a department store in *The Ladies' Field*, for instance, might appear facing the page containing 'Illustrated Dress Advice'.

'Saunters Through the Shops', in fact, constituted a tour of fashionable stores; a series of advertisements dressed up as a shopping expedition, with a running commentary to lend narrative interest. 'Among the present-day benefactors to womenkind at large must most assuredly be reckoned Messrs. Dickins and Jones, of Hanover House, Regent Street', began one such commentary:

> One glance at the enormous stock of exquisite fabrics, designed for the creation of all that is aerial and charming in ball and evening toilettes will make one long to linger admiringly in the immediate proximity of so much loveliness, and not rest satisfied till one of those gleaming, glistening robes has come into our possession.[25]

The advertorial conflated the language of philanthropy (a traditional female sphere of activity) with the language of consumerism (the assumed obsession of

[23] Edgar Morin, as cited in Clothilde de Stasio, 'Arnold Bennett and Late-Victorian *Woman*', *Victorian Periodicals Review*, xxviii, 1 (Spring 1995), p.44.

[24] Clothilde de Stasio, op. cit., pp.44-45.

[25] *The Ladies' Field*, 4, 21 January, 1899, p.286.

the contemporary female), in order to guarantee the advertiser the broadest possible appeal. One evening gown available at Dickins and Jones, a store which also advertised in *The Ladies' Field*, was depicted in a full-page illustration in the same issue, as the author was careful to point out.

The 'advertorial' or 'puff', in which specific shops or brands were recommended in the editorial pages, was derived from journals like *Myra's Journal*, and its use was hotly debated over the latter half of the nineteenth century. Yet such indirect appeals were so common by the early twentieth century that readers would have easily recognised the 'puff' for what it was.[26] A correspondent going by the name 'Perplexed', for instance, was advised by 'Beryl', editor of 'Illustrated Dress Advice':

> from practical knowledge of their merits I can assure you that Dickins and Jones's 'Specialité' corsets are as perfect in cut as any on the market, and will wear and retain their shape until the end, which the majority do not.[27]

'Mater' was advised to go to 'Peter Robinson's', who also advertised in *The Ladies' Field*, to obtain her boy's Eton suits. And 'A New Subscriber', complimented upon her tastefully chosen gown, was directed to Goodwood, another Newnes advertiser, for further purchases.

It was clear that 'Beryl', otherwise the counsellor of readers, was obtaining a commission from those retailers whose stock she praised. In March 1899, the column featured a revealing announcement:

> 'Beryl' would be exceedingly obliged if, when correspondents or readers act upon her advice as regards going to recommended firms and dressmakers, they would kindly mention her name and that of the paper.[28]

The Ladies' Field thus exemplified a process by which, especially in the woman's magazine, advertisers and newspaper proprietors became locked in a relationship of mutual dependence as a dynamic bourgeois commodity culture developed, and femininity became increasingly defined in terms of consumption.

If the female reader of *The Ladies' Field* was a consumer, however, the female sub-editor was a literary professional. The editor of this magazine marshalled together a company of expert female sub-editors, of which she was head, to advise readers about concerns relating to their femininity through a range of correspondence columns. The entrance of women into the journalistic profession was signalled by the establishment of the Institute of Women Journalists in 1895. Advice columns in women's magazines were constructed around an identified female persona, a practice 'Myra' Browne had pioneered

---

26 T.R. Nevett, *Advertising in Britain*, London: Heinemann, 1982, p.149.

27 *The Ladies' Field*, 2, 25 June, 1898, p.108.

28 *The Ladies' Field*, 4, 11 March, 1899, p.625.

with *Myra's Journal* and *Sylvia's Journal*. Pearson developed a series of magazines linked to 'Isabel', and *Woman at Home*, a popular magazine launched in the 1890s, was identified with the romantic novelist Annie S. Swan. The consultant-editors of *The Ladies' Field* - 'Ergane', 'Contessa', 'Beryl', 'Hygea' - were representatives of the process by which women assumed their place in the professional world. *The Ladies' Field's* 'Sale and Exchange' column also conjured up a range of female experts who offered their services as commercial consultants. One such advertisement read: 'LADY SPECIALIST for Complexion, figure, and reducing stoutness, by outward application; individual cases studied; most moderate charges'.[29] (Contrasting advice was offered to male readers by male experts of *The Captain* such as C.B. Fry and Eugen Sandow. Rather than offering to *reduce* stoutness, they explicitly advocated a version of it: solid muscularity.)

Yet the role of the writer, as Margaret Beetham has pointed out, was very much masculinised.[30] Andrew Lang, the arch-professional journalist of the period, employed his *Longman's* column to create a print version of the masculine ethos of the gentleman's club, an institution from which women were emphatically excluded. Editorial power remained almost entirely in the hands of metropolitan, middle-class men. No women appeared, for instance, in *The Strand's* 'Chronicles of the *Strand* Club', although female authors were included in the visual representation of the magazine's contributors. This is significant, given Beetham's argument that women's magazines tended to offer a definition of femininity, via an increasing emphasis on visual innovation and consumer culture, that revolved around physical appearance.

The issue of literary authority, complicated by gender relations, entered into the editorial column of *The Ladies' Field*. Mrs Macdonald, whom Newnes had appointed editor of the magazine, wrote in its second issue:

> As Editor, I must express my most grateful thanks for the splendid reception given to our first number. Letters and congratulations have reached me from all parts of the U.K., and the warm appreciation, not only of my own sex, but of clever men of the world, has given me the greatest possible pleasure. To my readers I appeal for co-operation, as without it my aim and cherished object to make the paper an influence in the world of cultured women cannot be accomplished.[31]

The paragraph demonstrated the difficulties facing the female editor as she attempted to establish her claims to editorial authority. She began confidently, employing a first person mode of address: 'As Editor *I* must express *my* most

---

[29] *The Ladies' Field*, 5, 25 March, 1899, p.106.

[30] Margaret Beetham, op. cit., p.128.

[31] *The Ladies' Field*, 1, 26 March, 1898, p.48. Mrs Macdonald is named as the editor of *The Ladies' Field* in *Public Opinion* (1904), but I have been unable to locate any biographical material on her.

grateful thanks'. Yet her independent self-assurance, revived in the phrase 'my aim and cherished object', was ultimately dissolved within a comforting notion of the collective identity of her 'own sex' and the 'co-operation' of 'women of culture'. The necessity of obtaining verification from 'clever men of the world' revealed the extent to which the role of the editor - the 'man of letters' - was still very much masculinised. The importance of their sanction lay both in the fact that they were 'clever', and in the fact that they were 'men of the world', and therefore had access to wider experiences than did 'cultured women', who inhabited a segregated, if privileged, world. These remarks conveyed a mixture of the editor's apprehension about the reception of the new magazine, and her apprehension about her gendered identity as a female editor in what was still predominantly a man's field.

The woman's magazine, however, came to represent feminised space; space which was defined by the woman at its centre and its separation from the masculine world of politics and economics.[32] Annie Swan's column in *Woman at Home*, 'Over the Teacups', according to Beetham, 'enacted a feminine dynamic of mutual support and created ... a community of like-minded readers who encouraged each other in the difficulties of everyday life'. Her capacity to *feel* for her readers was the source of the column's authority and popularity.[33] Similarly, the correspondence columns of *The Ladies' Field* created a forum in which women could share with each other the secrets of their femininity.

In 'Illustrated Dress Advice', 'Beryl' claimed to be 'delighted to answer any questions relating to dress, and when desired will give special designs to those correspondents sending photographs, and full particulars as to colouring, height, etc'. 'Hygea', a 'Specialist on all matters relating to the toilet', proffered advice on matters such as eye soreness, hair treatments, skin tonics and the like.[34] 'Contessa' was available as a consultant on etiquette, offering to 'solve any knotty points concerning manners and customs'. She was a persona characteristic of the mid-nineteenth-century ladies' paper, whilst 'Jeanne Jardine', who handled correspondence on cookery, represented a key figure of the domestic magazine. (Her given name, the French equivalent of 'Jane', drew upon the idea that France was the home of excellent cuisine, just as Italy was the model of a civilised society. And her surname suggested, perhaps, that her own garden provided her with the materials for her culinary expertise.) 'Portia'

---

[32] 'Mems by a Man', a column introduced into *The Ladies' Field* in 1899, which traded very much in sexual stereotypes, functioned as a kind of counterpoint to the dynamic complexity of the rest of the text. The name of the column's editor, 'Harry Adney', was a transparent play on the name of that subversive female figure 'Ariadne'. The term 'mems' served to link the column to Newnes's *Million*, which had featured a column entitled 'Mems for the Million', and to suggest that it contained ephemera. And the isolated position of the author was implicit in his impersonal generic identification. 'Mems by a Man' did not last long. The 'man' was ushered in only to be banished from feminine space.

[33] Margaret Beetham, op. cit., p.166.

[34] The name 'Hygea' was a derivation of that of the Greek mythological figure 'Hygieia'. As daughter of the god of healing, Hygieia personified health. In using such names, the magazine assumed that its readers were educated in their origins.

offered advice on 'Art in the House'. 'Ergane', meanwhile, was to 'receive for mention (if suitable) interesting items of news from at home and abroad' relating to 'Work for Gentlewomen'.[35] Identified by their fictitious first names, as if close family members, this company of personae addressed the reader as a friend, their columns suggesting a direct and intimate exchange between women about those skills which pertained to femininity. 'I suffer very much in the same way myself', wrote 'Hygea' in advising a sportswoman suffering from headaches and stomach problems to give up alcohol, drink Bovril and always have 'Cerebus' table salt on the meal table, 'and am only asking you to carry out my own golden rule of life'.[36] Like the subjects addressed - fashion, hygiene, etiquette - the tone of these columns was feminised. It was related to gossip, a form of speech associated particularly with women.

Palmistry was a female skill which was in increasing demand in the late nineteenth century. 'As a profession that enables its exponents to counsel, warn and guide those who come for advice', read one paragraph in *The Ladies' Field*, '[palmistry can] be turned to account in the most valuable manner by those wise enough to recognise its warnings, and profit by the self-knowledge gained from the deciphering of character and events by a skilled palmist.'[37] Even the King, always *dans le mouvement*, took an interest in palmistry, and had his 'hand told' by a celebrated Bond Street lady. For 2s. 6d. 'Cassandra', 'the well-known expert', provided palm readings through a column in *The Ladies' Field*.[38] The casting of a woman in the role of the palm-reader or mystic with special interpersonal and psychic skills constituted a reinforcement of gender stereotypes. This column reinforced the separation between the feminine sphere - personal, emotional, psychological - and that of the male - public, political, scientific. Thus the female editors of *The Ladies' Field* were characterised by their personal insights and by a confidential mode of expression. The editorial 'experts' that featured in *The Captain* and *C.B. Fry's Magazine*, on the other hand, were sportsmen, natural scientists and politicians who employed the language of sportsmanship, diplomacy and public school patriotism: the language of the public sphere.

The Ladies' Field represented both a repository of female wisdom and the pleasure of female company. 'Be sure and tell me all about the wedding, and do not hesitate to write to me again if I can be of use to you in any way', wrote a helpful 'Beryl' to one correspondent. Her column was characterised by very personal advice relating to colouring and style, as well as by an abundance of references to particular shops and firms. 'For your afternoon gown consult

---

35   *The Ladies' Field*, 1, 11 June, 1898, pp.618, 624, 628, 630. The name 'Ergane' was probably derived from 'Erginus', the Greek mythological figure who having been defeated by Hercules was forced to devote most of his ensuing years to recovering his prosperity, remaining wifeless and childless until old age.

36   *The Ladies' Field*, 1, 14 May, 1898, p.422.

37   *The Ladies' Field*, 1, 11 June, 1898, p.628.

38   Cassandra was a Greek prophetess. She appears in Shakespeare's *Troilus and Cressida*.

Madame Mathilde, of 16, Monmouth Rd, Westbourne Grove,' she advised
another reader, 'she has such a variety of exquisite materials, and is a born artist
in dress'. (Madame Mathilde also advertised in *The Ladies' Field*.) 'I am
wearing a gown of hers at the moment', continued the editor, in a confidential
manner, 'and never had one which fitted me better or was more comfortable. Let
her make your reception toilette also.'[39] Such responses evoked a sense of the
reading community and their advisors as a circle of confidantes, sharing
communally in the problems of femininity. Yet class consciousness continued to
intrude, on occasion, upon attempts to foster a shared ideology based on gender
identification. 'I cannot answer your second query until you give me a limit as to
price and your future husband's social position in India', was the editor's
slightly supercilious response to one reader's inquiry, 'as the size of your
trousseau depends a great deal upon that, naturally.'[40]

The 'ladies' field', moreover, was strictly divided amongst the various
consultant-editors, the text resembling a department store of the kind frequented
by the upper middle-class readers of the magazine and advertised in its pages. If
the rules of social engagement were the specialty of 'Contessa', inquiries about
these rules were not to be addressed to any of the other sub-editors. 'Not for a
year, at the very least; but you may go out a little this season, as the loss occurred
some months ago', wrote the editor of the 'Illustrated Dress Advice' column,
presumably referring to the loss of a husband. 'Another time', she continued, in
a firm tone, 'will you kindly address similar queries to " Contessa" who has
charge of the "Manners and Customs" department?'[41] Another reader was
redirected in a similar fashion: 'Your first query should have been addressed to
" Hygea", who has charge of the Toilet department.'[42]

Rosemary T. Van Arsdel has argued that interviews and biographical
sketches were crucial to the appeal and to the ideological and political purpose of
New Journalism, offering 'an intimate, close-up view of people ... who were well-
known, whose careers were valuable, who were determined to succeed, who could
be emulated'. The interview's 'freshness and rather gossipy tone sold
periodicals', and it could be used as 'a powerful new tool to educate, to inform,
and to move to action'.[43] Biographical sketches filled the columns of *The
Ladies' Field*, with Queen Victoria as the leading prototype of the successful,
public female figure. Yet one of the most prominent ways in which female role-
models were narratively and cumulatively constructed, with the participation of
readers, was through the correspondence columns. Through its discussions of
various fields of feminine concern - dress, the toilet, etiquette, cookery, household

---

[39] *The Ladies' Field*, 1, 21 May, 1898, p.486.

[40] *The Ladies' Field*, 1, 11 June, 1898, p.630.

[41] Ibid.

[42] *The Ladies' Field*, 1, 14 May, 1898, p.422.

[43] Rosemary T. Van Arsdel, 'Women's Periodicals and the New Journalism: The
Personal Interview', in Joel Wiener (ed.), *Papers for the Millions: The New Journalism in
Britain, 1850s-1914*, New York: Greenwood Press, 1988, pp.255-256.

management, and 'women's work' - the magazine negotiated and defined 'the ladies' field' and offered up a definition of femininity which publisher and editor deemed appropriate to its upper middle-class and upper-class readership.

'Cassandra's' column on palmistry produced a series of images which resonated with the ambitions, values and experiences of female readers.[44] 'Material comfort' and 'social success' (described in one reading as 'affluent circumstances and gratified ambition'), and skill in 'the management of a household and staff of servants' were characteristic features of the image. 'Changes of country' were occasionally predicted, and the vocational paths entering into 'Cassandra's' predictions included literature, acting, art and 'intellectual and philanthropic interests' - the kinds of callings that one might expect to fall within the ambitions and reach of the magazine's middle-class and upper-class readers. 'Marriage' was the consultant-editor's constant refrain. One example will serve to elucidate this point:

> marriage is marked to a man in good circumstances, who
> eventually makes a brilliant career for himself in his chosen
> calling[45]

'Delicate health', too, was a recurrent feature of the column's biographical plots.

Not all images offered by this magazine, then, were positive. According to an entrenched Victorian tradition, woman was a weak, frail, sickly creature with a poor constitution. She suffered from depression, headaches, listlessness and hysteria: what have been termed 'the fashionable diseases'. Ann Wood has argued that her health condition reflected her inferior position in society.[46] 'The Boudoir' tended to reinforce this image of feminine frailty. A succession of ladies with various ailments and apparently delicate constitutions were engaged in sympathetic discussions with 'Hygea', and given detailed personalised advice about tonics, pills, oils, diet and other treatments. Dyspepsia, obesity, nervous complaints, indigestion, anaemia and skin problems all featured regularly. Advertising, too, used and validated a professionalised medical discourse in which the female body became increasingly pathologised. The female frame, it emerged, was particularly liable to all manner of illness, weakness and debility, and other gender-specific but vaguely defined illnesses.

The Ladies' Field was, in fact, a site on which a number of different images of femininity were negotiated, all of them influential within the contemporary

---

44 Readers of Cassandra's column were informed that 'to obtain a delineation', they should send 'an outline of the back of the hand, placing the fingers well apart, and an impression of both palms'. They were instructed to rub oil or vaseline into their hand, paint lightly over it with liquid Indian ink, and make an imprint on a sheet of blotting paper. Their readings were printed in the column.

45 *The Ladies' Field*, 2, 12 November, 1898, p.406

46 Ann Wood, 'The Fashionable Diseases: Women's Complaints and their Treatment in Nineteenth Century America', *Journal of Interdisciplinary History*, 1973. This was an image evoked by Jane Austen with Mrs Bennet in *Pride and Prejudice* and with Mrs Norris in *Mansfield Park*.

cultural climate. A stereotype of the woman as wife, mother and domestic provider competed with a traditional notion of the leisured 'woman of culture'. And intruding upon both of these versions of the late Victorian and Edwardian 'lady' was the figure of the 'woman worker', a figure who complicated the discourses of femininity.

The first of these images was derived from the cult of 'glorified domesticity', one of the most successful features of the popular woman's magazine of the period. The mid to late nineteenth century saw a growing shortage of domestic servants, and this situation exposed deficiencies in the abilities of young, educated, otherwise fashionably accomplished women to assume the management of their households. At the same time, general price rises which forced women to economise in every area of housekeeping, and increasingly rigorous standards of nutrition, hygiene, health and child-care, led to increasing domestic demands being made upon women. A plethora of new women's magazines appeared. They were devoted to home topics such as health, housekeeping, cookery, needlework, child-care, home furnishing and the toilet, and fostered an image of the woman as domestic provider. *The Ladies' Field* reinforced this image with columns such as 'Menage and Means', 'Art in the House' and 'The Boudoir'. The fact that *The Ladies' Field* began to carry some requests for less costly menus suggested that some members of the upper classes were beginning to suffer from the gap between real income and social position.

Many of the magazine's competitions also reinforced this image, particularly the 'Menage and Means' competitions, which solicited entries marked, revealingly, '"Housewife", c/o Editor, *The Ladies' Field*'. These included a competition for the 'best set of Three Original Recipes for utilising a Pair of Fowls in such a manner as to provide three dishes: the first for dinner, the second for luncheon, and the third for breakfast', and one for 'the Best Original and Practical Scheme for Decorating a Round or Oval Dinner Table in white and yellow'. 'Mere extravagance in the design or costliness of the flowers used', it was stipulated, 'will not, irrespective of other points, be allowed to influence the award'.[47] Such competitions called for a combination of social accomplishment and economical pragmatism.

The Ladies' Field focussed considerable attention on housekeeping and motherhood. The situation of the married woman, as Patricia Branca has argued, was most representative of the Victorian and Edwardian middle-class woman's lifestyle, despite the historiographical focus on the single girl of the period. Furthermore, this woman spent most of her time in the home, her role in the family crucial.[48] For the upper-class girl, marriage was especially imperative. It was part of a girl's social duty to increase her status and influence through marriage. In fact, a girl's whole life from babyhood was oriented towards the role she had to play in the 'status theatre' of Society. Marriage was a crucial step in

[47] *The Ladies' Field*, 5, 25 March, 1899, p.106.

[48] Patricia Branca, *Silent Sisterhood: Middle-Class Women in the Victorian Home*, London: Croom Helm, 1975, p.2.

her career, her entire life defined by her progression through clearly demarcated social stages. (Her brother's life, by contrast, was defined by his progress in business or public life.) Such momentum towards the married state was clearly revealed in the paragraphs of the 'Palmistry' column, in which marriage was unquestioningly assumed to be the goal and destiny of the column's correspondents. And many of the questions addressed to 'Beryl' related to the wedding outfit.

A *Ladies' Field* column entitled 'Mothers in Council' elevated the concerns of motherhood to the realms of official dialogue. Its discussions, open only to 'mothers, teachers and guardians', and relating to issues such as 'girl's allowances', highlighted the maternal role of the contemporary woman. In 'The Children's Hour', a column aimed at attracting the juvenile market, the editor self-consciously exploited the possibilities of the maternal image in an attempt to characterise and market 'The Lady Editor'. 'Most of my young friends think they are writing to a man editor', she wrote, in soothing, maternal tones, 'but on the contrary, I am a mother, so know all about your troubles and pleasures, dear children.'

Having extolled the virtues of her sympathetic position as a mother, she then went on to appeal to the readers' sense of filial loyalty, writing in the letter format with which their schooling had familiarised readers, and presenting the column's next competition as a kind of party, with herself as hostess:

> Next week I am giving another competition, so be sure and look
> out for it, and try and interest all your friends and playmates in
> our 'Children's Corner'. By so doing, you will give very great
> pleasure to
> Your sincere friend,
> THE 'LADY EDITOR'[49]

Thus, an image of femininity which revolved around motherhood was exploited as a point of access to the juvenile market, as the editor experimented with the notion of gendered editorial identity. *The Captain*, established by Newnes in 1899, was to deploy different editorial personae - the thoroughly masculine public school 'gentleman' and the sportsman - and employ an almost conspiratorially 'chummy' editorial tone, derived from the colloquialisms of the English public school, to secure the interest of juvenile readers, mostly boys, but some girls as well.

The Ladies' Field, so it claimed, was designed for 'women of culture', and another resonant image that emerged from the text was that of the accomplished and socially active Society lady. Throughout the nineteenth century, as Leonore Davidoff has noted, upper and middle-class women played a central role in maintaining the fabric of Society, a remarkably formalised institution.[50] They

---

49 *The Ladies' Field*, 1, 14 May, 1898, p.414.

50 Leonore Davidoff, *The Best Circles: Society, Etiquette and the Season*, London: Croom Helm, 1973, pp.16-17.

were its semi-official leaders, and they acted as arbiters of social acceptance or rejection. They accepted the rubrics of Society and internalised its norms, voluntarily defining themselves within its circumscribed orbit. Excluded from public life, they maintained a rigid system of exact social classification which offered stability and security in the face of economic and political upheaval and social dislocation. It was women upon whom fell the burden of responsibility for maintaining many of the day-to-day social activities essential to the maintenance of Society. And they carefully studied the details of an elaborate system of etiquette, within which subtle shifts in fashionably correct behaviour were employed to mark the knowledgeable insider from the outsider. Magazines such as *The Ladies' Field*, offering regular advice columns on matters of etiquette, fashion and entertaining, acted to reinforce the social function of the upper-class woman, and revealed the ways in which class ideology impacted upon definitions of femininity.

The rules of 'good taste and the fitness of things' were defined by 'Contessa', editor of the column 'Manners and Customs'. 'You are quite mistaken', she chided one correspondent, 'everybody smokes now, and no woman is thought odd if she does so.' She went on to elaborate upon the proprieties of this rather *fin de siècle* habit, invoking the rituals of the highest of social circles:

> Cigarettes are smoked after luncheon and dinner in some of the best houses in London. A lady would not smoke at a public place such as a restaurant. It would probably be against the rules of the establishment, and certainly against those of good taste and the fitness of things.[51]

The column was filled with inquiries regarding the rules of calling, the duties of the hostess, the etiquette of mourning and many other concerns relating to the rules of social engagement.

'There are sets and there are sets', wrote 'Contessa' to another correspondent, 'and the small, smart world of London is a thing apart, with its own distinctive manners and customs.'[52] This magazine's preoccupation with Society and 'The Season' (and even with London department stores) was related to conditions of production. Women's magazines, unlike newspapers, were not published in provincial centres outside London. Throughout the nineteenth century, therefore, they produced an exclusively metropolitan version of femininity. By the 1890s, magazines such as this one were read across the empire, but they still offered an identity which bound readers to the culture of the capital.

The 'woman of culture', as she was presented in *The Ladies' Field*, sought to acquire the many elegant accomplishments that the daughters of the upper

---

[51] *The Ladies' Field*, 1, 11 June, 1898, p.628.

[52] Ibid., p.628.

classes of the period learned through governesses or boarding schools: some French, music, dancing, fancy needlework and, of course, the rules of etiquette. The magazine's upper middle-class readers were instructed through a series of columns and competitions. '*The Ladies' Field* Sketch Club' exemplifies this. Its aim:

> to encourage drawing and painting from nature, and to provide instruction based on the modern principles approved of on the Continent and at home for the pictorial treatment of figure, landscape and still life subjects.[53]

If Italy was the home of civilised values, and France the home of fine cooking, Europe more generally - 'the Continent' - was the home of painting. Entries in the Club's competitions were criticised by a teaching artist, and entrants were entitled to pose questions and mention difficulties, all of which were to be dealt with in the judge's criticisms, sent to the competitor. An 'eminent French critic' was employed, in connection with the Girls' Field Literary Club, to contribute a monthly article in French, discussing 'books worth studying, literary gossip, and pithy criticisms'.[54] Prizes were offered for the best translation of the article. The 'woman of culture' needed to be trained up to her social role, and *The Ladies' Field* took upon itself the role of governess.

The fashionable 'woman of culture' had substantial leisure time to engage in various activities (as the title of the column 'Saunters Thro' the Shops' implied), and competitions to design and produce a variety of objects from candlesticks to pin-cushions were a feature of women's magazines. In the Needlecraft Competitions, prizes were offered for embroidered photographic album covers, autograph album covers, pillow covers and, in one instance, for a cover for *The Ladies' Field*. Through 'The Arts and Craft Guild' *The Ladies' Field* posted a regular weekly challenge, offering to reward the competitor who produced 'the most original design for a pair of candlesticks, to be carried out in bent iron and copper work' one week, and she who sent in 'the most original design for a Silver Bowl or Cup, suitable for presentation to a lady at a dog or cat show' another. On one occasion, readers were urged to offer a time-table for a country house ('meant to hang in the guests' bedrooms, or by the post-box in the hall, to afford certain information which every visitor requires'). This competition was an indication that the magazine's readers were comfortable enough to own country houses, although not aristocratic enough to own rural estates. All prize designs became the copyright of the paper, the publisher deriving commercial benefit from a tradition of female accomplishment. (But then, competition winners also received money prizes.)

The competitions in *The Ladies' Field*, however, upheld a distinction between amateurs and professionals, in an age when the professional woman was

---

53 *The Ladies' Field*, 28, 20 May, 1905.
54 *The Ladies' Field*, 14, 15 June, 1901, p.2.

just beginning to make her presence felt. '*The Ladies' Field* Camera Club' competitions and the 'Menage and Means' competitions were open only to '*bona-fide* amateurs'. The 'woman of culture', it was implied, had the time, inclination and finances to cultivate these various skills as an amateur. Like the domestic and maternal woman, she too was nurtured by *The Ladies' Field*, her image reflected back from its pages.

Given the primacy of social goals and unpaid labour amongst middle and upper class women, the notion of paid work was problematic. The idea that work was actually degrading for 'ladies' had gained currency during the nineteenth century. Thus one gentlewoman wrote in 1881:

> Now allow me ... to pass by without notice all *democratic* and *low* arguments about *ladies* working. My opinion is ... that if a woman is obliged to work, at once she (although she may be Christian and well bred) loses that peculiar position which the word *lady* conventionally designates.[55]

The phrase 'working ladies' was therefore seen as a contradiction in terms. Governesses and lady companions were subject to chronic underemployment and exploitation. There was a distinct shortage of 'genteel' employment for women who found themselves without an income. That which was considered acceptable was generally marginal, makeshift and unremunerative, much of it in the personal service area, and involving the use of friends as clients or customers. 'Daffodils, 180 good blooms, foliage, 1s 6d., free [delivery]; Primroses, 1d. a bunch', read an advertisement in the 'Sale and Exchange' column of *The Ladies' Field*, 'Weekly orders solicited. "Ivy, Calbourne, Isle of Wight"'.[56]

Many women like 'Ivy' raised flowers or fruit to be used for table decoration. They competed, however, with trained gardeners and upper servants, and were poorly compensated for their efforts. Some pursued wider experiences in the semi-familial organisations attached to the Church, which took in lay workers by the end of the century. In *The Ladies' Field*, 'Eulalie' offered a column entitled 'Church and Charity' as 'a channel to assist, when possible, any really good public work brought to her notice'.[57] Such work tended to be voluntary, and it thrust women back into traditional social roles.

Nevertheless, the fashionable woman's role as the guardian of culture and social ritual was gradually eroded, as social life began to make provision for respectable women to meet in public places outside the home without chaperonage, women began to enter into paid employment and the suffrage

---

[55] [Mrs] E. Genna, *Irresponsible Philanthropists: Being Some Chapters on the Employment of Gentlewomen* (1881), as cited in Lee Holcombe, *Victorian Ladies at Work*, Newton Abbot: David and Charles, 1973, p.4.

[56] *The Ladies' Field*, 5, 25 March, 1899, p.106.

[57] The name 'Eulalie' is from the Greek, and means 'fair speech; one who speaks sweetly'.

movement gathered momentum.[58] In February 1899, the editor announced that *The Ladies' Field* would include a monthly feature entitled 'Women in Parliament', intended to address the growing influence of women in the sphere of public life: their 'work on boards and committees', their realisation of 'the duties and responsibilities of citizenship', their increasingly informed role in philanthropic and charity work, and their participation in women's political organisations. Her comments demonstrated the increasing friction associated with the rise of the professional woman within middle-class culture. This column aimed to educate women for the responsible practice of citizenship, claiming to offer a print version of the female debating societies that were rapidly being formed:

> The really important thing in all these matters is that there shall exist in the minds of women clear reasons for the faith that is in them, that they shall feel bound to take an intelligent interest in the current questions of the day, and that their opinions shall be formed not on prejudice or one-sided information, but after thoughtful investigation of a subject ... we hope to discuss fully and from all sides questions which are, or ought to be, of interest to women.[59]

The reader of this passage was, it was implied, engaged in transforming herself into a public and politicised figure. Yet she confined her education within the boundaries of feminine space, the established domain of the woman's magazine - 'questions which are, or ought to be, of interest to women' - and she assumed a subordinate, if responsible, role:

> It is only by educating ourselves as women, on the many important subjects which press for solution, that we shall rise in any worthy manner to the responsibility which all are agreed even now rests with women, in the forming and guiding of public opinion.[60]

Nevertheless, this column highlighted a series of more or less politically significant issues relevant to women such as 'The Education of Children Bill' and the meeting of the International Council of Women held in London in 1899.[61] *The Ladies' Field*, then, did introduce a new image of the woman as a public figure, albeit an image that was hedged in by the conservative leanings of the magazine and by traditional notions of feminine space.

---

58 See Leonore Davidoff, op. cit., p.67.

59 *The Ladies' Field*, 4, 25 February, 1899, p.519.

60 Ibid.

61 This organisation, formed from the federation of national councils or unions, was designed to promote 'unity and understanding between all associations of women working for the common welfare of the community'. It was divided into various sections and sub-committees, including a Professional Section, Social Section, Political Section, Educational Section, Literary Sub-Committee and Press Sub-Committee.

Harriet Martineau had drawn public attention to the problem of 'redundant women' in an article in the *Edinburgh Review* in 1859 in which she pointed out that there were over half a million more women than men in Britain. This group was composed of single women who could not hope to find economic security in marriage and widows whose husbands may not have provided for them. The number of women, including those of the upper and middle classes, forced to support themselves continued to grow as the century drew to a close.[62] These conditions acted as a spur to magazines such as *The Ladies' Field* to offer columns in which new ways of earning or supplementing inadequate incomes were discussed for the benefit of readers. Newnes's magazine ran a column entitled 'Women Workers', whilst *The Queen* offered 'Women's Employment' and *The Lady* established 'How to Live'.

In fact, the issue of women's access to paid work had surfaced across a range of women's magazines from the 1860s onwards, threatening the dominant discourse of even the most dedicated domestic magazines as well as 'ladies' papers'.[63] After 1900, a sub-genre of work-related magazines developed. The question of productive work for women intruded into the pages of *The Ladies' Field*, despite its constant equation of femininity with consumption, leisure and social ritual. The magazine ran stories about organisations which promoted the employment of women, such as the International Council of Women, and about areas of women's employment such as typewriting and millinery, advocated women's entry into male strongholds such as the factory inspectorate and offered a regular feature on 'Women Workers'. The editor reconciled the magazine's treatment of women's demands for economic independence with its more socially conservative thrust via the latter column's pictorial header: an image of two 'women workers' who were actually engaged in traditional, non-remunerative accomplishments (*see Figure 17a*).

Middle-class working women emerged out of the late nineteenth and early twentieth centuries as an increasingly diverse, well-trained, organised and professionalised group. This group produced a disruptive redefinition of the

---

[62] The number of unmarried women increased throughout the period before the first World War, the census of 1911 revealing that there were nearly 1,400,000 more women than men (Lee Holcombe, op. cit., p.11). Moreover the disproportion between the sexes was greater amongst the middle classes, a fact partly explained by the excessive emigration of men of this class to the empire and the wider world (a process documented and celebrated in *The Wide World Magazine*). The marriage rate fell in the first decade of the twentieth century to 15 per thousand in 1910, well below the average for the previous decade. Remarriage among the widowed was decreasing, whilst the number of divorces had risen by 20 per cent (Cynthia White, op. cit., p.81).

[63] *The Woman's Gazette*, a functional magazine designed to direct needy women to employment opportunities, was established in 1875. It changed its name to *Work and Leisure* in 1879, under which title it continued to supply employment advice and information about professional bodies, but also broadened its contents to include correspondence, competitions and fiction. Emily Faithfull's *Victoria Magazine* and the radical *English Woman's Journal*, since they already functioned to advertise both workers and employers, also addressed the problem of women's work. The Society for the Promotion of the Employment of Women developed directly out of the register of work in the *English Woman's Journal*.

structure of feminine behaviour. Through its 'Women Workers' column, *The Ladies' Field* documented and participated in the process of producing 'women workers', directing ladies to register with the Gentlewomen's Employment Club or the Central Bureau for the Employment of Women, publicising official inquiries into conditions in various industries in which women were employed, and advising readers of the means by which they could enter occupations such as typing, governessing, health work, teaching, weaving, dressmaking, nursing and floral decoration.

Shop assistants numbered almost half a million by 1914, and were by far the largest single group of middle-class women workers in Britain.[64] Whilst they received little attention in the 'Women Workers' column, the Fashion or Cosmetics sub-editor of this magazine represented a professionalised literary version of the shop assistant. Nursing had always been considered women's work, but was gradually transformed by female reformers into a respected and skilled (and popular) calling, and nurses earned the status of true professionals. 'For provincial hospitals', a *Ladies' Field* correspondent was informed, 'the New Infirmary, Birmingham, the Bristol Infirmary, and the Shrewsbury Infirmary have all very high reputations for the efficient and thorough training they provide for their nurses. In each case you should apply to the matron.'[65]

In a period characterised by the rhetoric of expertise, especially in the area of national health and hygiene, *The Ladies' Field* addressed many questions sent in by prospective health lecturers. The publication thus tackled the cultural preoccupation with national efficiency from the perspective of the budding female professional, whose special (and 'natural') gifts as a nurse and domestic manager, combined with professional training, equipped her to deal with the problem of national health. *The Captain* and *C.B. Fry's Magazine*, aimed at boys and at sportsmen and sportswomen, addressed the issue from a different angle, offering a solution to the problem of physical deterioration which revolved around physical training and sportsmanship.[66]

Teaching or 'governessing', the only calling considered respectable in the mid-Victorian period, remained one of the chief fields of employment for middle-class women. However, despite the fact that the issue of professional training received substantial attention throughout the 1890s, the majority of governesses continued to come from that class of ladies who were equipped for teaching by genteel poverty rather than by academic achievements.[67] 'Wanted', read one advertisement in the 'Educational' column of *The Ladies' Field*, 'gentlewoman, about 28-30, for Easter holidays, as companion-governess to boy 10, girl 13;

---

[64] Lee Holcombe, op. cit., p.103.

[65] *The Ladies' Field*, 1, 11 June, 1898, p.618.

[66] The Sanitary Institute offered lectures and demonstrations aimed at supplying practical training to female lecturers. Papers such as *Hospital* and *Sanitary Record* contained notices of vacant appointments. And the National Health Society co-ordinated the movement for national efficiency. See *The Ladies' Field*, 1, 11 June, 1898, p.618.

[67] A joint Oxford-Cambridge committee on teacher training was established in 1897, the year before *The Ladies' Field* was established.

must be good disciplinarian, fond of country, and willing to be generally useful'. 'Clergyman's wife recommends a doctor's daughter (20)', read another, 'for engagement as Companion or Mother's Help, where servants are kept; thoroughly conscientious, refined, musical, and most obliging; salary £15 to £20, and laundry'. The readers of this column, it must be assumed, retained a sense of identification with traditional social qualifications for 'women's work'.

Women were increasingly employed in the civil service as clerks, telephone operators, typists and inspectors.[68] Typewriting was, from the beginning, an almost exclusively feminine occupation, according to Lee Holcombe.[69] Well-educated, middle-class women began to enter the clerical occupations in increasing numbers in the years leading up to the first World War. With regard to clerical salaries, however, many female critics argued that the competition from the inadequately-educated and poorly-trained working classes kept levels of pay low. This discouraged capable, cultured, well-educated gentlewomen from seeking such work, and there were more well-paid positions open than there were women to fill them.

An article in *The Ladies' Field* on the conditions prevailing in typewriting as a female profession reinforced this view. The author attempted to assess why, whilst many girls were learning typing and shorthand on the understanding that there were 'plenty of openings' in the field, many found that they could only command very small wages. Her analysis represented a harnessing of Arnold's sense of 'culture for culture's sake' to a more utilitarian notion of practical application. 'Good openings', it was suggested, were available only to 'the educated and competent':

> A knowledge of typewriting and shorthand is, no doubt, of immense value in equipping a woman for making her own way in the world; but of what use is it without the basis of a sound, practical education? The knowledge will not, in itself, assist its possessor to write a clear business letter, or string together half-a-dozen sentences in good English.[70]

The author sought to assimilate a notion of women as workers to an image of femininity, characteristic of *The Ladies' Field*, to which 'culture' was central and the vocationally specific was marginal. This magazine's representation of women workers and women's work was complicated by its allegiance to a conservative notion of 'culture' and to the imperatives of class ideology. 'Business' and 'good English' were slightly uneasy bedfellows.

---

[68] The government inspectorate, in particular, offered an accessible (although increasingly competitive), respectable and secure field of employment for women of ability and education. The Board of Education made early use of women inspectors, as did the Local Government Board. Women acted as factory inspectors under the Home Office, and were employed in large numbers in the newly-created National Health Insurance Commission and Board of Trade Labour Exchanges.

[69] Lee Holcombe, op. cit., p.151.

[70] *The Ladies' Field*, 1, 11 June, 1898, p.618.

A paragraph on the occupation of the professional floral decorator revealed the difficulties attached to the task of accommodating work to the image of the 'lady'. The floral decorator's work, especially busy during 'the season', consisted in 'arranging the floral decorations at balls, parties and weddings, tending the flowers in drawing-rooms by day, filling and replenishing window boxes, and making up Court, bridal, and other bouquets'.[71] It was described variously as a field of 'women's enterprise', a 'business', a 'career', a form of 'feminine art' and, by implication, a kind of 'trade': a revealing collocation of terms. The ambivalence of the editor's treatment of such an occupation sprang from the difficulty of reconciling 'ladiness' with 'work', 'accomplishments' with professional 'skills' and 'art' with 'business'.

In January 1910, *The Lady* commented that women 'read more, they think more, and this shows in their conversation'. 'Subjects are discussed' it continued, 'which would not have been whispered about a generation ago.'[72] Women's magazines both fostered and reflected the widening social participation of women in the late Victorian and Edwardian periods, offering a textual and visual canvas of contemporary feminine 'conversation'. And the formal qualities of the woman's magazine - its personalised, intimate tone, its use of the paragraph or 'tit-bit' rather than the sustained argument, its provision of competitions for readers, its reliance on advertising, and its increasing use of illustration and novel formatting techniques - all linked it to the New Journalism.

Yet *The Ladies' Field* was, like *The Westminster Gazette*, a complex mixture of tradition and novelty. It incorporated features which reflected the best-established traditions of the nineteenth-century Society journal, alongside features which represented the latest novelty in women's magazines. Like *Tit-Bits*, it employed correspondence columns extensively, to interact with the feminine reading community. And like *The Wide World Magazine*, it engaged a number of popular contemporary cultural figures; in this case female figures.

This magazine merged an established emphasis on fashion intelligence with an expanded advertising section and new visual and journalistic techniques, to produce an image of femininity which married upper-class social ritual and bourgeois materialism - 'culture' and consumption - and was integral to the 'syncretism' of the text. The correspondence columns offered a version of feminine space that was a combination of gender ideology, class consciousness, professional and commercial rhetoric, and narrative trope, employing the rhetoric of intimacy and confidentiality to define and engage the magazine's readers. *The Ladies' Field* did not reflect any coherent notion of gender roles, but was a rather contradictory mixture of different elements of the profitable women's magazine: fashion, advertising, domesticity, correspondence columns, competitions and employment advice. Newnes's version of the 'ladies' paper' thus offered a multi-faceted version of femininity which, addressing various cultural developments and journalistic models, was designed to maximise the magazine's

---

71   Ibid.

72   *The Lady*, January 1910, p.126.

appeal within the limitations imposed by its price. It represented a synthesis of the ideologies of gender, consumption, class and 'culture'.

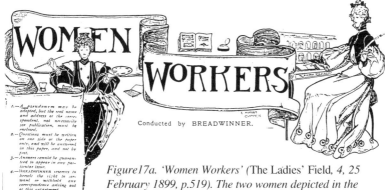

Figure17a. 'Women Workers' (The Ladies' Field, *4, 25 February 1899, p.519). The two women depicted in the column header are engaged in the traditional female occupations of painting and writing, and are elegantly dressed in the somewhat excessive and cumbersome fashions associated with a life which revolved around leisure and social ritual. They are far from radical figures. Yet the editor's pseudonym, 'Breadwinner', is an extremely loaded term, and it jars against the pictorial image.*

Figure 17b. 'Manners and Customs' (The Ladies' Field, *1, 11 June 1898, p.618).*

Figure 17d. 'Contents' (The Ladies' Field, *4, 7 January 1899, p.146).*

Figure 17c. 'Palmistry' (The Ladies' Field, *4, 25 February 1899, p.520).*

6

Respectable Anxieties, Role-Models and Readers

The Captain (1899)

'I said in No.1 that I hoped we should all be friends together', wrote the editor of *The Captain*, R.S. Warren Bell, in summing up the first six months of the publication. And he claimed that 'in barely half a year *The Captain* has made hundreds of thousands of chums, whom he intends, shall be his chums for always'.[1] This periodical, a sixpenny monthly boys' magazine, established by George Newnes in April 1899, was an outstanding commercial success. Juveniles represented a significant proportion of the expanding British population, and yet another segment of the reading market to which the periodical publisher could lay claim. 'Sir George Newnes', wrote C.B. Fry, 'who made as few mistakes as any magnate of the publishing world about new ventures, always maintained that a good magazine for boys ought to succeed.'.[2]

The Captain was a 'respectable' boys' magazine. Like Cassell's *Chums* (1892), it was clearly aimed at a reading community that was composed of middle-class, public school boys, and those who sought to emulate this class. The 'purpose' of the magazine, however, extended beyond the merely commercial. The editor suggested that:

> *The Captain* came into the world with a purpose, and I think he has achieved something of that purpose. He has succeeded ... in giving a goodly number a lift up the Path of Life, which is a stiff path to climb. He has helped many a young fellow on the career he will adopt, and he has filled many an hour which (if I may say so) might have been spent less profitably than in the perusal of a clean magazine. Out of doors he has instructed his readers in the gentle art of batting .... He has given you little song and sermon-snatches from the poets, and glimpses into the lives of men who have fought for, and won, fame, often against odds, always hardly.[3]

The Captain, 1, 6 (September 1899), p.670.

[2] C.B. Fry, *Life Worth Living: Some Phases of an Englishman*, London: Eyre and Spottiswoode, 1939, p.155.

[3] Ibid., p.670.

It was an apt assessment, pointing to all of the features that distinguished this popular monthly magazine: the confidential, 'chummy' tone of the editorial interjections; the concern of the editor with his readers' career prospects; the overtones of muscular Christianity and the ideal of a healthy (and well-stocked) mind in a healthy body; the sporting component of the paper; and the journalistic practice of constructing popular heroes for the edification and entertainment of readers. The editor's emphasis on the 'clean', utilitarian qualities of the publication was significant, situating the text within a contemporary debate about the 'pernicious' nature of many boys' penny weeklies.

On one hand, then, *The Captain* was a commercial product, and its editor and publisher employed a diverse set of strategies, images and features in an attempt to attract as wide a readership as possible. '*The Captain* was, I suppose', wrote C.B. Fry, 'the most successful boys' magazine that has ever appeared, and it lasted for many years.'[4] His observation, though not unbiased, was nevertheless widely echoed. *The Captain*'s use of public school language and images was designed as much to attract the enormous numbers excluded from public school education but imaginatively drawn to it, as the much smaller minority with actual access. In fact, the market for juvenile periodical fiction was vast. In the fifteen years from 1870 to 1885, the number of children receiving elementary education trebled, and juvenile periodicals proliferated. The vast proportion of such titles were aimed at an audience aged 10 to 20 years and over a third were specifically intended for boys.[5] The contents tended to vary little, and included adventure fiction, public school stories and, often, crime stories. In 1899, when *The Captain* was established, there was still considerable scope for expansion.

On the other hand, not only did this multitude of boys constitute a vast pool of potential readers, it constituted what was perceived to be a massive social problem. 'We have at the present time in Great Britain two million boys', wrote Baden-Powell making an anguished calculation in *Scouting For Boys* (1908), 'of whom a quarter to a half a million are under good influence outside their school walls.' 'The remainder', he estimated, 'are drifting towards "hooliganism" or bad citizenship for want of hands to guide them.' He ended with a plea: 'Cannot we find these guiding hands amongst us?'[6]

On the commercial side of things, the editor and publisher of *The Captain* employed a variety of techniques to appeal to potential readers, including advertising, competitions and visual material. Yet at another level, the narrative and promotional strategies, themes, motifs and features that characterised this magazine, and the subtleties of the rhetoric it employed, demonstrate the way in

---

4   Ibid., p.154.

5   Diana Dixon, 'Children and the Press, 1866-1914', in Michael Harris and Alan Lee (eds), *The Press in English Society from the Seventeenth to Nineteenth Centuries*, London: Associated University Presses, p.133.

6   Baden-Powell as cited in Geoffrey Pearson, *Hooligan: A History of Respectable Fears*, London: Macmillan, 1983, p.108.

which it both provided a crystallising focus for a vast array of contemporary anxieties and simultaneously sought to address them. It was a manifestation of contemporary society's anxieties as much as its enthusiasms.

The problems associated with youth, and especially male youth, constituted a major theme of cultural debate in the late Victorian and Edwardian periods. Public concern embraced attitudes to 'boy labour', psychological theories of adolescence and the social critique of the youth's personality. The boys' penny weekly or 'penny dreadful' (the term that was applied to boys' magazines of the lowest stratum by the 1880s) attracted a good deal of criticism. Critics of 'penny dreadfuls', concerned about the effect of educational reforms and the growth of mass literacy, and preoccupied with the prospect of increasing juvenile delinquency, argued that working-class readers were encouraged in anti-social attitudes and criminal behaviour by such publications. Sensational adventure and crime stories were considered to be a threat to society because they glorified physical aggression and encouraged disrespect for authority.[7] 'Penny dreadfuls', it was argued, offered apparently realistic heroes - disgruntled young clerks, errand boys, grocery assistants - with whom readers could identify, and depicted them as renegades. Readers were therefore inclined to emulate the irreverent, disrespectful, reckless, cruel, criminal, contemptible behaviour of such 'heroes'.

In 1879, the Religious Tract Society launched *Boys' Own Paper*. Addressing itself to youths, but meeting with general parental approval, this magazine defined itself against the highly-criticised traditions of cheap boys' literature as practical, respectable and 'wholesome'. It was widely emulated. In 1899, George Newnes established *The Captain*. It was the kind of journal that 'respectable' parents wanted their sons to read, and was promoted as morally unimpeachable. The editor urged readers of the magazine to 'buck *The Captain* up' all they could (implicitly representing the magazine as vulnerable and its readers as being in a position to help and encourage it). If every reader got 'every fellow they kn[ew] to take it in, as well as their girl cousins, sisters, friends, etc', not only would it 'soon have the largest circulation in the world', but its success would represent 'the knocking out of a lot of rotten periodicals that ought never to be allowed to disgrace the bookstalls'.[8]

The authors of *The Captain* were well-known writers, politicians, officers of field rank, headmasters, baronets and other gentlemen with M.A., F.R.S. and

---

7   Patrick A. Dunae, 'Penny Dreadfuls: Late Nineteenth-Century Boys' Literature and Crime', *Victorian Studies*, 22 (1979), pp.133-136. The most successful of the so-called 'penny dreadfuls' included Samuel Dacre Clark's *Bad Boys' Paper*, Charles Fox's *Boys' Standard*, John W. Allingham's *Boys' World*, and Edwin J. Brett's many publications: *Our Boys' Paper, Boys' Comic Journal, Boys of the Empire* and the extremely popular *Boys of England* (1866-1899). *Boys of England* reached a circulation of 250,000 in the early 1870s, and ceased publication in the year that *The Captain* was established. Crusaders of the National Purity League, alert for sexual innuendo and other forms of immorality, condemned such publications for espousing 'trickery, cheating, lying ... [and] laziness' as suitable for jokes. See *Cleansing of a City*, as cited in Harry Hendrick, *Images of Youth: Age, Class, and the Male Youth Problem, 1880-1920*, Oxford: Clarendon Press, 1990, p.136.

8   *The Captain*, 6, 32 (November 1901), p.190.

F.L.S. after their names. This magazine, like *The Wide World Magazine*, relied on the authority it derived from the social, intellectual and political standing of its contributors. *Captain* authors included P.G. Wodehouse, Frederick Swainson, E. Cockburn Reynolds, F.C. Selous, Bertram Mitford, E.J. Nankivell (the Philatelic Editor), C.B. Fry (the Athletic Editor), Edward Step, F.L.S. (the Natural History Editor) and Dr Gordon Stables. The magazine's illustrations, moreover, were executed by people who had been to art school, illustrators of training and reputation such as Tom Browne, R.I., George Soper, E.F. Skinner, Paul Hardy, Alfred Pearse and John Hassall. Both *The Captain* and *Boys' Own* employed leading sports personalities to write for them, praising great men in the sporting world and often emphasising the virtues of public school sport. *Boys Own* gained much popularity with W.G. Grace. *The Captain* replied with C.B. Fry, 'The Athletic Editor', who was widely popular, particularly, it appears, amongst the farmhands and labouring boys of rural Derbyshire in the 1890s. 'C.B. Fry was their hero', according to one contemporary. 'They saved up their pocket money to buy his magazine, *Captain* .'[9]

A change in the political and social climate of the 1890s fostered the development of new themes in juvenile papers. A growing preoccupation with empire, greater military awareness, and a newly-pronounced admiration for the muscular, meant that aggression, whilst co-opted by the newer periodicals, was re-directed into more acceptable outlets. 'Themes expressed in the old dreadfuls', as Patrick Dunae has observed, in an argument which relates directly to the thematic biases of *The Captain*, 'had been tamed, politicised, and redirected to serve the needs of empire.'[10] The heroes of *The Captain* were muscular sportsman, scouts, 'Empire Boys' (to borrow the title of Joseph Bristow's work on British boys' adventure fiction); manly, morally clean boys with a seemly respect for authority.[11] Far from undermining respect for authority, *The Captain* explicitly preached and inculcated its virtues.

Developments in juvenile (especially boys') periodical literature were intimately connected with the emergence of a concept of 'adolescence' as a distinct phase of life. In the 1880s, according to John Gillis, juvenile delinquency was still primarily associated with the children of the poor, as distinct from those from higher social strata. But in the 1890s, a stage of life called 'adolescence' was identified, and problems in handling this transition from childhood to adulthood emerged to replace class as the perceived cause of misbehaviour in young people, irrespective of their class. Juvenile delinquency was thus seen as

---

[9]   E. Saintsbury, *The World of Alison Uttley: A Biography*, as cited in Diana Dixon, 'Children and the Press', in Michael Harris and Alan Lee (eds), op. cit., p.145.

[10]   Patrick A. Dunae, op. cit., p.150.

[11]   It is significant that the magazine's title also called up Carlyle's phrase 'Captains of Industry' (*Past and Present*, Bk.4, Ch.4, title).

an attribute of maladjusted social and psychological growth rather than as a product of social and economic conditions.[12]

Class ideology continued to inform and condition the reformer's concept of adolescence. 'Hooliganism', for instance, associated with a particular code of dress, with anti-authoritarianism, gang warfare, restlessness and violence, was represented by contemporary commentators as a feature of working-class London street culture. The term 'hooligan' entered the language in 1898, the year before *The Captain* was established, and in the years leading up to the first World War, the Hooligan appeared, in name if not in person, before numerous governmental and semi-official bodies of inquiry. He figured large in fears about racial decline and physical inefficiency, in the Edwardian era's deliberations on the 'boy labour' question, in discourse about the demoralising influence of popular amusements and about the collapse of 'fair play' sportsmanship, and in allegations about the excessive 'freedom' and 'affluence' available to the young.[13] Yet concern over the 'youth problem' encompassed a variety of perspectives and strategies. And *The Captain* , directed primarily at middle-class and upper working-class readers, was set against this background of concern with the youth of all classes, the so-called 'boy problem' thoroughly implicated in the magazine's origins, tone, features and development.

The youth problem figured large in many of the numerous socio-economic inquiries and studies of the period which examined British working-class life and labour.[14] Theories of 'urban degeneration' which suggested that urban conditions were spawning an inferior race were in wide circulation from the 1880s.[15] Such theories were associated with a broader interest in Social Darwinism. Concern about urban ill-health continued to inform discussions about racial deterioration, imperial security, economic competitiveness and social stability. Hence *The Captain*'s reverence for the sportsman and its emphasis on muscularity. *C.B. Fry's Magazine* was to take up the issue of racial fitness and physical training still more passionately.

The industrial growth of Germany and the United States provoked a reappraisal of Britain's position in the world economy, whilst the Boer War served to underline Britain's fragility in military terms. *The Captain* was not aggressively militaristic, but its editor actively promoted School Cadet Corps and

---

[12] John R. Gillis, 'The Evolution of Juvenile Delinquency in England, 1890-1914', *Past and Present,* 67 (1975), pp.96-97.

[13] Anxiety about 'boy labour' was focussed on 'dead-end' or 'blind-alley' employment such as 'handy lads' in factories, van boys and messenger boys. Society anticipated a crisis in the social reproduction of work-discipline and skills arising from the absence of a regulatory system of trade practices and values.

[14] Helen Bosanquet discussed 'Little Drudges and Troublesome Boys' in her book, *The Standard of Life*, published in 1898, a year before *Captain* was established. E.J. Urwick, a resident of Toynbee Hall, edited a collection of essays entitled *Studies of Boy Life in Our Towns* (1904). And Rowntree and Lasker's inquiry into unemployment, *Unemployment, A Social Study* (1910), opened with a chapter on youth unemployment.

[15] In 1904 an Inter-Departmental Committee on Physical Deterioration was formed to inquire into the problem of urban degeneration.

demonstrated his concern with the issue of national strength by providing a plethora of competitions, articles, stories and editorials designed to foster a desire to serve the empire. Whilst the magazine's title was primarily a reference to the school rank of Captain of games or Captain (head boy) of the school, as the blazered figure on the cover of the annual suggested, it seems likely that its military connotations were intentional. In fact, a large number of contributors held field rank. The magazine's Athletic Editor, for instance (C.B. Fry), was a naval captain, as was F.S. Brereton, whose Great War sagas (*With Haig in Flanders, With Allenby in Palestine* and others) were later to be very popular.

Middle-class anxiety was also turned towards the public schools themselves. The public school's emphasis on athleticism and its insistence on the value of a classical education came under attack from education reformers in the late nineteenth century. Public school apologists responded to such criticisms with the assertion that the chief legacy of public school education was *character*. In locating 'manliness' within the themes of sportsmanship and gentlemanliness therefore, the editor of *The Captain* was resorting to a well-tried line of defence against contemporary anxieties. Yet the public school culture of games, emphasising vigorous discipline, loyalty, *esprit de corps* and the ideal of 'good form', did represent, for many, a solution to social instability. And the cadets and rifle corps, introduced into several public schools in the 1870s, but achieving widespread popularity during the Boer War, claimed to offer a substitute public school environment in which a boy would learn obedience, a sense of civic duty and corporate life, and the power of endurance and effort.[16] *The Captain*, devoting considerable space and attention to the public school cadet corps, and offering its readers the atmosphere of the public school, aimed to inculcate just these virtues.

The child psychologist G.S. Hall published a work entitled *Adolescence* in 1904. He theorised adolescence as a physiological and psychological state, and his theories were popularised by a variety of reformers, youth workers and educationalists. Such people sought to address the critical nature of the teen years. They tended to be desirous of *preventing* rather than *punishing* delinquency, depicting the contemporary youth as undisciplined and precociously independent by nature.[17] The boys' periodical offered the perfect means of influencing adolescents. Indeed, the press had long been seen as a mechanism of social control. *The Captain* was thus part of a comprehensive response to the cycle of anxiety that had begun with the founding of the first youth organisation in the late 1880s. It represented a mechanism of socialisation, instructing juvenile readers in the rudiments of social discipline through the provision of positive role-models and editorial advice, as well as channelling them into accepted youth

---

[16] From the 1880s, corps associated with the University Settlement Houses and Public School Missions recruited working-class boys as well.

[17] John R. Gillis, op. cit., p.113. Schooling lengthened the liminal period between childhood and manhood, and between home and work.

organisations such as the Boys' Empire League, of which it became the official organ in May 1904.

The Captain acted as a repository for respectable society's fears about a range of evils from 'pernicious literature' and juvenile delinquency to urban degeneration and imperial decline. These preoccupations were especially evident in the way in which a series of purified, moralised and nationalised role-models were created in the text for the entertainment and edification of readers. For *The Captain* was the textual site through which the Editor provided 'glimpses into the lives of men who have fought for, and won, fame, often against odds, always hardly', as he himself put it. The heroes that emerged from the textual interaction occurring through this magazine were sportsmen, 'gentlemen' and 'Empire Boys': heroes that were ideologically, morally and physically sound, and thus constituted suitable models for the potentially wayward adolescent, and the actually wayward Hooligan.

Such role-models were employed in the text through a number of themes and strategies. Firstly, the editor's responsive image and his personalised observations were designed to strengthen his ideological hold over his potentially wayward flock. Secondly, the public school component of the magazine served to bind readers imaginatively to the social, physical and moral image of the public school man. Thirdly, the sportsman was deployed as a role-model in the service of an ideal of gentlemanly behaviour and physical prowess. Fourthly, the editor concerned himself with reader's career prospects, his vocational advice a transparent cover for a series of sermons on 'manliness'.[18] And finally, *The Captain* fostered the themes of militarism and empire, invoking images of physical fitness and sportsmanship in order to encourage its readers in a desire to take up the national and imperial cause.

The Captain established a new type of relationship between the magazine editor and his juvenile readers. The editorials of boys' periodicals of the 1860s and 1870s tended to be authoritarian and patronising, editors maintaining a distance from their readers. 'The Old Fag' (the editor of *The Captain*), on the other hand, his name a public school tag, adopted a personal, relaxed and 'chummy' attitude towards readers. R.S. Warren Bell was, in fact, a master at a private school, possessed, according to C.B. Fry, of 'a great talent for writing school stories and reports'.[19] He represented himself, after the model provided by Thomas Arnold, as a kind of parental or guardian figure, handing down personal insights, friendly criticisms and 'ordinary, straightforward advice from a man of the world' with an air of sympathetic understanding.[20] He entered into the fortunes of his readers in their own familiar language: the distinctive slang of

---

[18] Twentieth-century urban sociologists, it is worth noting, have argued that in urban life, the place of the church is taken by the press. See Gareth Stedman Jones, *Outcast London: A Study of the Relations Between Classes in Urban Society*, Harmondsworth: Penguin, 1984, p.13.

[19] C.B. Fry, op. cit., p.154.

[20] *The Captain*, 4, 19 (October 1900), p.92.

the English public school. His attempt to establish editorial authority and reader response was disguised as a gesture towards intimacy. 'A thousand thanks for your good wishes', 'The Old Fag' remarked to one correspondent, conflating market loyalty and the loyalty of close personal allegiance. 'I knew you would make a "chum" of *The Captain.*'[21] It was part of a strategy to promote the magazine editor as an agent of socialisation.

In establishing himself in the role of mentor, the editor derived authority from a number of contemporary cultural sources, drawing on psychological theories of adolescence, on the language and ideology of the public school, and on the models provided by contemporary youth organisations. Developments in child psychology, popularising the uniqueness of the adolescent stage and theorising it as one of great turmoil, reinforced the importance of adult supervision and influence. And the editor of *The Captain* provided such guidance. The age categories that were strictly imposed in the competition columns to divide entrants ranged from an upper limit of 12 to a limit of 25, but demonstrated the magazine's concentration on the 14-20 years age bracket: the adolescent stage. This feature thus reinforced the classifications developed by child psychologists. Education reformers, influenced by child psychology and drawing upon its rhetoric, argued that the elementary school was the single most important agency of socialisation.[22] And the editor's title connected him to a public school system of fagging which was said to teach boys to submit themselves to authority and value the importance of service. Such was the discursive framework within which the editor sought to justify and popularise *The Captain*. Much of the rhetoric he employed was targeted at parents rather than their sons - in an effort to persuade them to pay for his magazine.

The Boys' Brigade, Christian in origin and founded in 1883, was probably the first of the youth organisations to emphasise the specific nature of 'boyhood', and develop a programme and philosophy designed to cater for it. Its founder, William Smith, took up a concept of 'manliness' derived from public school culture, as well as attempting to create the kind of *esprit de corps* that was typical of public school boys. Officers were advised to cultivate personal friendships with boys in an attempt to strengthen their influence, visiting and being visited by them.[23] Their activities were paralleled by *The Captain's* editorials. The tone of intimacy and familiarity which characterised the editor's communications to readers of *The Captain*, whilst it was characteristic of the New Journalism, was equally part of an attempt to provide adult guidance and apply accepted methods of socialisation to juvenile readers. In *The Ladies' Field*, on the other hand, the personalised editorial voice had been adapted and employed to create a sense of segregated, feminised space.

The editor of *The Captain*, then, appeared to be particularly responsive, meeting readers' requests for material and competitions with enthusiastic

---

[21] *The Captain*, 1, 3 (June 1899), p.335.

[22] Harry Hendrick, op. cit., p.123.

[23] Ibid., p.161.

promptness. The visual iconography of the editorial header cleverly reinforced the kind of relationship which the editor sought to establish with readers. 'The Old Fag' appeared in the guise of the scribe, dedicated to servicing the juvenile audience. The boy-reader was represented as a kind of market-muse (*see Figure 18*).

Matters of intellectual import and classical orientation, however, were beyond the scope of the magazine. 'DEAR OLD FAG', wrote one contributor, innocently:

> I hope you will not be offended if I make a suggestion. Why not have a mathematical and classical competition to run alternately, as some of your readers, who could not attempt the easiest of your competitions, could do the hardest problems in Euclid or algebra.

The editor's reply was designed to characterise his correspondent as eccentric and to earn him the approval of his readers: 'I hardly think such competitions as these would meet with general favour'.[24] If the readers of *The Captain* were admiring of material that was ideologically sound, they apparently did not covet material that was intellectually challenging. By the turn of the century, the classical education offered by the public schools was increasingly felt to be at odds with the pace and demands of modern life.[25] The editor's self-conscious comment brought this issue into focus. And he sought to secure his own pedagogical position by emphasising *The Captain*'s function as a vehicle of moral influence.

Captain editorials, in fact, read like a series of quasi-moral lessons. 'A healthy person should have an appetite for work and play, as well as for food', wrote the editor, repeating one of the maxims of the age; 'thus he will carry out the idea of a sound mind in a sound body.'[26] This lesson, a favourite of Newnes's, was to be reinforced in *C.B. Fry's Magazine*. 'Honest work, that gives one's conscience no twinge, is the only satisfactory form of labour', read another editorial admonition.[27] Moreover, the competition column was employed to reinforce the editor's pastoral role, and to teach the qualities of honesty and sportsmanship. Thus one prize winner, accused of having plagiarised from a Mark Twain story, was quoted as declaring that he had had no intention of 'cribbing': 'If I have erred, I have erred unconsciously, and beg sincerely to apologise.' His explanation and apology were accepted as having been made in good faith. So, however, was his offer to 'forego the prize awarded', and the

---

[24] *The Captain*, 1, 5 (August 1899), p.557.

[25] T.S. Eliot registered the incongruity of the two things in his attempt, in *The Waste Land*, to imagine the classically-educated 'Stetson' experience the horrors of the First World War. See T.S. Eliot, *Collected Poems, 1909-1962*, London: Faber and Faber, 1964, p.65.

[26] *The Captain*, 6, 31 (October, 1901), p.92.

[27] Ibid.

prize was awarded to another competitor. There was a caution in this for readers, and 'The Old Fag' was quick to draw attention to it:

> I must point out to all young writers that founding articles on old ideas is a dangerous experiment, especially when the similarity between the old and the new is made so apparent.[28]

Plagiarised excerpts had been the very substance of *Tit-Bits*, especially in its early years. And Newnes attempted to make the Tit-Bits Villa competition inclusive by explicitly allowing entrants to submit material 'cribbed' from other (more authoritative) sources, such as the Bible. In *The Strand*, Newnes utilised material from Continental authors to establish the magazine's reputation and format, thereby to promote the art of short-story writing amongst British authors. It was thus a sign of the increased resources, literary reputation and confidence of George Newnes, Ltd, as well as the moral and educational tone of *The Captain*, that 'plagiarism' was now to be denounced.

If the editor was a kind of friendly mentor figure, then *The Captain*'s 'Athletic Editor', C.B. Fry, was a schoolboy hero. The transformation of well-known sporting personalities into popular editorial figures was a discursive and journalistic practice that was associated with the increasing profile of the Victorian editor and with a developing tradition of hero-worship in the arena of mass spectator sports. Commercialism and the rise of the mass audience promoted both these developments. C.B. Fry and his successor in the Athletics editorial chair, P.F. Warner, were representative of a new kind of editorial personality - the popular sporting hero - their profiles as sportsmen harnessed to promote their influence as expert sub-editors.[29] In the public schools, lay staff had been finding appointments since the 1850s, and, under the influence of the doctrine of 'muscular Christianity', cricketing greats such as W.G. Grace were employed as specialist sports masters. *The Captain*, sustained by a practice of attracting popular support for model-heroes, was the journalistic equivalent of this process.

In 'The Athletic Corner', Fry was introduced as 'the first writer on athletics in the world'. He undertook, in February 1902, to write only for *The Captain*, amongst all other magazines 'intended for boys or athletes', and was thus placed under a contract to play for Newnes and *The Captain* exclusively. He also became, according to the editor, 'exclusively one of us'. In making this

---

28 *The Captain*, 6, 36 (March, 1902), p.573.

29 Fry was a famous cricketer, footballer and athlete. P.F. ('Plumb') Warner, who replaced Fry in 1905, was also a well-known cricketer. Both men captained English sides against Australia, Warner in 1903-1904, and Fry in 1912. Warner was manager of the English cricket team that toured Australia in the so-called 'Bodyline Series' (1932-1933). Given his association with *The Captain*, a magazine obsessed with 'form' and 'sportsmanship', it is not surprising that he was a harsh critic of Douglas Jardine's 'unsportsmanlike' tactic of bowling on a line with the batsman's body, a tactic aimed at wearing Donald Bradman and his compatriots down psychologically and preventing them from scoring runs.

observation, the editor attempted to foster in readers a sense of identification with Fry. And he further intimated that Fry himself read *The Captain* 'right through every month':

> In many ways this great athlete and idol of the cricketing public is quite a boy - that is, he has the enthusiasm and light-heartedness of a boy, combined with the solidity of purpose and wisdom of a strong man, in all senses.[30]

Thus the notion that *The Captain* represented a medium of positive influence for readers undertaking the transition from boyhood to manhood was made explicit. The magazine's career advice, addressed as much to fathers as to their sons, was to demonstrate a similar concern with this phase of life. Fry, who was to devote much of his life to training boys for naval service, considered his 'Answers to Correspondents' a great success. 'I sometimes re-read the intelligent questions, real as well as imaginary', he observed, revealing the fact that such columns were as much constructed as real, 'and the inspired answers with genuine appreciation.'[31]

Another aspect of *The Captain* was its large public school component, a component which served to bind readers imaginatively to the social, physical and moral qualities characteristic of the public school man. It featured illustrated series such as 'School Captains', 'Public School Cadet Corps' and 'Public School Football Captains', articles and stories about 'fagging', public school customs and school sports, and a page devoted to 'Reviews of School Magazines'. It was famous for the many school stories contributed by P.G. Wodehouse. Wodehouse broke with the tradition of English public school fiction by introducing a note of realism into his stories. He claimed to have been inspired to write by Fred Swainson's serial story, 'Acton's Feud', published in the first numbers of *The Captain*:

> It began, I remember, 'Shannon, the old international, had brought down a hot side to play the school ...', and if there has ever been a better opening line than that, I have never come across it. It was something entirely new in school stories - the real thing - and it inflamed me to do something in that line myself.[32]

Wodehouse went on to write many short stories for Newnes's magazine.[33] His 'Psmith' stories, however, were probably his most popular. Thus Arthur

---

[30]   *The Captain*, 6, 35 (February 1902), p.477.

[31]   C.B. Fry, op. cit., p.154.

[32]   Frances Donaldson, *P.G. Wodehouse: A Biography*, New York: Alfred A. Knopf, 1982, p.6.

[33]   Wodehouse hoped that the reputation he had earned with *The Captain* would put him in favour with the editor of *The Strand*. He had, in fact, written his first humorous article, entitled 'Men who Missed their own Weddings', for *Tit-Bits*. When he began writing for *The*

Waugh, father of Alec and Evelyn Waugh, wrote to Wodehouse of the enthusiasm he had inspired in 'public school boys' and 'old boys' (the boys' fathers), as *The Captain* described its readers:

> There was a time, in Alec's schooldays, when we used to read your books together with enormous enjoyment; and, though we are never long enough together nowadays ... we have still preserved a sort of freemason's code of Psmithisms, which continually crop up in our letters. Indeed, I can truly say, in emulation of Wolfe, that I would far rather have created Psmith than have stormed Quebec.[34]

The extension of the public school ethos of the period to those in less privileged environments occurred, in fact, largely through the medium of fiction. Robert Roberts, growing up in a slum neighbourhood in the 1890s, described this process as 'the Greyfriars experience'. Greyfriars was the public school invented by Charles Hamilton as the setting for his serial stories in *The Magnet* and *The Gem*. These stories were very popular, and *The Captain* imitated such publications with R.S. Warren Bell's 'Tales of Greyhouse School', some of the first tales to be serialised in its pages. Fred Swainson also wrote a series of public school stories, entitled 'Tales of " Eliza's"'. 'In our new volume', wrote the editor in introducing volume 7 of the magazine, 'several aspects of school life will be dealt with - what more want you?'[35] According to Roberts, he and his contemporaries in back-street Salford were 'avid' for the fictional world of Greyfriars school. It 'became to some of us our true Alma Mater, to whom we felt bound by a dream-like loyalty ... the public school ethos, distorted into myth and sold among us weekly in penny numbers, for good or ill, set ideals and standards'.[36] *The Captain* invested substantially in this ethos.

One reader of *The Captain* wrote to the editor that he 'yearned to have the public school and Varsity spirit', but 'owing to circumstances yearned in vain'. 'Reading *The Captain*', he said, 'made him recognise what a fine thing this "tone" is that a man gets by going to a public school and the University.' His ambition was simple:

Captain in 1900, Newnes paid £3 for a short story. Wodehouse earnt £50 for a serial entitled 'The Golden Bat', commencing in October 1903, £60 for 'The White Feather', commencing in October 1905, and £70 for 'Junior Jackson' in 1907. See David A. Jasen, *P.G. Wodehouse: Portrait of a Master*, London: Garnstone Press, 1975, pp.23, 45.

[34] Frances Donaldson, op. cit., p.79.

[35] *The Captain*, 6, 36 (March 1902), p.572. Such was the demand for school stories that Hamilton ('Frank Richards' in *The Magnet* and 'Martin Clifford' in *The Gem*), reputedly the most prolific author in the history of English literature, managed to sell some 72 million words' worth of fiction during his working life. See Peter Parker, *The Old Lie: The Great War and the Public School Ethos*, London: Constable, 1987, p.125.

[36] Robert Roberts, *The Classic Slum*, as cited in J.S. Bratton, 'Of England, Home and Duty: The Image of England in Victorian and Edwardian Juvenile Fiction' in John M. Mackenzie (ed.), *Imperialism and Popular Culture*, Manchester: Manchester University Press, 1984, p.76.

to have the ease and manner, of which the possessor is generally unconscious, that distinguished such men as Mike Jackson, Adair, and Psmith - to take three of Mr Wodehouse's characters.

The Captain, he claimed, was full of that indefinable 'public school spirit' which it was his overriding desire to obtain.[37] Not surprisingly, 'The Old Fag' applauded the reader's identification with the heroes of *The Captain*, urging that he could 'attain something of the public school spirit by modelling himself on certain public school men who have been held up in our tales as good examples of their class.' His advice reinforced the model of public school manliness which he sought to promote amongst readers. 'You expect a public school man', he claimed, 'to be *a sportsman* and *a gentleman*, and good sportsmanship can be cultivated by everybody and is to be found in all ranks of society.' Anxiety about the erosion of moral values throughout the 'ranks of society' pervaded the editor's comments. The image of the Hooligan was associated with discourse about the collapse of 'fair play' sportsmanship. Thus *The Captain*, allying itself to the ethos of the public school, mounted a rearguard action for the defence of 'sportsmanship'.

The most persistent and prestigious role-model promoted by *The Captain* was the sportsman. 'The Sportsman' was deployed in the service of an ideal of gentlemanly behaviour and physical prowess, and was glorified in a vast array of tales and articles about cricket, physical culture, athletics, football, rowing and boxing. J.O. Jones, hero of 'Tales of Greyhouse', was a muscular sportsman whose physical strength was demonstrated repeatedly in incidents scattered throughout the narratives. C.B. Fry contributed a series of articles on cricket and athletics. And a host of images of Fry, engaging in the various sports for which he was famous, visually reinforced the magazine's adoration of the sportsman (*see Figure 19*).

Eugen Sandow, a well-known proponent of 'physical culture', featured in various articles and a series of photos, preaching the virtues of physical fitness and muscular definition. 'A fellow is much better employed playing cricket or football', a correspondent inquiring about being in love was advised by the editor, 'than dangling round after some blue-eyed sylph, who only laughs at him when his back is turned'.[38] (Male camaraderie, it seems, was to be preferred to heterosexual mating rituals.) In October 1900, the sporting component of the magazine acquired an aura of permanence when C.B. Fry's column, a popular feature of the magazine's developing format, became 'THE ATHLETIC CORNER. Conducted by C.B. Fry'.

Fry was later to establish himself as the proto-type of the sportsman-editor, his editorial authority derived from both his prowess as a sportsman and his

---

[37] *The Captain*, 19, 110 (May 1908), p.184.
[38] *The Captain*, 6, 32 (November 1901), p.190.

social status as a gentleman-amateur. He was a public school educated, gentleman-amateur sportsman with a thorough knowledge of a variety of sports, a healthy regard for the principles of muscular Christianity and public school athleticism of which he was, in many ways, the ultimate embodiment, and a considerable public reputation. Politically, he was a Liberal, and he stood for Parliament three times, though without success. On this basis, George Newnes chose him as the editor and namesake of his new sporting publication, *C.B. Fry's Magazine*, and invested him with almost complete editorial control. Fry proceeded to pursue a variety of themes in the magazine over the next ten years, of which George Newnes, himself a middle-class, liberal-affiliated, public school educated editor and publisher of outstanding ability, with a strong belief in the principles of muscular Christianity, the value of an outdoor life and democratic reform, would undoubtedly have approved. Nevertheless, *Fry's Magazine* reflected the complexities and contradictions inherent in the contemporary debate over amateurism versus professionalism in sport.[39]

In a series of lectures delivered in 1840 and published in 1841, Thomas Carlyle had claimed that the history of the world was the history of 'Great Men'. His arguments, published under the title *On Heroes and Hero-Worship*, were a response to an increasing awareness that a progressively democratic society required extraordinary individuals in times of social tension and crisis. 'The Hero as King' was one of Carlyle's examples, and in *The Captain* the accession of Edward VII to the throne of England was enthusiastically celebrated as the King became one of the magazine's model-heroes. Had Carlyle been writing in the 1890s, however, he might well have added 'The Hero as Sportsman' to his list.

As the debate over the qualities of heroism progressed, Charles Kingsley offered an embodiment of the concept which combined physical and mental qualities. Kingsley's 'hero' was the muscular Christian, his admirable traits derived from public school athleticism:

> Games conduce not merely to physical, but to moral health; in the playing fields boys acquire virtues which no books can give them ... temper, self-restraint, fairness, honour, unenvious approbation of another's success, and all the 'give and take' of life which stand a man in good stead when he goes forth into the world.[40]

---

[39] See Ric Sissons, *The Players: A Social History of the Professional Cricketer*, Sydney: Pluto Press, 1988; Wray Vamplew, *Pay Up and Play the Game: Professional Sport in Britain, 1875-1914*, Cambridge: Cambridge University Press, 1988, p.200; E. Dunning and K. Sheard, *Barbarians, Gentlemen and Players*, Oxford: M. Robertson, 1979; E.A. Glader, *Amateurism and Athletics*, West Point, New York: Leisure Press, 1978; Tony Mason, *Association Football and English Society, 1863-1915*, Brighton: Harvester Press, 1980; J.A. Mangan, *Athleticism in the Victorian and Edwardian Public School: The Emergence and Consolidation of an Educational Ideology*, Cambridge: Cambridge University Press, 1981.

[40] Charles Kingsley, as cited in Bruce Haley, *Healthy Body and Victorian Culture*, Cambridge, Massachusetts; Harvard University Press, 1978, p.119.

The Captain's sporting heroes represented the combination of physique and character. ' " C.B." is a grand football player', wrote one contributor of the Athletic Editor, for instance, 'keen and alert; his judgement never seems to err; he is swift of foot, a good hard kicker, and never indulges in rough play, however badly he may be fouled.' Fry was also, in his estimation, 'as cool as a cucumber'. If appreciation for Fry as a sportsman and a gentleman was represented in terms of the rhetoric of muscular Christianity, however, admiration of his purely physical qualities was compromised by concerns about male homosexuality. ' " C.B." seems to stand out from the other players; his well-knit figure, and (may I say?) handsome face, catch the eyes at once', wrote the contributor.[41] There was a good deal of self-consciousness in the bracketed aside.

The rules of sportsmanship, and the virtues of honour, fair play and the spirit of competition were elaborated in the competition columns. And Henry E. Dudeney, editor of '*The Captain* Puzzle Corner', characterised and prompted his readers with a mixture of flattery and indulgence:

> few things give me more enjoyment than propounding posers for the amusement of boys .... I have found that, as a general rule, boys take their puzzles in the true spirit. Overgrown people often have a tendency to regard these things in too serious a light, but boys are enthusiastic, enter into the fun of the thing, like to play the game fairly, attack a puzzle on their own original lines, do not lose heart if they are beaten, and thoroughly appreciate their victory when they are successful.[42]

Thus, adolescence was redefined in the competition columns in a positive light, as the editor attempted to coax readers into social and temperamental identification with the kind of sound moral qualities which the magazine promoted, and to allay society's fears about the nature of contemporary youth.

If the editor preached the value of such qualities and aspirations, he also provided a variety of role-models in a series entitled '"What I Wanted to Be:" Some Boyish Aspirations of Famous Men'. The series consisted of a collection of 'the early impressions of famous men as to the callings they had decided to adopt on reaching the estate of manhood', and it was published, the editor claimed, 'for the *benefit* of readers of this magazine'. The 'estate of manhood', it was clear, was the reward for persevering with the rigours and temptations of adolescence. An article by Sandow about physical education and a series of portraits of his muscular physique, prompted one reader to send in photographs of his own muscular development and solicit Sandow's advice on the best method of improving his condition. And as a result of an interview published in *The Captain*, Tom Browne received 'a big budget of letters from boys who wish

---

41   *The Captain*, 6, 36 (March 1902), p.567.
42   *The Captain*, 3, 13 (April 1900), p.89.

to follow in his footsteps, and become popular black-and-white artists'.[43] If *The Captain* offered role-models, readers apparently took them up with enthusiasm.

The editor of *The Captain* explicitly preached the virtues of an ideal of masculinity of which moral fortitude, self-discipline, unaffected honesty and a somewhat abstract quality of 'manliness' were the salient features. 'There are many creatures in human shape going about in male attire who are not real men', he observed. (There was a hint of anxiety about the issue of homosexuality here. And the strength of the editor's reaction was implicit in his suggestion that such 'creatures' as dared to contravene the rules of 'manliness' were beyond the realms of the human.) 'But the real man', he continued, 'will battle with his weaknesses, and he will come through all right in the long run - scarred and singed, but still a man.'[44] The editorial resembled a sermon, drawing upon the biblical injunction (also alluded to in a well-known Victorian hymn which additionally advises the necessity of running 'the straight race'), to 'Fight the good fight' ('with all thy might' as the hymn has it). It thus demonstrated the extent to which 'respectable' boys' literature such as *The Captain* and *Boys' Own* represented the intersection between Christianity and imperialism, offering a combination of the spiritual and the worldly.

'In the Victorian public school', Norman Vance has observed, 'manliness passed from moral earnestness into vigorous "muscular Christianity", games mania, Grecian athleticism, and finally a recruiting campaign.' Manliness, he argues, 'reflected the changing atmosphere of Victorian society and largely disappeared, with some of the last vestiges of Victorianism, in the mud of the Somme'. In *The Captain*, this process of transformation was manifest. This magazine presented an ideal of manliness that was composed of a mixture of the muscular and the moral, or of the sportsman and the 'gentleman', and gradually transformed it into an ideal of manliness that was characterised by a commitment to military training and outdoor life, and a desire to serve the empire.

'Manliness', it appeared from *The Captain*, was a moveable feast, its substance dictated by changing conditions. Moreover, the ideal presented in the magazine was laced with a variety of contemporary anxieties relating to homosexuality, the philistinism of the games cult, the encroachments of the New Woman on the territory of the 'real man', and notions about the physical and moral deterioration of the British race. 'I don't want to make prigs of you', wrote the editor, entering sympathetically into his readers' journeys to manhood, 'but, at the same time, I would lay emphasis on the fact that dissipation is not the fine heroic thing that some folk imagine it to be':

> If it doesn't knock you over at the time, it tells on you later, and when this happens you can't blame anybody but yourself.[45]

43 *The Captain*, 1, 5 (August 1899), pp.558, 492-493.

44 *The Captain*, 12, 70 (January 1905), p.377.

45 *The Captain*, 4, 19 (October 1900), p.92.

In this instance, his comments carried a veiled reference to fears about the degenerative effects of excessive sexual, especially homosexual, activity.

The editor acted as a kind of surrogate parent to his readers, engaging with them in an atmosphere of imaginative sympathy and entering into their various vocational and moral dilemmas. His vocational advice, however, was largely a cover for a series of pedagogical pieces on the subject of 'manliness'. The generalised advice offered by the editor acquired a practical character in A.E. Manning Foster's column on the career prospects of readers, entitled 'When You Leave School'. The articles were geared towards the prevailing interest of readers in the professions, the military, and in vocational training. The column held out the carrot of upward social mobility and pecuniary advancement through training, self-discipline, conscientiousness and hard work. It constituted, in fact, a series of lessons in self-help. At the same time it reflected contemporary concerns relating to professionalism, urban industrial life, and the demands of imperial administration. 'Men are wanted, and now', urged Foster, betraying a sense of anxiety about imperial service, 'when we are all imbued with ideas of imperialism, and realising as never before that the strength and greatness of our country lie in our colonies - now is the time to bring the lesson home.'[46]

The keynote of all of this vocational advice, however, was struck by Foster in his summary of the first article in the series. 'First of all', he began, 'the boy who intends to go straight from school to the City should make the very most of his opportunities for acquiring a sound general education. It will stand him in good stead all his life.' There was an implicit tension here between admiration for a middle-class tradition of liberal education and the anxieties related to the 'usefulness' of a classical education.

Foster further advised boys to continue to pursue 'mental cultivation' in their spare time once leaving school, stressing the importance of further education, the touchstone of middle-class ideology. Yet his final strictures were the most revealing, tallying exactly with the image and aims of *The Captain* :

> cultivate while still at school business habits of promptitude and smartness. Don't put off till tomorrow what you should do today. Learn to make some definite progress, every day, and learn, above all, to make practical use of the knowledge you have previously gained. Take your life work in the proper spirit, not flippantly and lightly as a thing of small moment, but seriously and conscientiously, as befits one who is in earnest.[47]

The phrasing of the last sentence echoes the conception of marriage in the marriage service as something to be undertaken not 'unadvisedly, lightly, or wantonly ... but reverently, discreetly, advisedly, soberly, and in the fear of God'. And the degree of moral earnestness with which the advice is overlaid indicates the anxiety with which the problem of youthful behaviour was regarded.

---

46 *The Captain*, 1, 6 (September 1899), p.621.

47 *The Captain*, 1, 5 (August 1899), p. 305.

Concern about the developing youth culture was focussed on issues of leadership and authority. 'Learn to give and take, to submit yourself with good grace to authority', Foster had written, his advice to boys to enter into a kind of contract with their own consciences another echo of the marriage service, 'and so fit yourself for becoming in turn a leader'.[48] The great virtue of the fagging system, as 'The Old Fag' had pointed out in its defence, was the way in which it taught boys to submit themselves to authority and thus prepared them to exert authority themselves. 'Take your disappointments and failures bravely', Foster had written:

> So you shall learn life's hardest lesson - the lesson of self-dependence. So you shall become a true man, and never were manly men wanted more than at the present time.[49]

It was very much a moral model of manliness that was being offered. By the 1890s criticism from education reformers of the public schools was concentrated on their excessive emphasis on athleticism. But the public school, with its combination of athleticism and moral education, turned out leaders. This fact was crucial to its status.

The themes of militarism and empire were integral to *The Captain* from its early issues, although it was not a stridently militaristic publication. It was concerned as much with domestic and imperial defence as with military aggression. J.A. Hobson's influential critical work *Imperialism* (1904) both kindled anxiety about the demands of imperial administration and sharpened the defence of empire. As the new word 'Hooligan' became currency it attracted military connotations. It was never quite clear whether Hooliganism represented the end-point in the evolutionary deterioration of the Imperial Race, or whether Hooligans were just the kind of rough boys needed as a warrior class for imperial defence.[50] Some suggested that Hooliganism consisted in the misapplication of energy, and that youthful high spirits could be re-directed to serve military, rather than vandalistic or criminal ends.

Imperial fervour constituted a safe (if politicised) alternative to anti-authoritarian, anti-social aggression. The public schools, with their emphasis on moral character and discipline, inculcated through the cadet corp, on notions of duty and national strength, and on anti-intellectual athleticism, were associated, as Alan Sandison has argued, with the codification of imperial ideology. They acted as 'a mint for the coining of Empire-builders'.[51] The year in which *The Captain* had been established saw the commencement of the Boer campaign. Patriotic and imperialist fervour was running high. Little wonder, then, that the readers of *The*

---

[48]   Ibid.

[49]   Ibid., pp.306-307.

[50]   Geoffrey Pearson, *Hooligan: A History of Respectable Fears*, London: Macmillan, 1983, p.109.

[51]   Alan Sandison, *The Wheel of Empire*, London: Macmillan, 1967, p.400.

Captain who so strongly identified with the public school system, were caught up in admiration for heroes of the empire.

The editor fostered a sense of patriotic loyalty within the reading community in the correspondence columns of the magazine, in which, in some instances, he offered his readers a defence of Britain's imperial mission which approximated jingoistic swagger:

> You tell your German companions, when they jeer at you, that this Boer War is the toughest war ever undertaken by anybody. Any other country but Great Britain would have been licked out of the field long ago .... We absolutely rule the seas with our enormous fleet, and we have practically the carrying trade of the world, which means power and money such as no other country can lay claim to. No single European power could tackle us.[52]

There was more than a touch of defensiveness in his response, a defensiveness born of the national anxiety produced by the Boer War.

Literary serials about the navy and military proliferated. They included 'The King's Red Coat' (a story which concluded with the battle of Waterloo) and 'The Battle and the Breeze' (a depiction of life in the Royal Navy) by Dr Gordon Stables. 'The Three Scouts: A Story of the Boer War' was a serial narrative written by Fred Wishaw and illustrated by George Soper, which began in April 1900. Its two heroes, Geoff and Bernard ('generally known as Bunny') Bigby, aged 20 and 18 respectively, and both educated at an English public school (as Bernard's nickname foreshadows), were the kind of 'manly men' who were rallied to the imperial cause by Foster.[53]

The heroes of *Captain* tales were adventurers, hunters and imperialists: prototypes of frontier manliness. They embodied the qualities of youth, enthusiasm and physical fitness combined with those of moral fortitude and racial superiority. And the popularity of such tales was an indication of the extent to which readers identified with their protagonists. The readers of *The Captain*, then, were 'Empire Boys', caught up in youthful enthusiasm for imperialism and militarism. They may have purchased the '*Captain* Badge', introduced in April 1904. The badge, taking the form of an embossed picture of the world globe with the title 'CAPTAIN' spanning its circumference, was made to be worn on a hat or cap, as a brooch, in the lapel of a coat, or as a watch-chain pendant. It identified readers as a confraternity of surrogate British military 'captains', their interests

---

[52] *The Captain*, 6, 36 (March 1902), p.573.

[53] See *The Captain*, 3, 13 (April 1900), p.11. The younger brother, 'Bunny', may have been a play on E.W. Hornung's popular character. Hornung's 'Bunny' was offsider to the famous 'Raffles' in the Raffles stories, the first series of which was published in 1899. Bunny and Raffles were public school boys to the core, and the series ended, in 1903, with them going to serve their country in the Boer War, like Wishaw's heroes, in true public school spirit. See E.W. Hornung, *The Amateur Cracksman* (1899), *The Black Mask* (1901) and *A Thief in the Night* (1903).

and responsibilities extending around the globe. And *The Captain*, as revealed in the correspondence columns, did maintain a substantial overseas readership.

The imperial theme, though a feature of *The Captain* from the outset, acquired even greater significance at the conclusion of the Boer War with the accession of Edward VII to the throne. Queen Victoria, according to Joseph Bristow, represented the stability and purpose of the empire and the nation, fulfilling her symbolic function as a reassuringly constant maternal figure. Yet her very gender was a sign of imperial vulnerability, since as a female monarch she commanded the respect of her people but could not lead them into battle. The future of the empire depended upon the security of potent masculinity, and thus British culture invested much energy in glamourising male heroes in the pages of boys' periodicals and adventure fiction.[54] Bristow's argument is dramatically confirmed in *The Captain*.

The accession of Edward VII to the English throne resulted in a freer and more laudatory expression of British masculinity in Newnes's magazine, especially of the hunting, scouting, military variety. In the succeeding months *Captain* readers and authors indulged in an excess of patriotic enthusiasm for the monarchy. Under the bold title 'The King's Popularity', Edward VII was claimed as a prototype for *The Captain*'s heroic brand of sportsmanship, outdoor life, hunting, militarism, gentlemanliness and imperialistic enthusiasm. 'I think Edward the Seventh is one of the most popular monarchs that has ever occupied our throne', the editor observed, sending out a signal to readers:

> Your true Briton loves a sportsman, and the King is a sportsman to his fingertips. He is an outdoor King, and is the country squire all over when he is pottering about his estate in Norfolk. He has won the Derby, and he has won prizes for cattle bred under his own personal superintendence. He is devoted to horses and dogs; he hunted in his day; he is a good shot, and a keen yachtsman. He has the reputation of never forgetting a face. He is what is known as a 'particular' man, and a stickler for etiquette. And he is celebrated for his courtesy and tact. Such is Edward the Seventh, King of Great Britain and Ireland, and Emperor of India.[55]

Thus Edward VII was invested with all the qualities and virtues that *The Captain* valued and celebrated: sporting, social and personal. Readers were led into an almost cult-like bond of personal identification with the royal model-hero.[56]

The themes of militarism and empire were conflated with notions of sportsmanship and physical fitness already pervading the text to produce a

---

[54] Joseph Bristow, *Empire Boys: Adventures in a Man's World*, London: Harper Collins Academic, 1991, pp.224-226.

[55] *The Captain*, 7, 40 (July 1902), p.380.

[56] It is worth noting, in this context, that Newnes published a sixpenny magazine called *The King*, edited by A.J. Robertson, which contained illustrated articles on various sports such as golf, yachting and hunting.

concentration on hunting, scouting and the public school cadet corps. Cricket, rugby, athletics and other sports still featured, but more attention was devoted to the outdoor movement and the military. Some of the pictures sent in by readers demonstrated the new popularity of the outdoor theme. A series on public school cadet corps supplemented those on public school captains and sporting teams. Two articles appeared under the title 'Our School Army'. The national militia was the focus of a series entitled 'Some Official Crests of the British Army'. All of these features widened the scope of the magazine beyond its earlier concentration on English public schools. There was a new emphasis on naval competition too, with a glut of illustrated articles on sailors and the Navy (especially during the years of the Russo-Japanese War, 1904-1905).

In May 1904 *The Captain* became the official organ of the 'Boy's Empire League'. The B.E.L. was formed in 1901, during the Boer War, its intention 'To Promote and Strengthen a Worthy Imperial Spirit in British Boys all over the World'. By 1904, its membership numbered 7,000 boys residing in all parts of the British Empire. The aims of the B.E.L., as set out in its official papers, included the specification that:

> Every member undertakes, by some direct effort, to make himself a direct and worthy representative of the British race at home and abroad .... to show by his physical development, his intelligent knowledge of the Empire, his loyalty to British institutions, and to the King, that the British race is worthy of its proud position in the world.[57]

The 'noble spirit of Fairplay' was invoked, too, at the B.E.L. meeting held to declare *The Captain* the official organ of the League.[58] The League thus epitomised the spirit of *The Captain*.

Earlier, George Newnes had asked Fry's opinion on a proposition put to him by Thompson Seton, who had organised camping clubs in America called the 'Thompson Seton Indians'. The clubs operated according to a code of physical and moral procedure, embodied in maxims, which later became the basis of the Boy Scout movement. Thompson Seton had suggested that Fry would be the person to promote a parallel movement in England, and *The Captain* the best organ. But Fry felt that such a movement would be artificial in England, a country which didn't have the space and terrain of America, and was sceptical of any form of training for boys which wasn't essentially founded in discipline. He preferred such organisations as the Church Lads' Brigade.[59] The scout movement, however, borrowing much from Seton's system, subsequently burgeoned in England, led by Lord Baden-Powell.

---

[57] *The Captain*, 11, 64 (July, 1904), pp.xiii- xiv.

[58] Ibid., p.xiv.

[59] C.B. Fry, op. cit., p.155.

The shift in *The Captain*'s focus and the emergence of the 'Empire Boy' as the dominant type of role-model was the result of a changing cultural climate. The absence of a conscript or regular reserve army in Britain gave rise to concern about defence in the early twentieth century. Powerful pressure groups such as the militarist National Service League argued that compulsory training would act as a tonic against the physical and moral degeneracy attendant upon industrial civilisation. In the public school context, Edmund Warre campaigned for some form of compulsory military training within schools, and Field Marshall Lord Roberts, popularly considered the saviour of the Boer War and a hero of schoolboys, promoted conscription of some kind to be led from the top. He wrote to public school headmasters inviting 'their co-operation in bringing the deficiencies of the Volunteer force before their pupils'.[60] Roberts was to be one of the figureheads of *C.B. Frys' Magazine*. Established in 1904, *Fry's Magazine* offered a version of sporting culture that was morally responsible, socially integrational and staunchly nationalistic.[61]

Boys' magazines particularly addressed themselves to the need for military recruitment, and this theme attracted increasing attention as 1914 drew nearer. Northcliffe's publications were the most blatantly propagandist. The appearance, on the cover of *Chums*, of a bugler on a rearing horse, set against a military vessel, signified the way in which the magazine had developed a military emphasis. *The Captain* responded to Lord Roberts by promoting the Public School Cadet Corps.

'Giving boys the lead' in the spirit of militarism became a major preoccupation of such magazines, as A.C. Doyle was profoundly aware. He felt obliged to volunteer for military service in the Boer War because, as he told his mother:

> I have perhaps the strongest influence over young men, especially young athletic sporting men, of anyone in England (bar Kipling). That being so, it is really important that I should give them the lead.[62]

Such were the duties incumbent upon the role-model. And *The Captain* recognised the sacrifices of these men. In March 1915, the editor printed a picture of Lieutenant A.J.N. Williamson, a teacher from Highgate School, and the first public school master to be killed in the First World War. 'Everybody recognises the fact that the spirit of discipline and sportsmanship inculcated in our schools', he wrote, emphasising the very public school virtues which *The Captain* attempted to promote throughout the years of its publication, 'is bearing

---

[60] Lord Roberts, as cited in Peter Parker, *The Old Lie: The Great War and the Public School Ethos*, London: Constable, 1987, p.66.

[61] See Kate Jackson, 'C.B. Fry: The Sportsman-Editor', in *Victorian Periodicals Review*, (Winter 2000).

[62] Arthur Conan Doyle as cited in Peter Parker, op. cit., p.130.

rich and glorious fruit on the stern fields of duty.'[63] (Invoking a vaguer and more generalised 'spirit of ... sportsmanship' was less problematic in this context than invoking 'the noble spirit of Fairplay'.)

In 1910 a 'Scouts Corner' was introduced into *The Captain* to provide a defined and regular space for the discussion of issues such as tracking, riding and fire-making. It was a natural product of the hunting, sporting and military emphasis of the magazine. The 'Corner' was inevitably accompanied by an 'Answers to Correspondents' section and a 'Scouts Competition'. And a variety of advertisements for Scout outfits, 'Tabloid' First-Aid Outfits and other items of outdoor equipment appeared in the advertising pages. Baden-Powell's *Scouting for Boys* first appeared in 1908, and became one of the twentieth century's best-sellers. It marked the climax, rather than the origins, of a process by which images of frontier manliness, from a dispersed and varied set of imperial environments, were assembled in a variety of popular cultural forms. One of these was the boys' periodical, of which *The Captain* was an outstanding example. The rapid growth of the Boy Scouts serves as a reminder that Edwardian Britain was preoccupied with its youth, and as an indication of the anxiety as well as the enthusiasm associated with the youth movement. Like *The Captain*'s, the movement's major recruiting base was among middle-class and lower middle-class youths, rather than actual slum youth, although it drew its inspiration from the problems of urban slum life.

The Captain functioned as a repository for the moral and social anxieties of a generation preoccupied with a range of issues relating to communications, youth culture, sexuality, education, urban life, empire and, increasingly, national defence. *The Captain* both expressed and addressed anxieties about popular entertainments, adolescence, Hooliganism (and juvenile delinquency in general), public school education, urban degeneration, the erosion of traditional authority structures, imperial ideology and national military strength. This network of concerns constituted an implicit frame of reference for the publisher, editor, authors and readers of the magazine.

'Everyone who reads to any extent', one reader prefaced his contribution on 'My Favourite Character in Fiction',

> almost involuntarily chooses some particular character in fiction whose trials and fortunes and the way in which he meets them, rouse sympathy and admiration. This particular one is sometimes elected umpire in questions which one would, perhaps, not care to submit to anyone in the flesh.[64]

His use of the term 'umpire' indicated the extent to which sporting culture was brought to bear on morality. The text of the boys' periodical became the site on which such 'questions' were negotiated and readers' moral and imaginative lives

---

63 *The Captain*, 32, 191 (March 1915), as cited in Peter Parker, op. cit., p.261.

64 *The Captain*, 3, 16 (July 1900), p.333.

were played out. In this particular feature, Marcus Brutus was offered as the embodiment of all that was heroic: a perfect paragon of 'love, trust, faithfulness, and constancy'. And Bulwer Lytton's 'Zanoni' was a favourite of contributors because he represented 'a being perfect *bodily, morally, and mentally*'; 'Apollo Christianised' (a kind of popular hybrid of Arnold's Hellenism and Hebraism).[65] *The Captain* provided an enviable collection of role-models for its readers, through a range of features. Its reputation and appeal lay in the way in which it offered editorial, visual and fictional fodder for the practice of hero-worship, and thus represented a foil to concerns about contemporary youth.

As the twentieth century dawned and *The Captain* established itself amongst its readership, those qualities which Gillis has identified with the 'rituals of misrule' - the high-spirited rowdyism and hooliganism that had been associated with such events as Guy Fawkes Night - were appropriated for patriotic purposes.[66] The traditions of a generation of youths trained in military drill and imperialist enthusiasm acquired a conservative political cast. The 'Hooligans' of the new century channelled their pent-up enthusiasms into occasions of patriotic significance such as Mafeking Night (1900), the announcement of peace at the end of the Boer War, the accession of Edward VII to the throne of England, and ultimately the military parades of the First World War. *The Captain*, like youth organisations such as the Boys' Brigade and Boy Scouts, fostered a politicised impulse to serve the empire. The heroes of *The Captain* were not the reckless, cruel, criminal heroes of the 'penny dreadful'. They were sportsmen, gentlemen and 'Empire Boys': purified, moralised and nationalised heroes.

---

[65] My italics. *The Captain*, 11, 61 (April 1904), p.38.

[66] John R. Gillis, op. cit., p.106.

Figure 18. 'The Old Fag' editorial header. The header illustration for the editorial column of The Captain *was symbolic of the responsive and intimate tone adopted by the editor.*

C.B. Fry in various guises. 'The Sportsman', as this collection of images of Fry demonstrates, was well-represented in The Captain's *visual material.*

Figure 19a. The Captain, *6, 33 (December 1901), p.281.*

Figure 19b. The Captain, *6, 36 (March 1902), p.567.*

MR. C. B. FRY,
(Taken at Eastbourne—Sussex v. Oxford University—by G. B. Lye.)

"C. B. F."
(As seen by Southamptonians.)

Figure 19c. The Captain, *6, 36 (March 1902), p.511.*

HOW TO START.
(Photographed specially for THE CAPTAIN *by Geo. Newnes, Ltd.)*

Conclusion

George Newnes was one of a handful of great late Victorian and Edwardian print media entrepreneurs who successfully purveyed and shaped culture for profit through their innovations in a new type of journalism. He began his periodical publishing career in 1881, in Manchester, as the editor and publisher of a penny paper. He had studied the field of popular journalism as a reader, had experienced commercial and urban conditions in London and Manchester, and had a flair for novelty and an instinct for marketing and promotion. He developed into a wealthy philanthropist, Liberal MP and newspaper proprietor, publisher and editor of national and international renown, producing a variety of innovative periodicals, and commanding enormous respect as a man of high social and professional position with political connections and a reputation for commercial success within periodical publishing, despite the setbacks and failures that blighted the last years of his career. This book has traced this progression, through some of the most popular and distinctive periodicals established by Newnes and the discursive, journalistic and cultural contexts in which they were embedded.

After a rich and varied periodical publishing career, Newnes's final years brought disappointment and failure. He was a victim of diabetes, drink and a failing mind. In the last years of his life, he received a letter from the Prime Minister, intimating that his name was being put forward for a barony. He showed the letter to Sir Grimwood Mears, an old barrister friend who had been in the Indian civil service for many years. He decided to be known as Lord Wildcroft. At the Speaker's Dinner at the House of Commons, however, he drank to excess and had to be led away. His name was absent from the next Honours List. Sir Grimwood later recalled Frank Newnes's reaction: 'He has ruined my life.'[1] Lady Newnes enlisted the aid of the Reverend R.J. Campbell to help restore her husband's sense of responsibility to his family, his friends and his business. But the attempt was a failure, and Newnes acquired a habit of disappearing for extended periods without notice, leaving important decisions in suspense.

---

[1]   Reginald Pound, *Mirror of the Century: The Strand Magazine, 1891-1950*, London: Heinemann, 1966, p.112.

When, in the General Election of January 1910, Frank Newnes lost the seat that he had held for four years as MP for Bassetlaw in Nottinghamshire, Newnes was bitterly disappointed. He died on 9 June, at Hollerday House, and was buried at Lynton.[2] When his will was published it was apparent that most of the family fortune had gone. Made in 1895 on a sheet of foolscap paper, it was proved at £174,753, an amount which went towards debts to the company. Lady Newnes was to receive £3,000 a year. The bequest could not be made. Frank Newnes, still a board member for George Newnes, Ltd, was forced to seek a personal loan guarantee for £1,000 from Leicester Harmsworth.[3] Frank was to spend most of his life paying back the debts left by his father.

Despite the injurious effects of these latter events on the company's affairs, many preferred to remember Newnes for his contribution to publishing, his acts of public benevolence, and his generosity to the vast numbers of people whose lives were touched, in various ways, by his activities. 'The news of Sir George's death', according to one North Devon paper, 'caused a profound feeling of regret in Lynmouth and Lynton, where flags were flown at half-mast as a sign of public grief':

> By all classes he was beloved for his broadmindedness, generosity, and particularly for his kindly interest in the working people, which was a most notable trait in his character. Large as his private benefactions were, his gifts to Lynton were on an almost princely scale.[4]

George Newnes was remembered as publisher, proprietor and editor, paternalist, gentleman and squire. But he was also remembered as an innovator, as the *Daily Graphic* emphasised in its obituary of him:

> Something more than a notable figure in journalism has passed away with the death of Sir George Newnes. An innovator has gone, though he has left his influence behind .... it was the application of Sir George Newnes of innovation to the monthly magazine, to the picture photograph, and to other subjects connected with journalism, that turned his enterprises into gold.[5]

Newnes has frequently been associated with the legendary Greek king Midas. He employed a creative approach to publishing and journalism which resulted in

---

[2] Hollerday House was destroyed by fire on 4 August, 1913. See John Travis, *An Illustrated History of Lynton and Lynmouth, 1770-1914*, Derby: Breedon Books, 1995, pp.105-107.

[3] Wandsworth and Putney *Borough News*, 12 August, 1910, p.144; Reginald Pound, op. cit., p.113.

[4] Cited in Hulda Friederichs, *The Life of Sir George Newnes, Bart*, London: Hodder and Stoughton, 1911, p.296.

[5] Ibid., pp.144-145.

the accumulation of a vast fortune, and in this way represented an ideal of entrepreneurialism that had gained remarkable currency in the nineteenth century.

Newnes, of course, did not devote himself equally to each of his publications, once they were conceived and established. He maintained a very active and visible presence in the early years of *Tit-Bits* (1881), *The Million* (1892) and *The Strand* (1891) as journalist, editor and publisher. *The Westminster Gazette* and *The Wide World Magazine*, founded in the 1890s, although they were inspired and shaped by his beliefs, commitments and experiences, were less closely controlled by Newnes. And he made only rare appearances in the texts of these publications. As he added more and more publications to his stable around the turn of the century, Newnes's participation was limited to identifying niche audiences who could be readily exploited, devising plans for a new publications to target them, and choosing editors to undertake each project.[6] The name 'George Newnes' came to symbolise the diversification of the magazine industry. Newnes's role as a publisher thus evolved and changed as his business expanded.

This analysis has offered many images of Newnes as he appeared to the readers of his various publications. To 'Tit-Bitites' and 'Millionaires', he was a benevolent paternalist (as he was at Lynton, where the title 'Sergeorge the Giver' was conferred on him), but one who was attuned to the progress of democracy. He was host to the *Strand* circle, and liberal sponsor of *The Westminster Gazette* (albeit that mentions of his role as partisan proprietor were tempered by a strong sense of journalistic propriety). But ultimately, George Newnes perfectly represented the self-made entrepreneurial ideal that was one of the lynchpins of late nineteenth-century middle-class culture in Britain. He employed a creative approach to publishing and journalism which, when combined with sound and confident business practice and an intuitive sense of the popular taste, resulted in the creation of dozens of successful periodicals that catered to a variety of audiences.

Harold Perkin has argued that the capitalist of the entrepreneurial type was the ideal citizen for the bulk of the middle class, representing 'the active owner-manager of the Industrial Revolution, not the passive or remotely controlling financier of later corporate capitalism'.[7] The dichotomy between active and

---

6   *Fry's Magazine* offers a case in point. It continued publication until 1914. Its last year was on an independent basis, since Fry and Lord Riddell (the recently-appointed Managing Director of George Newnes, Ltd) could not agree on who had control over the conduct of the magazine. Riddell obviously did not adopt the laissez-faire approach employed by Newnes as regards the production of the magazine. Newnes had been sure of the commercial potential, qualifications and commitments of his editor. Riddell operated by different principles of management. Not for him Newnes's approach, as Fry put it, of 'leaving the whole thing entirely to me' as a process of experimentation and editorial creativity. Not for him Newnes's confidence in the figure of the editor-manager, learned from his own experiences with *Tit-Bits* and the host of publications that followed. See C.B. Fry, *Life Worth Living: Some Phases of an Englishman*, London: Eyre and Spottiswoode, 1939, p.159.

7   Harold Perkin, *The Origins of Modern English Society, 1780- 880*, London: Routledge and Kegan Paul, 1969, p.221.

passive leadership is one that has flavoured the historiography of late nineteenth and early twentieth-century journalism. Alfred Harmsworth, for instance, defending, in 1922, the status (recently established) of the professional journalist as against the purely capitalistic role of the 'millionaire-amateur' press magnate, proffered a distinction between 'the absentee proprietor behind whose edicts there is no authority save that of the purse', and the trained journalist, possessing in abundance the qualities of 'professional competence and professional morality'.[8] More recently, Piers Brendon has invoked the opposition between personal and purely financial investment in his study of nineteenth-century press barons.

Late nineteenth-century British journalism was dominated, Brendon has shown, by a handful of innovative and idiosyncratic 'press barons'. They were independent and autonomous, in contrast to the vast and anonymous 'communications corporations' and 'media conglomerates' by which they were superseded in the economic climate of the twentieth century:

> The arduous feat of creating and sustaining a prosperous publication was almost always achieved by a lone pioneer of outstanding journalistic ability, a man of mercury who invested his entire personality in his newspaper .... Between them they created the amazingly rich variety of newspapers which was such a distinctive feature of British and American life before the coming of today's monopolistic companies .... What they lacked in integrity they made up for in idiosyncrasy .... The history of modern journalism is the sum of their biographies.[9]

George Newnes could not have been accused of lacking integrity. Yet he was a 'press baron'. And Brendon's 'press barons' were entrepreneurs, their contributions to modern journalism a combination of 'journalistic ability', 'personality' and 'investment'. This book has sought to add an account of Newnes's periodical publishing career to the 'sum' that is the history of modern journalism.

There was nothing particularly mercenary about Newnes, nor anything 'cheap' or 'low' about his publications, commercially successful though they were. Publishers had always aimed to make money out of their enterprises. They just made more, in this period, through the exploitation of more readers, appealing to a diverse cross-section of the market by using a variety of entrepreneurial techniques. Newnes created and sustained a series of publications

---

[8]   Viscount Northcliffe, *Newspapers and their Millionaires: With Some Further Meditations About Us*, 18th ed., London; Associated Newspapers, 1922, pp.23-24. There was more than a touch of arrogance about Northcliffe's arguments: 'The well-meaning and public-spirited amateur, who does not understand journalistic values and has not grasped the subtlety of that faculty which enables some men to know what their readers want much better than the readers know it themselves, has no place in the journalistic world' (p.24).

[9]   Piers Brendon, *The Life and Death of the Press Barons*, London: Secker and Warburg, 1982, p.3.

which were both 'rich', in literary terms, and 'prosperous' in commercial terms. He confirmed the belief of his contemporaries in the dynamic *cultural* and *economic* role of the entrepreneur. The entrepreneur was not a mere capitalist. He made creative and productive use of capital. Newnes's entrepreneurial reputation and his journalistic success were established by his use of a variety of promotional and marketing techniques involving novel circulation-boosting and publicity schemes, and of innovative advertising techniques, his technological progressiveness and thoughtful staffing, and his active involvement in specialisation and diversification in the late nineteenth and early twentieth-century press.

According to the prevailing orthodoxy, the entrepreneur was the lynchpin of society:

> The entrepreneur was the impressario, the creative force, the initiator of the economic cycle. He it was who conceived the end, found the means, bore the burden of risk, and paid out the other factors of production .... If the worker was the horse and the landlord the non-paying passenger, the entrepreneur was driver, conductor, pathfinder, caterer and provider of all provender all rolled into one.[10]

The entrepreneur was thus one of the ideal figures of the period, and George Newnes, actively involved in the creation of a vast network of periodical publications from virtually no starting capital, fitted the mould exactly.[11] He was well aware of the fact, and cultivated the image.

Newnes cast himself - as editor, publisher and proprietor - in the role of hero. 'To publish a newspaper requires the skill, the precision, the vigilance, the strategy, the boldness of a commander-in-chief', wrote Newnes in *Tit-Bits*, his first publication. He went on:

> To edit a newspaper, one needs to be a statesman, an essayist, a geographer, a statistician, and, so far as all acquisition is concerned, encyclopaedic. To man and propel a newspaper requires more qualities than any other business on earth.[12]

---

[10] Harold Perkin, op. cit., pp.221-222.

[11] The rhetoric of entrepreneurialism pervaded contemporary debates within and about the developing capitalist press. The entrepreneurial ideal was, for instance, the publisher's line of defence against the attacks of Walter Besant and the Society of Authors in a dispute that raged in the press in the early 1890s. In *The Athenaeum*, Besant's criticisms of a system in which the author's rights were unequal, his profits from production inadequate and thus his legal and financial position in relation to his publisher subordinate were met with a series of responses in which the publisher was defended in terms of the financial risk incurred in the search for profit, the machinery, facilities and thus capital provided, and the publisher's active and responsible role as 'agent, manufacturer and distributor'. See *The Athenaeum*, 14 October-11 November, 1893.

[12] *Tit-Bits*, 1, 24 (March 1882), p.5.

Newnes's use of the professions - army officers, diplomats, 'men of letters' - as the source of his analogies belies the continuing tension between entrepreneurial and professionl ideals in this period, a tension which was to permeate *The Strand Magazine*. The publisher of *Tit-Bits* was the 'commander in chief', deploying armies of correspondents to provide material for the paper and armies of newspaper boys to advertise and sell it, instituting circulation-raising schemes and competitions, and investing money, human resources and leadership skills in his campaign.

Newnes's private correspondence reflected a similar confidence in his abilities. Separating from W.T. Stead, he emphasised the entrepreneurial skill and self-confidence which created and underwrote the value of any publication. 'A valuer', he said of the *Review of Reviews*, 'might treat it as a nine days wonder.'

> This we know to be false and that it will last your and my lifetime and a good deal longer. At least it might do. Many people prophesied that Tit-Bits would never keep up the enormous sale which it obtained the first four months. I knew better about Tit-Bits and I know better about R of R. Therefore the man who buys must be a man who believes it will last as I do.[13]

Although Newnes claimed elsewhere that he was 'the average man' (both an expression of humility and an attempt to identify with the audience of *Tit-Bits*) he was, according to Reginald Pound, 'an almost offensively comfortable-looking entrepreneur, replete with the artfully controlled self-esteem that marked the successful man in whom business acumen was mingled with the public spirit'.[14]

C.B. Fry, the famous sportsman and journalist, and editor of *C.B. Fry's Magazine*, wrote of this 'notable man' that he had two characteristics of greatness:

> He not only just thought about and round about whatever he happened to have in mind; he thought it right out. This capacity to think a subject right out is rare .... Another feature of George Newnes's mind was an instinctive knack of simplifying: a knack of not seeing any part of a question at issue that did not matter.[15]

Newnes, according to Fry, was energetic, alert and precise. But most significantly, he was original, and many of the periodical forms which he invented were later developed by 'an army of copyists'. He was, in fact, 'destined to modify in the most profound degree, the intellectual, social and

---

[13] George Newnes to W.T. Stead, 21 March, 1890, Newnes-Stead Correspondence, Churchill College Library, Cambridge.

[14] Reginald Pound, op. cit., p.25.

[15] C.B. Fry, op. cit., p.155.

political tone of the press as a whole', in the words of the official historian of *The Times*.[16]

With *Tit-Bits*, Newnes established the first widely-circulating penny miscellany paper. *The Million* pioneered coloured illustration in the cheap popular press. *The Strand* was a prototype of the sixpenny short-story magazine in which illustrations were featured frequently and prominently, as they were in American magazines. *The Ladies' Field* (and *Country Life*) set new standards in pictorial printing. And Newnes utilised new techniques of photographic reproduction developed in these two magazines in *The Wide World Magazine*. This was the original 'true story magazine', and its format was to be extensively copied in the twentieth century. *The Captain* was an early and successful example of the 'respectable' boys' paper, its use of acknowledged authorities and real sporting heroes a new technique in soliciting readers. And *C.B. Fry's Magazine* was one of the first magazines to employ the sportsman-editor, writing under his own name, to produce an authoritative sporting journal.

Many of these new formats were implicated, in a very tangible way, in the cultural and discursive environments from which they emerged. *Tit-Bits*, for instance, was rooted in the rhythms of industrial life, even as it sought to provide readers with relief from the urban reality that hemmed them in. Its format echoed the temporal and spatial conditions experienced by its readers who 'plodded on from day to day', commuting to the city by rail, and possessing only timed leisure in which to digest the paper's paragraphic portions. It was no coincidence that *Tit-Bits* was established in Manchester, a busy, densely populated northern 'city of stone and iron', as Reginald Pound has observed, 'echoing the intimidating clangour of the industrial revolution'.[17] The short-story magazine, too, was clearly a product of a society in which commuting was widespread and time-discipline was an increasingly accepted part of life. The short story could be easily consumed in a railway journey. And, as Grant Allen pointed out in an interview in *The Million*:

> For the public, short stories are undeniably the best, for why should they trouble to wade through three weary volumes when the pith of the tale can be put into twenty pages.[18]

Industrial time produced new temporal categories such as 'the dinner hour', and later, 'office hours' and 'travel time'. Columns like 'The Children's Hour' (*The Million* and *The Ladies' Field*) reflected such developments, anticipating policies of segmentation that were later to characterise radio and television broadcasting.

This study has revealed the cultural diversity and historical developments that characterised late Victorian and Edwardian society, through the comparisons it has made between Newnes's periodical publications. In *Tit-Bits*, millionaires

---

[16] Reginald Pound, op. cit., p.16.

[17] Ibid., p.19.

[18] *The Million*, 2, 36 (November 1892), p.129.

and swindlers were featured in two popular biographical series: 'Millionaires and How They Became So' (1883) and 'Big Swindles' (1884). Such features were evidence of the concern of lower middle-class readers with social and economic mobility, and with the relationship between individual and national wealth in the political world that they were to have a part in shaping.

The biographical component of *The Strand* was focussed on 'celebrities' of the middle and upper classes, many of them professionals. It offered a strategy for finding security in a rapidly changing world, and served to emphasise the rise of professional society. It symbolised the way in which the middle class redefined respectability and asserted their rights to public esteem in terms of the skills (as opposed to the capital) they possessed. *The Strand*'s emphasis on the 'intellectual class' was also a kind of rearguard action as far as elevating the fields of literature, art and theatre in a democratic age was concerned. This magazine was central to the development of a type of literature that was essentially middle-brow.

The protagonists of *The Wide World Magazine* were travellers, missionaries, hunters and exiles, explorers, army and navy officers and empire-builders. They represented the development of imperial ideology, and new notions of time and space. *The Captain* presented heroes (Henley's 'Great Men' and Carlyle's 'Heroes') who fulfilled society's need for role-models, especially male role-models, in the context of war, and of the threats to potent masculinity posed by physical deterioration, homosexuality, hooliganism and other social problems. 'Sportsmen' were some of the most potent heroes of *The Captain*, a fact which prompted Newnes to establish *C.B. Fry's Magazine* in 1904, with the famous sportsman C.B. Fry as editor. Such sporting figures gained popularity with the rise of mass culture and new forms of entertainment.

As the twentieth century wore on, the 'celebrities' of *The Strand* were replaced by the 'stars' of the new cinema. Editorially, their rise to prominence was celebrated in a series entitled 'Stories of the Film Stars', and new sepia half-tones conveyed their images. Alma Taylor, Chrissie White, Blanche Sweete, Anna Nilsson, Alice Joyce, Gabrielle Robinne and Marie Pickering were some of the new 'stars' of *The Strand*. Like the sportsmen of *Fry's*, they were the emissaries of mass entertainment. Such transitions in biographical nomenclature and focus, evident in an examination of the range of Newnes publications, are a poignant record of historical and cultural change.

What also emerges from this study is a narrative of journalistic consistency. This narrative underlines the ways in which Newnes's periodicals represent a stable of publications, all of them bearing the mark, to differing degrees, of their creator and of those that might be called 'Newnes people', and each of them a mixture of ideology and profit. As his publishing business expanded, Newnes gathered around him a company of editors, authors and illustrators who contributed to a range of his publications. It was these people, who had 'been associated with [him] so intimately at the offices of George

Newnes, Ltd', who signed the celebratory volume presented to Newnes for the Thousandth Number of *Tit-Bits* in 1900.

Illustrators such as Tom Browne, Paul Hardy, E.F. Skinner, Alfred Pearse and F.C. Gould created the pictures that were to characterise *The Strand*, *The Westminster Gazette*, *The Wide World Magazine*, *The Captain* and *C.B. Fry's Magazine*. Authors and journalists such as P.G. Wodehouse, Grant Allen, W.W. Jacobs, R.S. Warren Bell, Edward Step, Raymond Blathwayt and Harry How wrote material for a number of different Newnes periodicals. Writers whose careers Newnes had promoted and who became closely associated with his publications, such as Arthur Conan Doyle of *The Strand*, became close personal friends. And editors such as H. Greenhough Smith, J.A. Spender and C.B. Fry became essential to the character and appeal of Newnes's publishing innovations. Greenhough Smith, whom Newnes had chosen as the Literary Editor of *The Strand* at the outset, continued to control the literary side of the magazine until 1930. Spender edited *The Westminster* for thirteen of the sixteen years that Newnes was its proprietor and was central to its 'personality'. And Fry was so successful as the Athletic Editor of *The Captain* that Newnes employed him to promote and develop another Newnes periodical, bearing his own name. These people, generally on friendly terms with the head of the firm, were integral to the development and success of the House of Newnes. George Newnes's skill lay partly in his aptitude for selecting and maintaining staff and his continuing personal relations with them.

There was, in fact, a substantial amount of cross-fertilisation, inter-textuality and cross-marketing involved in Newnes's various periodical publications. When Grant Allen won a *Tit-Bits* competition for writing a novel, to be published in serial form in *Tit-Bits*, he was interviewed in *The Million*. He commented that his story ('What's Bred in the Bone') was 'a popular story for popular consumption, introducing a good deal of the scientific element in an unobtrusive form, which is what I like best to do.' It was designed to 'hit the taste of a wide body of readers'.[19] Thus *The Million*, with a target audience very similar to that of *Tit-Bits*, was utilised by Newnes to market and interpret the character of *Tit-Bits*, and to reinforce its ethos. In the early issues of *The Strand*, Newnes utilised figures and diagrams representing the scope and output of his periodical publishing career in order to establish his own professional credibility and thus the credibility of his newest publication. The increasing diversity of Newnes's publishing operations meant that he could utilise the pages of one periodical to advertise another similarly targeted publication, and thus capitalise on readership continuities.

An exploration of the more overt ideological element of *The Westminster Gazette* facilitates a better understanding of the kind of liberal-democratic idealism and socio-cultural concerns underpinning journals like *Tit-Bits* and *The Million*. Both of these publications, if they employed many of the tactics of the

---

[19] *The Million*, 2, 36 (November 1892), p.129.

New Journalism, were underwritten by notions of political suffrage and collectivism. *The Captain* and *C.B. Fry's Magazine*, too, were broadly liberal popular publications. There was a strong link, through Newnes and his identification with liberal journalism, between Newnes's more commercially successful papers - *Tit-Bits, The Million, The Wide World Magazine, The Captain* and *C.B. Fry's Magazine* - and the so-called 'political' journalism of *The Westminster Gazette*. This highlights the fact that, whilst all of Newnes's publications purported to be inclusive, this inclusivity was underpinned by a particular perception of the new mass market, and did, in fact, promote a particular class ideology.

By exploring the intricate connections between editor, proprietor and political community in *The Westminster*, and understanding the sense in which this paper was a record of their world and circle, it is possible to penetrate Newnes's collaboration and identification with the more literary and artistic circle of *The Strand*. *The Westminster Gazette* simply represented another social milieu to which Newnes belonged as a successful editor and publisher, another aspect of his world view, and hence another journalistic prototype amongst the many with which he engaged.

The term 'reading community' is a particularly appropriate description of the way in which Newnes imagined and created the readerships of his various periodicals. It is a curious fact that whilst the capitalistic development of the late nineteenth-century press entailed an increase in the distance between the organisational hierarchy of the publishing company and the mass reading public that fed its progress, the New Journalism was characterised by its personalised tone and its dependence upon the individual identities of editors, authors and illustrators. Vast increases in circulation meant that it was actually impossible for a publisher or editor to 'know' his audience in any real sense, but successful publishers like Newnes attempted to recreate the old communal relations of eighteenth and early nineteenth-century Britain (Raymond Williams' 'knowable community') within various 'reading communities' with shared values and experiences: the public 'image', both of the editor and of the reader, became as significant as the 'real' person behind it. All of Newnes's magazines represented the attempt to maintain an interactive relationship with readers and to manufacture a community of interest, through editorials, correspondence columns, competitions and other features, in place of the organic neighbourhood in which rural people had enjoyed close personal involvement. In an industrialised society, relations between people were becoming increasingly impersonal. In the pages of newspapers, as Piers Brendon has suggested, 'local gossip was writ large and the anonymous citizen became a living, breathing participant'.[20]

Both *Tit-Bits* and *The Million* offered the security of a close community of loyal lower middle-class readers, and the protection of a paternalistic and responsive editor-proprietor. They reflected and exploited the developments in

---

[20] Piers Brendon, op. cit., pp. 17-18.

the national community brought about by the extension of literacy and the popular press, the democratic extension of political suffrage, urban conditions and new notions of fellowship, cooperation and collectivism in politics and law. (Although, whilst they purported to be inclusive they did, in fact, promote a particular class ideology in relation to the new mass market and market segmentation, revealing the apparent conflict between Newnes's aspirations towards 'community' and 'fellowship' and his representation and market exploitation of 'class'-based notions of culture.) *The Strand* offered the corporate life of the professional community and the social cohesion of the middle-class club. *The Westminster Gazette* appealed to a close-knit circle of educated and like-minded gentlemen readers. Even so, its editor, J.A. Spender, maintained that in writing leaders for the paper, he felt as if he were delivering addresses to 'the fog-filled street below'. Spender was a 'citizen householder' at Toynbee Hall. He took a lively part in the public life of East London, serving as whip of the Progressive party on the municipal authority at Mile End, managing three big council schools and taking part in many East End agitations. He saw his role as overcoming the tyranny of distance which divided society into Disraeli's 'two nations'. 'No share in the government of this country is worth anything', he wrote, 'which is not based on immediate, practical experience of the lives of the toiling millions who are the real people of England.'[21] He was thus intensely interested in notions of community and fellowship. At the same time, he was obviously interested in asserting the value of his liberal-democratic approach to social problems and his own authority as a journalist.

The Wide World Magazine enacted a diminution of the distance between individuals and nations, and demonstrated the development of a new notion of community: international, temporal and spatial. It offered the reader membership of white, western, 'civilised', English-speaking society, and, through material that confirmed the motto 'Truth is Stranger than Fiction', made that version of community personal, visual and contemporary. *The Ladies' Field*, by contrast, created a version of segregated feminine space, inhabited by advisors, friends and confidantes, and defined by social ritual and increasingly by consumerism. *The Captain* recreated the atmosphere of the English public school, and its editor attracted boy readers by offering them the friendship of a 'chum' and wooed their middle-class parents by cultivating the authority of a mentor. Both *The Captain* and the later *C.B. Fry's Magazine* identified with their readers through their own system of shared values: the values of sporting culture, spectatorism and mass leisure. R.J. Holt has offered an illuminating account of the way in which, as the industrial city expanded, the fact of being a loyal football team supporter came to offer 'a sense of place, of belonging and of meaning that could never come from the formal expression of citizenship through the

21 J.A. Spender, *Life, Journalism and Politics*, London: Cassell, 1927, vol. 2, pp.87-88.

municipal ballot box'.[22] *The Captain* and *Fry's Magazine* drew upon this sense of collective identity to create reader loyalty.

The methodological model which interprets the periodical as a socio-historical text has proven particularly relevant to the study of Newnes's periodicals. Each publication, it has been established, was integrally connected with the contemporary discursive and cultural conditions within which it functioned both interactively and historically. Both creating and reflecting contemporary culture, the periodical can only properly be viewed as a combination of production and reception. From the promotional techniques, formatting, illustrations and regular columns which distinguish them, to the rhetoric employed by their editors, and the themes that recur through their various features, Newnes's periodicals *realise* contemporary society, in all its diversity and dynamism, and thus represent a sequence of useful and inter-connected points of access to this interesting period in British history. It was in this way that J.A. Spender resolved the question of the status and significance of journalism as a form of cultural production, writing of the journalist: 'his task is literally for the day and his glory is to be a good ephemeral'.[23] And with specific reference to Newnes's periodical publishing career, Arthur Conan Doyle said of his contribution to British literature and society, in a tribute of 1902, that he had 'done for the public of this country, a most important thing striking deeply into the very roots of national life'.[24]

What this study clearly reveals is the way in which Newnes balanced and synthesised various potentially conflicting imperatives within his periodical publications, creating a kind of synergy between business and benevolence, popular and quality journalism, old and new journalism, and, ultimately, culture and profit. It is worth noting that other so-called 'New Journalists' also combined ideology and profit in various ways. John Goodbody has argued cogently that O'Connor's *Star*, the first daily paper to aim at a mass readership in Britain, combined radical politics with a high circulation.[25] Joseph Baylen, on the other hand, has suggested that there was an important distinction between journalists such as Stead, whose journalism represented moral and social convictions, political ambitions and the 'projection of a Nonconformist

---

[22] R.J. Holt, 'Football and the Urban Way of Life', in J.A. Mangan (ed.), *Pleasure, Sport and Proselytism: British Culture and Sport at Home and Abroad, 1700-1914*, London: Frank Cass, 1988, p.83.

[23] J.A. Spender, op. cit., p.163.

[24] 'A Tribute to Sir G. Newnes', *The Times*, 9 September 1902, p.2. This is an account of the speech made by Conan Doyle at the unveiling of a bust of Newnes at Lynton, in recognition of his services to the village, and especially his donation of the town hall.

[25] John Goodbody, 'The *Star*: Its Role in the Rise of the New Journalism', in Joel Wiener (ed.), *Papers for the Millions: The New Journalism in Britain, 1850s-1914*, New York: Greenwood Press, 1988, pp.143-163.

conscience', and Harmsworth, whose journalism he characterises as blatantly sensationalist.[26]

In *Tit-Bits* and *The Million*, Newnes combined business and benevolence, offering the lower middle-class audience periodical literature that was a mixture of commercial transaction and cultural exchange. These magazines were commercial in origin and format, relying heavily on competitions and circulation-boosting schemes, and effectively making Newnes's fortune in publishing. But their attraction was, at the same time, the way in which they offered connection, representation and creative potential to readers, and enabled Newnes to establish a responsive and benevolent editorial presence.

In *The Strand*, Newnes offered a compromise between artistic 'quality' and journalistic innovation, providing material that was authenticated through a system of 'quality control' that comprised the guarantee of the publisher's established reputation, the patronage and participation of a range of well-connected social figures, the code of professional standards governing the corporate body of contributors, and the general popularity attained by the magazine amongst the educated middle class. Through this magazine, Newnes pioneered a new definition of 'quality' journalism which encompassed the contributions of a range of specialists in the various 'branches' of literature and illustration, the adjudications of expert art and literary editors, and the maintenance of high standards of production. Yet in terms of circulation and of its deliberate attempts to, in Raymond Williams' terms, 'win favour with the people', *The Strand* was very much a piece of popular journalism.[27] *The Strand* was, in fact, neither 'high' nor 'popular', but 'middle-brow' journalism.

The Westminster Gazette was a Liberal evening newspaper which straddled the ground between the political press and the commercial press, combining the traditions and attachments of the old journalism with the modernising techniques of the New Journalism. It represents the combination of political commentary and journalistic technique and the cross-pollination between the old journalism and the new. And as for the combination of culture and profit, all of Newnes's periodicals reflected this combination, but perhaps none more so than *The Ladies' Field, The Captain* and *C.B. Fry's Magazine*, all of which both exploited the niche audiences of consumers at which they were targeted for profit, and at the same time expressed, focussed and to some extent alleviated their anxieties, fulfilling their psychological and cultural needs as readers.

The periodical publications of George Newnes were firmly rooted in contemporary culture, fostering and sustaining the ideas, values, preoccupations and self-reflections of publisher, editors, authors, illustrators, correspondents, competitors and readers alike, all of whose moral, political and imaginative lives were played out in their pages. They expressed a kind of consensual reality. Yet they also represented, of course, the commercial exchange between producer and

---

[26] Joseph O. Baylen, 'The "New Journalism" in Late-Victorian Britain', *Australian Journal of Politics and History*, 18 (1972), pp.369, 375.

[27] See Introduction.

consumer, bringing readers' pennies and sixpences, advertising revenue and share income to the publisher, and payments and retainers to their contributors, and providing readers with entertainment and instruction, goods and services through their columns, features and advertising pages. They were as much the purveyors of profit as the vehicles of culture, and were deeply implicated in the rise of commercialism and consumer culture. If nineteenth-century British society was precariously poised between 'culture and anarchy', as Matthew Arnold suggested, then Newnes's experiments in New Journalism were successfully poised between 'culture and profit'. Newnes's brand of journalism at once democratised Arnold's 'culture' and, by both representing and educating the tastes and interests of Arnold's 'populace', defused the anarchy which was its postulated alternative.

George Newnes

Biographical Summary

1851   Born at Matlock, Peak District, England, to Thomas Mold Newnes (a Congregational minister) and his Scottish wife Sarah Urquhart.

1857-1866   Entered Silcoates, a Congregational school near Wakefield, Yorkshire, in 1857 (aged 6). Then attended Shireland School, Cape Hill, Birmingham, and finished his education at City of London School, where he spent only two terms, spring and summer 1866.

1867-1880   At age 16, apprenticed to a haberdashery firm in London, where he served most of his five years in the basement 'Entering Room'. Lived, during these years, at 33 Colebrook Row, near the Angel at Islington. Towards the end of his apprenticeship, was transferred to Manchester to open up business for the firm. Then took a similar job as the local representative of a London firm of haberdashers in Manchester and Liverpool. Married Priscilla Jenney, daughter of Reverend James Hillyard, of Leicester, in 1875, by whom he had two sons, one of whom died at age 8. The family lived in a semi-detached villa in Stretford, Manchester.

1881   Opened a vegetarian restaurant in the basement of 2 Pall Mall, Manchester. In a few weeks, his 'Vegetarian Company's Saloon' had a turnover which enabled him to sell at a net profit of £400. *Tit-Bits* established.

1882   National Liberal Club, of which Newnes became a member, founded. (Opened first premises in June 1887.)

1885   Offices of *Tit-Bits* moved from Manchester to Farringdon St, London, and Newnes family settled at Putney Heath. Newnes elected to Parliament as the Liberal member for the Newmarket division of Cambridgeshire.

1886   Offices of *Tit-Bits* moved to Burleigh St, off The Strand. Newnes regained his seat in the General Election fought over Home Rule. Stood against Mr Bullock Hall, Chairman of the Liberal party and a staunch Unionist.

1890   *Review of Reviews* established with W.T. Stead. Cliff railway (Lynton-Lynmouth), proposed and largely funded by Newnes, opened by him.

1891   *The Strand Magazine* established. George Newnes, Ltd floated as a limited company with £400,000 capital. Newnes paid for a cricket ground and pavilion in Valley of the Rocks, Lynton.

1892   *The Million* established. Newnes returned to Parliament for the third time.

1893   *The Westminster Gazette* established. Newnes's mansion at Lynton, Hollerday House, completed.

1894   *Picture Politics* established. Newnes opened a new golf course at Lynton which he had helped to pay for.

1895   *Woman's Life* and *Navy and Army Illustrated* established. Newnes lost his seat in the House of Commons. Awarded a baronetcy for his political services to Liberalism and the 'good work' he had done 'in the cause of healthy popular literature' (as Lord Rosebery wrote to him).

1897   *Country Life* established. George Newnes, Ltd capitalised at £1,000,000.

1898   *Ladies' Field* and *Wide World Magazine* established. Newnes wrote two travel narratives for *The Strand*. Borchgrevink Antarctic expedition, funded by Newnes, left England. Borchgrevink named a promontory westward of Cape Washington Newnes Land after the expedition's benefactor. Lynton-Barnstaple railway, of which Newnes was a leading financier, opened.

1899   *Captain* and *Under the Union Jack* established. Putney Library, a free public library donated by Newnes, opened. Newnes published his own pamphlet, *Cairo and Egypt: Comprising An Illustrated Account of a Trip up the Nile*.

1900   *Sunday Strand* established. Newnes re-elected to Parliament as the member for Swansea. Performed ceremony at opening of Lynton Town Hall, which he had donated to the town.

1902   Bust of Newnes installed at Lynton Town Hall and unveiled by Arthur Conan Doyle.

1904   *C.B. Fry's Magazine* established. Newnes donated a new bowling green to Lynton. New Congregational church at Lynton opened. Newnes donated the site and paid for its construction.

1906   Became one of the directors of the British Commonwealth Oil Corporation which obtained leases in the Wolgan Valley, New South Wales. Site of oil shale mine was named Newnes after him. Personally contributed an undisclosed sum to increase the profits of George Newnes, Ltd.

1910   Died and was buried at Lynton, Devon. Inhabitants mourned his death, and many laudatory obituaries appeared in the press.

Select Bibliography

PRIMARY SOURCES

Newnes Periodicals
C.B. Fry's Magazine (1904)
The Captain (1899)
Country Life (1897)
The Ladies' Field (1898)
The Million (1892)
Navy and Army Illustrated (1895)
Picture Politics (1894)
The Strand Magazine (1891)
Sunday Strand (1900)
Tit-Bits (1881)
Under the Union Jack (1899)
The Westminster Gazette (1893)
The Wide World Magazine (1898)
Woman's Life (1895)

Manuscript Sources
Interview with International Publishing Company Secretary, John Gore.
Newnes to Henry Campbell-Bannerman, 27 November, 1905, Campbell-Bannerman Papers, BL, Add. Ms. 41238, f.89b.
Newnes to Herbert Gladstone, 24 October, 1903, Viscount Gladstone Papers, BL, Add. Ms. 46061, f.31b.
Newnes to Herbert Gladstone, 19 December 1905, Viscount Gladstone Papers, BL, Add. MS. 46063, f.227b.
Newnes to John Burns, 30 May, 1895, Burns Papers, BL, Add. MS. 46295. f.104b.
Newnes-Hoyle Correspondence, Lynmouth and Lynton Lift Company, Lynton (three letters between 25 and 29 November, 1887).
Newnes-Stead Correspondence, Churchill College Library, Cambridge (nineteen letters between 7 January, 1890 and 6 June, 1893).

Books
Arnold, Matthew, *Culture and Anarchy* (ed. and intro. J. Dover Wilson), London: Cambridge University Press, 1960.
Baden-Powell, R.S.S., *Scouting for Boys: A Handbook for Instruction in Good Citizenship*, London: Horace Cox, 1908.

Besant, Walter and G.E. Milton, *The Fascination of London: The Strand District*, London: Adam and Charles Black, 1903.

Borchgrevink, C.E., *First on the Antarctic Continent. Being an Account of the British Antarctic Expedition, 1898-1900* (Intro. by Tore Gjelsvik), London: C. Hurst, 1980.

Cambrose, Viscount, *British Newspapers and their Controllers*, London: Cassell, 1947.

Dark, Sidney, *The Life of Cyril Arthur Pearson, Bt, G.B.E.*, London: Hodder and Stoughton, 1922.

Dicey, A.V., *Lectures on the Relationship Between Law and Public Opinion During the Nineteenth Century in England*, London: Macmillan, 1905.

Doyle, Arthur Conan, *Memories and Adventures*, London: Greenhill, 1988.

Escott, T.H.S., *Masters of English Journalism: A Study of Personal Forces*, London: T. Fisher Unwin, 1911.

Friederichs, Hulda, *The Life of Sir George Newnes, Bart*, London: Hodder and Stoughton, 1911.

Lucy, Henry, *Sixty Years in the Wilderness*, London: Smith, Elder, 1909.

Northcliffe, Viscount, *Newspapers and their Millionaires: With Some Further Meditations About Us*, 18th ed., London, 1922.

Pemberton, Max, *Lord Northcliffe. A Memoir*, London: Hodder and Stoughton, 1922.

Raymond, E.T., *Portraits of the Nineties*, London: T. Fisher Unwin, 1921.

Simonis, H., *The Street of Ink: An Intimate History of Journalism*, London: Cassell, 1917.

Spender, J.A., *Life, Journalism and Politics*, 2 vols, London: Cassell, 1927.

Whyte, Frederic, *The Life of W.T. Stead*, 2 vols, London: Jonathan Cape, 1925.

Willing, J., *Willing's Press Guide and Advertisers' Directory and Handbook*, London, 1903.

Articles in Contemporary Periodicals

Arnold, Matthew, 'Up to Easter', *The Nineteenth Century*, XXI (May 1887), pp.629-643.

Dicey, Edward, 'Journalism, New and Old', *Fortnightly Review*, LXXVII (May 1905), pp.904-918.

Escott, T.H.S., 'Old and New in the Daily Press', *Quarterly Review*, 227, 451 (April 1917), pp.353-368.

Newnes, George, 'From Cairo to Cataract', *Strand Magazine*, 15, 87 (March 1897), pp.305-316.

Newnes, George, 'A Journey to Jerusalem', *Strand Magazine*, 15, 87 (April 1898), pp.436-442.

Newnes, George, 'Personal Impressions of the Author', *The Wide World Magazine*, 3, 15 (June 1899), p.227.

O'Connor, F., 'The New Journalism', *The New Review*, 1 (1889), pp.423-424.

Stead, W.T., *The Contemporary Review*, XLIX (May 1886), pp.653-674.

SECONDARY SOURCES

Books

Altick, Richard D., *The English Common Reader. A Social History of the Mass Reading Public*, Chicago: University of Chicago Press, 1963.

Beare, Geraldine (comp.), *Index to the Strand Magazine, 1891-1950*, Westport, Connecticut and London: Greenwood Press, 1982.

Beetham, Margaret, *A Magazine of Her Own? Domesticity and Desire in the Woman's Magazine, 1800-1914*, London and New York: Routledge, 1996.

Benson, John, *The Rise of Consumer Society, 1880-1980*, London and New York: Longman, 1994.

Boyce, George, James Curran and Pauline Wingate (eds), *Newspaper History from the Seventeenth Century to the Present Day*, London: Constable, 1978.

Braithwaite, Brian, *Women's Magazines: The First 300 Years*, London: Peter Owen, 1995.

Brake, Laurel, Aled Jones and Lionel Madden (eds), *Investigating Victorian Journalism*, New York: St Martin's Press, 1990.

Branca, Patricia, *Silent Sisterhood: Middle-Class Women in the Victorian Home*, London: Croom Helm, 1975.

Brantlinger, Patrick, *Rule of Darkness: British Literature and Imperialism, 1830-1914*, London: Cornell University Press, 1988.

Brendon, Piers, *The Life and Death of the Press Barons*, London: Secker and Warburg, 1982.

Bristow, Joseph, *Empire Boys: Adventures in a Man's World*, London: Harper Collins Academic, 1991.

Brown, Lucy, *Victorian News and Newspapers*, New York: Oxford University Press, 1985.

Buzard, James, *The Beaten Track: European Tourism, Literature and the Ways to Culture, 1800-1918*, Oxford: Clarendon, 1993.

Dancyger, Irene, *A World of Women: An Illustrated History of Women's Magazines*, Dublin: Gill and Macmillan, 1978.

Darwin, Bernard, *Fifty Years of Country Life*, London: Country Life Ltd, 1947.

Davidoff, Leonore, *The Best Circles: Society, Etiquette and the Season*, London: Croom Helm, 1973.

Dictionary of National Biography.

Freeden, Michael, *The New Liberalism: An Ideology of Social Reform*, Oxford: Clarendon Press, 1978.

Gilmour, Robin, *The Victorian Period: The Intellectual and Cultural Context of English Literature, 1830-1890*, London and New York: Longman, 1993.

Haley, Bruce, *The Healthy Body and Victorian Culture*, Cambridge, Massachusetts: Harvard University Press, 1978.

Hall, Catherine, *White, Male and Middle Class*, Cambridge: Polity Press, 1992.

Harris, Jose, *Private Lives, Public Spirit: Britain 1870-1914*, Harmondsworth: Penguin, 1993.

Harris, Michael and Alan Lee (eds), *The Press in English Society from the Seventeenth to Nineteenth Centuries*, London: Associated University Presses, 1986.

Hendrick, Harry, *Images of Youth. Age, Class, and the Male Youth Problem, 1880-1920*, Oxford: Clarendon, 1990.

Herd, Harold, *The Making of Modern Journalism*, London: Allen and Unwin, 1927.

Herd, Harold, *The March of English Journalism, The Story of the British Press from 1622 to the Present Day*, London: Allen and Unwin, 1952.

Hobsbawm, E.J., *Industry and Empire*, London: Penguin, 1968.

Hoggart, Richard, *The Uses of Literacy* (Intro. Andrew Goodwin), New Brunswick: Transaction Publishers, 1992.

Houfe, Simon, *The Dictionary of British Book Illustrators and Caricaturists, 1800-1914 with Introductory Chapters on the Rise and Progress of the Art*, Woodbridge, England: Antique Collectors Club, 1978.

Houghton, Walter A. (ed.), *The Wellesley Index to Victorian Periodicals, 1824-1900*, Toronto: University of Toronto Press, 1966.

Hutt, Allen, *The Changing Newspaper: Typographic Trends in Britain and America, 1622-1972*, London: Gordon Fraser, 1973.

Kern, Stephen, *The Culture of Time and Space, 1880-1918*, Cambridge, Massachusetts: Harvard University Press, 1983.

Knight, Stephen, *Form and Ideology in Crime Fiction*, Bloomington: Indiana University Press, 1980.

Leavis, Q.D., *Fiction and the Reading Public*, London: Chatto and Windus, 1932.

Lee, Alan J., *The Origins of the Popular Press*, London: Croom Helm, 1976.

Leed, Eric, *The Mind of the Traveller: From Gilgamesh to Global Tourism*, New York: Basic Books, 1991.

Linkman, Audrey, *The Victorians: Photographic Portraits*, London: Tauris Parke, 1993.

Mackenzie, John M. (ed.), *Imperialism and Popular Culture*, Manchester: Manchester University Press, 1984.

Mangan, J.A., *Athleticism in the Victorian and Edwardian Public School: The Emergence and Consolidation of an Educational Ideology*, Cambridge: Cambridge University Press, 1981.

Mangan, J.A. (ed.), *Pleasure, Sport and Proselytism: British Culture and Sport at Home and Abroad, 1700-1914*, London: Frank Cass, 1988.

Matthew, H.C.G., *The Liberal Imperialists: The Ideas and Politics of a Post-Gladstonian Élite*, Oxford: Oxford University Press, 1973.

Morrison, Stanley, *The English Newspaper: Some Account of the Physical Development of Journals Printed in London Between 1622 and the Present Day*, Cambridge: Cambridge University Press, 1932.

Nevett, T.R., *Advertising in Britain*, London: Heinemann, 1982.

Ohmann, Richard (ed.), *Making and Selling Culture*, Hanover and London: Wesleyan University Press, 1996.

Parker, Peter, *The Old Lie: The Great War and the Public School Ethos*, London: Constable, 1987.

Pearson, Geoffery, *Hooligan: A History of Respectable Fears*, London: Macmillan, 1983.

Perkin, Harold, *The Rise of Professional Society: England Since 1880*, London and New York: Routledge, 1989.

Perkin, Harold, *The Structured Crowd: Essays in English Social History*, Sussex: Harvester Press, 1981.

Pound, Reginald, *Mirror of the Century: The Strand Magazine, 1891-1950*, London: Heinemann, 1966.

Pound, Reginald and Geoffery Harmsworth, *Northcliffe*, London: Cassell, 1959.

Rose, Jonathan, *The Edwardian Temperament*, Athens, Ohio: Ohio University Press, 1986.

Said, Edward W., *Culture and Imperialism*, London: Vintage, 1994.

Sandison, Alan, *The Wheel of Empire*, London: Macmillan, 1967.

Searle, G.R., *Corruption in British Politics, 1895-1930*, Oxford: Clarendon Press, 1987.

Searle, G.R., *The Quest for National Efficiency: A Study in British Politics and Political Thought, 1899-1914*, Oxford: Basil Blackwell, 1971.

Shattock, Joanne and Michael Wolff (eds), *The Victorian Periodical Press: Samplings and Soundings*, Leicester: Leicester University Press, 1982.

Sullivan, Alvin (ed.), *British Literary Magazines: The Victorian and Edwardian Age, 1837-1913*, Westport, Connecticut and London: Greenwood Press, 1984.

Swinglehurst, Edmund, *The Romantic Journey: The Story of Thomas Cook and Victorian Travel*, London: Pica Editions, 1974.

Thompson, E.P., *The Making of the English Working Class*, London: Penguin, 1968.

Thompson, Paul, *The Edwardians: The Remaking of British Society*, London: Weidenfeld and Nicolson, 1975.

Thorpe, James, *English Illustration: The Nineties*, London: Faber and Faber, 1935.

Tompkins, Jane P. (ed.), *Reader Response Criticism: From Formalism to Post Structuralism*, Baltimore and London: Johns Hopkins University Press, 1980.

Travis, John, *An Illustrated History of Lynton and Lynmouth, 1770-1914*, Derby: Breedon Books, 1995.

Tye, J. Reginald, *Periodicals of the Nineties*, Oxford: Oxford Bibliographical Society, 1974.

Vann, J. Don and Rosemary T. Van Arsdel (eds),*Victorian Periodicals: A Guide to Research*, New York: Modern Language Association of America, 1978.

Waterloo Directory of Victorian Periodicals, 1824-1900, Waterloo, Ontario, 1976.

White, Cynthia, *Women's Magazines, 1693-1968*, London: Michael Joseph, 1970.

Wiener, Joel H. (ed.), *Innovators and Preachers: The Role of the Editor in Victorian England*, New York: Greenwood Press, 1985.

Wiener, Joel H. (ed.), *Papers for the Millions: The New Journalism in Britain, 1850s-1914*, New York: Greenwood Press, 1988.

Williams, Francis, *Dangerous Estate: The Anatomy of Newspapers*, London: Longman, Green, 1957.

Williams, Raymond, *Keywords*, London: Fontana, 1983.

Articles

Baylen, Joseph O., 'The "New Journalism" in Later Victorian Britain', *Australian Journal of Politics and History*, 18 (1972), pp.367-385.

Baylen, Joseph O., 'The Press and Public Opinion: W.T. Stead and the "New Journalism"', *Journalism Studies Review*, 4 (July 1979), pp.45-49.

Baylen, Joseph O., 'W.T. Stead and the New Journalism', *Emory University Quarterly*, XXI (1965), pp.196-206.

Beare, Geraldine, 'Indexing the Strand Magazine', *Journal of Newspaper and Periodical History*, 11, 2 (Spring 1986), p.20.

Beetham, Margaret, 'Open and Closed: The Periodical as Publishing Genre', *Victorian Periodicals Review*, XXII, 3 (Fall 1989), pp.96-100.

Block, Bernard, 'Romance and High Purpose: the *National Geographic*', *Wilson Library Bulletin* (January 1984), p.334.

Brake, Laurel and Anne Humpherys, 'Critical Theory and Periodical Research', *Victorian Periodicals Review*, XXII, 3 (Fall 1989) pp.94-95.

Dunae, Patrick A., 'Penny Dreadfuls: Late Nineteenth-Century Boys' Literature and Crime', *Victorian Studies*, 22 (1979), pp.133-136.

Gillis, John R., 'The Evolution of Juvenile Delinquency in England, 1890-1914', *Past and Present*, 67 (1975), pp.96-97.

Jackson, Kate, 'C.B. Fry: The Sportsman-Editor', *Victorian Periodicals Review* (Winter 2000).

Jackson, Kate, 'Securing the Suffrage of the Crowd: George Newnes and *The Million*', *Nineteenth Century Prose*, 24, 1 (Spring 1997), pp.17-38.

Leavis, Q.D., 'Gissing and the English Novel', *Scrutiny*, VII, 1 (June 1938), pp.73-81.

Pykett, Lyn, 'Reading the Periodical Press: Text and Context', *Victorian Periodicals Review*, XXII, 3 (Fall 1989), pp.101-109.

Smith Schuneman, R., 'Art of Photography: A Question for Newspaper Editors of the 1890s', *Journalism Quarterly*, 42, 1 (Winter 1965), pp.43-52.

Stasio, Clothilde de, 'Arnold Bennett and Late-Victorian *Woman*', *Victorian Periodicals Review*, XXVIII, 1 (Spring 1995), pp.40-53.

Thompson, E.P., 'Time, Work-Discipline and Industrial Capitalism', *Past and Present*, 38 (1967), pp 56-97.

Index